KENTUCKY FRONTIER

to

COMMONWEALTH

KENTUCKY FRONTIER *to* COMMONWEALTH

HISTORICAL ARCHAEOLOGY *at* DANIEL BOONE'S *and* HUGH McGARY'S STATIONS

NANCY O'MALLEY

Scholarly publisher for the Commonwealth,
serving Bellarmine University, Berea College, Centre College of Kentucky, Eastern Kentucky University, The Filson Historical Society, Georgetown College, Kentucky Historical Society, Kentucky State University, Morehead State University, Murray State University, Northern Kentucky University, Spalding University, Transylvania University, University of Kentucky, University of Louisville, University of Pikeville, and Western Kentucky University.

Editorial and Sales Offices: The University Press of Kentucky
663 South Limestone, Lexington, Kentucky 40508-4008
www.kentuckypress.com

Unless otherwise noted, illustrations are courtesy of the William S. Webb Museum of Anthropology at the University of Kentucky.

Cataloging-in-Publication data is available from the Library of Congress.

ISBN 978-1-9859-0228-2 (hardcover : alk. paper)
ISBN 978-1-9859-0305-0 (pbk. : alk. paper)
ISBN 978-1-9859-0239-8 (epub)
ISBN 978-1-9859-0240-4 (pdf)

This book will be made open access within three years of publication thanks to Path to Open, a program developed in partnership between JSTOR, the American Council of Learned Societies (ACLS), University of Michigan Press, and The University of North Carolina Press to bring about equitable access and impact for the entire scholarly community, including authors, researchers, libraries, and university presses around the world. Learn more at https://about.jstor.org/path-to-open/

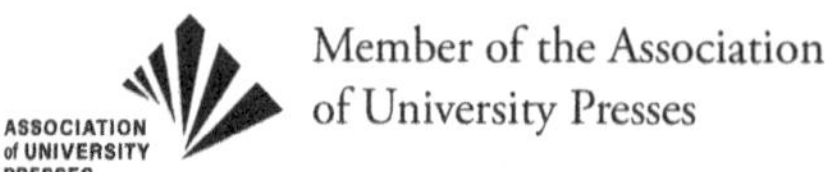

Member of the Association
of University Presses

Every individual is part and parcel of a great picture of the society
in which he lives and acts, and his life cannot be painted
without reproducing the picture of the world he lived in.
—Harriet Beecher Stowe

Contents

List of Illustrations

Figures

Tables

Introduction

Historical archaeology is a unique profession where the humanities and the social sciences come together to make sense of the recent human past. "Recent," in this context, means the period of human culture after the invention of writing. Historical archaeologists receive their professional training in anthropology and are, at heart, social scientists who analyze physical artifacts and sites as primary data and couple it with historic archival sources. So we must also be well versed in history and historical method. My journey from a college freshman who decided to take an introductory archaeology class at The University of Texas at Austin in 1971 to a professional archaeologist specializing in historic sites was not a straight-line path. While I was exposed to both precontact and historic archaeology early in my career, my original intent was to pursue precontact research as a specialty.

My early career in contract archaeology necessitated my becoming proficient in both subdisciplines, but it was not until the mid-1980s that my career path took a detour. After moving to Kentucky to take a job at the University of Kentucky Program for Cultural Resource Assessment in 1979, I had the opportunity to survey many historic sites during contract projects. I had to learn Kentucky history so that I could interpret the sites I encountered. In the process, I discovered the late eighteenth-century sites known as "pioneer stations." Stations were temporary residential solutions designed to provide protection from the natural elements and from Native American attacks, primarily during the Revolutionary War period. They generally were somewhat isolated, were occupied for short periods of time and usually abandoned when their owners built permanent homes elsewhere, and left little or no substantial physical evidence of their structures. Identification of archaeological remains is the best and, in many cases, the only means of locating and studying the architectural and archaeological footprint of these sites. Archival sources are also essential to understanding who lived in the stations, what life in times of conflict and danger was like, how long stations were used, and what happened when the danger passed.

I became fascinated with these ephemeral, short-term sites that had an outsize influence on the successful settlement of the Kentucky frontier. The cast of characters was colorful and diverse, including the Euro-American settlers, who crossed the Appalachian Mountains in search of land, and Native American tribes, who strongly resisted the invasion of their lands by these interlopers. The clash of cultures played out against the broader context of a war waged by American colonists seeking independence from their mother country, England. You could not ask for a more fraught storyline—one that had the added benefit of being true. From this interest grew my research into the early historic period of Kentucky and its Revolutionary War beginnings.

As my expertise evolved, I had the opportunity to investigate two station sites in particular, one settled by the iconic Daniel Boone, and the other by a lesser-known, though equally interesting, man named Hugh McGary. Daniel Boone looms large in the Kentucky historical settlement story for many reasons, not the least of which are his skillful leadership, humility, courage, and tolerance for cultural differences. While he had his detractors, the collective verdict on his character and personality is one of an honest, amiable, trustworthy man who did not avoid difficult situations, who helped his fellow settlers on every occasion, and whose historical legacy is legendary. His place in history was assured as early as 1784, when John Filson first published his biography of Boone. Subsequent biographies further burnished his reputation.

Hugh McGary is barely present in the pantheon of notable historical figures, both heroes and villains, in Kentucky and American history. He was personally acquainted with many of Kentucky's earliest historical leaders: Daniel Boone, James Harrod, Benjamin Logan, and George Rogers Clark, to name a few. McGary was instrumental in the establishment of Harrodsburg, Kentucky's earliest settlement. He served in various civic capacities during the early settlement of Kentucky, faithfully helped defend the frontier, and acquired a very respectable fortune. He was a complex man—emotional, impetuous, headstrong, and possessed of indomitable self-confidence and personal courage—who seemed to have inspired either respect or disgust. Nineteenth-century historians relegated him to pariah status, and there his reputation has been mired with no substantive evaluation of his character, personality, or achievements—good or bad.

While the contrasting personalities of Boone and McGary fascinated me, other players in the drama that unfolded during Kentucky's early settlement era are equally important. Principal among them are the Native peoples: the Shawnee, Cherokee, Wyandots, Mingoes, and other tribes, who resisted the encroachment of Euro-American settlers in the trans-Appalachian territory that the British set aside for them with the Proclamation of 1763. Euro-American settlers, for the most part, considered all Native Americans under the broadly generic term "Indian" and had little concern for their tribal identities. However, there were many differences between the tribes in terms of how they reacted to the flood of settlers who came to Kentucky seeking land and fortune in the late eighteenth century. Where I was able to determine proper tribal names, I used them. I restricted the use of the term "Indian" to instances when I am directly quoting a settler or other historic individual. Otherwise, I use the terms "Native" or "Native American" for those instances when the specific tribe is unknown.

My excavations of Boone's and McGary's Stations were undertaken on a financial shoestring, with volunteers and students providing the labor in the field and lab and hours of my own time snatched when and where I could manage it around my other work responsibilities. It was not until my retirement from the University of Kentucky in 2018 that I was able to turn my attention exclusively to this research. I did not initially intend to combine the two sites within the same book, but the longer I thought about it, the more sense it made to me. The two men knew each other well. They interacted during militia raids and battles. Both served not only as militia officers, leading other men of lesser rank, but also in civic capacities. They and their families experienced the privations and dangers of the wartime Kentucky frontier in equal measure. Comparing and contrasting their lives through the lens of archaeological and archival analysis seemed obvious.

The preservation of the two sites also offered interesting possibilities. The archaeological footprints of Boone's and McGary's Stations differ primarily regarding the preservation of architectural features. Each one contributes significant archaeological evidence of station architecture and the material culture (artifacts) in use during the frontier settlement era. Integrating the archaeological and historical information from these two sites is a major goal of this book. Boone and McGary are representative of Kentucky settlers in general, and studying their sites offers a snapshot of colonial life on the western border of the American frontier in the late eighteenth century. Their places of residence were at once homes and sanctuaries that had to be protected from outside forces that sought to dislodge them. In this context, studying their station sites reveals aspects of their frontier experience that can be extrapolated to a larger historical pattern of behavioral response to unfamiliar, adverse circumstances.

Embodied in the history and archaeology of the two sites is another instructive lesson. The frontier period, during which settlers came into an unfamiliar territory, claimed land, fought off Native American attacks during a time of war, and ultimately prevailed, was remarkably short. The long view is that the conflict between the British, Native Americans, and Kentucky settlers started around 1773, when settlement surveys for Kentucky land began. It continued throughout the Revolutionary War, as the British enabled their Native allies to be their proxies in the western theater of Kentucky, and beyond the Treaty of Paris in 1783 until 1794, when the Battle of Fallen Timbers finally vanquished the Shawnee and peace was attained. The presumption is that people remained in a state of constant vigilance against Native American attacks during this time throughout the Central and northern Kentucky region.

History is not that tidy, nor was the situation in Kentucky. There is no question that some Native American hostilities continued after the conclusion of the war in 1783. But it is also true that the raids were so attenuated as to be largely inconsequential to the process of settling farms, communities, and towns. By the late 1780s, houses of stone construction that could only be built by trained stone masons over extended periods of time were starting to appear all over the Central Kentucky area, including at Boone's Station. The area around Lexington became stable and safe first, and growth started there. The territory along the Ohio River remained at somewhat greater risk because of its proximity to tribes north of the Ohio River who were not willing to give up their claim to the Kentucky territory and continued to fight even though they were no longer supported by the British. But despite the threat, settlements such as the town of Washington, in Mason County, located just four miles from the Ohio River, were successfully established a year after the Treaty of Paris in 1783. The Native American tribes did not prevail, and the practical outcome of the battle at Fallen Timbers was that the threat to Kentuckians was reduced to essentially zero after 1794. But for many Kentuckians living in the Central Kentucky area around Lexington, this threat had been negligible for ten years. And in those ten years, they transitioned from a defensive position, where they simply survived, to an actively capitalist stance that developed agricultural, industrial, and commercial networks and established government, civic, and social norms to support the towns and communities that took form.

The process is exemplified in the archaeology of Daniel Boone's and Hugh McGary's Stations. McGary abandoned his station a few years after the Revolutionary War ended and, as many settlers did, went elsewhere to build his fortune. Boone, too, left his station when the war ended, but a series of families continued to occupy the site for over sixty years longer. Remarkably, these later occupants did not tear down the station completely but continued to use the station cabins as part of a large farmstead. Thus, while McGary's Station is an archaeological time capsule, Boone's Station is a palimpsest of lives lived on the same spot over decades, adding and subtracting artifacts and cultural features, figuratively writing, erasing, and rewriting the site's history.

Finally, while this book is a detailed look at the structure and material culture of two archaeological sites occupied by a diverse cast of characters, the conclusions I draw from my research point to cultural patterns that reflect the broader sweep of our national history. The westward expansion of the American colonies and, later, the fledgling United States of America, was inexorable and, to a great degree, inevitable. Historians have spoken of Kentucky as part of the "First West," where the pattern was set for "ensuing expansionist processes across that vast domain stretching from the Appalachians to the Pacific." Native American tribes fought for their land and resources, sometimes banding together to present an effective collective response, other times pursuing objectives that suited their particular tribal interests. Even within tribes, there were factions that differed in their views and strategies. British support aided Native American objectives during the Revolutionary War, but the loss of this support after the war was a devastating blow that ultimately led to the tribes' relinquishing their claims. The primary motivation of the Kentucky settlers was to acquire land and build their fortunes. They benefited from access to European technology, such as superior firearms, had strength in numbers, and possessed an understanding of political organization that would be critical to establishing a settled society. The chapters that follow examine, at micro- and macrolevels, the elements of the adversarial conditions of Kentucky's settlement period and the rapid transition to a settled society characterized by a complex system of wealth and social status girded by the adoption of slavery.[1]

PART ONE

Documentary Evidence

1

Daniel Boone and Hugh McGary

Early Connections Lead to Kentucky

Daniel Boone was a commercial hunter from North Carolina who plied his trade on "long hunts." These extended trips lasted as long as two years, during which he and a companion or two hunted white-tailed deer and harvested their skins for sale in the eastern markets. An encounter with trader John Findley in 1769 fueled his determination to explore the mysterious western country beyond the Appalachian Mountains. His initial foray into Kentucky with Findley, his brother-in-law John Stewart, James Mooney, Joseph Holden, and William Cooley in 1769 was both an exploration and a business venture, the aim being to harvest as many deerskins as they could. The men took a series of well-worn hunting trails to reach the famous Cumberland Gap, a V-shaped notch in the mountains along a noted trail, the Great Warrior's Path, that opened the way into Kentucky.

Eight months of hunting yielded several hundred dollars' worth of deerskins packed in 250-pound bales and familiarized Boone with the lay of the land. The men had seen no sign of Native Americans at the start of their trip, but early in December, a group of Shawnee led by a warrior named Captain Will surrounded Boone and Stewart while they were away from camp. Their attempts to warn their camp tenders and lure their captors away from the main camp failed and, forced to return to camp, they found it deserted and their skins unguarded. Captain Will appropriated their accumulated skins and equipment, loaded them on the horses, and left the two men with two pairs of moccasins each, some patch leather, a trade gun, and enough ammunition to feed themselves on their way out of Kentucky. Captain Will admonished

Boone to "go home and stay there," but Boone and Stewart followed the Shawnee men on foot, stole back their horses, and rode through the night. The Shawnee soon tracked them and took them captive again—this time, with the intention of taking them north of the Ohio River. Once again, Boone and Stewart escaped, grabbing guns and ammunition, and fleeing into a canebrake. This time, the Shawnee did not try to pursue them, and the men headed south to find their companions. They found them on the way back east. With them were Daniel's brother, Squire, and Alexander Neeley, with fresh supplies and horses. Findley and the camp tenders heeded the Shawnee's warning and returned east, but the other four men headed back into the Kentucky country to make up their hunting losses. Tragedy soon struck the expedition party: John Stewart failed to return after checking beaver traplines. The men feared the worst, and Neeley had had enough. He returned to the settlements.[1]

Daniel and Squire Boone persevered and remained in Kentucky for over a year longer. Squire was tasked with replenishing their supplies and selling their skins—once leaving Daniel alone for several months. In the spring of 1771, they finally returned to their homes in North Carolina, but not before being relieved of their deerskins, rifles, horses, and equipment by yet another group of Native Americans. Two years of arduous work were wiped out, and the trip could hardly have been called profitable. But despite the financial losses, Daniel Boone returned home with invaluable information from his many months of exploring eastern and Central Kentucky.[2]

Boone's hunting trip to the Kentucky country must be viewed in a larger geopolitical context that recognizes the differing motivations of Native American tribes who defended their land and resources and hunters like Boone and later settlers. The Shawnee claimed Kentucky as part of their territory and, in their view, had royal law on their side by virtue of the Proclamation Line of 1763. This all-important boundary was meant to prevent Euro-American settlement beyond the Appalachian Mountains. However, the Treaty of Fort Stanwix, executed between Superintendent William Johnson, who administered the northern section of royal lands for the English Crown, and the Iroquois Confederacy in 1768, established the Ohio River as a new boundary that eliminated Iroquois claims to the south of the river. It also shut out Shawnee and other tribal claims to the same land without their taking any part in the negotiations. The Shawnee refused to honor the treaty and detained Boone and his companions on the grounds that they were trespassing and stealing their resources. Under the circumstances, their response was quite lenient when they confiscated the ill-gotten deerskins but provided the basic necessities for Boone and Stewart to return unharmed to their homes. Boone did not heed the lesson: his future encounters with Native Americans were much more violent and sometimes resulted in tragedy. Meanwhile, incursions on Native lands continued as expansion of colonial settlement pushed westward.[3]

McGary may have met Boone as a consequence of their living near one another on the Upper Yadkin River in Rowan County, North Carolina. Daniel Bryan, a kinsman of Boone's wife, Rebecca, claimed McGary was a neighbor to Boone, who had been a longtime resident there. The relationship between the two men is first documented in the historical record in the fall of 1772, when McGary joined Boone, Samuel Tate, Benjamin Cutbirth, and perhaps another North Carolinian man (whose name is unknown) on a hunting trip to Kentucky. Little is known about the trip, which seems to have been conducted without any noteworthy incidents.[4]

Unlike Boone, "McGary" is not a household name. What fame (or infamy) his life possesses today is largely due to his poor judgment during one seminal event in Kentucky history, and even that is a small footnote in historical research of the settlement era. The only published source on McGary is Mary Powell Hammersmith's publication, based on decades of painstaking research. Sources differ on McGary's place and date of birth. He was probably born in Augusta County, Virginia, to John and Sarah McGary. Transcribed names and dates from a Bible that was reportedly brought into Kentucky by the McGarys list his birth date as March 10, 1747. The birth year may have been mistranscribed, since McGary himself stated his age as fifty-two years in a deposition he gave in Bourbon County, Kentucky, on April 18, 1796, indicating his birth year as 1744. McGary's parents moved to North Carolina in 1763, likely taking their son, then nineteen years old, with them. He was certainly in North Carolina by 1769, when he witnessed a deed transaction between David Caldwell and James and Robert Bunton (also spelled Buntin) in Rowan County on Beaver Dam Branch. His association with the Buntin family was formalized by his marriage to Mary Buntin Ray, a widow with three sons by her marriage to John Ray, who died between August and November 1764 in Amherst County, Virginia. McGary married his wife sometime between November 1764 and January 1767, when their first son, Robert, was born. As Mary was pregnant with her third son, John, at the time of her first husband's death, her second marriage and subsequent pregnancy may have occurred around 1765 or 1766; however, no marriage license or bond has been found.[5]

Not long after the 1772–1773 hunting trip, Boone joined forces with Captain William Russell, who lived in southwestern Virginia at Castle's Wood on the Clinch River, for a settlement attempt. Once again, Boone ignored the royal policy that prevented settlement in the Kentucky country, but, this time, he paid a heavy price. Leaving in late September 1773, Boone led the large pack train of families and single men slowly along the trail while Captain Russell remained behind to finish up some business. Their slow progress induced Boone to send his eldest son, James, and John and Richard Mendinhall for additional supplies. They procured the supplies from Captain Russell and set out, their party including Russell's son Henry, two enslaved men, Charles and Adam, a hired man named Drake, and Isaac Crabtree, an experienced woodsman. The supply party was asleep when they were attacked by fifteen Delaware, two Cherokee, and two Shawnee. The initial attack killed the Mendinhalls and wounded Crabtree and the hired man, who managed to flee. James Boone and Henry Russell were immobilized by bullets through their hips. The Native Americans ran into the camp to steal the horses and took the helpless boys captive, slashing them with knives. One of the Cherokee was Big Jim, whom James knew. He tore James's fingernails and toenails out, clubbed his head, and finally shot both boys with arrows. The enslaved man Charles was also taken captive, leaving the other enslaved man, Adam, who had hidden nearby, the only eyewitness; he wandered off in shock and finally returned home eleven days later. Charles was later found dead in the woods. James, Henry, and the Mendinhalls were found by a member of Boone's party, who had stolen a pack of deerskins and was returning to the settlements. His gruesome discovery sent him riding quickly back to Boone's camp to alert the party. The dead were buried along the trail, and the tragedy ended the settlement attempt. Boone then settled his family in a cabin belonging to David Gass on the Clinch River. The suddenness of the attack and the shocking violence of Big Jim's treatment of the boys stand in stark contrast to Boone's earlier encounter with Native warriors. What prompted Big Jim's actions, and why did he not extend leniency to the settlers? History does not record an explanation, but an important factor had to have been that this was not a hunting party that stayed only long enough to accumulate animal hides but rather a large group of people, including women and children, who intended to establish a permanent settlement on Native lands. To the Native point of view, this was a provocative expansion of the encroachment that the tribes had been fighting for years. The violence sent a message that settlers should expect resistance if they persisted in their settlement goals.[6]

McGary did not participate in Boone's tragic first attempt to permanently settle in Kentucky. Little is known about his life in the two years that passed between his hunting trip with Boone in 1772–1773 and 1775, when he crossed paths with Boone once again while they were both living in Rowan County, North Carolina, on the Yadkin River. Daniel Bryan claimed that McGary served as sheriff of Rowan County, North Carolina, prior to the American Revolution. Among a sheriff's duties was to serve as a peace officer, tax collector, vendue master, and master of elections.[7]

In an insightful article on the role and power of the office of sheriff in colonial North Carolina, Julian P. Boyd states:

> There was probably no other office in the colony, and certainly there was none under the jurisdiction of the county court, who exercised such plenary executive and administrative powers as the sheriff did. . . . It is also equally true that there was no other office who made efficient royal government impossible quite so much as the sheriff did. He frequently misappropriated and embezzled great quantities of the public money. He was a controlling factor in the elections, and at times returned the person of his choice rather than that of the electorate.[8]

Despite the opportunities for increasing one's personal wealth at the expense of fellow colonists, there were drawbacks to being a sheriff, principally in the role of peace officer. Insecure jails and hardened criminals, as well as frequent threats of riots and insurrections by enslaved persons, all were part of a sheriff's burdens. Clearly, it was not a job for the fainthearted. At the same time, given what is known of Hugh McGary's personality, the office of sheriff seems to have been uniquely suited to his abilities and temperament.

One of the important aspects of the office of sheriff was its relationship with the county court, which, increasingly through the colonial period, held true political power. Significantly, the justices of the court usually nominated a fellow justice for the office of sheriff. This practice was made mandatory in 1739 but was repealed in 1742, though it continued to be a common practice. Other practices virtually insured that the choice of sheriff lay in the hands of the county court, and it behooved politically ambitious candidates to curry favor with the justices.[9]

McGary's later appointment in Kentucky as justice to the Lincoln County Court in 1781, and his continued service on the Mercer County Court, indicate he was aware of the importance of civil service. That it was a lucrative position is perhaps indicated by the many times he acted as a surety for promissory notes. He frequently sued his debtors to force payment of these loans, and he frequently won judgment. Public officials often make political enemies, and McGary's service on the court may have been another source of irritation for people who disliked him.[10]

McGary bided his time in North Carolina before taking the plunge to move to Kentucky permanently. Many surveying parties traveled to Kentucky between 1773 and 1775 to mark land for colonial governments and private interests. Virginia Governor Dunmore claimed the Kentucky lands as part of his colony's territory, while the colony of Pennsylvania claimed overlapping sections of the Ohio valley.

Dunmore, as a servant of the Crown, was officially tasked with enforcing the Proclamation of 1763, which prevented English settlement west of the Appalachian Mountains. However, privately, he encouraged both private and public surveys, circulated a proclamation that warned of impending war, and promoted violence in pursuit of his own interests. Dunmore's War ensued in June 1774, when the governor ordered the erection of garrison forts to protect the settlers, sent rangers to patrol the waterways, and prepared for war against tribes of the Ohio River valley. Captain Russell, acting on the governor's orders, sent Boone and Michael Stoner to search Kentucky and warn any surveyors they found. While there, Boone took the opportunity to mark some land for later claims but found neither Native Americans nor surveyors. Boone's subsequent involvement in the short-lived but bloody Dunmore's War established him as a natural leader, and he was promoted from lieutenant to the rank of captain by Virginia surveyor William Preston, who was a colonel in the Virginia militia. Dunmore's short conflict had another important effect on the subsequent settlement of Kentucky. The governor used militia forces to defeat the Shawnee and their allies at the Battle of Point Pleasant. The Shawnee were forced to accept the Ohio River boundary line established by the Treaty of Fort Stanwix signed in 1769 that they had previously rejected, to restrict their hunting to the north side of the river, and to fulfill other requirements until a permanent peace was negotiated the following spring. The outbreak of the American Revolution in April 1775 prevented the peace conference from happening and convinced the American colonists that they could settle in the contested area on their own terms.[11]

The opening of the Revolutionary War exacerbated an already tense situation as Native Americans pondered the best course of action to take: neutrality, alliance with the British, or some accommodation with the Americans. Many Shawnee tried to remain neutral when the Revolution first broke out, but continued American encroachments divided the five subtribal divisions, with the Chillicothe and Piqua groups becoming more militant while leaders like Moluntha and Chief Cornstalk in the Maquachake division advocated peace. By 1777, the war supporters gained strength among the Shawnee villages, and warriors accepted a war belt from Governor Henry Hamilton at Detroit to join the Mingoes in raids against the Americans. Many more Shawnee joined the British when Chief Cornstalk was murdered by American militia in the same year. Their alliance with the British made perfect sense, given the adversarial relationship between Native tribes and American settlers.[12]

The opportunity for more conflict reared its head when Boone and McGary joined forces to bring their families to Kentucky for permanent settlement in 1775. Boone initiated the process when he participated with Judge Richard Henderson and his partners in the Transylvania Company. The Transylvania Company had illegally purchased approximately sixteen million acres covering most of what is today Central and western Kentucky from the Cherokee. The partners hoped to gain approval for the purchase from the British Crown and establish a new colony. They employed Boone to cut a road to their new purchase and establish a capital on the Kentucky River at a site Boone had selected a year earlier. In the spring of 1775, Boone guided his party of road cutters, along with his daughter Susannah and an enslaved woman named Dolly, to the site, following existing paths for part of the way and cutting new trails where necessary. Boone's party was attacked en route, but he persevered and arrived at the future site of Fort Boonesborough on April 1. He and his men constructed lean-to shelters and tents initially and laid out town lots. Henderson's party arrived on April 20 and began construction of a large, stockaded fort at a higher elevation south of Boone's camp. Several weeks later, Boone returned east to bring his family and others out. Among the settlers in the party were Hugh and Mary McGary and their children. The large party led by Boone arrived in Kentucky in late August.[13]

The 1775 trip included several families besides the Boones and the McGarys. One of James Ray's sons, Dr. John Ray, later stated that he thought there were twenty or thirty families in the company. Among these were Thomas Denton, Richard Hogan, and their families. The Dentons were apparently related to Mary McGary. McGary brought a herd of forty horses with him. Cattle, pigs, and perhaps sheep also made up part of the company.[14]

The party divided at the head of the Dix River, with Boone taking most of the families to Boonesborough and McGary intending to take the remainder of the party to the Harrodsburg area. Here the stories of the McGary and Boone families diverge as each family established residence in different counties. While Boone and McGary may have occasionally encountered each other over the next few years, history is silent on the possibility. However, both participated in George Rogers Clark's punitive expedition against the Shawnee in the fall of 1780, following the destruction of Martin's and Ruddell's Stations in June. Details of possible interactions between the two men during that expedition have not been uncovered. Their next recorded encounter did not take place until 1782.

2

The McGarys Settle in Harrodsburg

In 1775, Hugh McGary and the families that traveled with him headed west, intent on settling at the fledgling settlement Harrodsburg, named after its founder, James Harrod. The settlement was a scattered arrangement of cabins with no defensive fort yet built. En route, even though McGary had directions to the Harrod settlement, the party "got bewildered" and became lost, ending up at the mouth of Gilberts Creek, which empties into the Dix River in present-day Lincoln County, Kentucky. There McGary left his livestock with his stepson James Ray and two other boys, John Denton (Ray's cousin) and John Hays, promising to return in three days. McGary then took the remainder of the party and left to locate the Harrod settlement. However, they had difficulty finding a place to cross the Dix River. McGary got across by himself and ended up at James Harrod's Station, six miles south of present-day Harrodsburg, where the fort was later built. At Harrod's Station (also called Boiling Spring), McGary received assistance, returned to collect the rest of the party, and finally retrieved his livestock and the boys two weeks after he had left them at Gilberts Creek. The McGary party completed their trek to Harrodsburg on September 8, 1775. The fort at Harrodsburg was begun during the winter of 1776 and was completed the following spring.[1]

The McGary family lived in Harrodsburg from 1775 to 1779, when they moved out to Shawnee Springs. While the assumption has been that they lived in the large, stockaded fort from the time it was finished to 1779, it is plausible that they may have erected a cabin for themselves when they first arrived, since the stockaded fort was not yet built. Whether McGary's first settlement was stockaded is unknown. Once the fort was built, the McGarys moved there because the danger of living outside its protection was too great.[2]

Once established, Hugh McGary immediately began to participate in the settlement's civic affairs. At the time, the settlements at Harrodsburg and Boonesborough both lay within Fincastle County, Virginia. While Richard Henderson's renegade purchase of the area from the Cherokee was illegal, he managed to persuade some settlers, like Daniel Boone, to accept his proprietorship and fall in with his policies and governance—but he had no such luck persuading the settlers at Harrodsburg. The Committee of Fincastle County sent a petition dated June 15, 1776, to the Virginia Assembly expressing their objections to Henderson's Transylvania Company and asked to be taken under the protection and government of Virginia. This petition was signed by Isaac Hite and John Gabriel Jones as agents of the committee. A second petition, dated June 20, asked that Jones and George Rogers Clark be recognized as delegates from Fincastle County. Hugh McGary was one of fourteen signatories.[3]

A few months later, in December 1776, Kentucky County was formed out of western Fincastle County, encompassing Boonesborough and Harrodsburg, with the latter serving as the county seat. Hugh McGary was named chairman of the Committee of the County of Kentucky. His committee sent a petition dated February 27, 1777, to the governor and the Honorable Council of Virginia "setting forth the distressing situation of the inhabitants, and praying that some method be devised for guarding against attacks of Indians." The petition referenced an attack on Christmas Day of 1776 against a party of ten, killing John Gabriel Jones, James (Joseph) Rogers, William Gradon [Gordon], and Josiah Dixon, as well as an attack against John McClelland's Station a few days later, resulting in McClelland's and another man's death, the destruction of many cattle, and the stealing of horses. The station was abandoned as a result of the attack. The inhabitants of Fort Harrod were particularly concerned because these raids happened during the winter, when hostilities were generally halted. The petition concluded with a fervent plea.

> We are surrounded with enemies on every side; every day increases their numbers. To retreat from the place where our all is centered would be little preferable to death. Our Fort is already filled with widows and orphans; their necessities call upon [us] daily for supplies. Yet all this would be tolerable could we but see the dawn of

> peace; but a continuance of our woes threaten us: A rueful war presents itself before us.
>
> The apprehension of an invasion on the ensuing spring fills our minds with a thousand fears. The brave despise danger, even death, upon their own accounts; it is the state of weak infancy and helpless widowhood that set heavy on [us] . . . we most humbly present this our most dutiful Petition praying that the Hon. Governor and Council would take into serious consideration our distressed state and devise some method to guard us against the attacks of our merciless enemy, till our country, strengthened by new adventurers, shall be in a capacity to defend itself.[4]

Barely a week later, the McGary family was one of the first to experience the tragedy predicted by the petition. McGary had claimed land at Shawnee Springs about five miles northeast of Harrodsburg, and on March 6, he sent his two stepsons, James and William Ray, another young man named Thomas Shores, and an older man named William Coomes to boil maple tree sap for sugar and clear ground at the springs. The area supported a rich stand of sugar maples, and a small camp for boiling syrup was established at the Great Blue Spring. Around noon, James, William, and Thomas gathered to rest at camp, leaving the older man to continue working alone.[5]

The boys, hearing noises in the surrounding forest, saw forty-seven Shawnee warriors running toward their camp. Since only William Ray had his gun with him, James told the other boys to run in one direction while he ran to get his gun, but he was cut off before he could reach it and ran to catch up with William. James was a very fleet runner, but William, burdened by a heavy gun and "being a fleshy young man," could not run as fast. James told him to throw down his gun and surrender, but William refused. The two most detailed accounts of this incident differ slightly. Both accounts agree that William was shot while James was still with him. James Ray's son John reported years later that William aimed his gun at his pursuers and was shot before he could fire. Dr. C. Columbus Graham, James Ray's physician, stated that William, shot through the breast, attempted to keep up with James but grew faint, at which point James advised William to throw down his gun and surrender. William instead faced his pursuers and "shot down the nearest." Graham also reported that James Ray saw the Shawnee tomahawk his brother.[6]

James continued running back to the fort at Harrodsburg, only stopping at the base of a hill behind a large tree to cut the lacings of his leather leggings when they impeded his progress. Some of the warriors pursued him, shooting into the treetops above his head and hurling their war clubs at him. James's pace foiled the Shawnee's efforts to overtake him. When he realized he was no longer being pursued, he turned back to see if he could determine the fate of his brother. Being unable to safely do so, he resumed his retreat to the fort four miles away, reaching it around dusk.[7]

His report of the incident impelled the men at the fort to send word to other settlers out on their land improvements to return to the safety of the fort. The chain of events that took place at this point is somewhat confusing due to varying accounts. In one version, McGary and James Harrod argued over McGary's insistence that a party of men be sent out to try to rescue William. Harrod was against this plan because he felt it would be too dangerous. The altercation nearly became violent when both McGary and Harrod raised their guns. Intervention by Mrs. McGary prevented bloodshed. This version of events goes on to state that a party traveled to Shawnee Springs, where William's body was found "horribly mangled." John Ray implies that the party did not go to Shawnee Springs for at least a day, with William's fate being unknown. The timing of the trip to Shawnee Springs to find William is important, as further details will show.[8]

Early the next day, with the aim of drawing the men out of the fort, the Shawnee set fire to a building that was used to store flax about one-quarter mile away. "This was Indian Cunning, which the whites at that day had but little anticipation of—It had the desired effect."[9] The resulting skirmish lasted about an hour, leaving five or six Shawnee dead and several settlers injured, including McGary, whose arm was fractured. When McGary recognized the shirt one warrior was wearing as belonging to his late stepson, he killed him. The Shawnee warriors retreated, and the men returned to the fort.[10]

When the settlers went to Shawnee Springs, Thomas Shores was nowhere to be found, and the settlers speculated that he may have been taken captive. When they found William Ray, he was dead, stripped, and scalped. Jacob Stevens, who was not present at the time but related the story as he heard it, said that William's body had been cut in pieces and hung on the bushes. He is also the sole source for the report that McGary cut up the warrior wearing William's shirt and fed the body parts to the dogs. Mutilation and dismemberment of human body parts were among several gruesome wartime practices committed by both Native Americans and settlers. Stevens knew McGary and the Rays well and later was related to both McGary and James Ray through marriage (Stevens, McGary, and Ray all later married daughters of Matthias Yocum). He probably heard accounts of the incident frequently. Stevens was also more disposed to make allowances for McGary's behavior, as was clear from his account of the Battle of Blue Licks, in which he took part. Given his intimate association with McGary, his account appears credible.[11]

The only surviving eyewitness to William's death was the older German man, Coomes, described by Dr. John Ray as a "Non-Compos-Mentis loon." Lincoln County settler William Whitley described Coomes as an "old Clumpsey" person. Coomes was a Catholic and probably spoke with a German accent, traits that set him apart from most of his fellow settlers. Whitley's and Ray's disparaging adjectives may reflect more on local prejudices against people of Germanic origin rather than accurately describing Coomes's mental capacities. After all, Coomes had the wits to hide, remain quiet, and make his escape. His account, though filtered through his detractors, tells a chilling tale.[12]

According to John Ray, Coomes heard guns being discharged and, his shotgun Beelzabub in hand, went back to the camp to see what was happening. The camp was empty when he reached it, but he felt that there was danger about. After looking around, he hid "in a concave spot some ten paces from the camp, in which a Tree had fallen & broken off & sunk down in the cavity which afforded a kind [of] hiding place."[13] He watched as the warriors returned with William and tomahawked and scalped him. He made no mention of any further mutilation even though he remained in his hiding place until the Shawnee left.[14]

Coomes's son, Walter, related his father's version of events slightly differently. He stated that his father was clearing land when the boys took a break to get a drink of "sugar water." When they did not return, he became concerned and went to look for them. He saw fifteen Shawnee warriors coming from the direction of the sugar camp and concealed himself behind a fallen tree with his gun cocked, thus escaping detection. After these warriors passed, he went to the sugar camp and hid in the branches of a fallen hickory tree whose yellow leaves were nearly the same color as his buckskins. He watched as forty Shawnee, joined by the fifteen he had seen before, came to the camp. They were joined by others until their party numbered about seventy. Coomes did not witness William Ray's killing or James Ray's escape, nor was he at the fort when McGary and Harrod argued. Coomes's account relates that a party of thirty men was raised that same day and reached the sugar camp sometime before sunset. He described McGary's reaction on viewing his stepson's "mangled remains" as having nearly fainted. After burying William, the party returned to Fort Harrod, arriving around sunset. If this is a more accurate account of the sequence of events, then the reports of McGary's dismemberment of the Shawnee warrior the next day may be correct. However, the report of his having broken his arm during that skirmish still raises questions about his ability to carry out this mutilation. If it did happen, it would not be surprising if McGary was assisted by other settlers who considered his actions justifiable and retaliation appropriate.[15]

Subsequent events in McGary's life provide ample evidence of his hatred of Native Americans, and some have speculated that his stepson's death and subsequent treatment of his body spurred his intense enmity. If McGary's treatment of the Shawnee warrior's body was motivated by revenge over the treatment of his stepson, this incident may indirectly support the version that a party of men from Fort Harrod went to Shawnee Springs on the evening of William's murder rather than waiting until the following day. Only by having made the trip to Shawnee Springs and finding his stepson could McGary have known the fate of William's body. Native Americans customarily carried their dead away with them for burial. John Bradford, editor of the *Kentucky Gazette*, later observed that their leaving of slain comrades was "a thing never done if they can avoid it, and . . . the best evidence of defeat." If McGary and his settlers made a trip to Shawnee Springs that evening, they may have also caused the Shawnee to leave hastily without their dead. However, this same account turned the short skirmish outside the fort into a more prolonged battle and failed to mention Coomes. Suffice it to say, there seem to be some details missing in the tale.[16]

William Ray's death signified the end of any perceived peace on the frontier and was the opening salvo of an onslaught of Native American raids against the settlers that were so numerous and had such fatal consequences that 1777 came to be known as "the year of the bloody 7s." On a more personal level, local folk history relates that William's mother, Mary Buntin Ray McGary, was so overcome with grief over her son's death that she took to her bed and declined in health, dying at age forty-five in 1780. Local historical tradition identifies the cause of her death as tuberculosis. If this is accurate, she could have been ill before William's death or contracted the disease later, but grief and the difficulties of frontier life may have hastened the progress of her illness, for which there was no effective treatment at the time.[17]

The increased danger from Native American raids caused many settlers to retreat to the eastern colonies in 1777, leaving only a handful of forts and stations still occupied. Fort Harrod was one of these sites, and the McGarys and Rays remained here throughout that terrible year. They—particularly the men and boys who had to leave the fort to hunt—found themselves in constant danger. Even going to the town spring for water was a fraught endeavor. So successful were the Native Americans that year that they prevented the Fort Harrod settlers from raising any corn. The situation became desperate as food supplies dwindled.[18]

James Ray, then only a teenager, was reputed to be one of the best hunters in the fort. He left the stockade in the middle of the night, "[rode] with rapidity till he thought he was out of reach of the Indians," and hunted until he had all the meat he could carry. Then he would come back to the fort around dawn and make a dash into the stockade. According to his son, he made these trips twice weekly for several months without injury. However, on at least one occasion, Ray did not return to the fort when expected, and everyone was convinced he was dead. As it turned out, he had been chased by four or five warriors, but he was able to escape being captured and returned the next evening. When two other settlers offered to take over his hunting duties, he acquiesced but was forced to resume his activities when the two were killed the first night they ventured out. Ray's expert marksmanship also came in handy around the fort, resulting in the deaths of several Native Americans. General Robert B. McAfee wrote, "My old uncle, James McAfee, used to say, You may rely upon it, that that little Ray has a sharp eye, his gun never snaps when there is an Indian to shoot at."[19]

Nor was McGary lax when it came to defending his fellow settlers. There are several recorded incidents in which he brought women and children to safety or retrieved the bodies of settlers killed outside the fort. He also participated in George Rogers Clark's campaign in 1778 to capture Vincennes as well as in other retaliatory strikes against Native American groups living in the Ohio Territory.[20]

3

The McGary Family Settles at Shawnee Springs

Since the main reason for coming to Kentucky was to acquire land, Hugh McGary wasted no time. The desire for land was strong in the settlers who came to Kentucky, but they did not all come with equal opportunities to acquire it. For example, those with military certificates in hand, either acquired by military service or purchased, were much more likely to be able to acquire land. The timing of one's arrival was also important. Lincoln County, Kentucky, was one of the earliest settlement areas (from which Mercer County was formed in 1786) and was quickly carved up into grants of fourteen hundred acres or more.

Shawnee Springs first enters the historical record in the early 1770s, when Central Kentucky was explored by Daniel Boone, James Harrod, the McAfee brothers, and many others. Freshwater springs are abundant in the Mercer County area, and for a time, several springs vied for the name. But by 1779–1780, the springs system that now carries the name was a "place of considerable notoriety" to the settlers. As such, McGary's presence on the Kentucky frontier in 1775 conferred a great advantage—that is, he used his early presence in Kentucky to his advantage by raising a corn crop at the springs in 1776 and filing a claim with the land commissioners in 1779.[1]

Shawnee Springs is an impressive series of freshwater springs that form part of the headwaters of Shawnee Run, a tributary of the Kentucky River. The springs became a prominent and famous landmark early in the history of Kentucky's settlement and were well known to both Native Americans and settlers. The term "Shawnee Springs" was used by most settlers to refer to three springs concentrated at the headwaters of the Shawnee Run valley. The springs' mutual proximity and plentiful water supply made them an asset to incoming settlers, and they were quickly claimed. So famous were the springs that even modern maps continue to label them. The use of the term "Shawnee" pushes the notoriety of the springs even further back to times when the Shawnee and other tribal groups roamed Kentucky untroubled by land-hungry settlers. Shawnee Springs has been a place of meaning to many people in many times.[2]

A visit to the springs is a return into nature. The springs originate from three major openings in the rock formation at the headwaters of Shawnee Run. Walking upstream along Shawnee Run just below the springs, one first encounters the Great Blue Spring emanating from a cave once visible in the rock cliff. The cave was sealed off in the late nineteenth or early twentieth century, but originally, a person could walk into it. Water emerges from the cave source and pools in the bottomland, where watercress grows in a sheltered sunny spot along the margins of the pool. Proceeding further up to the head of the run, visitors come to a rocky slope where two strong streams of water emerge and flow noisily down the hillside, joining to form the Shawnee Run. Around them secondary-growth trees long undisturbed by axe or crosscut saw are tall and broad, replacing the forest cover that settlers encountered when they first saw the springs.

McGary claimed a prime piece of real estate on Shawnee Run that included the Shawnee Springs at the headwaters of the tributary. His original intention was to claim a 400-acre settlement and a 1,000-acre preemption around Shawnee Springs, but conflicting claims prevented him from getting that much land. However, he successfully claimed the land surrounding the springs themselves as well as a substantial area on either side of the run, totaling 575 acres.[3]

He also acquired additional grants or was assigned property by other men who sold him their claims to specific tracts. These then could be resold or reassigned. This process of land trading and selling took place well prior to the legal steps to acquire clear title and led to frequent instances where improvements, such as building a cabin or planting a corn crop, may have been made by one man but eventually used by another as evidence of his right to that particular claim. McGary seems to have come to Kentucky well prepared to acquire significant tracts of land.[4]

At the time McGary came to Kentucky, it was officially part of Fincastle County, Virginia. According to his settlement entry, he did not plant a corn

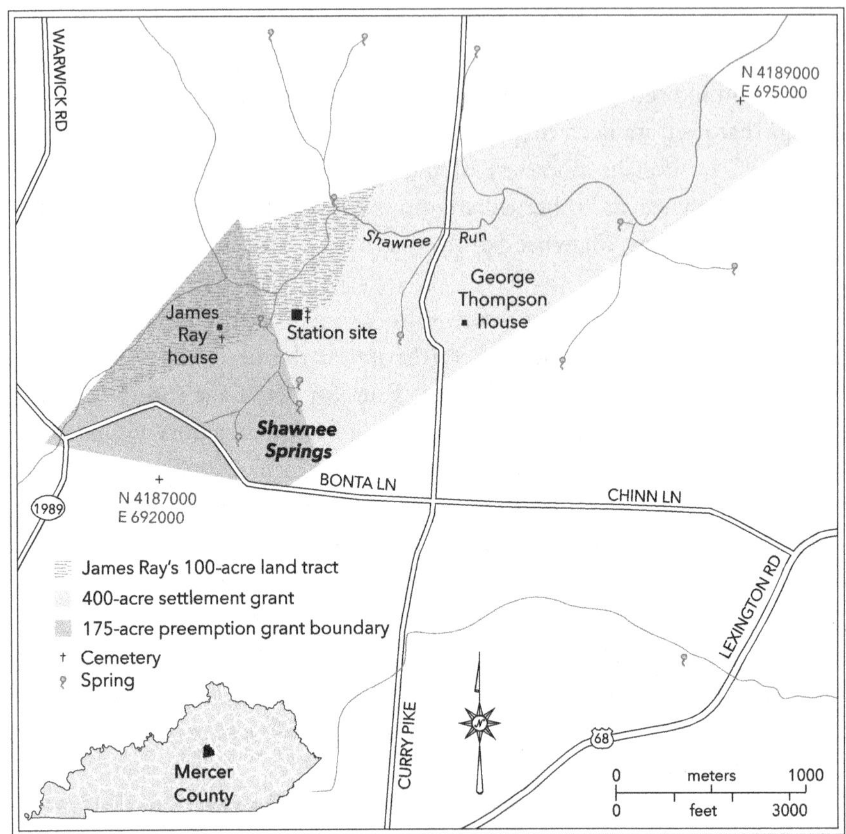

Map showing Hugh McGary's land grants at Shawnee Springs, station site, and James Ray's and George Thompson's house sites. Author's Collection.

crop at Shawnee Springs, the legal requirement for land improvement, until 1776. In December 1776, Fincastle County was abolished, and Kentucky County was created. However, it was not until May 1779, after a land law was passed, that settlers could register their claims for land. A land court was established for this purpose, with several commissioners' courts being held in 1779 and 1780. McGary attended one of these courts in Harrodsburg on October 27, 1779, where he applied for a settlement certificate on Shawnee Springs. McGary attended two courts in 1780, at Harrodsburg and Bryant's Station, where he served as a claimant's representative for Joseph Robertson and Lewis Holmes. His Kentucky County entries include the following:

1. 400-acre settlement on Shawnee Springs, dated November 3, 1779
2. 400-acre settlement on Silver Creek, dated February 21, 1780, and assigned to Joseph Robertson
3. 400-acre settlement on the Kentucky River, dated March 1, 1780, and assigned to Richard Porter
4. 400-acre settlement on Shawnee Run, dated March 1, 1780, and assigned to Lewis Holmes
5. 400-acre treasury warrant on Rolling Fork River, dated May 9, 1780, and assigned to J. Myers
6. 1,000-acre preemption on Shawnee Run, dated April 26, 1780, which was contested and only a portion was received

Virginia land grant records credit McGary with four tracts of 400 acres each, one 802-acre tract, a 175-acre tract, and a 74.5-acre tract assigned to him by Matthias Yocum. Of these tracts, McGary assigned one 400-acre tract each to Samuel Davis in 1784 and to Walter Beal in 1786; both of these tracts were outside Mercer County. The remaining tracts were all in Mercer County and included his two tracts totaling 575 acres at Shawnee Springs, granted by the land court in 1780, and two tracts of 802 and 400 acres on the Kentucky River, granted in 1783 and 1785. The 74.5-acre Yocum tract was granted in 1787. These dates document when the title became legal, but it is important to understand that McGary had, in most cases, control of the land much earlier. A good deal of business concerning land was carried out before legal title was gained in Kentucky.

Native American raiding began to slack off in 1778, and settlers resumed their attempts to clear their land and plant crops. McGary settled on his 400-acre settlement grant at Shawnee Springs. Henry Wilson told Lyman C. Draper that the McGary family built a "regular station, stockaded . . . in the fall of [1778] and moved there in the spring of 1779." Describing the station location in a court deposition, John Ray said that "McGary settled at . . . the Upper Shawnee spring near the old mill in 1779 in a cabbin east of a north course within about 100 or 150 yards of that spring." McGary's move to the station and the necessity of raising crops in the spring of 1779 prevented him from accompanying John Bowman on his campaign against the Shawnee town of Old Chillicothe in 1779. Wilson named the John Denton and John Yocum

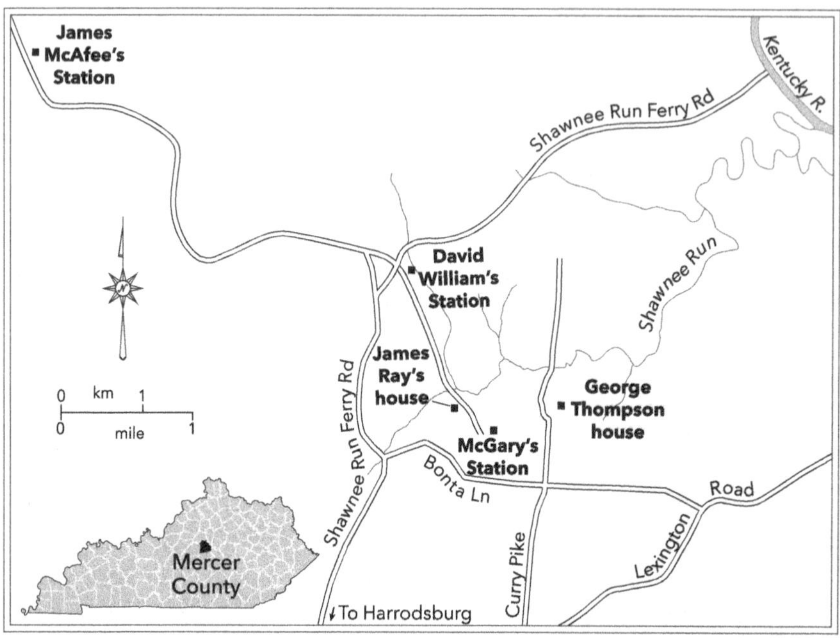

Generalized map showing possible road alignments (McGary's to McAfee's Station, Shawnee Run Ferry Road). Author's Collection.

families as two of "some dozen" families that lived there briefly until they could build stations of their own on their land claims. Others who lived there included the families of Thomas Denton, Matthias Yocum, and George Corn. Peter Jordan moved his family to the station in the spring of 1780 and lived there for five years. Various young men were assigned to the site which, like other stations, served to house "spies," young men who patrolled the countryside looking for signs of impending attack. An unknown number of enslaved persons probably lived at the station at various times as well. The "great blue spring" where the sugar camp was established is located near where James Ray later built his house on one hundred acres he purchased from his stepfather in 1787. Ray lived in the station until he finished his house, and McGary was still living there when he sold the remainder of his property the following year. This evidence suggests that the station was near one of the other springs.[5]

Due to conflicting prior claims, McGary was granted only 175 acres adjoining his 400-acre settlement around Shawnee Springs, but the court allowed him to claim the remaining 825 acres in another location on the

Kentucky River that included Harrod's Landing. In the course of entering, withdrawing, and reentering this claim, he described the land as being "on the landing road leading from the said McGary's Station to Harrods landing." The landing road probably ran north from McGary's Station past David Williams's Station, connecting with present-day Munday's Landing Road. From this juncture, a traveler could head east to the Kentucky River, west to the Salt River, or north to Harrod's Landing at present-day Oregon (an unincorporated community in Mercer County, Kentucky) on the Kentucky River. This road probably ran near or was the same as the private paved road that runs south from the antebellum house called Walnut Hall past David Williams's Station to Shawnee Springs. It may be part of a road that was ordered to be routed in 1786 from Harrodsburg to Harrod's Landing. The road surveyors reported that they marked a route through the land of Peter Hawkins, Henry Higgins, James Ray, David Williams, Simeon Moore, and Walter Beall. Subsequent appointments of surveyors suggest that sections of the road actually had to be built rather than following existing trails.[6]

Harrod's Landing is on the Kentucky River at Oregon. The first four men listed (Hawkins, Higgins, Ray, and Williams) all owned land south of Munday's Landing Road. A possible route of this early road could have been along or near present-day Warwick Road to its juncture with Bonta Lane, then along this lane to its first curve (which is also one of James Ray's boundary lines, formed by the one hundred acres McGary sold to him), then leaving Bonta Lane and running northeast to pass James Ray's house and then north through David Williams's land. The road could have then reached Harrod's Landing by following the general route of present-day Unity Road. If this route is generally correct, then the segment of Warwick Road from Bonta Lane to Munday's Landing may have been built later.

McGary's Station was also on a road running between it and James McAfee's Station. This was an old road in 1790 when Patrick Jordan saw an improvement marked for David Williams next to it. Since Williams's land was north of Ray's and McGary's, this road may be a segment of the Harrodsburg-Harrod's Landing Road. James McAfee's Station could have been reached by taking the Harrod's Landing Road to Munday's Landing Road, then the Unity Road to Dunn Lane, then traveling north to the road on which the community of Talmage is located. McAfee's Station is located north of Talmage.[7]

Still another road runs from Shawnee Springs to connect with the McCroskey Pike. The date of this road is not certain, but it also runs near or along the north boundary line of James Ray's four hundred acres. The land bequests James Ray made to his children, Jane, Harvey, and Jefferson (dating 1835–1847), all mention a road running from Harrodsburg to the mouth of Shawnee Run as the Shawnee Run Ferry Road. Although the exact placement is slightly problematic, the road, or parts of it, that these deeds best fit is present-day Warwick Road between Bonta Land and Munday's Landing Road. It is possible that when the Warwick Turnpike was organized in the 1830s, segments of existing road may have been incorporated into the new route. The Shawnee Run Ferry Road was described by John Mahan of Jessamine County as the road used to reach Harrodsburg from Lexington.[8]

McGary's land was heavily wooded, as was most of Central Kentucky at the beginning of the frontier era. His metes-and-bounds description for his settlement and preemption lists Spanish and white oaks, sugar maple, wild cherry, beech, ash, and hickory trees for the corners. Sugar maples grew in large quantities around the springs, probably on lower elevations, where they would have been well watered. Other frontier surveys nearby list additional tree types such as honey locust, hackberry, walnut, red oak, elm, and even dogwood. Although the settlers appreciated the value of Kentucky's woods for use as raw material and fuel, their mental blueprint for developing the agricultural potential of their land demanded large-scale clearing of the forests. The use of wood to construct houses, outbuildings, and other items, and the voracious demands for fuel to stoke the inefficient fireplaces of late eighteenth- and early nineteenth-century residences all contributed to the demise of the forested Kentucky landscape at the hands of early settlers.

Life at McGary's Station was bustling with activity in the late 1770s and early 1780s. In addition to labor-intensive agricultural chores, the men at the station also had military service that sometimes took them away from their homes for several days or weeks. James Ray stayed busy as a "spy," spending many hours on horseback patrolling the region. McGary was sent to Pittsburg in 1777 by Gen. George Rogers Clark to deliver a list of stolen horses with their descriptive marks in the hope that an expedition ordered by the Virginia General Assembly might recover them for their owners. He traveled all over Central Kentucky for various purposes and took up duties as a justice of the peace for Lincoln County in 1781, so he was frequently away from home. He served in the militia as a lieutenant, and by 1781, a major. He participated in the Battle of Blue Licks and Gen. George Rogers Clark's campaign to Chillicothe and Piqua in 1782 and was involved in many other skirmishes.[9]

McGary's first wife Mary, until her death in 1780, and his second wife, Catherine (Catey or Catesey) Yocum, whom he married in August of the same year, reared children and managed their households and matters of daily living at the station. Between the two women, McGary was stepfather to three sons and biological father to two more sons and two daughters by Mary and four sons and three daughters by Catesey by the time he sold his station land and moved away between 1788 and 1792. Archaeological artifacts recovered from the station offer insights into the material culture of his large, blended family.

The Yocum family, led by Matthias Yocum, came to Kentucky in the fall of 1779, living for a while at McGary's Station. They established their own station in 1780. Sarah Graham, in an interview with Reverend John Dabney Shane around 1844, passed along a local tale about McGary's courtship of his second wife that does not reflect well on his character but is a good example of the checkered nature of his reputation and the willingness of people to pass along unsavory gossip even long after his death. Mrs. Graham related that "it was said he would go to see her, two miles off, while his first wife . . . lay sick; and that one of the boys, Ray's, as it was thought, used to stop him in the road . . . and appear to him as a spectre, wrapped up in sheets, and talk to him of it, as the spirit of his present wife. Twas said the widow Ray could manage McGary when a whole army could not do it."[10]

Nathaniel Hart Jr. also left very unfavorable impressions of McGary, stating that one of his wives had two illegitimate children and that McGary fathered a child by one of his daughters, who was herself illegitimate. While there are gaps in the McGary family genealogy, Hart's accusations appear to be more spiteful than accurate and are very likely based on secondhand gossip and innuendo. A letter sent to the Harrodsburg Historical Society by Cornelia L. Elliott in 1927 described a Bible that was in her possession, having been passed down through the family from Daniel McGary, Hugh's son. It was purported to have been brought to Kentucky by McGary in 1775. McGary's children and stepchildren are listed along with other family members. Several Yocums are listed alongside McGarys, Rays, and other surnames. However, familial relationships are not indicated. Family history lists Mary McGary as having had four children by Hugh McGary, including, by birth order, Robert, Daniel, Mary Ann, and Rosanna. Children attributed to Catharine Yocum McGary while she was living at the station include John (born February 6, 1780, the year Mary died), William Ray, Hugh Jr., Nancy, Jesse, Catharine, and Elizabeth. If John's mother was Catherine, he may be one of the illegitimate children Hart mentioned. However, Mary Ray McGary may have been John's mother. While her death is attributed to tuberculosis, pregnancy would have exacerbated her condition, and she may have died shortly after giving birth. McGary's rapid remarriage after his wife's death was common on the frontier. Without more precise primary documentation of the exact date of Mary McGary's death and the maternity of John, it is difficult to resolve these issues. McGary's attitude toward women and marital fidelity is unknown, but in general, the available documentary evidence suggests that he had something of a soft spot for women and was solicitous of, and concerned about, their welfare. At the same time, a chronically ill wife had to be a liability on a frontier, particularly with young children in the household. The shortage of adult women at the station must have presented difficulties managing a household while McGary was on the road performing his military and civic duties.[11]

John Ray (James Ray's son) wrote that James Ray married Catherine's sister, Amelia (called Milley), in 1779 at Yocum's Station. They lived at McGary's Station but since the other families were moving out to establish their own stations, the female contingent at McGary's was far outnumbered by the male household members. Amelia was probably delighted to have her sister join her. Both women began adding to the family, Amelia with sons William and Jesse before her death in 1785, and Catherine with four more sons and three daughters before she died, around 1800.[12]

The McGary household may have been assisted in the tasks of daily living by enslaved persons. Both James Ray and McGary were owners of enslaved persons when they died. McGary may have brought some enslaved people with him when he first moved to Kentucky. He certainly acquired them after he arrived because he stated in a deposition in 1794 that he had sold 420 acres for "seven negroes nearly grown." McGary sold enslaved people on other occasions as well and may have done so on a regular basis although what evidence exists dates to the period after he sold his station site.[13]

The trade in enslaved persons was considered an unsavory business, although many white persons sold slaves when they deemed it necessary. Enslaved persons were generally sold to settle an estate, to be rid of a recalcitrant or disobedient individual, or to settle debt. The extent of McGary's involvement in this trade is not known, but, as in many other aspects of his life, rumors arose over his treatment of enslaved persons. Nathaniel Hart Jr. referred to the trade of land for enslaved people (although he incorrectly named John Thompson rather than George Thompson as the other party in the transaction), and further stated that "these McGary treated most inhumanely." Hart claimed that McGary caused the death or serious injury of one enslaved man by beating him to unconsciousness and allowing him to fall against a burning log. The source of this story is unclear. Hart's daughter, Sarah Hart, became the third wife of George C. Thompson, son of Col. George Thompson who bought McGary's property in 1788. This marriage took place many years after McGary's departure from Mercer County and his death in Indiana. While Colonel Thompson may well have been in a position to know if McGary mistreated an enslaved person, Nathaniel Hart must have heard it secondhand or even thirdhand. Under the circumstances, it would not be surprising if the story grew in the retelling. Nevertheless, the account is grim and highlights the helplessness of enslaved persons when confronted with a violent owner.[14]

In addition to his military service and clearing and improving his land, McGary also served as justice of the peace, being listed as such on January 16, 1781, in the first order book for Lincoln County. He was a regular attendant at court and missed very few meetings in 1781. He and the other justices performed many duties, including the appointment of committees for various reasons, setting tavern rates, hearing civil cases, and recording military commissions for the local militia.

Not surprisingly, McGary took a keen interest in the politics of the time. One issue that sparked the creation of several politically motivated groups was the question of separation from Virginia, a move that was favored by some largely because they disliked the system of land distribution currently in place but also for other reasons. Some of the separatists were in favor only if it was done constitutionally with Virginia's consent and on mutually agreed terms. More impatient partisans (as Watlington's 1972 study refers to them) wished to separate unconditionally and then have the freedom to adopt land and other policies that were more favorable to their interests. This position left open the possibility of some land grants being canceled and was strongly contested by men who already had been granted land they did not wish to lose. Finally, a radical faction favored a declaration of independence and then negotiation for an association with a foreign power, which could be the United States or some European country with American interests. While the partisans were not very numerous, they did stir up considerable discussion by having meetings, circulating petitions, and writing letters.[15]

One of the partisans was a man named John Kinkead, who lived near Harrodsburg. In the fall of 1781, he and others of similar mind held a meeting at

Harrodsburg with the purpose of petitioning Congress to take Kentucky land away from Virginia and reapportion it more equably. John Cowan, an early settler in what is now Boyle County, Kentucky, described the partisans in a letter to Levi Todd as "a discontented few, most of whom had no land" and further said that "they were dispersed in a forseable [forcible] manner . . . by Col. Hugh McGary." James Ray wrote to Todd about the same meeting, referring to "the spirited conduct of Col. McGary and a party who Join'd him." There were many landowners who no doubt applauded McGary's actions.[16]

The forcefulness of McGary's personality is obvious to any student of history. Because he seems to have had a complex, mercurial character, his actions generated widely varying reactions from his fellow settlers. His peers deemed him sufficiently competent to serve as a justice of the peace, yet he was also capable of provoking a fistfight by insulting a fellow settler. While seemingly solicitous of women and children, going out of his way to look after widows and orphans or to rescue people stranded outside Fort Harrod, his frequent reaction to sensitive situations was violent or hasty, or both, whether it involved a political controversy, a personal conflict, or a military action. Descriptions by later historians offered increasingly negative views of him. Humphrey Marshall wrote in 1824, "It may be said with truth, that for enterprising and daring courage, none transcended Major Hugh McGary." Yet only ten years later, Mann Butler described McGary as "a man of courage, almost too fierce for Indian battles, much less for pacific society." By 1847, John Mason Peck characterized McGary as "a man of fierce and daring courage, but of a fiery and ferocious temper, void of humane and gentle qualities, a quarrelsome and unpleasant man in civil life."[17]

Was McGary the blackguard that history has painted him? On the one hand, he willingly participated as a militia officer on Gen. George Rogers Clark's Kaskaskia campaign in 1778 and his sacking of Shawnee villages in 1782 as well as many other skirmishes, rescues, and encounters with Native Americans. On the negative side, he behaved reprehensibly at the Battle of Blue Licks (see chapter 7) and committed other acts that brought censure against him. His descendant, Mary Hammersmith, thought some of the claims about his bad character were overdrawn and, in some cases, untrue. As she wrote, "And what if, in the end, some distasteful stories about some members of the family may happen to be true? . . . In coping with this aspect of the dilemma, I came in time to realize that if a person understands he can't take credit for his ancestors' achievements, he doesn't have to feel embarrassment or responsibility for his ancestors' shortcomings. With that attitude, detachment becomes easier. . . . Hugh McGary's young stepson was murdered and mutilated by Indians. This doesn't excuse McGary's subsequent behavior, but it does explain it."[18] The truth about Hugh McGary's character and personality is a shifting target that moves toward or away from either a negative or positive assessment of him, depending on how the evidence is weighted. Do his misdeeds outweigh his achievements and acts of bravery and concern for his fellow settlers? There is no clear answer.

4

The Boone Family Settles at Fort Boonesborough

Settling at Fort Boonesborough in 1775, the Boones made their home there for most of the next four years. Their sojourn at Fort Boonesborough was punctuated by many stressful and dangerous events. In July 1776, Jemima Boone, Daniel and Rebecca's second daughter and fourth child, and the daughters of Richard Callaway, Frances and Betsy, were taken captive by five Shawnee and Cherokee men while they canoed on the Kentucky River. The two distraught fathers led separate parties, Boone on foot and Callaway on horseback, to rescue the girls. Boone reached them first and was successful in rescuing them without injury or loss of life to the rescue party. Their captors were less fortunate as two of them were mortally wounded. The incident may have been, in part, why Boone did not have a cordial relationship with Callaway, as later events made clear.

The two were not social equals. Callaway was affluent, owned enslaved persons, and was politically well connected. He considered himself a social equal to Richard Henderson and his Transylvania partners, outranked Boone, and was twenty years older. He likely thought Boone was his social inferior. Boone's natural abilities as a leader who was someone people called upon in times of strife may well have irked Callaway, who may have wanted such recognition himself. The circumstances of his daughters' kidnapping may have exacerbated matters, since the girls took the fort's sole canoe out for a joyride and seemed to have been heedless of the potential danger. One of the Callaway girls was sixteen and engaged to be married and should have known better, but Callaway may have placed much of the blame on Jemima, who wanted to take the canoe so that she could soothe a foot injury by dipping it in the river. Part of his distress stemmed from his fear that his daughters might be sexually molested by their captors. The fact that Boone and his men reached the girls first and rescued them without Callaway's assistance probably rankled as well.[1]

The incident heralded the opening of intense hostilities between the settlers and the tribes that characterized the incessant violence of 1777. The Boones stayed throughout the conflict that drove many other settlers back east, but not without many sacrifices and privations.

By early 1778, the settlers at Fort Boonesborough were nearly out of salt to preserve their primary food source, wild meat. Boone led a party of thirty men to the Lower Blue Licks to process the mineral-charged spring water for salt. A large party of Shawnee warriors encountered Boone as he hunted for meat to feed his salt makers, who were still at the springs. Forcing him to take them to the lick, they threatened to kill everyone but were persuaded by Boone to take the salt makers prisoners instead. The captives were divided up and sent to different places, some to Native American villages, and others to the British outpost at Detroit. Boone spent four months in captivity at the Shawnee village of Chillicothe, where he was adopted by Chief Blackfish and treated with considerable leniency. His preferential treatment did not sit well with some of the captives who were in the same village. Learning of plans for a large multitribal expedition to attack Fort Boonesborough, he escaped and spent a harrowing four days to cover the 160 miles, mostly on foot, to the fort. There he helped ready the fort's defenses for the looming attack.[2]

The Siege of Fort Boonesborough became one of the most famous incidents in Kentucky history. The settlers, estimated to number sixty able-bodied white men, seventy-five women and children, and an unknown number of enslaved people, held out for nine days against a superior force of more than four hundred Native Americans accompanied by several French-Canadian militia. Among them was Chief Blackfish, who called on Boone to surrender the fort as he had promised when negotiating for the lives of his salt makers. Boone had never intended to make good on his promise, but the perceived perfidy did not impress Callaway, who put the worst possible interpretation on Boone's actions. After the siege was lifted and the attackers left in defeat, Boone was subjected to a court-martial called by Colonel Callaway and another militia officer, Benjamin Logan, who headed another fort nearby. Callaway accused Boone of treason and treachery, arguing that he offered his men up as captives, cooperated and even consorted with the British during his captivity, and exposed the fort's leaders to ambush during the siege when the two sides met to negotiate peace. Boone countered by saying that he surrendered his men to prevent the Native Americans from coming to Fort Boonesborough when it was in a poor state of defense, that he deliberately misled the British and the Shawnee, and that his actions during the siege should exonerate him of any charges of treason. Two other salt makers who had escaped their captivity offered additional testimony in his favor, and he was acquitted. Although exonerated by the tribunal of militia officers who even promoted him to major, Boone felt humiliated and offended by the accusations. Soon afterward, he returned to North Carolina, where Rebecca, thinking he was dead, had taken most of his family to live. There he stayed for an uncomfortable year as he pondered his next move. John Filson, Boone's biographer, quoted him as saying, "The history of my going home, and returning with my family forms a series of difficulties, an account of which would swell a volume." His son Nathan believed that Rebecca was opposed to taking any more risks in Kentucky, an understandable attitude given that she had already lost one son and nearly lost her husband to death at the hands of Indigenous foes.[3]

5

Daniel Boone Builds a Station on Boone's Creek

His wife's opposition notwithstanding, Daniel Boone did not give up his plans to settle west of the Appalachian Mountains. In 1779, he had good reason to return to Kentucky in pursuit of land and to better his fortunes. The Virginia Assembly had passed a land law in 1778 that laid out a legal path for settlers to claim land, and Governor Thomas Jefferson appointed land commissioners to go to Kentucky to confirm the claims in 1779–1780. Boone had numerous parcels that he had improved or where he raised a corn crop before January 1, 1778, so he was in an enviable position to acquire significant quantities of land. He had to return to Kentucky to make the claims. Many of his Boone and Bryan kinsmen also decided to make the trip. The circumstances probably tipped the balance for Rebecca, who agreed to return with him. The large company of some one hundred people left in mid-September 1779 and arrived at Fort Boonesborough in late October. There Boone had to wait until he could file his claims at the commissioners' proceedings in December.[1]

Boone was involved in many land surveys for himself and for his family members and as a land jobber who received pay for his services for other men. His surveying activities preceded the newly passed land law, but the law enabled him or the claimants for whom he had surveyed to seek legal title by presenting evidence of military service and improvement of the land claimed. The land on which he built Boone's Station was originally awarded to Boone's son, Israel, and consisted of a four-hundred-acre settlement and an adjoining thousand-acre preemption by virtue of his son raising a corn crop there in

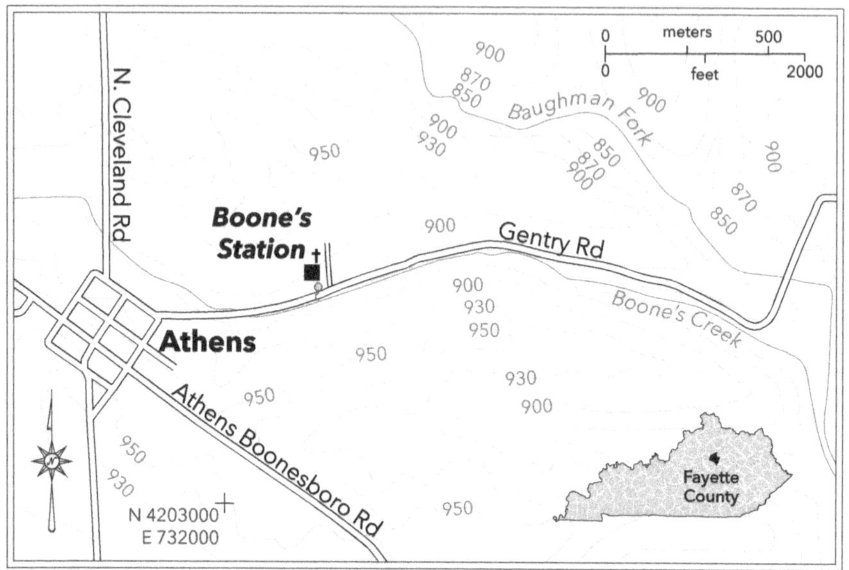

Map showing Daniel Boone's Station. Author's Collection.

1775 and 1776. The acreage was described as "between and joining [James] Hickman's two surveys on the said [Boone] Creek." The land court issued a certificate on December 24. The Boone family immediately set off for Boone Creek, arriving on December 26.[2]

The station population, at the time of its establishment in 1779, included Daniel and Rebecca Boone and their five children still at home (Israel, Levina, Rebecca, Daniel Morgan, and Jesse Bryan) as well as several families related to them. Including Daniel and Rebecca Boone's family, at least six families were living at the station at its inception. Daniel and Rebecca's daughter, Susannah, and her husband, William Hays, were there with their two young daughters, Elizabeth and Jemima. Susannah had at least two—perhaps three—more children while at the station: William Hays Jr., born in 1780; Susannah, born in 1782; and possibly Boone, born in 1783. Another daughter, Jemima, married Flanders Callaway, possibly in 1779, and had her first child, Sarah (Sally) Callaway, in 1780. Her second child, John Boone Callaway, was born on July 4, 1781, shortly after Daniel Boone finished his first session as the representative for Fayette County at the Virginia General Assembly. She may have had a third child, James, in 1783, before moving away.

Two of Daniel Boone's brothers, Samuel and Edward, made the move with their families. Edward and his wife, Martha Bryan Boone (sister to Rebecca Bryan Boone) had six children (Mary, George, Joseph, Sarah, Jane, and Charity) who may have all still been living with their parents in 1779. Older brother Samuel and his wife, Sarah Day Boone, had six children, some or all of whom were at the station. The birth years of two of their sons, Samuel Jr. (1758) and Squire (1760), indicate they were twenty-one and nineteen years old in 1779. The birth years of the other children, Thomas, Rebecca, Mary (Polly), and Levi, are not known, but they were probably younger. Thomas was definitely at the station, because he accompanied the other station men to the Battle of Blue Licks in 1782, where he was killed. Some or all of the children of Rebecca Boone's cousin, James, and his deceased wife, Rebecca Enox Bryan, were raised by Daniel and Rebecca Boone after their mother died. Their father, James Bryan, never remarried and was involved in the settlement of Bryan's Station in 1779. His older sons, David, Jonathan, and Henry, were twenty-two, twenty, and eighteen years old, respectively, in 1779 and may have been with their father. The three youngest children, Susan, Mary (Polly), and Rebecca, were sixteen, fourteen, and twelve years old in 1779 and were most likely at Boone's Station, since they all married while there.

Boone's cousin, William Scholl, and his wife, Leah Morgan Scholl, brought their large family to the station, and two of their sons married Boones while there. Peter, who was born in 1754 and may have been the oldest, married Mary, daughter of Edward Boone, at the station around 1782. Joseph, born in 1755, married Levina, Daniel's daughter. Other children included John, Sarah (Sally), Elizabeth, Rachel, Aaron, Isaac, Abraham (born in 1765), Jacob (who died in infancy), and William. Peter Scholl stated that he lived there for five years (1779–1784). He probably left with his parents when they moved to a fourteen-hundred-acre settlement and preemption in Clark County, Kentucky that became the community of Schollsville. Rachel Denton said William Hays and Joseph Scholl left in the fall of 1784 and settled their families on Marble Creek about five miles distant.[3]

Other families that were not related to the Boones also took up residence at the station. Asa C. Barrow and James McMillan were there with their families, and George Muir may also have been, since his daughter was born there. The precise dates of their tenure at the station are not known.

The Boones and their relatives began building on Boone Creek on a cold December day. Peter Shull (Scholl) deposed in a Bourbon Circuit Court case that he "raked the snow off the ground to commence building the fort." One of the station inhabitants, Rachel Denton, recalled years later to historian Lyman C. Draper that they first erected "half-faced camps made of boards and forked sticks." These crude shelters, open to the elements, with fires maintained near their openings, were all the settlers had between them and the cruelly cold temperatures of the "Hard Winter" of 1779–1780. The winter was so bad that the buffalo, bears, deer, and turkeys that formed the bulk of their meat diet were very poor and lean. Boone brought "a considerable supply of corn" to share with all the settlers. Snow remained on the ground from December to March before temperatures abated enough for it to melt. When the weather broke, the settlers built a rectangular enclosure of log cabins with gun ports, each structure joined by a stockade to its neighbor. There was access to the interior by means of one or more gates. The station stood at an upland elevation about sixty meters northeast of the freshwater spring that could be utilized for water. There was also a well located inside the enclosure.[4]

The size of the station was determined in part by the number of cabins needed to house the families that lived there. Sarah Boone Hunter, daughter of Edward and Martha Boone, remembered that fifteen families lived in the half-acre enclosure. Some of the cabins may have been double pen (two main rooms), with room for more than one family. Archaeological excavation in 1999 confirmed the presence of three cabins, and remote sensing, metal detection, and shovel probe surveying indicated possibly four more within the area surveyed.

Once the weather allowed, the settlers at Boone's Station turned their attention to planting corn, vegetables, and other necessary crops. They tapped a nearby grove of sugar maples for their sap to boil down for sugar. Mrs. Denton recalled that "the poor miserable buffalo" came to the sugar-making camp to drink the sugar water and could hardly be driven off, so desperately hungry they were. The children were sent to gather rotted nettles that were used to make fiber for warping the women's looms. Buffalo hair was used to compose the weft of the fabric when sheep's wool was unavailable. Wild fruits such as pawpaws, grapes, and plums, as well as nuts, were particularly plentiful that year, and the cultivated corn and pumpkins also thrived. After the privations of the cold winter, the abundance of wild and domesticated food must have been very welcome.[5]

As the family worked to make the station habitable and ensure an adequate food supply, Boone prepared for a trip to Williamsburg, Virginia, to file certificates signed by the land court commissioners for himself and some of his neighbors. He traveled with two other men, whose names are unknown, and arrived at the home of Adam Byrd a few miles from Williamsburg on March 20, 1780. That night, the men were robbed of many of the certificates they carried and the cash they intended to use to pay for filing the warrants. Boone suspected that they had been drugged and that the theft had been perpetrated by Byrd, but he had no proof. Boone did not lose his own certificates, but the incident was devastating for the men who lost their certificates and money as well as for Boone, who felt responsible for the loss. Boone later filed a memorandum listing the names of the men whose certificates were stolen with Levi Todd, clerk of Fayette County, who certified it to the Register of the Land Office so that the warrants could be procured. The memorandum lists the following names: William Hicks; Edward Bradley; William Hays, assignee of James Forbush; John Bullock; Nathaniel Bullock; Nicholas George; Lewis Enow; Thomas Swearingen; three certificates in the name of Abraham Chaplin, Joseph Essex, and Nicholas Proctor; Nicholas Proctor; John Snoddy; James Wharton; John Boyles; Robert Preston; Moses Thomas, assignee of William Criddlebough; John Bundrum; James Guthery; Robert Boggs; and a military warrant granted to Phillip Chapman and assigned to Henry Smith. Some of the men held Boone responsible for the losses, and he worked hard to reimburse them over the next few years.[6]

In June, following Boone's return to Kentucky, John Martin's and Isaac Ruddell's Stations were attacked by a large enemy force. At the time of the attack, Ruddell's and Martin's Stations were two of five stations in the area later constituting the present boundaries of Bourbon and Harrison Counties. Ruddell's Station, located on the South Fork of Licking River near the later boundary between Bourbon and Harrison Counties, was the more exposed of the five, being the farthest north. Martin's Station was located nearly seven miles to the south of Ruddell's on Stoner Creek, a tributary of the South Fork of the Licking.

The attack was conducted by a combined British, Canadian, and Native American army under the command of Captain Henry Bird. It was notable for the size and composition of the army and the use of heavy artillery. Bird led a company of an estimated one thousand men, comprised of British soldiers, Canadian volunteers, and hundreds of Native American men from several tribes, by boat down the Licking River to a point where navigation became difficult, then overland on a trail that became known as Bird's War

Road. The expedition carried with them several pieces of heavy artillery capable of destroying the log stockade and cabin enclosures that constituted the stations. Reaching Ruddell's Station on June 22, Bird discharged one of the fieldpieces as an opening salvo, then demanded the station's surrender. Captain Ruddell assented on the condition that the prisoners be under British protection, after which he opened the gates. Despite Bird's promise, the warriors rushed in and seized the settlers, separating families and gathering up property. Some prisoners were killed. Bird was outraged by the warriors' conduct but had little recourse because of their greater numbers. He refused to continue to Martin's Station without reassurances that the warriors would take only plunder while Bird maintained control of the prisoners. Martin's Station fell without opposition.[7]

In stark contrast with the usually much smaller attacks by a few Native American warriors against settlers caught outside the protection of their stations, Bird's army attacked two sizable stations and captured the largest number of settlers ever taken in Kentucky in a single encounter. Several hundred prisoners were marched to Detroit (some dying of exposure along the way), where most of them remained captive for several years. A contingent of warriors broke off from the main body and went to John Grant's Station in present-day Bourbon County, Kentucky and, finding it abandoned, burned it. The attack had a chilling effect on the occupation of the South Fork Licking drainage as many settlers moved closer to Lexington and abandoned their improvements and stations.[8]

The scope and magnitude of the attacks on Ruddell's and Martin's Stations threw the Kentucky settlers into a panic, and many called upon Gen. George Rogers Clark to conduct a retaliatory raid. General Clark put out a call for volunteers to accompany him for an invasion of the Native American villages north of the Ohio River. In the spring of 1780, Col. George Slaughter arrived at the Falls of the Ohio with nearly 100 Virginia regulars. Clark was then in the process of building Fort Jefferson on the Mississippi River far to the west. He returned to the Falls shortly after the capture of Ruddell's and Martin's Stations. Clark was partially dependent on militia companies from the various stations and forts to man his army and collaborated with Col. Benjamin Logan who took the place of Col. John Bowman as second in command. The two officers assembled and organized 970 men into two divisions comprising four-fifths of the able-bodied men in Kentucky at the time. Clark named the mouth of the Licking River as the meeting place for the various companies.

Maj. James Harrod led four small companies totaling 124 men to the Falls of the Ohio to join Clark's 80 Virginia regulars under Colonel Slaughter's command, as well as two small militia regiments of 200 and 233 men, led by Col. John Floyd and Col. William Lynn, respectively. Serving as a captain under Major Harrod, Hugh McGary led one of the Harrodsburg companies on the north side of the Ohio River with orders to hunt for game, while the main army marched under George Rogers Clark on the other side. Colonel Slaughter supervised boats for transporting men and supplies, including a brass cannon that Clark captured at Vincennes, up the Ohio. At a point near the present town of Warsaw in Gallatin County, Kentucky, McGary's party found nineteen paddles and more in the process of being made, accompanied by Native American "budgets" (bags holding provisions or other items). The Native Americans who were making the paddles were absent. McGary's men were between the mouths of the Kentucky and Licking Rivers when warriors fired upon them as they reentered the boats, killing 9 and injuring several.

At the mouth of the Kentucky River, Clark picked up Squire Boone and the men from his station in present-day Shelby County, Kentucky. The remainder of the party, forming eight companies and containing 328 men, came from the Central Kentucky stations and was commanded by Benjamin Logan. The militia companies varied in size from Capt. Robert Patterson's 90 men to 43 men commanded by Capt. John Holder, and 32 men each in companies led by William Whitley, John Logan, Levi Todd, John Kennedy, John Doherty, and Samuel Scott. Daniel Boone signed on as a scout and was probably attached to Patterson's or Todd's company.

The force of about 970 men rendezvoused on the Licking River and arrived on August 2 at the Ohio River at present-day Cincinnati. They reached Chillicothe on August 6 and found it abandoned and burning. After cutting down several hundred acres of corn, they proceeded to the Piqua villages, about twelve miles distant, in pouring rain. The Native American trail that the expedition followed crossed the Mad River downstream of Piqua, and there the militiamen were attacked. Clark ordered Colonel Logan to take 400 men and march up the east side of the river to the upper end of the town, while another contingent under the command of Colonels Lynn, Floyd, and Harrod marched to the west side of the town. General Clark and Col. George Slaughter led their Jefferson County troops along the road directly to the town. The western division of men came under attack and was forced to engage about a mile from the town, fighting until late in the day, when the

Shawnee withdrew. The other divisions saw little to no action and reached the town to find quantities of food cooking in large kettles, indicating that the Shawnee had not expected the militia to reach the town as quickly as they did. General Clark concluded his retaliatory raid by destroying the extensive corn fields, vegetable gardens, and dwellings, and by collecting horses for the march home. Lack of sufficient provisions prevented Clark's army from doing even greater damage, but the campaign cemented his reputation for swift and brutal retaliation.[9]

The fall of 1780 saw the Boone family harvesting crops and preserving meat for the coming winter. Daniel Boone spent much of his time hunting, and it was on one of these hunting trips that he suffered his next tragic family loss. As all accounts were from people who heard about the event secondhand from various sources, the details vary, but the following can be pieced together as a plausible scenario: Daniel and his younger brother, Edward, familiarly known as Ned, were returning from a hunt in the Upper Blue Licks area. They stopped to rest their horses, which were heavily loaded down with buffalo meat, in an area known as Grassy Lick in the eastern part of present-day Bourbon County, Kentucky. Edward remained with the horses, cracking nuts to pass the time, while Boone went into the nearby woods to hunt. He had just shot a bear when he heard shots ring out from his brother's location. Convinced that his brother was dead and that warriors were on his own trail, Boone ran for about three miles, then fled into a canebrake as the warriors pursued him with a dog. The canebrake provided him with sufficient cover to elude capture, but he was forced to kill the dog as it neared. He managed to make his way back to his station on foot, where he broke the news of Edward's death to his wife, Martha, and the other station inhabitants.

Edward and Martha Boone had six children, Charity (twenty years old), Jane (eighteen years), Mary (sixteen years), George (thirteen years), Joseph (twelve years), and Sarah (nine years). The youngest children were likely at the station when their father was killed, but no record was found to confirm that all the children were living there. The youngest, Sarah Boone Hunter, was present and was later in contact with Lyman C. Draper to whom she described her father's death: "My father Edward Boone was killed 40 miles from the station. He was stabbed in 7 places, his fingers were horribly cut with the Indian's knife. He was scalped—part of his clothing were taken off, I think his coat & pantaloons."[10]

Boone gathered men from his and other stations in the area to form a burial party for Edward and to attempt pursuit of the Native Americans responsible for his death. Several of these men later relayed the experience, in varying detail, to Draper. John McIntyre listed, in addition to himself, Charles Gatliff, James Estill, James Ray, and William McConnell as members of the party and said there were sixty or seventy men altogether. Peter Scholl, who later married Edward Boone's daughter, Mary, mentioned that Israel Boone and Israel Grant were members of the party as well. Daniel Boone said Jacob Strucker was in attendance, and James Ray corroborated that claim. Col. James Davidson added William and George Boone to the list of men. George Boone was another brother to Edward and was, according to Davidson, "much affected" when he saw his brother's mutilated body. Several published references claim that Edward Boone was beheaded but, on this point, they are contradicted by Sarah Boone Hunter's recollection, as well as others who state he was scalped, and his body mutilated.[11]

In pursuit of their enemy, the men followed a series of well-known trails. James Ray deposed that the men pursued the warriors to the Upper Blue Licks and then on to the Lower Blue Licks, then went along a "plain road" to another road near Limestone (in present-day Maysville). Boone described in considerable detail the route from the Upper Blue Licks, describing it as a "war-road" that forked at Fleming Creek three or four miles from the Licks. The upper fork led a northerly course to a clay lick on the North Fork of the Licking River, continuing north and crossing the fork twice until it reached Cabin Creek. The road followed Cabin Creek to Stone Lick and continued to the creek's mouth, where it debouched into the Ohio River. Nine or ten of the men, including Jacob Strucker and Charles Gatliff, stopped at the Stone Lick. John Stephenson said that the bulk of the company reached Cabin Creek near the Ohio River, only to find that the Native Americans had crossed the river and were out of reach. Peter Scholl spoke in greater detail about the warriors' trail and mentioned seeing where they had stopped to roast the meat they took from the Boones. He related that some "spies" were sent forward to see if the Native Americans had crossed the Ohio River, while the rest of the company remained behind upstream of the mouth of Cabin Creek.

Boone traveled some twenty miles by foot to reach his station by the following morning. He immediately began to gather a large number of men from his station, as well as from Bryan's Station and perhaps elsewhere, to return to the scene, bury Edward, and then attempt a pursuit. No one mentioned how long the return, gathering of the men, and burial took, but it must have taken at least twenty-four hours if not more. One might justifiably ask why they tried to follow and overtake the Native Americans. They were not going to be successful given the amount of time the warriors had to reach the Ohio River and cross it. Why did they still attempt it? The answer may simply be that retaliatory expeditions were a common response to Native American attacks. Edward Boone had been in Kentucky for less than a year and apparently had not made any earlier trips before he emigrated. He'd lived only at Boone's Station and probably did not know very many settlers outside of his relatives at Boone's and Bryan's Stations. Nevertheless, his death prompted many men to follow the warriors' trail in the hope that they could engage them before they crossed the Ohio River. His connection to Daniel Boone may have been a motivation in addition to the knowledge that participation in these raids was a collective offensive strategy with potential benefits for everyone.

After the excitement of Edward's murder, winter set in, and Native American raids lessened as the weather worsened. Settlers sought sanctuary in their stations and lived off the food they had grown or gathered while awaiting a new year. On the home front, Rebecca Boone was pregnant with her last child, a son named Nathan, who was born on March 2. Daniel and Rebecca's daughter, Jemima Boone Callaway, was also pregnant with her son, John Boone Callaway, and another daughter, Susannah Hays, had delivered a son, William Hays Jr., the previous year. The war continued but the wheels of government intent on establishing order in the Kentucky frontier rolled on. In November 1780, the Virginia Assembly divided Kentucky County into three parts, naming the new counties Fayette, Jefferson, and Lincoln. The new counties needed militia officers, sheriffs, and representatives. Boone was chosen to be county lieutenant, lieutenant-colonel of the militia, sheriff of Fayette County, representative of Fayette County, and was named as one of several deputy surveyors.

Daniel had to travel to Richmond, Virginia, to attend his first session of the General Assembly that was scheduled to convene on May 7. He was accompanied by Benjamin Logan, a representative from Lincoln County, and Charles Gatliff, who seems to have been traveling for personal reasons. Boone and Logan had crossed paths in 1778, when Logan joined Richard Callaway in the court-martialing of Boone that ultimately ended in acquittal and a promotion in rank for Boone. In 1780, Boone served as a scout under Logan for Gen. George Rogers Clark's retaliatory raid after the attack on Ruddell's and Martin's Stations. By 1781, Richard Callaway was deceased, having been killed by Native Americans in 1780. Although Boone and Logan lived in different parts of Kentucky County, they would have likely interacted to some extent during their militia service. Perhaps Boone and Logan settled their differences in the aftermath of the trial.[12]

The most direct route from Kentucky to Richmond, Virginia, was via the Wilderness Road. This famous route was not a road in the modern sense. At the time Boone made his trip, it was little more than a trail, passing through a wide range of physiographic conditions, from relatively easy rolling hills to mountainous areas with deep ravines. Unsuitable for wagon traffic, the trail traversed numerous waterways and long stretches where no sign of human habitation could be found. No details of his journey have been preserved, but his experience was probably similar to other, better-documented trips around the same time. His was an expeditiously executed trip with stops to rest his horse or horses (he may have led a second horse as a backup and to carry supplies), eat a meal, and perhaps stay at a private house or inn along the more inhabited sections. He needed to allow enough time to reach Richmond by May 7 while also anticipating possible delays along the way.

Leaving his station, he would have traveled a little more than eight miles to Fort Boonesborough where he followed the road that he and his road cutters had opened in 1775. The next 211 miles took Boone through rugged wilderness country, devoid of settlement, which was a challenge to traverse. The road led south about 55 miles to Hazel Patch, then southeast 73 miles to Cumberland Gap. Turning slightly northeast, the road continued for another 75 miles to a place called the Blockhouse. This site marked the point where travelers heading east left the wilderness and entered more settled country. Traveler William Brown covered about 27 miles per day when he followed most of this section of the road in 1782. Boone's rate of travel was probably comparable. The remaining 188 miles to Richmond, Virginia, were much easier traveling, with plenty of places to rest and resupply. He may have stopped at Atkins Tavern, Fort Chiswell, Long's Tavern, or any number of private houses and small towns. William Brown took his time along this section of the route, traveling on average only about 8 or 9 miles per day, but he did not have the deadline Boone faced. Boone's rate of travel once he left the wilderness could have been as much as 40 miles per day. At such a rate of travel, the entire trip could be completed in approximately two weeks. If he left in early April, and experienced no significant delays, he could have easily arrived well before the Assembly convened.[13]

Boone was one of two representatives from Fayette County, the other being Thomas Swearingen. Swearingen had served as a burgess from 1756 to 1758 in Frederick, Virginia. He first came to Kentucky from Berkeley County, Virginia (present-day West Virginia), in the spring of 1779 with his son, Van; brother Benoni; Maj. George Michael Bedinger; Col. William Morgan and his son Ralph; John Taylor; John Strode; James Duncan; John Constant; and Samuel Dusee. Thomas and Benoni each brought an enslaved person as well. Their purpose was to locate land and file claims under the land law that the Virginia General Assembly had passed in May. The Swearingens initially stayed at Fort Boonesborough but moved to John Strode's Station (in present-day Clark County, Kentucky), where they spent the winter of 1779 and cleared five acres of Strode's land. Both Swearingens were accomplished surveyors. Thomas eventually filed twenty-two land grants totaling 19,413 acres. He also acted as an agent for the men whose money and land warrants were stolen from Boone's room in 1780.[14]

Boone arrived in Richmond, Virginia, sometime in April (probably toward the end of the month). The Assembly was trying to execute its governmental responsibilities against the backdrop of active military conflict in the eastern theater of the Revolutionary War. The session convened on May 7 but was adjourned for three days because an insufficient number of legislators were present. On May 10, the legislators received word that British Col. Banastre Tarleton, accompanied by 180 dragoons and 70 mounted infantry, was advancing toward Richmond. The session reconvened in Charlottesville on May 24, and Boone took his oath on that day. The Attendance Book for the House of Delegates documents that he attended all twelve days that the legislators met in Charlottesville but only six days in Staunton. He is not mentioned by name in any of the minutes for the session that ran from May 24 to June 23, usually convening at 10:00 a.m. or noon, and meeting every day except Sunday. He may have simply been learning and observing how the delegates did business, but part of the time, he was in the custody of the British.[15]

The session was briefly adjourned on June 4, when another enemy invasion threatened. John "Jack" Jouett was at the Cuckoo Tavern in Louisa, when Colonel Tarleton and his troops rode by on their way to Charlottesville. Jouett rode to Charlottesville on a swift horse by an alternate route, stopping on the way at Monticello to warn Governor Thomas Jefferson before alerting the delegates of Tarleton's approach. Most of the delegates, as well as Jefferson, eluded capture, but seven men were taken into custody, according to Tarleton's account of the 1780–1781 campaign. Boone and Swearingen were among them, as was Col. John Syme of Hanover County, Virginia. Two men who were not delegates were also detained: a member of the South Carolina Congress named Francis Kinlow or Kinlock, and Capt. Joseph Saunders, who had traveled from the Falls of the Ohio to get money and supplies for George Rogers Clark's troops. As the legislators fled, Boone and Swearingen lingered to load public records in a wagon and take them to a safe place. Encountering one of the dragoon units on June 4, Boone appeared unimpressive in his "common jeans suit, with the buckskin leggings neatly beaded" but was taken into custody when Swearingen addressed him by his rank within earshot of one of the British officers. Nathan Boone told Draper that his father was taken to the British camp, presumably in Charlottesville, and held in a coal house until the next day, when he met Colonel Tarleton. Nathan surmised that Boone "very probably explained his title of captain by referring to his old Dunmore commission" and may have "pretended contentment and sung songs while confined" in the hope that Tarleton would conclude that he was in sympathy with the British and let him go.

Boone researcher Ken Kamper wrote that Boone was held by the British for nine days, presumably from June 4 to June 12. Colonel Tarleton mentioned the incident in his history of the 1780 and 1781 campaigns but did not refer to Boone by name. His account of his campaigns of 1780 and 1781 states that seven members of the Virginia Assembly were captured on June 4 and were joined by twenty other prisoners who had been soldiers of the Saratoga army. Tarleton left that afternoon, "with his corps and the prisoners, down the Rivanna, towards the Point of Fork." Presumably, Boone was among the prisoners who accompanied Tarleton, and he may have encountered a relative by marriage during his captivity. His wife's brother, Samuel, was a colonel who served under Tarleton and could hardly have been unaware that his brother-in-law was one of the prisoners.

Tarleton claimed that he treated the captive "gentlemen" with "kindness and liberality." Moreover, his history stated that "in different conversations with Lieutenant-colonel Tarleton, on the state of public affairs, they generally and separately avowed, that if England could prevent the intended cooperation of the French fleet and army with the American forces during the ensuing autumn, both Congress and the country would gladly dissolve the French alliance, and enter into a treaty with Great Britain." Such sentiments might be construed as treasonous by the rebels but may have simply been a ploy to gain favorable treatment and parole. For it appears, from Tarleton's account, that more than one captive made these claims. Tarleton also secured promises from "the captives of note, both civil and military," "not to quit the camps or line of march of the light troops till they joined the army, which they faithfully complied with." The captives of note undoubtedly included the assemblymen or the "gentlemen" of which Tarleton wrote. Despite Boone's backwoods attire, his rank and his relationship to Col. Samuel Boone must have placed him in the "captives of note" category. His extended period in captivity is probably explained by his transfer with the other prisoners to the Point of Fork and, perhaps, accounts for the time required for questioning. Tarleton's history states that "the prisoners of note brought down the country were, in general, dismissed, on giving their paroles."[16]

Boone returned to the Assembly when it reconvened on June 17 in Staunton and served from June 18 to June 23. On June 21, he probably presented a petition filed on behalf of the inhabitants of Lexington to authorize the charter first filed in 1779 for the establishment of the town. At the conclusion of the session, Boone returned to his station in Kentucky to spend the summer at home until he was required to return east for the fall session.[17]

While Boone's name did not appear in any of the spring session minutes, he was privy to a wide variety of matters that came to the attention of the delegates. Much of the business of the House concerned both the rules by which horses and supplies could be impressed for use in the war and rules under which men served in the militia. Concerning the former, the *Journal of the House of Delegates of the Commonwealth of Virginia* often mentioned the Honorable Major General Marquis de Lafayette and authorized him to impress horses and determine the use of public arms and ammunition. The delegates received many letters informing them of the state of the war, depreciation of money, and other matters, as well as petitions that were referred to committees of privileges and elections and courts of justice. The committees often produced bills for the House to debate and either pass or reject. There were frequent communications with the Senate concerning bills that originated in the House. Individual counties brought specific grievances before the house, and even individual citizens could apply for relief. One matter that personally involved Boone was the first reading of a resolution on June 11, which gave the Speaker of the House authority to issue a writ for the election of a substitute if a member became a prisoner of the enemy. The resolution was read a second time on June 13 and agreed to. However, Boone was released before his replacement became necessary. On June 15, the House heard and passed a resolution that pertained to Fayette, Lincoln, and Jefferson Counties. The resolution asked that poor residents of these counties be permitted to "take up and locate such quantities of vacant land as may suffice them for settlements and plantations, not exceeding four hundred acres for one family" and have two years' credit for the land at twenty shillings per hundred acres plus office fees. The session ended on June 23, as the Speaker signed twenty-three bills.[18]

In contrast to the absence of Boone's name in the minutes of the spring session, the *Journal* mentions Boone several times in the minutes for the fall session. The fall session began on October 1 and attempted to meet for three days but failed to achieve a quorum and voted to reconvene on November 5. Boone seems to have been absent along with many other delegates. On his way to the fall session, he stopped to see relatives in North Carolina. James Boone recorded on October 20 that Daniel was with his family. In the interim between the date that the session was supposed to start and when it did, General Cornwallis surrendered in October. The fall session met for a total of fifty-three days from November 5, 1781, to January 5, 1782. A persistent problem was members who were absent without authorization, leaving the House unable to do any business because it lacked a quorum. On November 8, a long list of absent members was announced, and the sergeant at arms was empowered to find them and take them into custody. The next eight days of sessions were spent rounding up and compelling the absent members to attend or give an acceptable reason for their absence. Boone was not among the members listed as delinquent.[19]

The House was finally able to get on with business on November 19. They began by appointing officers and establishing standing committees on religion, privileges and elections, courts of justice, trade, and propositions and grievances. Boone was appointed to the Committee of Propositions and Grievances, which handled petitions from citizens that ranged widely in topic. On November 29, Daniel was appointed with two other committee members to bring a bill that empowered the registrar of the Land Office to appoint a deputy for the westernmost counties. On December 5, he was added to a committee "to whom the letters from General [George Rogers] Clarke were referred." Thomas Swearingen also served on this committee. Additionally,

Boone served on a committee tasked with responding to various petitions by the inhabitants of Lincoln, Fayette, and Jefferson Counties. On December 18, he, Swearingen (rendered as Swearingham in the published *Journal*), and others were instructed to bring a bill or bills "for the better administration of government in the western country." This was in response to a petition by citizens of Fayette, Jefferson, and Lincoln Counties who complained that they did not participate in the common benefits of government because of their "detached and remote situation" and asked that the legislature make provision for their future good government.[20]

All through the fall session, the minutes include lists of members absent without authorization, notations of their return, and payment of fines or exemptions—depending on whether they were able to explain the reasons for their absence. On December 28, all but one of the members from Fayette, Lincoln, and Jefferson Counties were listed as absent without authorization. In addition to Boone, Benjamin Logan and John Edwards of Lincoln County, Kentucky, and Isaac Cox and Willis Greene of Jefferson County, Kentucky, were called to account for their absences. Swearingen, the other Fayette County member, was apparently never absent without an acceptable excuse. Isaac Cox, Benjamin Logan, and John Edwards had appeared on the list of delinquent members several times before, but Daniel only appeared once. Some of the members on the delinquent list produced acceptable excuses for their absences. Acceptable excuses included sickness and employment in the service of the state elsewhere, among others. Others on the delinquent list were seated once they had paid fees or fines. The fall session ended on January 5, 1782.[21]

6

Kentucky's "Year of Blood"

1782

Although British general Cornwallis's surrender in October 1781 after a three-week siege had effectively ended the conflict back east, the war continued to rage in the western settlements. The conflict was hardly one sided; the Kentucky settlers waged attacks directly against Shawnee villages numerous times in the twelve years following the Treaty of Paris. The British in Detroit did not hear of the surrender until April 13, 1782, and spent the winter planning more attacks on the Kentucky settlers. Shawnee runners were sent to every northwest tribe to invite them to a grand council planned for August at the Shawnee town of Chillicothe (near present-day Xenia, Ohio). The goal was to launch a joint expedition against the Kentucky settlements. Joining the Shawnee, Delaware, and other Ohio River tribes who had been raiding Kentucky throughout the war were the Wyandots, known for their ferocity and prowess in armed conflict. The Wyandots were in no mood to wait until the summer, however, and they began attacking Kentucky in the spring.[1]

March opened with an attack on Strode's Station (near present-day Winchester, Kentucky) by a band of twenty-five Wyandot warriors who killed two men. On March 19, Fort Boonesborough settlers sent an alert to Benjamin Logan at his station near present-day Stanford in Lincoln County, Kentucky, to warn him of possible Native American activity. Logan sent fifteen men to James Estill's Station with instructions to augment the party to forty and look for evidence of Native Americans in the area. Estill gathered the necessary twenty-five additional men from his and nearby stations, and the party of forty men left Estill's Station defenseless while they investigated. While they were gone, Wyandots attacked Estill's Station, killed a young girl named Jane Gass, and took an enslaved Black man named Monk Estill prisoner. The Wyandots decided to retreat north when Monk convincingly claimed that the station was heavily defended. When James Estill learned of the attack against his station, he and his twenty-five men pursued the Wyandots to a place called Little Mountain (in present-day Mount Sterling) where, on March 22, a battle ensued that killed James Estill along with six or seven others and badly wounded six.[2]

The dangerous situation on the Kentucky frontier grew even worse in August when the planned joint Native American expedition was launched against the Kentucky settlements. British Captains Alexander McKee and William Caldwell, assisted by Simon and James Girty (white brothers who had lived among Native peoples for most of their lives), called a grand council at Chillicothe. Representatives from the Wyandot, Mingo, Ottawa, Potawatomi, Miami, and other Indigenous bands attended. Simon Girty delivered an inflammatory speech, reminding the assembled warriors of the settlers' encroachment onto their Kentucky hunting grounds and urging them to use their combined strength to conduct a major campaign into Kentucky. A force of three hundred warriors composed mostly of Wyandots along with some Delaware, Shawnee, and Mingoes formed under the leadership of Captain Caldwell, who also took along thirty rangers, the Shawnee chief Moluntha, and Wyandot interpreter Simon Girty.[3]

The campaign opened when Captain Caldwell sent a detachment of seventy warriors to attack Hoy's Station (in present-day Madison County, Kentucky), where two boys were captured. The warriors with their captives moved slowly toward the Ohio River, expecting and hoping for a pursuit by the settlers. Captain John Holder assembled a party of men from his station on the Kentucky River (in present-day Clark County, Kentucky) and gathered up more men from David McGee's and John Strode's Stations as he headed north in pursuit. Holder and his men fell into the trap that the warriors had intended for them when they met at the Upper Blue Licks on the Battle Run Branch. Forced to flee, they left a wounded man behind, who later died, and barely made it back with the other three injured men.[4]

Hearing of Holder's defeat, men from the stations in and around Lexington were preparing to rendezvous at Hoy's Station to render aid to John Holder's party. Several historians wrote that Daniel Boone went to Fort Boonesborough to raise men there. Historian John Bakeless asserts that Boone "practically stripped Boonesborough of its defenders" but provides no primary source citation or any estimate of the number of men there. Robert McMillan deposed that between twenty and thirty families lived at Fort Boonesborough in the latter part of 1782 and 1783. In Boone's absence, Captain William Ellis assembled about ten men from Boone's Station. William Hays, husband of Susannah Boone (Daniel Boone's daughter), assumed command of the party. Joseph Ficklin, who was a young boy living at Bryan's Station, said there were forty-four men capable of fighting, but his estimate included only the men who lived at the station.[5]

Caldwell and McKee brought their Native American allies and Canadian support staff to Bryan's Station on the night of August 15. The force surrounded the station under the cover of darkness, and their presence was initially undetected. The original intent was to situate a decoy party at one end to fire on the station and so draw out the station men, allowing the larger group of warriors the opportunity to attack an undefended target. Anticipating that men from the various stations would go to the aid of Holder's men, McKee and Caldwell hoped to find Bryan's Station undefended.[6]

However, the Bryan's Station men had not yet left. Historians differ on how the settlers became aware that they were surrounded, but William Tomlinson Sr., who lived in a cabin outside the stockade, may have given the alarm. Joseph Ficklin, who was living in the station at the time, said that settlers who "first opened their doors" on the morning of the 16th were fired upon. Another eyewitness, John Gatewood, claimed that two enslaved men named Lancaster and Daniel (owned by Capt. Robert Johnson and Capt. John Craig, respectively) were fired upon when they left the station to gather provender for the station's hogs. Elizabeth Johnson Payne, then a ten-year-old child, corroborated Gatewood's account of Lancaster being fired upon but said he left the station for firewood. They escaped injury and made it back to safety. John Bakeless offered two possibilities: scouts alerted the station, or one or more captives from the 1780 attack on Ruddles's and Martin's Stations (whom the Native Americans brought along) may have broken away and sounded the alert. In any event, the station inhabitants found themselves in a precarious situation. Alarmingly, the enemy outnumbered the station's men by a large margin. Initially, however, the Native American force held off from an additional attack. Two men, Thomas Bell and Nicholas Tomlinson, managed to make it through enemy lines on horseback and headed to Lexington for reinforcements.[7]

The leader of Bryan's Station, Robert Johnson, along with ten men from the station, was in Virginia at the time. Captain John Craig Sr. assumed leadership in Johnson's absence. Bryan's Station had recently been enlarged by the addition of more cabins to the stockaded enclosure, but the stockade sections between the new construction had not yet been installed. Fortunately, the ditches had already been dug and the puncheons for the stockade split. The men quickly built the stockade sections between the cabins to secure the enclosure completely.[8]

The women and enslaved people of the station were responsible for gathering water from one of two springs nearby but outside of the protective stockade. Water gathering was normally a routine task that took place every morning at every station, but this chore, on this day, under the hazardous conditions of a potential Native American siege, inspired later historians to transform this routine task into an epic tale of heroism. Eyewitness accounts of the siege (which itself was not prolonged and barely fitted the definition) mentioned gathering water but placed no great emphasis on it. From John Gatewood: After Bell and Tomlinson left for Lexington, "the men went to work & got all the cattle into the fort—fastened the gates—& water was got for a siege." Mrs. John Arnold, who was a member of the party of women who went to the spring, merely referenced taking in water and "fix[ing] up the doors, etc." by late Saturday. Ellison E. Williams said that the settlers knew that the Native Americans were camped near the spring but believed they would hold their fire to conceal their presence. The two springs associated with the station were called the Big Spring (or the Spring under the Hill) and the Little Spring. The Big Spring was located on the easterly side of the station, very near North Elkhorn Creek, about sixty steps away. Contemporary accounts place the Native American encampment around this spring. The Little Spring was located to the north of the station and was fed by a tributary of North Elkhorn Creek. Joseph Ficklin, who lived at Bryan's Station at the time of the siege, drew a map for Lyman C. Draper that clearly showed the locations of the two springs, which still exist today. The Big Spring is closest to the road between the station and Lexington (now known as Bryan Station Road). The Lexington chapter of the Daughters of the American Revolution marked the Big Spring with a memorial enclosure wall inscribed with the names of the women thought to have made the journey for water on that fateful day. However, historian Bessie Taul Conkwright argued in 1916 that the wrong spring was commemorated and that the women actually gathered water from the Little Spring north of the station and were protected to some extent by a "covered way" to the spring.[9]

By the evening of August 16, all preparations that could be made were completed, and a party of thirteen men led by Jeremiah Craig left the station to see what had prompted the gunfire in the morning. They encountered Native American warriors one hundred yards away and exchanged gunfire but safely retreated without injuries. This engagement induced the larger party of warriors waiting in the calf-pasture near the spring to rush the fort, under the impression that all the men had been enticed from the station. They took possession of ten cabins and outbuildings that stood outside the station stockade and set them on fire. Receiving heavy gunfire, the warriors retreated with some losses. Among the settlers, Michael Mitchell was killed in his cooper's shop, and John Adkins was mortally wounded and died a few hours later. The burning cabins nearly ignited the station enclosure, but a brisk wind changed course and blew the flames away from the station. The rest of the evening passed somewhat quietly, only occasionally punctuated by yelling and firing by the warriors.

Bell and Tomlinson returned to the station around noon and were able to enter without interference. They described how they had reached Lexington only to find that the Lexington men had already left. They caught up with them at Boone's Station. Between fifteen and seventeen mounted men and about thirty footmen reversed course and came to Bryan's Station, where they met enemy fire about an hour after Bell and Tomlinson had returned. The horsemen, riding in a great cloud of dust, made it safely into the station, but the men on foot were routed and suffered two killed and four wounded. Most of the surviving party fled back to Lexington.[10]

The reinforcements increased the number of fighting men at Bryan's Station to approximately sixty-one men. Settler deaths reduced the number by four, and the injured men may have been too impaired to be effective fighters. Over the next day, the Native Americans continued to direct gunfire at the station but made little headway. They spent most of their time killing livestock. Joseph Ficklin said that 80 cattle, 150 hogs, and 30 sheep were killed—some for food, but most were slaughtered to inflict as much destruction of valuable property as possible. Only one settler, Nicholas Tomlinson, was slightly injured during this stage of the conflict.

As the day wore on and with no easy victory in sight, Simon Girty tried a final strategy. Nearing the fort and standing in the protection of a tall stump, he called for Capt. John Craig to surrender the station. He said that he expected cannons to arrive by nightfall and that, if the station had to be taken by force, he could not be held responsible for how the warriors might behave. He predicted destruction and a bloody massacre with great loss of life, particularly of the women and children. Captain Craig spurned his entreaties, but the station inhabitants were terrified by Girty's threat. Regardless, a young man named Aaron Reynolds jumped up on a stump and expressed his contempt, saying he had two worthless dogs named Simon and Girty and that the warriors should be the ones to be afraid. Reynolds's taunting cheered up the settlers, and Girty finally gave up, knowing that his bluff had failed.[11]

That night, Girty and most of the Native American force left and headed back north to their villages on the other side of the Ohio. Thirty or forty warriors remained and harassed the station through the night, but they eventually left before sunrise. The Native Americans' inability to breach the station walls by either gunfire or attempts to set the cabins and stockade on fire over a period of two days (August 15–16) led to their abandonment of the attack, but not before they had killed nearly all the station's livestock. As sieges go, this one was quite short but the uncertainty surrounding how long the Native Americans may have stayed was undoubtedly an alarming factor. The Girtys may also have had difficulty convincing the warriors to stay longer when their attempts to take the station failed and the settlers had a tactical advantage of being behind protective stockade. Known Native American casualties numbered five killed and two wounded.[12]

7

Daniel Boone and Hugh McGary Meet Again

The Battle of Blue Licks

The victory at Bryan's Station must have come as a relief after the previous defeats earlier that year. But the siege of Bryan's Station was a prelude to one of the worst defeats ever suffered by Kentucky settlers. Within hours after the departure of the main Native American force from Bryan's Station, men from Lexington, Fort Harrod, Strode's Station, Boone's Station, and other area settlements gathered at the station to launch a retaliatory expedition against the British and Native forces. Militiamen were drawn from two of the three counties that then constituted the former Kentucky County: Fayette and Lincoln. Further away, Jefferson County was the headquarters of General George Rogers Clark, who oversaw the protection of all three western counties, though he was not involved in the recruitment of men for the upcoming expedition. Within Fayette County was Lexington, as well as Bryan's, Strode's, Boone's, McGee's, Hoy's, and Holder's Stations. The recent attacks that began early in August had already prompted the recruitment of men from the Fayette County settlements to respond to Holder's defeat and the attack on Hoy's Station, as well as the most recent engagement at Bryan's Station. Some of these men had been wounded and were unable to help, while others remained behind to provide defense and protection for the stations. The infusion of additional men from more populous Lincoln County drew primarily from the Harrodsburg/Danville area stations of John Gordon, Stephen Trigg, Hugh McGary, John Bowman, Matthias Yocum, James Laurence, and George Corn, Jacob Coffman's Station in present-day Lawrenceburg, and from Benjamin Logan's Station (near present-day Stanford).

Men from Fayette County and from the Harrodsburg area stations arrived at Bryan's Station on August 17. Although the historic records on the total number vary somewhat, most agree that approximately 182 men gathered that day. An estimated 135 men came from the Harrodsburg area of Lincoln County while 47 men gathered from the Fayette County stations. Benjamin Logan was expected to bring 45 more men but had not yet arrived. Daniel Boone's Station had contributed 10 men to the Bryan's Station incident, and some of these men may have continued to form part of the larger force. William Hays and Samuel Stinson were both wounded while trying to enter Bryan's Station and could not join the force marching to Blue Licks; another member of the party, Charles Hunter, was mortally wounded and died the next morning. Besides Boone, other men from the station who fought at Blue Licks included Boone's son Israel; his nephews, Samuel Boone Jr., Squire Boone Jr., and Thomas Boone; relatives by marriage, Abraham, Joseph, and Peter Scholl; and three other settlers, Samuel Brannon, James Hays, and John Morgan. Hugh McGary was accompanied by his stepson, James Ray, and Hugh Cunningham.[1]

By Sunday morning, August 18, the forces from Fayette and Lincoln Counties had gathered at Bryan's Station, lacking only the men assembled by Logan. The ranking officer was Col. John Todd, who lived near Lexington. Col. Daniel Boone was second in command under Todd. Col. Stephen Trigg was the ranking officer for Lincoln County in the absence of Logan. Second in command from Lincoln County was Major Hugh McGary. Other officers included Majors Edward Bulger and Silas Harlan, both from Lincoln County (present-day Mercer County, Kentucky), and Levi Todd from Lexington, who was John Todd's brother. Ten captains, five lieutenants, an ensign, and a commissary constituted the remaining officers. Interpersonal relationships between the higher-ranking men played a role in how and what decisions were made, as did prior experience with Native American warfare. These dynamics were also key to determining their decision to embark on what, in hindsight, was a disastrous expedition.[2]

Early on, there was the question of whether Colonel Logan outranked Colonel Todd and would have taken command of the force had he reached Bryan's Station in time. The force of 182 men was dominated by Lincoln County militia, who may have preferred to serve under Colonel Logan, whom they knew. Boone also knew Colonel Logan well, but their relationship was strained when Logan joined Richard Callaway in calling for Boone's court-martial in 1778. Logan was reportedly displeased by Boone's acquittal, and Boone may have preferred to serve under Todd as a result. McGary considered Colonel Logan his superior officer and may have resented Stephen Trigg because Trigg was promoted over him.[3]

Even among men of lower rank, who had little or no say in decisions taken by higher-ranking officers, loyalties, grievances, and prior military experiences colored their responses and reactions. While some Kentucky settlers had prior military experience with a regular army that involved training and the instillation of military discipline, many experienced their first armed conflict as members of the county militias. The system of county militias was an ancient British tradition that was revitalized in America for fighting Native Americans. Each of the thirteen colonies enacted laws making militia service compulsory for every able-bodied, free male between the ages of seventeen and sixty. Although militia units were organized by county and officers were usually elected locally, the units were generally a source for recruiting individuals for specific operations or expeditions. County militias cooperated with one another when they shared a common interest in a particular expedition. "As a part-time civilian army, the militia was naturally not a well-disciplined, cohesive force comparable to the professional army of the age." Militiamen did not like long periods of service and expected to be paid for their services and fed while on duty. They had to provide their own arms and ammunition and were expected to be ready to respond to emergencies, such as Native American attacks. Training was inconsistent and did not always prepare the men for Indigenous methods of warfare, such as the use of cover and concealment and of ambush. Kentucky settlers who had fought Native Americans elsewhere had an advantage over men who had no such experience. Going into battle with men inexperienced in Indigenous warfare was a recipe for disaster. Add to that a strong sense that frontier violence required a retaliatory response on the grounds that the Native American threat could only be extinguished by total annihilation. A common response after a raid or attack was to assemble a party and pursue the offending party in hopes of engaging and defeating them before they escaped over the Ohio River to their home ground, where the militia was at a disadvantage.[4]

The officers held a brief, fractious meeting to discuss how to proceed on August 17. The chief bone of contention was whether to wait for Logan and his reinforcements or to proceed without him. McGary wanted to wait for Logan to arrive. When Capt. John Craig, then in temporary command of

Bryan's Station, assured Colonel Todd that the enemy's numbers were "inconsiderable," Todd wanted to get started on the pursuit immediately, arguing that any delay would give the warriors time to cross the Ohio River and escape. He may have insinuated that McGary was being overly cautious and that there were enough brave men to go ahead without him. For a man like McGary, sensitive to any suggestion of cowardice, this response would have been like lighting a match to gasoline. History does not record his reaction at being overruled by Todd, but it would be completely in character for him to have nursed a grievance as the men set off in pursuit.[5]

Historian Mann Butler described the scene.

> It is due to the memory of Major McGary (who was a man of courage, almost too fierce for Indian battles, much less for pacific society) to state, that he is said to have counseled a delay at Bryant's for twenty-four hours, until Logan could arrive with his powerful reinforcement. This was rather tauntingly rejected as it is alleged, by Colonel Todd, who, in the honorable ambition of a brave man, was fearful of the escape of the Indians and was apprehensive that he should lose this opportunity of distinguishing himself, by the arrival of his senior Colonel. McGary unhappily, and too fiercely resented this treatment; and in a spirit of lamentable revenge, determined to force a battle at the hazard of any consequences to his fellow-soldiers and to his country.[6]

The men moved out between midmorning and noon on August 19 and rode until they reached the abandoned station of Isaac Ruddell on the Licking River (in present-day Harrison County, Kentucky, bordering Bourbon County). Reaching the station site around 2:00 p.m., the officers concluded that the enemy forces were much greater in number than they had initially thought. What they did not appear to know was that about one hundred warriors broke off from Caldwell's force of slightly more than three hundred at Ruddell's Station. Author Neal Hammon asked the question in his analysis of the battle: "Where were the trackers, spies, and cavalry scouts when the militia reached the Indian camp that afternoon?" Reasoning that one hundred warriors "cannot just disappear without leaving any trace," he concluded that "scouts were either not sent out, or were incompetent." In any event, as the ranking officer of the group, John Todd made the decision to follow the trail of the larger force traveling under Caldwell, even though he thought they considerably outnumbered his men. The men continued their march, moving at a slow pace for sixteen miles until they reached a point on Stoney Creek a few miles distant from the Lower Blue Licks at 3:25 a.m. Robert Patterson said that their progress was slow because they were traveling at night and through dense woods. They stopped to rest for a couple of hours on Stoney Creek.[7]

The men resumed their march early the next morning, August 19, following the buffalo road along the Stoney Creek drainage for two or three miles, then taking one of two forks that traversed over and around a hill, both leading to the Licking River, where two spatially distinct salt licks formed what was known as the Lower Blue Licks. Captain Caldwell had stationed some Native American spies on the hill to watch for the approaching army. After ascertaining that the militiamen were indeed in pursuit, the spies retreated down the hill to the ford over the Licking River and crossed it to the north side.

Silas Harlan was placed in command of an advance guard of about twenty-six experienced men who, as Harlan reportedly said, responded to his question, "Who'll go with me for Indian bait?" Among them were Maj. Edward Bulger, brothers John and Henry Wilson, James Elijah Woods, Lewis Rose, Samuel Scott, George Corn, William Barbee, John Pitman, Jacob Stevens, and James Hays. Colonel Todd sent Edward Bulger, Silas Harlan, George Corn, James Hays, and Jacob Stevens ahead to reconnoiter, and they saw the Native American spies wading the river at the ford and continuing north up the hill on the other side. The scouts reached the river, forded it, and looked for additional signs but saw nothing and reported their findings back to Todd.

Two conflicting versions of what happened next appear in the historic record. The most frequently stated version is that Todd called a halt at the top of the hill above and on the south side of the river and assembled his officers for a consultation. This version states that most of the officers, including Boone, called for a delay in launching an attack. Boone recommended waiting for Logan's reinforcements. McGary, who according to the story had nursed his resentment at being overruled at Bryan's Station, angrily challenged their decision, accused them of cowardice, and called on the other men to follow him. Seeing that some of the men were following McGary, the other leaders acquiesced and followed. A variation on the story states that the army rushed ahead in a disorganized fashion, was confronted by an ambush, and was defeated. Humphrey Marshall, writing forty years later, presented this version, and many other subsequent histories adopted this interpretation.[8]

The other version of the story is that the counsel on the hill never happened, the force made an organized crossing at the ford, and then it re-formed on the other side into an advance party led by Silas Harlan and three companies, which were led by Boone on the left, McGary in the center, and Trigg on the right. Reports written after the fact by surviving officers all described the army's actions in this way and omit any mention of McGary's outburst; however, Boone's son, Nathan, who must have heard his father speak of the battle, related the version that included McGary's challenge and further claimed that McGary accused Boone of cowardice, leading Boone to declare that "[he could] go as far as any man." McGary himself wrote a letter to Logan after the battle, acknowledging his "bad conduct" and the postdefeat censure he was receiving and requesting an official hearing, which never took place. Contemporary accounts by survivors confirm that the army made the crossing and formed on the other side, maintaining their organization of three lines and an advance party as they approached Caldwell's force.[9]

Boone's men initiated the planned strategy with very heavy fire, but the enemy was so strong that they broke the right flank of the line and attacked from the rear, prompting a retreat with heavy casualties. If McGary can be credited with any noteworthy action in the battle, it was carried out at the end when, having told his own men to flee for their lives, he risked his own life to warn Boone of the rear guard attack. According to Nathan Boone, McGary rushed up to Boone on horseback, saying, "Col. Boone, why are you not retreating? Todd & Trigg's line has given way, & the Indians are all around you."[10]

The retreat was chaotic with every man trying desperately to reach the ford and cross the river. Those on foot were at a disadvantage, and many were killed by Wyandots wielding tomahawks and knives, who fought with a ferocity that many of the Kentucky men had not encountered before. Colonel Todd, Colonel Trigg, Maj. Silas Harlan, Maj. Edward Bulger, and ten other lower-ranking officers, as well as Commissary Joseph Lindsay and sixty-six enlisted militia, died in the battle or later from their injuries. Of the men from Boone's Station, Daniel's son, Israel, and nephew, Thomas Boone, were killed at the battle. Another nephew, Squire Boone Jr., received a gunshot that shattered his femur. Samuel Brannon was killed while helping Squire escape. James Hays was wounded in the shoulder and carried the bullet for the rest of his life. John Morgan was taken captive at the battle but later returned. McGary and James Ray both survived. Hugh Cunningham from McGary's Station was captured but later returned to Kentucky.[11]

There were many instances of bravery during the short battle, and a few were immortalized later by the survivors. One of the best known is when Aaron Reynolds found Robert Patterson on foot, trying to reach the ford. Reynolds gave up his horse to allow Patterson, who was still disabled from injuries received in 1776, to reach the ford and safety. Reynolds narrowly eluded capture and reached Lexington on foot. Samuel Brannon found Squire Boone (wounded with a broken femur), tied him onto his horse, and then jumped on behind him. Brannon was shot and killed as the two men climbed the hill after fording the river. Squire made it safely back to Boone's Station three days later. Benjamin Netherland, who had the reputation of being cowardly, reached the south shore of the Licking River unharmed. Rather than continuing his retreat, he rallied other men with him to fire on the warriors cutting off fleeing militiamen who were trying to ford the river. His action allowed many to reach safety who would probably not have succeeded otherwise.

A lesser-known incident involved James Morgan, who had left his wife hiding under the floorboards of their cabin outside the stockade of Bryan's Station. She had been taken captive and was with the warriors during the battle at Blue Licks. She escaped during the confusion of battle and as she traveled along the main buffalo road, she miraculously encountered her husband, wounded and left behind by his comrades. She took care of him until he recovered enough to travel, and the two made their way safely back to Bryan's Station.[12]

In the aftermath of the battle, surviving officers attempted to explain why the battle was lost and who was responsible. A letter to Governor Harrison dated September 11, 1782, and signed by nine officers of Fayette County complained of their militia being called to "do duty . . . that has a tendency to protect . . . Louisville, a Town without Inhabitants" while leaving their own area "open & unguarded." Boone was more explicit in his report when he said he was instructed by General Clark "to send [his] men to the Falls of the Ohio in order to build a strong garrison and a row galley, thus by weakening one end to strengthen another, the upper part of the country was left exposed and the enemy intercepting our designs, brought their intended expedition against the frontiers of Fayette." General Clark responded with a letter dated October 18 that strongly denounced "that imprudent affair at the blue licks" and the "extremely reprehensible" conduct of the officers involved. Another of Clark's letters, dated November 30, targeted Col. John Todd and his militia as having failed to adequately patrol along the Ohio River and thus allow the enemy to penetrate and attack. Col. Levi Todd acknowledged that the officers' conduct had been censured as imprudent but explained the loss by writing that "as we had no chance to know their number, we thought ours was not much Inferior & supposed we should by a fierce attack throw them in confusion & break their Lines."[13]

Even though McGary was not blamed in any of the official reports, he found himself the object of censure and wrote a letter to his superior officer, Colonel Logan, explaining his side and offering to attend a hearing on the matter.

> 28th August 1782
>
> Dr. Sir—
>
> There has been some partys a-spying about the Magazine at Harrodstown some nights past, and as all the powerful men at that place is lost, I think it would be good to move the powder to Col. Bowman's, though such orders you send shall be put in force.
>
> Sir, I understand I am much sensured for incouraging the men to fight the Indians when we came up with them. I should have informed you of a grand Scheam that was planed [planned] when I saw you only I thought perhaps it would cause a Riot and you may Judge the matter yourself only it is hard to Judge dead men, you saw Trigg did not wright [write] to you untill he was shure you could not come up with us, and Todd took captn. Craig's word for the number of Indians, so we Marched in order to gain great applause with our men, as it was well known you would have [had] the Command, as almost all the men was of our County, and their Scheam met with a sad misfortune which I am sorry. So I suppose you have heard of my bad conduct, perhaps by some person that was conserned in the scheam and if you think I am faulty I should be fond to have a hearing in the Matter. Sir, if any thing should happen we have not one lb. of Lead. Captn. Denton's Station Breaks up this day or tomorrow. I have had no chance to send your Letter to Gen'l Clark. I hope you will instruct me in any thing you want done in this end of the County and you may depend on me as far as in me lies.[14]

Both Trigg and Todd, mentioned in the letter, were killed, so they could not defend themselves against McGary's version. However, in the coming months, McGary must have had ample opportunity to experience the aftermath of his behavior. Still charged with his duties as a justice of the peace, his absence in court was conspicuous in the latter half of 1782 when many of the wills left by the battle's casualties were presented for settlement. Numerous lawsuits were abated by the court in early 1783 because of the death of the plaintiff, in many cases, at the Battle of Blue Licks. McGary's life after the battle could not have been very pleasant.[15]

Only one letter from Col. Arthur Campbell to Col. William Davies, written as a private, unofficial communication on October 3, mentioned McGary as partially responsible, along with strong criticism of the other officers. "Never was the lives of so many valuable men lost more shamefully than in the late action of the 19th of August, and that not a little thro' the vain and seditious expressions of a Major McGeary [McGary]. How much more harm than good can one fool do. Todd & Trigg had capacity, but wanted experience. Boone, Harlin [Harlan], and Lindsay had experience, but were defective in capacity. Good, however, would it have been, had their advice been followed." Campbell also criticized Logan, describing him as a "dull, narrow body, from whom nothing clever need be expected," and faulted him for taking six days to reach the battlefield as well as for spending insufficient time to find and bury the dead. Of General Clark, Campbell wrote, "He has lost the confidence of the people, and it is said become a Sot; perhaps something worse." Campbell was told of the circumstances of the battle and McGary's behavior by Col. William Christian, who did not move to Kentucky until three years later. Campbell's views on the battle, and the people he deemed responsible for the defeat, were colored by other people who, as Mary Hammersmith observes, "do not appear to have had the highest qualifications to evaluate the action."[16]

If a single event can be said to have served as a watershed episode in McGary's life, the Battle of Blue Licks would have to be that event. Although blame was meted out to many as a result of that battle, McGary alone has been made the principal cause of the defeat by later historians. Yet it is worth examining briefly the situation that prompted the battle and caused the defeat. Samuel M. Wilson published a concise and evenhanded analysis of the battle in 1927. He made several important points that both corrected common misperceptions about the outcome of McGary's behavior and put in proper context the military strategy used and why it was unsuccessful. He states, "However dreadful may have been the repulse and defeat at the Blue Licks or however disheartening the effects of that disaster, it cannot be denied that it was a fair fight, according to the methods then in vogue, or that the Kentuckians were the immediate aggressors in that fight." He also points out that none of the commanding officers who survived to make reports on the battle mentioned McGary's behavior as having any significant impact on the outcome of the battle. In fact, McGary was not identified in any published record as having had a significant negative role in the battle until historian Humphrey Marshall so targeted him in 1812.[17]

More recently, Neal Hammon published a detailed analysis of the battle and events that led up to and followed it. He concludes:

> Readers will notice that only a few quotations from participants of the battle are used in this book. Likewise, perhaps less is said about the alleged conduct of Maj. Hugh McGary than might be expected. These omissions are because I have no confidence in their validity. In studying the reports and statements, it becomes obvious that some of the men who gave accounts of the Battle of Blue Licks were trying to appear important, and others clearly wanted it to be known that they were acquainted with various leaders, especially Daniel Boone. Even worse, some invented all or parts of their stories. Every private soldier who left an account claimed to have been at the officers' council, but curiously none of the officers seemed to remember it.[18]

Hammon goes on to recount conflicting statements that cannot be reconciled, among them McGary's behavior at the battle. Numerous accounts indicate that it was the choice of a frontal attack, always a risky military maneuver, that ultimately led to the defeat. It is also true that the commanders of the expedition were perplexed by the behavior of the enemy, who left ample indications of a potential ambush. When Colonel Todd and his troops reached the Licking River at Blue Licks, they were sufficiently confused over what to do that Todd called a meeting of his fellow officers, one of whom was McGary. During the course of the discussion over how to approach the enemy, McGary is reported to have lost his temper at what he saw as undue caution and delay (particularly since he had counseled delay at Bryan's Station and had been rejected) and said something to the effect of "Delay is dastardly; all who are not cowards follow me, and I will show you where the Indians are!" Jacob Stevens, then a private in the battle, reported McGary as asking, "By Godly" (apparently an expression that he used when he was "in earnest"), "what came we there for? . . . Then let's fight them. They that ain't cowards follow me." Hammon questions how a private could have witnessed this behavior firsthand since it took place in the context of a meeting between the higher-ranking officers that would not have been open to low-ranking privates.[19]

Benjamin A. Cooper, who claimed to have fought as a lieutenant with the Fayette troops and witnessed McGary's behavior, reported, "The action was forced on us by the act of Major Hugh Magarey [*sic*], who broke from the council, and called upon the troops who were not cowards to follow him, and thus collecting a band, went without order, and against orders, into the action, and in consequence of this act a general pursuit of officers and men took place, more to save the desperate men that followed Magary [*sic*] than from a hope of a successful fight with the Indians." However, Cooper failed to explain, as many other eyewitness accounts did, that the men formed into three lines and an advance guard and did not rush blindly behind McGary into disorganized combat. Hammon exposes inaccuracies in other parts of Cooper's testimony and suggests that his entire account is suspect.[20]

Another account by Joseph Scholl, Daniel Boone's grandson, related that

> Col. Boone rather blamed himself in some degree for the Blue Licks battle. He said . . . at the council preceding the crossing the river . . . "You see the Indians have shown themselves on the hill beyond the river, loitering, as if to invite pursuit . . . It is not wise for us to heedlessly run into the trap set for us. Now, I propose taking a party and reconnoitering in their rear by going around for that purpose." This was opposed by one (McGary) [who] insinuated that, perhaps, Boone was afraid to meet the Indians. This so nettled Col. Boone that he retorted: "If you are determined to go and meet the enemy at this great disadvantage, go on: I can go as far into an Indian fight as any other man." His caution was misconstrued into cowardice, and he let his zeal get the better of his judgment.[21]

It is important to point out here that McGary was in as much danger as anyone else. The fact that he not only survived but emerged from the battle without wounds certainly must have infuriated those who were prone to put the worst possible interpretation on his behavior. As Wilson concludes, "In the very act of following [McGary's] unauthorized and mutinous lead, all became implicated in the blunder, not to say the wrong, that he committed. Morally, McGary was primarily responsible; but, unless he was ready to admit that he had been spurned and overruled by a willful subordinate, Col. John Todd, as commander of the expedition and from a strictly military standpoint, was mainly responsible; and his responsibility must be shared, in some measure, by all of his brother officers." Hammon sums up the incident in this way: "Perhaps what was really lacking . . . was good leadership, and not soldiers' abilities, courage or proper equipment. The most important thing in combat is to be commanded by capable officers who understand the talents and limitations of their own men and the ability of the enemy, and who know how to take advantage of the weapons at hand. Men under capable officers can often defeat an enemy who would rout a similar force commanded by incompetent officers. But this was not the case at Blue Licks. Even the famous Daniel Boone could not save that day."[22]

The Blue Licks defeat was a stunning blow for virtually every settler in Fayette and Lincoln Counties since many families either lost a loved one there, knew someone who perished, or both. When Logan and a party of 470 men, including Boone but apparently not McGary, finally reached the battle site on August 24, they found and buried 43 men but acknowledged that there were many more bodies that they did not find and, as Boone wrote, "Could not Tarry to search very close, being Both Hungry and weary, and some what Dubious that the enemy might not be gone quite off." Logan's tally of missing men was much higher: 50 men from Lincoln and 15 from Fayette (others set the total higher still). He spoke little of the condition of the dead (mentioning only that Stephen Trigg had been quartered), yet others were not so reticent. Levi Todd described the scene to his brother, Robert: "They were all stript naked, scalped & mangled in such a manner that it was hard to know one from another. Our Brother [John] was not known." Andrew Steele, writing to Governor Harrison on August 26, reported that some of the captured men were found at the river ford, "tied & Butchered with knives & spears." In his autobiography, Boone related that the burial party "found their bodies strewed everywhere, cut and mangled in a dreadful manner . . . Some torn and eaten by wild beasts; those in the river eaten by fishes; all in such a putrified condition, that no one could be distinguished from another."

Among the dead were Daniel's son, Israel, and nephew, Thomas. Daniel's son, Nathan, thought his father recognized Israel and buried him separately from the rest; other members of the family thought Israel was buried in the mass grave. Some of the dead were recognized: Stephen Trigg by Logan, and John Todd and Silas Harlan by Henry Wilson. Although Nathan claimed, according to his father, that the bodies were not "torn or eaten by varmints," this conclusion was contradicted by several witnesses, including Boone himself. Henry Wilson further made the point that the bodies were too decayed to be moved ("skin slipping off"). Unburied bodies were left to decay in place and a few years later, human bones were visible on the surface when William Clinkenbeard carried chains for a survey through the area.[23]

Amid the acrimonious aftermath of the Battle of Blue Licks, as the rank and file censured McGary for his insubordinate behavior, higher-ranking officers like Boone, Logan, and Levi Todd faulted George Rogers Clark for failing to adequately protect the Central Kentucky settlements and focusing too much attention on the Falls of the Ohio area where he was based. Among the criticisms was Clark's failure to build a fort at the mouth of the Kentucky River as he had been instructed to do by Governor Harrison earlier in the year. Governor Harrison even wrote a letter to Clark, rebuking him for his conduct. In response, Clark began to plan an invasion of Native American territory. He attempted to mobilize militia from all three counties with the goal of assembling 950 men. But he was unable to realize his plans for a September expedition. Finally, he was able to collect 1,128 men from thirty-nine militia companies. The Lincoln County militia led by Logan was to meet at Bryan's Station, while John Floyd oversaw the Jefferson County militia. Boone was promoted to county lieutenant of Fayette County and led his battalion as a full colonel. The army began marching to the rendezvous point at the mouth of the Licking River on November 1, 1782. They crossed the Ohio River on November 4 and marched to the Shawnee town of New Chillicothe on the Miami River. The Shawnee were alerted ahead of time and abandoned the town, leaving Clark to burn the settlement to the ground. He torched the town of Piqua as well and sent Logan and 150 mounted men to destroy Loramie's Fort, the British trading post at the head of the Miami River. The destruction of the recently harvested crops was particularly devastating to the Shawnee and promised hungry times for the coming winter. After waiting a few days for a counterattack that never occurred, Clark's force returned with ten scalps, seven Native prisoners, and two settler captives who had been taken earlier.[24]

Boone and McGary both accompanied General Clark on his expedition to the Shawnee towns on the Miami River, along with James Ray. After this expedition, Boone and McGary returned to their respective stations, and they seem to have led largely separate lives thenceforth. The close of 1782 ended a year of great strife and tragedy, and the articles of peace negotiated at the same time as Clark's expedition extinguished the British role as instigators and suppliers of Native American offensives against the Kentucky settlers. Native American concerns about the rapid expansion of Euro-American settlement were hardly extinguished by the British withdrawing from their former American colonies. However, the loss of British support for Native American resistance against the Kentucky settlements was a major blow for the Shawnee in particular, who struggled to fight until 1795. Their efforts made the settlement process more fraught but could not ultimately stop it. Settlers began to accelerate their plans to develop their farms, produce marketable goods, and build prosperity. Boone and McGary followed the same path along separate tracks.[25]

8

Postwar Life at McGary's Station

The "year of blood" finally ended, and 1783 marked a turning point in the fortunes of the Kentucky settlers. McGary returned from the retaliatory raid that leveled the Shawnee settlements at Chillicothe, Piqua, and Wills to resume his life at Shawnee Springs. His family now included his second wife, Catherine (nicknamed Catesey or Caty); his stepsons, James and John Ray; his children by his first wife, Robert, Daniel, and Mary Ann; his child by Catesey, William Ray (born April 4, 1782); and two step-grandchildren, William and Jesse Ray, whose parents were James and Amelia (Yocum) Ray. James married Amelia Yocum on July 5, 1781, but she died on December 21, 1783. James next married Elizabeth Talbot in 1787. They eventually had seven children, of whom an unknown number were born at the station. Others, probably mostly single young men, occasionally stayed at the station as well.

McGary's activities over the next five years undoubtedly involved developing his landholdings, raising crops, and adding to his prosperity. He had raised hogs and horses in North Carolina and brought forty horses with him to Kentucky (he probably raised other livestock as well). McGary also likely owned enslaved people whom he occasionally sold or traded, though the historical record is sparse on evidence.

Continuing his activity in civic affairs, McGary was serving on the Lincoln County Court when, in late spring of 1783, he was indicted for betting and winning a mare worth twelve pounds (indicating it was probably an older horse) from a man named Foster on a race at Hagan's Path. McGary was found guilty on August 21, with the following judgment: "It is the opinion of the Court that the defendant be deemed an infamous gambler and that he shall not be eligible to any office of trust or honor within this state, and that he pay the costs of this presentment." The charge is rather ironic considering the long, deeply ingrained cultural history of gambling and horse racing in Virginia. Gambling of all kinds was so pervasive that it penetrated all levels of society, from rich plantation owners to impoverished farmers and soldiers. However, the ills of gambling appear to have been the impetus for the 1779 passage of the Virginia anti-gaming law that ensnared McGary. "An Act to Suppress Excessive Gambling" prohibited gambling "on any horserace" that exceeded five pounds or equal value in winnings as well as wagering that took place in "a tavern, racefield, or other place of publick resort." The value of five pounds in 1783 equals about $871 today, so McGary's winnings, equaling $2089 today, clearly exceeded the minimum amount allowed by law. Despite the verdict, McGary was not removed from the court immediately, as he was still serving as a justice in September 1783. However, his appearances in court for the rest of the year were for lawsuits in which he was involved, not as a justice.[1]

Litigation for many reasons was commonplace in the late eighteenth century, and McGary both sued as a plaintiff and was called out as a defendant. He sued Manoah Singleton, Samuel Davis, and Barney Stagner for debt in 1783 and 1784, and he and his stepson, James Ray, were sued for trespass by William Overall (both were found not guilty). His conviction as an "infamous gambler" was the most unusual of the suits involving him and occurred almost exactly a year after the battle, begging the question, was he singled out because of his behavior at Blue Licks?[2]

McGary was apparently stripped of his position on the county court until April 1785, when he was again appointed. He served on the court in 1785 and 1786 and was commissioned as a lieutenant colonel on September 5, 1786, where the record referred to him as a "gentleman." A month later, he got into trouble again when he participated in Benjamin Logan's expedition against the Miami villages north of the Ohio River. Native American raiding parties from the Wabash River valley (spanning present-day Illinois, Indiana, and Ohio) had been particularly troublesome in the spring of 1786, prompting Governor Patrick Henry to write to Logan authorizing him to meet with all the militia commanders in Kentucky and devise a plan for defense. Logan and the commanders met at Harrodsburg and determined to use militia troops to respond to the raids. Despite some discussion as to the legality of mounting military expeditions against Native tribes outside of Virginia's borders, a plan was devised to mobilize half of the militia by means of conscription and launch an attack against the Miami villages on the Wabash River. Logan assumed command when George Rogers Clark refused to take command of the drafted army on the grounds that militia law required that individuals consent to leave the state. If taken against their will, they were not bound to obey orders, nor could they be legally punished for disobedience, desertion, or other offenses.

Under these unsatisfactory conditions, the militia leaders ordered the companies to rendezvous at the new town of Clarksville, opposite the Falls of the Ohio River. Out of an expected force of twenty-five hundred, only twelve hundred men reluctantly appeared. Clark consented to take the available men and proceed to Vincennes (in present-day Indiana) while an officer from each of the other counties rounded up the delinquents and deserters. (By then, these new counties included Bourbon, Madison, and Mercer, in addition to more established Jefferson, Fayette, and Lincoln.) Clark also called up half of the remaining militiamen, assigning Logan to lead this force against the Shawnee towns on the Miami River. Both McGary and Daniel Boone accompanied Logan, McGary with the Mercer County men and Boone with the Fayette County contingent. The force of about eight hundred men crossed the Ohio River on September 30 and then marched in regiments headed by John Logan's Lincoln County men on the right, Robert Patterson's Fayette County men on the left, a rear guard led by Major John Hinkston, and an advance guard led by Benjamin Logan. As they neared the Shawnee villages on October 5, Logan ordered that the men march as quietly as possible, take no plunder until granted permission, and receive any person approaching the army "in a friendly manner." His intent was to protect recently captured white prisoners and prevent their being killed inadvertently if mistaken for the enemy, as well as to give the Shawnee the opportunity to send emissaries to sue for peace.[3]

When Logan's army reached the first Shawnee village on October 6, no peace emissaries appeared, and the Shawnee did not show any signs of trying to escape. Logan began to worry that the men might not fight as vigorously as he anticipated would be necessary. He modified his original instructions by riding through the lines and telling the men that they were to spare white persons but were free to do as they pleased with the Shawnee. Seven villages, Mackacheck, Wappatomica, New Piqua, Will's Town, McKee's Town, Blue

Jacket's Town, and Moluntha's Town, constituted the Shawnee settlements along the Miami River, and Logan divided his force so each town could be attacked simultaneously. As Logan's men neared the villages, they encountered very little resistance. Many of the Shawnee warriors were absent, having gone to the Wabash to fight General Clark's army. The men then burned over two hundred houses and fifteen thousand bushels of corn, took plunder worth nearly £1000, and gathered and slaughtered hogs. Ten warriors were killed, among them Big Jim, who had tortured and killed Boone's son, James, in 1773. Thirty-two prisoners, most of them women and children, were rounded up. The Kentucky men suffered one fatality, two men were mortally wounded, and two were slightly injured.[4]

One of the captives was an elderly chief named Moluntha, who was head of one of the destroyed villages. Moluntha had headed a peace delegation the previous year and signed a treaty with the United States, promising to accept its sovereignty and live in peace. His village was flying an American flag when he, his wife, and some women and children surrendered to Logan's force. While Moluntha and his wife sat in custody, McGary asked the chief if he had been at the Battle of Blue Licks. When Moluntha replied in the affirmative, McGary seized the wife's small axe and buried it in the man's head, killing him and wounding his wife when she tried to intervene. According to William Sudduth, who was also on the expedition, some of the men under McGary's command killed another warrior the next morning. They did not apparently suffer any consequences for their actions. McGary's killing of Moluntha, however, outraged his fellow officers, and he further inflamed the situation by "insulting and abusing" Lt. Col. James Trotter of Fayette County for "taking measures to prevent the Prisoners being murdered" then vowing to chop down any man who hindered him.[5]

The following March 21, a general court-martial was convened at Bardstown to consider both McGary's behavior and a counter complaint that McGary made against Col. Robert Patterson and Lt. Col. James Trotter. Col. Alexander Scott Bullitt presided over a court of twelve men while John Steele served as the judge advocate. McGary stood accused of four charges: murdering Moluntha; acting in disobedience of orders to spare the prisoners; behaving in a disorderly manner by insulting Col. Trotter and swearing to harm anyone who interfered; and finally, "abusing several Field Officers in a public manner, but who were absent at Limestone on the return of the Expedition." The final charge seems to have been added because McGary cursed his fellow officers publicly but not to their faces afterward. McGary was found guilty of murdering Moluntha, not guilty of disobeying orders, guilty of abusing Colonel Trotter, and partly guilty of the fourth charge. The court agreed that McGary's conduct was "unbecoming the character of an officer and a Gentleman" and sentenced him to be suspended from military service for one year. McGary's countercharge claimed that Colonel Patterson and Lieutenant Colonel Trotter opened a barrel of rum at Limestone where the troops crossed the Ohio River and killed twenty beeves (cows) without the authority of the commissary, thus delaying the army for more than one day. He also claimed that Lieutenant Colonel Trotter gave orders for his men to shoot any man who killed a Shawnee captive, presumably after McGary had killed Moluntha. The court dismissed the rum charge on the grounds that it was not a military matter and found Patterson guilty of not applying to the commissary concerning the beeves, recommending a severe reprimand. The court found no evidence to support the charge against Colonel Trotter.[6]

McGary's punishment was quite mild considering he took a life, but the court may have felt that their options were limited. Colonel Logan's change of orders concerning the treatment of Shawnee was not written down, and McGary clearly felt justified in his attack of Moluntha, whom he singled out because of his involvement in the Battle of Blue Licks. Although the battle was four years past, McGary had apparently not gotten over the criticism and censure he received for his conduct on that fateful day. McGary's court-martial seems to have been prompted more by his conduct against his fellow officers than his murder of a Native American, particularly a chief who was known to have waged war against Kentucky. Given the generally negative views that most settlers held against Native Americans, the court's verdict is, while reprehensible to modern sensibilities, understandable in context. The punishment he received removed him from military service for a year but did not affect his standing as a member of the Mercer County court, where he continued to serve. Nonetheless, the outcome of the trial must have continued to rankle, particularly since McGary's countersuits against James Trotter and Robert Patterson only resulted in a reprimand for Patterson. Historian John A. McClung blamed McGary for precipitating the rush into battle, citing an anonymous "gentleman of Kentucky" who claimed to have spoken with McGary several years later at one of the circuit courts. He said that McGary acknowledged that he was the cause of the defeat, but he was still resentful that his superior officers did not follow his advice and felt that they deserved the deaths they received. McClung's description of the battle had several major errors, not the least of which being his report that the men followed McGary in a disorganized manner. Both Samuel Wilson and Neal Hammon cast doubt on his account. Nevertheless, while McGary was not officially blamed in any of the contemporary reports sent to the governor after the battle, his reputation was checkered at best by this event and others, causing people to view him with prejudice.[7]

In 1787, McGary began to sell off his Mercer County land. One of the purchasers was his stepson, James Ray. On February 7, 1787, Ray, by then a widower, married Elizabeth Talbot, and in 1782, he had been granted a 400-acre settlement tract as an assignee of McGary, who had himself been assigned a certificate for the land by Lewis Holmes. This tract connected to McGary's 175-acre preemption on the west and flanked what is today Warwick Road. Ray also owned property near and on the Salt River in what is presently western Mercer County. However, he purchased 100 acres for fifty pounds from Hugh and Catherine McGary in 1787, filing the deed a few months after his remarriage. This tract was roughly diamond-shaped and was taken from the northwesterly portion of McGary's settlement and preemption. A portion of the tract's southern line exists today as a section of Bonta Lane. A portion of the north line of the tract served as one of the boundary lines of a later farm that became part of the much larger Anderson Circle Farm. Enclosed by this tract is the Great Blue Spring (where William Ray was killed), the cemetery in which James and his second wife (as well as other people who do not have inscribed gravestones) were buried, and the spot where James Ray built the house he occupied until his death. While the deed does not indicate if he had already built his house prior to filing, it is likely that he moved in sometime in 1787 or 1788.[8]

On April 25, 1788, Hugh and Catherine McGary filed a deed of sale for the remaining 475 acres of the settlement and preemption to George Thompson of Fluvanna County, Virginia. George Thompson did not move to Kentucky permanently until May 1792, but he made frequent visits. He may have allowed the McGarys to remain at their station for a time after the land sale was finalized. McGary owned land that he had purchased in 1788 from Matthias Yocum that may have become their home for a few years. He still owned property on the Kentucky River, where he served as a trustee for the small port of Warwick, established to provide a shipping point for farm products destined for sale in New Orleans or other places downstream. The

George M. Bedinger Papers include an unattributed note by Lyman C. Draper that the McGarys lived at Warwick in 1787, but no source is cited, and the possibility is not corroborated elsewhere. In 1794, the McGarys sold three tracts of land to John Adair. The deed describing the land has a transcription error that reads "whereon the now lives" so it is not clear if the McGarys or John Adair were living there at the time of the transaction. In 1795, the McGarys bought lots in Harrodsburg and operated a tavern on Main Street. They may have also built a brick house on one of the lots. By 1798, McGary had sold almost all of his Mercer County property in preparation to relocate. He later moved to Henderson, Kentucky, and then to Indiana, where he died in 1806. Although his subsequent history is not relevant to Shawnee Springs during the postfrontier period, he continued to stir up controversy.[9]

The Shawnee Springs in the Postfrontier Period

After the departure of the McGarys, the land around the Shawnee Springs was owned partly by James Ray and partly by George Thompson, both prominent, highly respectable citizens. Both built homes on their land and passed their estates on to their children. McGary's Station was abandoned, its structures removed or allowed to decay, and the land was put to agricultural use.

James Ray lived at his home above the Great Blue Spring for the rest of his life. He was remembered by his family doctor as "neighborly, kind & pleasing . . . unassuming and modest, a kinder and better hearted man never lived." His son, John, said, "My father was a man of Stern integrity and all Matters emanating from considered unexceptionable." Though he received no formal education, he was literate, and his estate inventory indicates that he was a reader of history, geography, and politics. One of his contemporaries described him as "never a professor of religion but was of quite a different stamp from McGary. The law of kindness ruled in his heart. He had a great faith in dreams." His inventory included a book entitled *Life of Christ*, suggesting that he had an interest in spiritual matters even if he may not have attended church regularly. Yet he also owned enslaved people and, at his death in May 1835, continued by will the servitude of all but two enslaved folk. In this contradiction between his reputation of kindness and modesty and his belief that owning enslaved people was acceptable, he was like many of his contemporaries.[10]

James Ray had by his first wife, Milly Yocum, two sons, William and Jesse. In a curious aside, a notation in the Draper manuscripts states that his son,

James Ray's portrait. Courtesy of the Wisconsin Historical Society.

William, shot him with the view of killing him, leaving a facial scar that he carried to his death. Yet his son was given $100 by his father's will, so seemingly the incident did not alienate them completely. His second wife, Elizabeth Talbot, bore him eleven more children, according to John Ray (James Jr., John, Harvey, Jefferson, Mary, Catherine, Jane, Lucinda, Martha, and two whose names are not known). Elizabeth died in 1810, and James never remarried.[11]

Except for two more episodes of military service, James Ray settled down to a life of industry and civic responsibility. He led a battalion during General Harmar's 1790 campaign and served in the War of 1812 even though he was advanced in age, receiving a commission of major general. He was active in local civic affairs, serving on juries, viewing new road routes, directing work on road maintenance, appraising estates, and testifying in land suits. A major part of his later life was spent as a competent but not spectacular representative in the Kentucky Assembly. He was elected twelve times between 1801 and 1818. Fiscally conservative, he frequently voted against measures that cost money. He supported moving Transylvania University to Harrodsburg and was involved in the time-consuming controversy regarding the location of the state capitol. He voted in favor of a bill preventing freed men of color from entering the state in 1807. In 1810, he voted against a bill that prohibited the importation of enslaved persons into the state. He also opposed a bill regulating the behavior of the enslaved. He owned enslaved persons, and his votes seemed to support the increase of the enslaved population by importation but sought to limit the increase of freed men of color. His attitude was not unusual among those who owned enslaved persons, who felt that free people of color were dangerous to the status quo of white people maintaining control over the Black population.[12]

Ray was not a wealthy man, but he was prosperous enough to remain in "easy circumstances," and "did not seem to thirst for Wealth." Ill throughout his later years, he died on May 9, 1835, at home near the beautiful spring where some of the most tragic and the happiest events of his life had taken place. He was buried in a family cemetery on a prominent ridge near his house. He had already divided much of his land among his grown children, and his will reflected these prior bequests. His will is a curious document largely because it reflects an unequal distribution of land, enslaved persons, and personal estate among his children. For instance, five of his children received land ranging in size from 100 to 200 acres, as well as enslaved persons, while his son James just received a watch, and three of his other sons received only $100. Jefferson Ray, one of his youngest children, received about 180 acres of land, which included Ray's house, several enslaved people, the balance of his stock, and all his personal property. Jefferson was charged with helping out his siblings if they were in need; however, his business management must not have been very competent since he later acquired so much debt that he had to convey his property to Beriah Magoffin in 1847.[13]

Of the children, Harvey, Jane (Wilson), and Jefferson were given land out of Ray's home farm; the other offspring either did not receive land or were given land from Ray's holdings on the Salt River. Some land from Ray's home farm was parceled out by the heirs to their other siblings later.

His inventory also offers evidence of his farm operation and household. He owned a yoke of oxen that he probably used as plow animals. He also raised other cattle, perhaps to sell yearly for beef. Among his cattle were eight cows who produced calves and milk, but no bull is listed. He may have used his neighbors' bulls to service his cows, as was common practice. He owned a total of thirteen horses, a rather high number for most farmers, suggesting that he also sold horses as part of his income. His livestock was further diversified by the presence of sheep and hogs as well as eleven beehives. He produced hemp and wool, the former undoubtedly for sale as part of the farm income, the latter probably for family use. His agricultural equipment was modest compared to the contemporary inventories of other farmers. Given his landholdings and livestock, this list may not have represented all he owned but rather what was left over after his children took what they wanted or needed. For instance, no clothing items are listed.[14]

The household inventory taken after Ray's death lists four beds (one "fancy," two "common," and one with curtains) with their accompanying linens, along with two dining tables, six Windsor chairs, and two bureaus to hold clothes and personal belongings. Two extra coverlets and other household linens were stored in a press. A bookcase held his books, which included a dictionary, two volumes of the *History of the Revolution*, one volume of the *Life of Christ*, one volume of Guthrie's *Geography*, and two volumes of *Journals of the Kentucky Legislature*. A mantle clock and watch were also listed, along with a loom that had probably belonged to his wife and may have been used by enslaved females to weave wool sheared from his sheep. He was a coffee drinker and owned a coffee mill. He was also sufficiently affluent to keep enough sugar on hand (an expensive commodity) that he needed a lockable

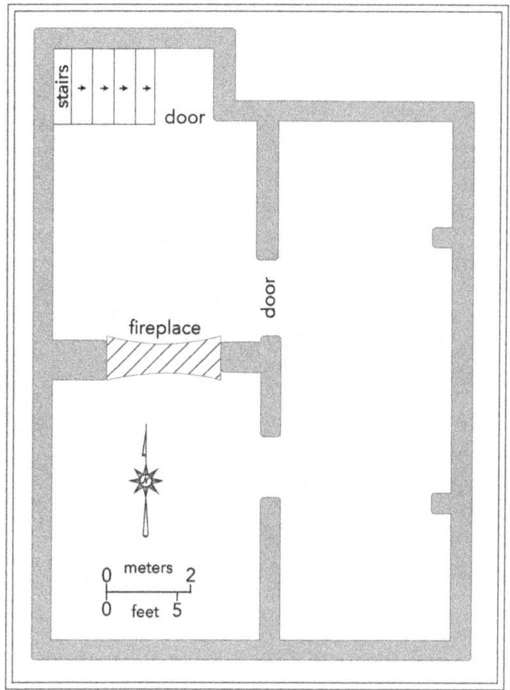

Floor plan of the James Ray house.

sugar chest to store it in. Unspecified kitchen and table "furniture" referred to such items as dinnerware, flatware, cooking implements and containers, and other common items that were of too low value to individually list. In keeping with his pioneer beginnings, he kept a muzzle-loading rifle and shot pouch and had a considerable quantity of gunpowder on hand, although a little sport hunting or pest control was probably its chief use in his later life. His son Jefferson inherited his house and the contents that were not disbursed in his will to his other offspring; an inventory was not strictly necessary but was probably done so that each heir would receive an equal portion of the estate.

As was common for many men of modest means, he occasionally made loans to his friends and family in the form of promissory notes. In a society where cash was sometimes scarce, promissory notes were the legal tender of the day. Only one of his loans was sizable, $300 to Samuel Keller, who was his son-in-law (married to his daughter, Catherine).

His house, the foundation of which still exists, was not particularly large but typical for the time and his status. The stone foundation of the house

Col. George Thompson's house at Shawnee Springs. (2008ms020: Item 1562, Clay Lancaster Slide Collection, 1939–1992, University of Kentucky Special Collections Resource Center)

forms a basement that is divided into three rooms. The east room, which is the largest, extends the length of the foundation. The two rooms on the west side of the foundation have a common wall, with a fireplace in the southernmost room. The northernmost room of the pair may have also had a fireplace, but it was not well preserved. Door openings connected each of the rooms on the west side to the larger room on the east side. Stairs on the north exterior wall of the foundation led down to the basement. The orientation of the house is not self-evident from the foundation, and the house may have had more rooms that were not underlain by the basement.

A former farm manager described the house as being of brick construction and very similar in style to the nearby George Thompson house. This house, which was enlarged and embellished by Thompson's son after he inherited it, stood until 1982, when it was destroyed by a fire. The original house, two stories in height and originally facing north, had a front facade laid in Flemish bond with glazed headers and glazed bricks laid in a Dutch cross bond on the side elevations. The house was reoriented to face south when George C. Thompson added a large Greek Revival addition and the

Col. George Thompson's and George C. Thompson's portraits. Courtesy of Rafinesque Manuscript Collection, Transylvania University Library.

original house was incorporated as the west wing, its rear elevation becoming part of the front elevation of the larger structure. An extant photograph shows four windows, larger on the first floor, smaller on the second, arranged symmetrically in vertical pairs.

George Thompson was a wealthy businessman and politician who, after making several visits to Kentucky, moved permanently in May 1792. The land he purchased from McGary in 1788 included the station site and the two springs southeast of James Ray's spring at the head of the run. Colonel Thompson, as he was called, served in the Virginia Assembly from 1779 to 1781, was an aide to General Lafayette during the American Revolution, and later served in the Kentucky House of Representatives. He built a house he called Shawnee Springs on Curry Road that stood almost directly in the middle of the 475-acre tract he purchased from McGary. He continued to buy property and amassed a large estate by the time of his death.[15]

In a letter he wrote for his grandson, Thompson told of being born on the Solitude plantation on the North Fork of the James River (called the Rivanna River) in Albemarle County, Virginia, on February 12, 1748. His parents were Joseph Thompson, son of Roger and Ann Foster Thompson, and Sarah Claiborne, daughter of Thomas Claiborne and his wife, whose surname was

Fox. Colonel Thompson married Rebecca Barton on December 6, 1773, on the James River in Virginia. They had two sons: Samuel, who died as an infant, and George Claiborne, who was born on April 30, 1778. Mrs. Thompson died shortly after the birth of George, and Colonel Thompson never remarried, rearing his only surviving son with the help of enslaved persons.

Son George married three times. He married his first cousin, Sally Thompson, in 1806. She died within a few years of marriage, leaving no children, and George married Mary McClung McDowell in 1809. Mary bore three children: Mary, who married Frank Kinkead; George Madison, who died at the age of seventeen; and William, born on May 16, 1814. Mary Thompson must have died soon after William's birth, because George married a third time to Sarah Hart, daughter of Nathaniel Hart Jr., and stated in 1849 that he had been married to her for over thirty years. Two daughters, Letitia and Susan, were born to his third wife before the winter of 1823–1824. Letitia was the youngest.

Like James Ray, with whom he was friends, George C. Thompson served in the Kentucky House of Representatives. His family lived with his father, Colonel Thompson, on the Shawnee Springs plantation in the house that once stood on Curry Road. George C. Thompson's last wife did not get along with her father-in-law. During the winter of 1823, she left the Shawnee Springs house and, taking her two daughters, returned to her father's house. Colonel Thompson had never given his son any part of his estate, which was the basis for his daughter-in-law's unhappiness. In January 1824, Colonel Thompson conveyed over one thousand acres of land and about fifty enslaved persons to his son and expressed his intent to build a new residence for either himself or his son. This action appeased the young wife, and she returned to the Shawnee Springs house. Colonel Thompson kept his promise and built for himself a new house that he called Pleasant Fields. He died on March 22, 1834. He left Pleasant Fields to his grandson, William, along with enslaved people and considerable personal property.[16]

George C. Thompson died in 1856 and left a will that attempted to divide his estate among his children and provide for his widow. Surviving children included William, who had been amply provided for in his grandfather's will and so received only a gold-headed cane and watch from his father. Mary was unable to have children and so received less from her father's estate than the other children. Nonetheless, she received land and enslaved people valued at $19,000. Susan, who married Morgan Vance and had returned to live with her father and mother in the years before George C. died, had been previously deeded part of the Shawnee Springs tract, and the will acknowledged this gift. Letitia received the residue of the land, road stock, and other considerations, including her mother's dower.

Although the language of the will clearly indicated George C. Thompson's intent to treat all his heirs fairly, its conditions were contested by his widow in court. The crux of the disagreement hung on the conditions under which George C. Thompson owned the Shawnee Springs plantation and the enslaved persons he received from his father. This gift was given as a life estate so that it could not be considered part of the estate subject to the widow's dower. While George C. could have given part of his land and enslaved persons outright to his wife, he did not do so. The appeals court affirmed the original verdict that Mrs. Thompson was not entitled to dower in the property under question.

The disagreements over inheritance caused a rift in the family. This is further confirmed by a lawsuit brought by Letitia's husband, William L. Vance, against Morgan and Susan Vance. In 1849, Morgan and Susan Vance lived on the Mississippi River below Memphis, Tennessee. George C. Thompson, then in poor health and missing his daughter's company, asked her and her husband to settle on a part of his land known as the Ray tract. This was the land that James Ray had purchased from McGary and on which he had built a house. In a long letter penned to her father during a visit to his home in October 1849, Susan outlined "feelings of misunderstandings" that had arisen between her and her sisters, Mary and Letitia, over their father's plan. Her father answered her with another letter in which he set out his reasons for dividing his property. Specifically, he stated his intent to leave his home to his widow for the remainder of her life or until remarriage or voluntary relinquishment. Upon the expiration of the widow's right, the property was to go to Letitia and Susan, but rather than dividing it, commissioners were to be appointed to set a value so that one of the sisters could buy out the other. His wish was that Susan would buy out Letitia and settle at the Shawnee Springs house permanently. He had already given Susan two tracts of 143 and 40 acres in 1847. In 1850, Morgan and Susan were living with Colonel and Mrs. Thompson in the Shawnee Springs house and expected to inherit the property upon the colonel's death. But something must have happened to make George C. Thompson change his mind.[17]

George C. Thompson survived over six years after the correspondence of 1849. When he died in 1856, his will did not reflect the intent of his earlier letter. Instead, he left the Shawnee Springs house and part of the tract originally purchased by his father from McGary to Letitia and her heirs in fee simple and excluded his daughter Susan. His will stated he had already given her "a good deal" and "I will give her no more." Other than the land he had given her in 1847, the record is silent on other transactions, suggesting that his generosity took the form of cash gifts. His widow received her dower calculated only on the property that was not part of her husband's inheritance from her father. Since he had not amassed much more property beyond what he had inherited, her share was considerably smaller than it might have been had the conditions of Colonel Thompson's will been different.[18]

Resulting court cases clearly indicate that both the widow Sarah and daughter Susan were unhappy over the conditions of the will. Sarah filed suit, renouncing the will, and laying claim to the Shawnee Springs house, land, and enslaved persons. Her claim was not upheld in court. Morgan and Susan sued the estate, claiming that George C. Thompson's 1849 letter constituted a valid, binding contract. The court agreed, but the verdict was overturned when Letitia and William Vance filed an appeal. The appeals court implied in their ruling that conditions alluded to in his 1849 letter that would cause George C. Thompson to change his will had probably arisen and that he was entitled to alter his intent "upon the happening of events that might render it proper, and of which he to a very great extent must necessarily have been the judge." These conditions may have been related to Morgan Vance's business dealings. Susan mentioned in her letter to her father that she did not want her husband to have business dealings with her family. Although she did not give any reasons, the fact that accusations and gossip had already arisen within the family concerning her (and perhaps her husband's) motives suggests that there was dissension among the family women.[19]

Morgan Vance's business dealings during the 1850s are unknown, but lawsuits filed against him in the first few years after the end of the Civil War hint at a variety of deals gone sour. The land he purchased from Joseph A. Thompson in 1847 was never fully paid for, and Thompson had to bring suit in 1866, 1867, and 1871 to recover unpaid installments. Partnerships Vance made with other individuals failed, and the assets were ordered sold between 1869 and 1874. The Civil War may well have been the final blow to his financial house of cards, especially if he was using enslaved people as collateral and acquiring debt. If George Thompson gave his daughter and son-in-law money that was lost in poor investments, he may well have viewed his son-in-law unfavorably. In any event, George changed his mind and took steps to ensure that the plantation begun by his father and lovingly maintained by him did not go to Susan and Morgan Vance. Letitia and William Vance emerged as the winners in the dispute over the land, and in 1860, they were living in Mercer County at the Shawnee Springs house. Morgan and Susan Vance were living on the property they had been given, as well as purchased, with their four sons aged one to eight years, and Sarah S. Thompson, Susan's mother. Since Sarah Thompson had been given the use of the Shawnee Springs house for her lifetime (if she did not remarry) in her husband's will, she must have voluntarily relinquished her claim to it. She certainly seems to have taken her daughter Susan's side in the controversy. At the time of the 1860 census, Morgan's real estate value was $62,000, and his personal estate was worth $50,000—a tidy sum for the time. But brother-in-law William reported a real estate value of $186,300 and a personal estate value of $289,200—clearly trumping Morgan by a staggering amount. While these totals probably represent other assets that William had separate from his wife's inheritance, the contrast is striking and could not have improved matters with his brother and sister-in-law.[20]

Morgan's financial fortunes continued to decline during the early 1870s. His holdings of enslaved persons disappeared with the Union victory, amounting to a considerable loss in assets. Morgan and Susan, their four sons, and a daughter moved to New Albany, Indiana, during the war, and Susan's mother, Sarah, lived with them in 1870. An 1874 deed referenced two cases in which Morgan Vance and his partners were the losers; this deed conveyed 185 acres adjoining the old Ray tract where Vance had formerly lived. Morgan Vance died on June 8, 1871, at the age of fifty-seven. His widow, Susan, was living with her mother, Sarah Thompson, her grown sons, and her underage daughter (born in 1865) in New Albany, Indiana, in 1880. In 1881, Susan Vance and her family sold sixty-five acres of the Mercer County property to R. H. Cecil. In 1887, Susan, then living in New York City, sold her fifty-acre dower tract to W. W. Goddard. The land contained a graveyard with the interments of some of her children, probably two young daughters named Mary (aged four) and Sallie (aged two) who had been living with their parents and grandparents in 1850 but do not appear in the 1860 census. This parcel probably included the house built by James Ray above the Great Blue Spring.[21]

After passing through several owners, the land was acquired by Thomas Marksbury and remained in his family until 1944, when Ethel C. Spilman purchased it. The Spilmans had already purchased most of the land that James Ray had owned from J. W. McCray in 1917. They moved out of Mercer County, and the land was leased for many years before Mrs. Spilman sold a tract of 359.639 acres in 1986 to Ralph C. Anderson, who added it to his Anderson Circle Farm holdings. This tract contained virtually all of the land James Ray left to his children as well as the springs section of the tract that McGary sold to Col. George Thompson, thus uniting once again under one owner the famous Shawnee Springs. After Ralph Anderson's death in 2010, his heirs sold the entire Anderson Circle Farm to Justice Family Farms.[22]

9

Postwar Life at Boone's Station

Daniel Boone was living at his station on Boone Creek at the time of the Battle of Blue Licks in August 1782 but moved to a tract on Marble Creek in Jessamine County that was claimed by his son-in-law, William Hays. Daniel Bryan told Lyman Draper that he visited his uncle Daniel on Marble Creek in the fall of 1783. Boone attempted to gain title to the station land when he filed a four-hundred-acre settlement survey on April 7, 1784, and a thousand-acre preemption survey a week later, on April 15, and submitted the survey in the name of Daniel Morgan Boone, who had inherited Israel Boone's estate after Israel was killed at the Battle of Blue Licks. The settlement tract survey calls cornered on James Hickman, William Madison, Jonathan Martin, John Boofman, and William Gillespie and referenced an entry date of January 17, 1780, with the land court. The four hundred acres were within William Madison's thousand-acre military survey that Deputy Surveyor John Floyd had surveyed in 1775. The Madison survey was well known, and Boone undoubtedly knew about it since he was in contact with John Floyd and was locating land in the same area for James Hickman at the same time. His later placement of his son's four-hundred-acre settlement on Madison land may have been a mistake, or he may have thought erroneously that claims made under the 1779 land law would take precedence over earlier military claims. In any event, Madison had the elder claim, and Boone's claim would never have prevailed. The thousand-acre preemption referenced an entry date of December 11, 1782, and was an unusually complex shape, suggesting that Boone was attempting to place it on vacant land between other earlier surveys.

The survey calls referenced Jonathan Martin, Levi Todd (who also served as a marker), Waller Overton, Robert Todd, and Isaac Shelby as neighbors. There was less interference with this land, but it still overlapped with one of James Hickman's claims. Nonetheless, Boone went ahead with plans to establish a station on the property in 1779. By 1783 or perhaps earlier, Boone and his family pulled up stakes and moved, even though he apparently did not give up all hope of gaining title until sometime later.[1]

Later in 1790, a court case was filed by Christinah Boofman against James Hickman, and the resulting trial records elucidated the complicated and chaotic land claim process that resulted in Boone losing his claim to the land. The case dragged on for years. Although Boone never resorted to litigation to claim the station tract, he was called to depose in the case in 1794. He was then living at Point Pleasant in Kanawha County (in present-day West Virginia). Boone stated that he had consulted John Floyd, deputy surveyor for William Preston of Virginia, concerning where to place his survey. Floyd assured him that William Preston would not grant a survey that Floyd had not validated, but James Hickman insisted on Floyd giving him the field notes for the land in dispute. Another deponent, Thomas McClanahan, stated that Boone felt "grossly imposed on by Floyd" whom he blamed for surveying errors that caused overlaps in the various surveys.[2]

Although Boone and his family left the station on Boone's Creek, the site was not abandoned. William Madison sold the station tract in 1781 to John Gordon, who occupied his own station in Mercer County. Boone probably knew about the land transfer but perhaps worked out an arrangement with Gordon to remain there until he could make other arrangements. John Gordon was killed at the Battle of Blue Licks in 1782, and his son Ambrose inherited the land.[3]

Ambrose Gordon sold five hundred acres of the Boone's Station Tract in 1795 to Robert Frank and his wife, Elizabeth. The Franks had a large family of ten children, three of whom were still underage when the Franks moved to the property. The other children were adults, and most of them were married. Robert Frank built a stone house on the property, where he lived with his wife, his three youngest children (Ann, Margaret, and Thomas), and several enslaved people. Although the deed was dated December 8, 1795, Robert Frank moved onto the property by 1788 and bequeathed portions of the tract to his wife and children when he wrote his will on May 1, 1792. His will made clear that the land was already laid out for each of his offspring. His daughter Mary and her husband, John Bledsoe, received one hundred acres and took up residence there. Another one hundred acres went to his other daughter, Elizabeth, married to George Sharp, while Philadelphia, married to Abraham Simpson, received seventy acres. His son, Robert, received part of the tract his father was living on that did not contain the station site. That tract and the stone house were given to his wife, Elizabeth, for the remainder of her life along with all the "household furniture, plantation tools, live Stock and three grown Negroes, Will, Dinah and Jenny." In return, Elizabeth Frank was to "nurse, cloathe, and School" the three youngest children, Ann, Margaret, and Thomas, until they reached their majority. Once Thomas reached the age of twenty-one years, he came into possession of the home tract on which the stone house and the station site were located.[4]

Other bequests in Frank's will dispersed enslaved persons and livestock. Catherine Jones was given an enslaved boy named Cozer. John Frank was given an enslaved boy named Ben, a gray mare, and a colt called the Ranter mare. His underage daughter, Margeret, received an enslaved girl named Suckey; an adult daughter, Sarah, was given an enslaved boy named George; and yet another underage daughter, Ann, was given an enslaved girl named Aggy. One enslaved boy, Tom, was to live on the farm and assist Elizabeth Frank in rearing the underage enslaved children. Based on the bequests included in the will, Robert Frank's holdings of enslaved persons amounted to nine individuals, four of whom remained on the home tract with Elizabeth Frank. An additional boy named Jefry was mentioned in the estate inventory taken after Elizabeth Frank's death in 1807; he must have been born after Robert Frank died. The enslaved people living with Elizabeth were to be sold after her death, along with a thousand acres of land near the Big Bone Lick and the proceeds divided equally among the heirs. Significantly, Robert Frank named his "beloved friend Samuel Boone Jnr." as his executor. Robert Frank died in 1798, and his will was produced for probate in the June Court of that year by Samuel Boone and Elias Sharp.

By the time Elizabeth Frank died in 1807, the children were all adults, and the administration of her estate was handled by her son-in-law, George Sharp. Thomas Frank became the sole owner of the station site. If the four enslaved persons listed in Elizabeth's inventory and appraisement were sold as Robert Frank's will directed, Thomas may have been left without anyone to help operate the farm unless he purchased the enslaved people from the estate or acquired them by other means. Thomas gave a bond to John S. Cockrell

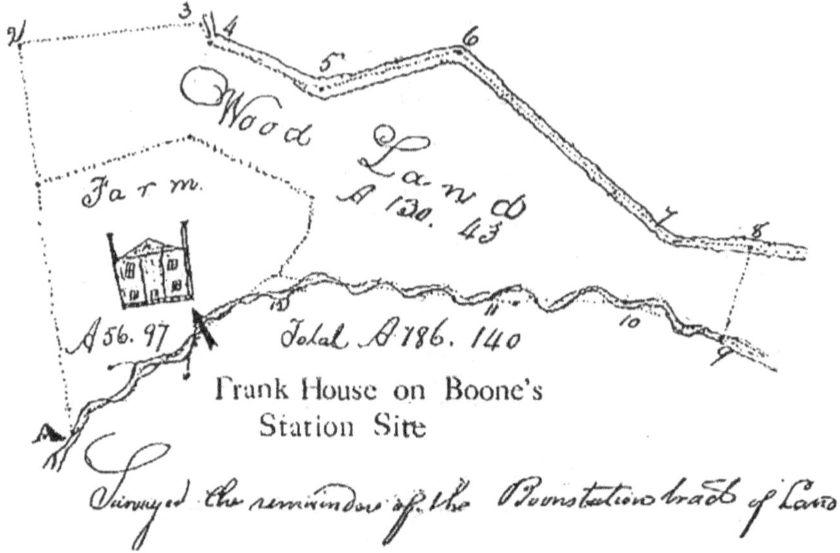

Map showing Robert Frank's home tract and stone house (John Hendley vs. Edmund Bullock, John S. Cockrell [deceased], Hamilton Jenkins and Thomas Franks, Fayette County Land Trial Book F, 184–86).

for 240 acres that included the station tract at an unknown date but probably after his mother died in 1807. Cockrell resided at the site until 1809, when he died. No deed was ever filed between Cockrell and Frank, most likely because the land was still mortgaged. Cockrell left instructions in his will to his executor, Edmund Bullock, to sell the land and settle his debt. Hamilton Jenkins bought the bond for $1,800 and assigned it to John Hendley, who ran a tavern in Cross Plains (later renamed Athens) in 1808. Hendley sued Edmund Bullock, Hamilton Jenkins, and Thomas Frank in 1815 on the grounds that the land he purchased contained slightly more than 181 acres rather than 240 acres as specified on the bond to Cockrell. Hendley successfully sued to gain an injunction concerning the insufficiency and claimed a mill seat within the tract. The case went to court in September 1815, and the defendants were successful in having the injunction dissolved on the grounds that Hendley was aware of the correct acreage at the time of sale and that the mill seat had never been part of the transaction since it had been bequeathed to George Sharp by Elizabeth Frank.[5]

Thomas Frank's inherited land was bounded on the south by Boone Creek and on the north by Boffman's Fork. A survey included among the court case filed by Hendley showed Thomas Frank's land as having a 56.97-acre tract in the southwest corner labeled "Farm" and a 130.43-acre tract labeled "Woodland," totaling 186.140 acres. A two-story house with end chimneys and a centered door flanked by two windows on each side was drawn on the farm tract. This house was the stone structure built by Robert Frank, where Elizabeth lived until her death. The map represented the land that Thomas Frank sold to John Cockrell and was presented as evidence that Hendley was aware of the amount of acreage that he purchased from the Cockrell estate. Hendley sold the land to Charles Grimes in 1815 for 362 barrels of "super fine flour." Charles Grimes lived in a large stone house and was the proprietor of a stone mill that currently serves as the headquarters of the Iroquois Hunt Club on Grimes Mill Road in Fayette County. Grimes never occupied the house on Boone's Station, and it may have stood empty or was rented out while he owned it. In 1824, the Fayette County Circuit Court issued an execution fieri facias in favor of David Castleman, who had sued the Estate of George E. Monroe, Charles Grimes, and John Gess for $2,019.04. The county sheriff put the 181-acre Boone's Station tract up for auction and sold it to Simeon, Harvey, and Robert Bledsoe, who were partners in Simeon Bledsoe & Co. for four dollars per acre, payable in gold or silver. The Bledsoes ran a store in nearby Athens, and Harvey Bledsoe served as postmaster and was one of the trustees who laid out the Athens town plan in 1826.[6]

Sometime before October 1827, Simeon Bledsoe died, leaving his two brothers as the remaining partners. Robert Bledsoe was a distant partner and lived in Georgia by 1818, remaining there until his death in 1854. Harvey was the only partner living in Kentucky, and he is the best candidate for having occupied the site from 1824 until sometime before September 1833, when he died. Another brother, John Bledsoe, briefly held an interest in the land by virtue of his inheritance from his brother Simeon, but he sold his interest to Robert and Harvey in 1827. Harvey left no will, but documents appraising and selling his personal property were filed in the circuit court as his estate was settled.[7]

Robert Bledsoe became the sole owner of the Boone's Station tract. Since he was living in Georgia, he appointed Garrett Watts as his power of attorney to handle his Kentucky landholdings, particularly his Fayette County property, in 1842. Robert Bledsoe wrote his will in 1846 at the age of sixty-three and named Waller Bullock and Garrett Watts as the executors for his Kentucky holdings. Two years later, he sold 172 acres of the Boone's Station tract to Garrett Watts. In 1849, Watts sold 96.5 acres of the tract, containing the station site, to Thomas F. and James R. Barker. Thomas F. Barker took 76 acres from the west side and became the sole owner of Boone's Station. The Barkers had a familial connection to the Boone family. Their grandmother, Rebecca Boone, was the daughter of Samuel and Sarah Day Boone who had lived at the station with Daniel and later married Roger Jones. Their daughter, Nancy, married Joseph Barker and gave birth to Thomas F. and James R. The Barker family was aware of the Samuel Boone connection and passed that knowledge down through the family. Historian William Henry Perrin interviewed Thomas F. Barker for his 1882 *History of Fayette County, Kentucky*. Barker did not know where the station was located and seemed to be unaware of the stone house built by Robert Frank. As discussion of the archaeological evidence will demonstrate (see part II), the stone house and old station cabins were probably torn down prior to the Barkers' acquisition. Thomas Barker's son, Robert, received the land from his father's estate and transferred it to his daughter, Mrs. Joseph N. Strader, who lived with her family in a frame house on the hill overlooking the station site. Their son, Robert Channing Strader, inherited the farm and willed it to the Commonwealth of Kentucky. The property served as a passive recreational park until 2018, when it was transferred to David's Fork Baptist Church during Governor Matt Bevin's administration.[8]

PART TWO

The Archaeological Evidence

The archival evidence for the occupation of the two pioneer station sites by Daniel Boone, Hugh McGary, and others offers invaluable information about the inhabitants and their experiences both at the site and away from it. The archival record is an essential part of historical archaeology and functions as a form of artifact itself in the sense that bits of information are conveyed in the form of enumeration, description, and recorded knowledge. Historical documentation reveals the names of the people who lived on the site, how long they were there, their relationships to one another, events that took place, and other information. But archaeology is unique in its focus on the physicality of material culture that embodies a wide variety of human activity, from the remains of dwellings and outbuildings to fragments of household, personal, and other types of goods. Archival and archaeological data have their strengths and their weaknesses as information sources. The survival of both archival and archaeological data is dependent on many factors that are beyond the control of either the historian or the archaeologist who seeks to reconstruct the past. The people who created the sites were not thinking of the future archaeologist when they built their homes, prepared their meals, sewed their clothes, or performed myriad other tasks of everyday living. Preservation factors affect both sources; paper documents may be missing, biased, or never created, while material culture is affected by physical preservation of architectural and artifactual evidence. Postoccupation activities such as plowing or erosion erase physical context. The result is a tangle of data that must be carefully examined and sorted into a coherent order. Neither material culture nor archival data alone reveals as much as the two sources do together.

Daniel Boone's and Hugh McGary's Stations share some commonalities that make them ideal subjects for comparison. They were built at the same time, and both employed defensibility in their architecture, following the standard use of stockade and log buildings formed in a quadrilinear arrangement common at the time. Both families were constrained in the acquisition of goods and merchandise during the Revolutionary War and its immediate aftermath because of their distance from eastern markets. The limitations on commercial market availability narrowed the variety of manufactured goods that could be acquired until more robust mercantile systems were developed locally. This had the practical effect of limiting differences based on social class and the ability to acquire goods. In the case of Boone and McGary, their wealth status was more equivalent than disparate; both farmed and kept livestock, McGary owned and traded enslaved persons, while Boone worked as a commercial hunter and land surveyor. The desire to obtain manufactured goods, particularly those that signaled wealth or class status, may have varied between the two men. Boone's reputation as a woodsman who lived simply may suggest a lack of interest in acquiring material trappings of social status, but his wife and family may have had different views. Archaeological artifact analysis can shed some light on how families used material goods to signal their social class. The McGary's Station artifact assemblage is eminently suitable for this type of analysis because it is dated within a short time frame and was generated almost exclusively by the McGary family. The Boone's Station assemblage is less suitable because several families lived on the site in the late eighteenth century and recognizing the material culture of a particular family is problematic.

Differences between the sites are equally important to recognize and evaluate. McGary's Station was abandoned around 1788 or a few years afterward; the lack of later occupation created an artifact assemblage that is a veritable time capsule for stations occupied during the Revolutionary War and the years immediately following it. Boone's Station was occupied for several decades beyond the Revolutionary War, and its artifact assemblage reflects this extended occupation by numerous people. Preservation of architectural evidence also varied between the two sites. Owing to postoccupation agricultural activities (principally, deep plowing and removal of stone foundations), McGary's Station is preserved largely as an archaeological artifact assemblage dating to a short time frame. Boone's Station, in contrast, retained significant evidence of its defensive residential architecture, which was preserved by virtue of its extended and continued use by later families. Grafted onto the earlier station architectural plan was a later stone house that retained and incorporated the rectilinear arrangement of the station cabins minus the stockade into its site plan.

10

Locating Archaeological Evidence of Hugh McGary's Station

The complicated reapportionment of the land that Hugh McGary owned, and where he established his station, was typical of land redistribution in the Bluegrass during the late eighteenth and nineteenth centuries. However, the deeds that were generated from this process failed to mention McGary's Station. The only clue to the location of the station was John Ray's deposition in a court case that stated it was about 100 or 150 yards east of the upper spring from which water emanated and flowed north. Only one of the springs collectively known as Shawnee Springs at the headwaters of Shawnee Run fits that description. The area indicated by John Ray occupies a ridge that encircles the Shawnee Run valley. Using Ray's estimated distances from the spring, I designated an upland area on the east side of the springs' headwaters as the most likely location of the station. There is a historic cemetery containing graves marked by rough field stones close to this area as well. I was not able to determine who is buried there, but its location close to the station site may mean that its interments were related to the station. The cemetery may also have been used after the station was gone, perhaps for burials of enslaved persons.

I utilized special survey techniques to find the site because it was occupied for a short period of time (from 1779 to c. 1788–1792) and because sites dating to the frontier period generally have sparse quantities of artifacts, making them difficult to detect. The area where the station was located was heavily cultivated in the past, although it has been in pasture for much of the twentieth century and since then. Plowing typically mixes the top twelve inches of soil and can also cause soil erosion on slopes. Any surface structural remains, such as stone foundations, may be severely modified or even destroyed by cultivation. Deeper cultural features such as post molds (the cylindrical soil stain marking where a post once stood) or storage cellars are often still preserved since they extend below the surface deeply enough to escape being plowed.

I began field investigations in 1994 to identify the site in concurrence with clues from John Ray's court deposition. Fieldwork continued in 1995 and 1996, using funds provided by then-landowner Ralph Anderson. The investigation began with a remote sensing survey that measured soil conductivity. Professional archaeologist and former State Archaeologist Dr. R. Berle Clay, then employed by the University of Kentucky Department of Anthropology, provided the equipment and expertise to carry out the soil conductivity survey.

Dr. Clay used an EM38 Geonics soil conductivity meter to see if buried features such as root cellars, stone foundations, or other structural remains might be present. A soil conductivity meter sends electrical current through the soil and records readings on the rate of conduction of the current. When applied to archaeological sites, conductivity surveying identifies areas of low and high conductivity that may indicate the presence of cultural features like stone foundations, grave shafts, privy or outhouse shafts, storage pits, or cultural midden with a high humic content. Because soil is an unconsolidated medium, electricity can readily pass through it. If the soil is high in clay, electricity passes through it more quickly than in less clay-rich soil. Where soil has been disturbed or altered from its natural state—for example, when a cellar is dug and filled in or stone foundations are put in place—the electric conductivity normal for that soil is changed in that location. By systematically taking conductivity readings over a land tract, the meter records conductivity values at each grid point; these values, when loaded into a computerized mapping program, are generated as a contour map. Areas of higher or lower conductivity are expressed as anomalies in the soil. This procedure was followed for a tract measuring sixty by eighty meters in the field east of the upper spring. I used the metric system for all mapping, unit placement, and excavation on both sites because it is easier to calculate in the field and is the most commonly used means of measurement in modern archaeology. The resulting conductivity map contained numerous anomalies but no clear linear patterns that could be attributed to cultural features such as a house foundation or a stockade. The destructive effects of plowing on the soil conductivity appeared evident, particularly when the map was compared to two other conductivity maps of pioneer stations that had never been plowed.

While the remote sensing was underway, Mr. Anderson mentioned that a guest, Stanley Felix, who was staying at the farm, had recovered artifacts from the field. Stanley was a metal detector hobbyist who possessed a high level of acumen and skill. He used his metal detector in several places on the farm and, at Mr. Anderson's request, turned over his finds. The artifacts that Stanley found dated to the late eighteenth century and corroborated the existence of the station in the field east of the northernmost spring. The difference between archaeologists and "metal detectorists" is that archaeologists do not keep or sell their finds, as some metal detectorists do. Under other circumstances, Stanley may have been able to keep the artifacts he found, but Mr. Anderson, at my request, prevented him from doing so. Yet Stanley was more interested in my research and helping me than he was in keeping the artifacts, and he offered his considerable expertise in metal detecting to help me investigate the site, determine its size, and collect an artifact assemblage that dates to the brief period in which the McGary family lived on the property.

Archaeological fieldwork on pioneer stations in West Virginia previously verified the usefulness of metal detectors to find artifacts like nails, buttons, and other metal items. Mr. Felix used his metal detection skills to identify "targets" (the locations of metal artifacts identified by the instrument), which were each marked with a pin flag. My field crew and I mapped the distribution of pin flags and hand excavated each point to retrieve the metal artifact. The distribution of eighteenth-century artifacts indicated that the artifacts were spatially concentrated along the western third of the conductivity map and beyond the limits of the map to the west toward the spring, covering an area measuring approximately 40 by 60 meters (equivalent to 0.6 acres).[1]

As crew members excavated the metal detection targets, I realized that cultivation of the site caused soil erosion downhill, in an area where the higher section of the ridge sloped downward to the edge of the valley containing the springs. The erosion carried some artifacts downhill, concentrated them in greater numbers at the base of the slope, and left the higher areas devoid of the original topsoil. At first, this seemed to be bad news for the preservation of the site. However, erosion did not affect the higher, more level part of the site. Since McGary, like most people, preferred to build on level ground rather than on a slope, the lack of erosion on the level part of the ridge was

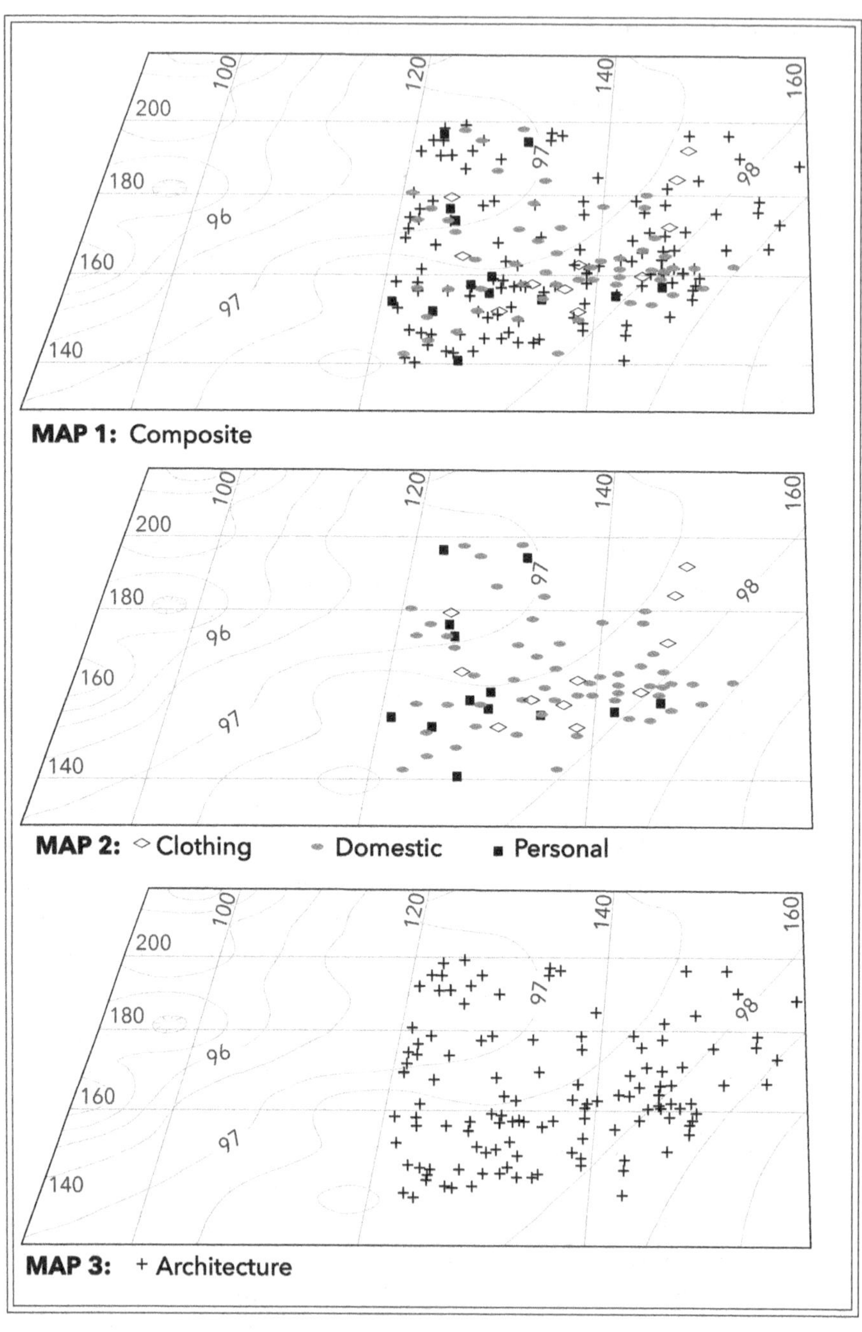

Artifact distribution map of McGary's Station.

encouraging evidence that cultural features associated with the station construction might be preserved. The metal detector survey was instrumental in collecting artifacts that indicated not only the types of household belongings the McGarys and other station occupants owned but also how big the site was. My subsequent artifact analysis identified a diverse assemblage of late eighteenth-century metal artifacts in addition to a few nineteenth- and twentieth-century artifacts attributable to later agricultural activities. I determined the size of the site by plotting the specific location of each artifact on a site map. Most artifacts were contained within a 40 by 60 meter (131 by 197 feet) area, amounting to about three-fifths of an acre or just under one-quarter of a hectare.

During the excavation of shovel probes to retrieve artifacts located by the metal detection, we encountered a soil zone with lots of wood ash and charred wood that lay below the plow-disturbed soil layer. I designated the location as Feature 1. Paleobotanist Jack Rossen identified the larger pieces of charred wood as black locust. Artifacts from the feature include a pig mandible and other unidentifiable animal bone and a few ceramic sherds. We also recovered two cut stones within this feature, suggesting that the chimney of a log cabin might have once stood there. I concluded that the area had served as a hearth of some kind.

A large proportion of the artifacts were distributed in an arc that circled around to the west and north from the cultural hearth feature on the east. This distribution suggested that the station stood on the level area just east of the slope, approximately midway between the edge of the valley going down to the spring, and the historic cemetery to the east. While this area was not at the highest elevation of the ridge, it was located near enough to the spring that water did not have to be hauled very far. Additionally, the area was at a high enough elevation to give the occupants a reasonably clear view of the surrounding countryside. Since Native American raids were a fact of life for much of the time the station was occupied, being able to see people approaching the site was a considerable advantage that could spell the difference between life and death.

Archaeological excavation to determine if cultural features such as storage pits, hearths, or foundations were preserved began in 1996, and additional excavation was conducted in 2005 in collaboration with an archaeological field school class taught by Professor Christopher Begley of Transylvania University. Excavation of thirty-eight square meters in the densest part of the

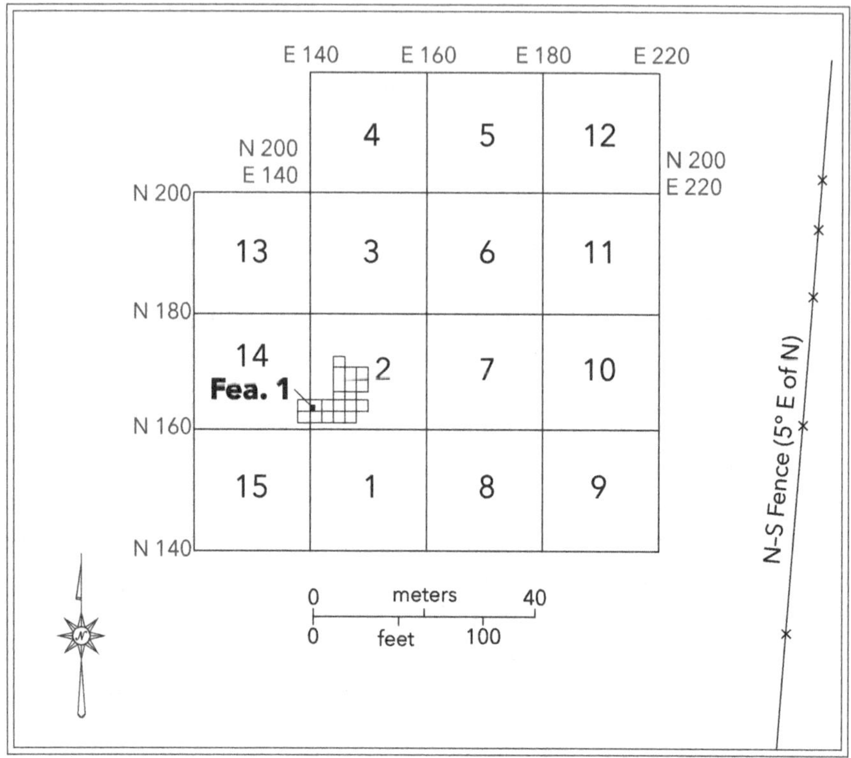

Map of metal detection areas and excavations at McGary's Station.

artifact concentration identified, in addition to the probable hearth, two shallow midden-filled depressions (Features 2 and 3) that may have once served as storage pits; however, plowing has destroyed the upper portions of these features. Excavation revealed that the site had been heavily cultivated in the past, probably plowed with a chisel plow which completely mixed the top fifteen centimeters or so of soil. The base of a single post mold (Feature 4—the filled-in hole where a post once stood) was located east of the hearth and pit features. A denser concentration of larger limestone rocks was recorded a short distance west of the post mold. These features were located near one another and probably indicate the remains of a log structure. However, their poor preservation and the lack of an identifiable structural foundation make interpretation somewhat tentative. The station cabins were probably not very substantial buildings and may not have even had stone foundation piers. Rather, it was customary to erect rather crude, notched log structures in which the only stone used was for the base of the chimney (the upper part of the chimney being stick-and-daub). Later plowing would have not only mixed the topsoil but also destroyed cultural features, such as chimney bases. Farmers routinely threw out larger rocks when they impeded the progress of plows, and it is likely that the same practice was carried out here. Deep plowing also destroys shallow features such as storage pits and shallowly set posts.

Lyman C. Draper's interview with settler Henry Wilson in 1843 described the site as "a regular station, stockaded in" that initially housed "some dozen families." Other than the McGarys, Wilson identified only two other families, the Dentons and the Yokums, who lived briefly at the station before establishing their own.[2]

Poor preservation of cultural features associated with station architecture prevented me from identifying the number of cabins that constituted the station, or the construction details of the stockade. However, the artifacts recovered from the metal target probes and excavation units were consistent with an occupation date of 1779–1788/92 indicated by the archival analysis, and they include a diverse variety of functional classes.

11

The McGary Station Artifact Assemblage

Despite the scarcity of cultural features, the artifacts from McGary's Station represent a tightly dated assemblage that offers abundant insights into what pioneers owned. Pioneer assemblages generally contain limited quantities of artifacts for several reasons. First, settlers coming to Kentucky in the 1770s and 1780s could only bring what they could carry or pack on horses, because the roads were not suitable for wagon travel until the 1790s. Second, there were no stores from which to buy manufactured items. Settlers instead had to rely on either occasional traveling peddlers from whom they could purchase goods or friends to bring needed items into Kentucky—or settlers could return to the east themselves. Typically, a family might own a few iron cooking pots; some utensils (such as metal spoons, knives, and forks); cooking, processing, storage, and serving ware; an axe and other woodworking tools; a limited supply of clothing; bedding and furniture; a gun and ammunition; and a few agricultural tools.

An inventory taken of John Floyd's belongings after he was killed by Native Americans in 1783 is illustrative of the kinds of household items McGary probably owned as well, as the two men were social equals. Among the kitchen and serving items are listed four iron pots weighing from thirty-eight to forty-four pounds, a Dutch oven and two iron kettles weighing twenty and twenty-seven and a half pounds, candle molds, a collection of worn pewter plates and dishes, a pewter basin, pewter spoons, a set of ten knives and forks, a copper tea kettle, and four tin canisters. Seven "delf" (delft) plates as well as a teapot with four teacups and saucers are the only ceramic serving ware listed. The list also included a large bottle, perhaps made of glass and intended to hold liquor. Other household items included three beds with their linens and mattresses, a table and two tablecloths, a chest, three old trunks, a spinning wheel and reel (for measuring warp threads used on a loom), two brass candlesticks, a fire shovel, and a smoothing iron. Floyd, who was an officially designated deputy surveyor for Virginia, also owned a compass, chain, and other instruments for surveying land, a saddle, a "rifle gun," and a smoothbore gun. His livestock included cattle, horses, and pigs, as well as nine beehives. He also had six acres sown in wheat and rye. Tools included four old hoes, two old axes, two plows with the wagon hardware, hames, chains, collar and clevises to hitch a horse to a plow, sixteen harrow teeth, a crosscut saw, and a whipsaw. The personal estate was valued at £218, fifteen shillings and two pence, an amount equivalent to nearly $43,000 in 2025.[1]

Local wood supplied the raw material for large items such as stools, chairs, bedsteads, and other furniture that were too bulky to carry on the long journey from the eastern colonies. Even serving and eating vessels such as cups, spoons, trenchers, and bowls could be made from wood or horn. These materials do not generally survive to be found later by archaeologists. The cabins were constructed of logs and could have been completed without the use of nails although nails made installing a roof or door hinges much easier.

Ceramic dishes and glass containers are infrequent in pioneer assemblages, largely because of the difficulty of transporting them but also because of their cost (particularly in the case of glass containers, which were expensive in the late eighteenth century). As a result, pioneer assemblages tend to contain more metal than any other material class. Metal artifacts expected to occur in pioneer sites include (but are not limited to) buttons and other clothing fasteners, sewing tools, handwrought nails, and parts of such items as horse harnesses and other equine equipment, iron, brass, or copper cooking vessels, utensils, and other tools. Other artifacts that may occur include gun flints and parts, and wild or domestic animal bone discarded from meals.

Finally, pioneer assemblages may be quite sparse if a site was occupied for only a few years. McGary's Station was occupied from the fall of 1779 to at least 1788, when McGary sold the land to George Thompson. While Thompson could have occupied the station during the construction of his house, he probably did not have any use for it after his own residential complex was completed. By 1788, McGary's Station cabins may well have been showing signs of dilapidation that were not worth trying to repair. It was also located at a considerable distance from Thompson's house, and quarters for Thompson's enslaved persons would have been more practical closer to his residence.

My analysis of the artifacts recovered from McGary's Station verified that the majority of them dated to the late eighteenth century with only a few nineteenth-century artifacts that were lost on the site during the years it was cultivated. Analysis also indicated that the late eighteenth-century artifacts were from a domestic context, again reinforcing the conclusion that this site was indeed McGary's Station. The artifacts could have been the property of any of the several families that lived at McGary's Station, but since the McGarys and Rays lived there the longest, they probably contributed the most to the assemblage.

Identifying the artifacts by their original function is a good way to interpret how people lived at the station. The major functional categories that the artifacts represent include architectural or construction related, clothing and personal, kitchen and household, and munitions and miscellaneous classes. Each of these classes is discussed separately since each represents a different aspect of station life.

Architectural and Construction-Related Artifacts

Nails and other fasteners fall under this category. The nails found at McGary's Station are all handwrought, with the exception of two machine-cut nails dating to the early nineteenth century and eight twentieth-century wire nails that were probably discarded or lost on the site during later agricultural activity. The nails occur in various sizes and have several different types of heads that are associated with different uses. Many of them are very crudely made and very battered from use (and perhaps reuse).

Wrought nails were made individually by a blacksmith on a forge from a nailrod in which impurities in the metal were stretched out lengthwise as the iron was worked into a rod. Nail shafts were cut with the grain, which gave them greater strength. Although their invention predates the development of the machine-cut nail, wrought nails continued to be used in specific contexts well into the nineteenth century. For example, wrought nails were superior to early cut nails in contexts that required clinching (driving a nail fully through wood then bending back the protruding end).

Table 11.1 lists the different types and sizes of wrought nails. The shaft of a wrought nail has four tapering sides. The point of the nail was sometimes

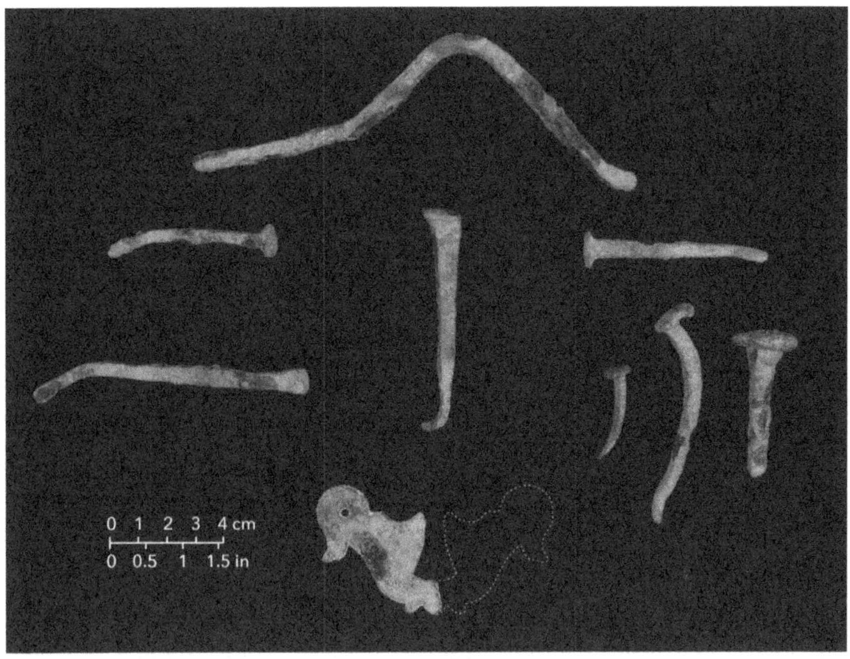

Wrought iron nails and escutcheon plate from McGary's Station.

flattened into a spatulate shape that helped keep the nail from bending when it was hammered into wood. This is called a chisel point. Nail types found on McGary's Station include all of the more common head forms as well as very irregularly made nails. In fact, irregularly headed nails are the most frequent nail type in the collection. Their prevalence in the assemblage, along with the recovery of slag, nailrods, and four large circular, or ovate, headed nails that may have been part of a bellows, strongly suggest that someone at the site had rudimentary blacksmithing skills and operated a small forge.

Nails were often used for more than one function. Thus the three most numerous categories, rosehead, irregular, and L-head, could have been used in cabin or furniture construction or many other contexts. The function of other types, such as the expanded head and headless, is less clear. The expanded head nails are similar in shape to horseshoe nails but are much longer. They may represent unused horseshoe nails. Headless nails may have been used as finishing nails. In a log cabin, nails would have been useful for attaching flooring, for door hinges, or for framing woodwork around doors and windows. The T-shaped nails may have been used for flooring and are called plancher nails.

The sizes of the nails are also important in interpreting their use. Considered as a whole, the most common nail sizes in the assemblage, expressed as pennyweights, are 3d, 6d, and 8d. However, in general, the middling sizes, 6d, 7d, and 8d, collectively are most frequent. This range of sizes is useful for many different contexts. Very small nails, as well as a few very large ones, are also present in the assemblage and suggest more specialized uses. For instance, very small nails were commonly used in document boxes and other artifacts collected from the site indicate that at least two document boxes or storage trunks were part of the family belongings. Very large nails may have been used to fasten heavy log members or where a strong join was necessary.

The condition of the nails at the time of their loss or discard can also indicate contexts in which they were used or other site activities. The presence of clinched nails indicates that these specimens were used in situations where greater holding power was needed, such as in doors or shutters. Because these units moved when they were opened or shut, they put much greater pressure on the nails that held their component parts together. Clinching a nail, that is, driving it completely through the component parts and then bending the point and driving it back into the wood, locked the pieces together and prevented them from loosening. Only four clinched nails were identified, including one 3d, 6d, and 10d, as well as a fragment. This may indicate that contexts where clinching was desirable were uncommon. That is, the cabins undoubtedly had doors for entry but may not have had shuttered windows.

Pulled nails are often indicative of the practice of disassembling a wood construction to recycle the nails (and perhaps also the wood) or to make repairs. I identified 22 pulled nails (out of a sample of 108 analyzed nails), or about 21 percent of the assemblage. This percentage seems fairly high, considering that wrought nails were expensive and would not have been discarded even if bent. Perhaps the cabins were dismantled so that the wood could be salvaged for fuel or some other purpose.

A fragmentary metal escutcheon plate was also recovered. This decorative plate surrounded a keyhole on a piece of furniture. Its style is typical of the Chippendale "bat's-" or "angel's-wing" pattern popular between 1750 and 1775. Given the difficulty in transporting large pieces of cabinetry into the Kentucky frontier, this escutcheon plate may have adorned a smaller piece, such as a sugar chest.[2]

Table 11.1. Nail Statistics from McGary's Station

Head Type	2d	3d	4d	5d	6d	7d	8d	9d	10d	12d	17d	Fragments	Total
Wrought Nails													
Unidentified head	15		2	2		1							20
Headless nails			1		2	1			1	1		1	7
T-head nails	3	2		2	3	1		1				4	16
Irregular T-head nails		1											1
Rosehead nails	2	1	1	3	3		4		1			12	27
Irregular rosehead nails	2	2					1					6	11
Irregular head nails	19	7	12	2	3	3	4	1	1			27	79
L-headed nails	2		1		1	1	2		1			9	17
Expanded head nails		2	1	1		1	1				1	7	14
Large, circular/ovate headed nails		2			1			1					4
Recto-ovate headed nails		2					1				1		4
Unfinished nail													1
Nail fragments												82	82
Cut nails	1	1											2
Wire nails										2		6	8
Unidentified nails										1		2	3
												Total:	296

Clothing and Personal Artifacts

This group is a particularly evocative one because it contains items that reflect a settler's personal tastes and habits, as well as how they chose to appear to others. Clothing, jewelry, and other personal artifacts speak to gender- and age-related roles, class, personal appearance and habits, and other aspects of identity construction. The construction of one's personal identity is intimately allied with the "centrality of the body" as a "scene of display." I identified nineteen buttons, two buckles, three items of sewing equipment, two clasps (possibly for garments), two pieces of jewelry (a finger ring and a pin), three straight razor blades, a handle, a box key and three nameplates from three different chests (possibly document or money boxes), part of a padlock, a folding knife, a ceramic smoking pipe bowl sherd, and six flat glass fragments that probably were from a hand mirror.[3]

Clothing is represented primarily by buttons, many of which are most likely from men's clothes. Late colonial male attire for civilians included three types of breeches, a long-sleeved smock shirt with an open collar, and various outer coverings such as a sleeveless weskit or long vest, a tight sleeved coat, a "capote" (a heavy winter coat made from a woolen blanket), or a cloak. Buttons were used to fasten breeches, weskits, and coats. Some Kentucky pioneers favored buckskin clothing, which was made with a minimum of buttons. Leggings, made from hide, were also worn to protect the legs from briars and undergrowth. These were laced onto the leg. James Ray was wearing laced leggings that he had to cut off when he was trying to outrun the Shawnee who killed his brother in 1777. Despite the popular notion that all Kentucky pioneers wore buckskins, documentary and archaeological evidence indicates that this was not always the case.

The McGary's Station buttons include several styles and sizes. Many of the metal buttons can be classified using Stanley Olsen's system in which he places buttons in chronological periods according to the method of attachment. Olsen based his chronology on manufacturing modifications, buttons from dated garments, and archaeological examples from dated shipwrecks. Carolyn L. White classified buttons by size, using the metric system, and by garment type. Her size classes include small (less than 12 mm in diameter), medium (12–18 mm), and large (more than 18 mm). According to her analysis, coat buttons usually measured between 18 and 35-plus millimeters. Waistcoat buttons measured between 14.5 and 19.5 millimeters in diameter.

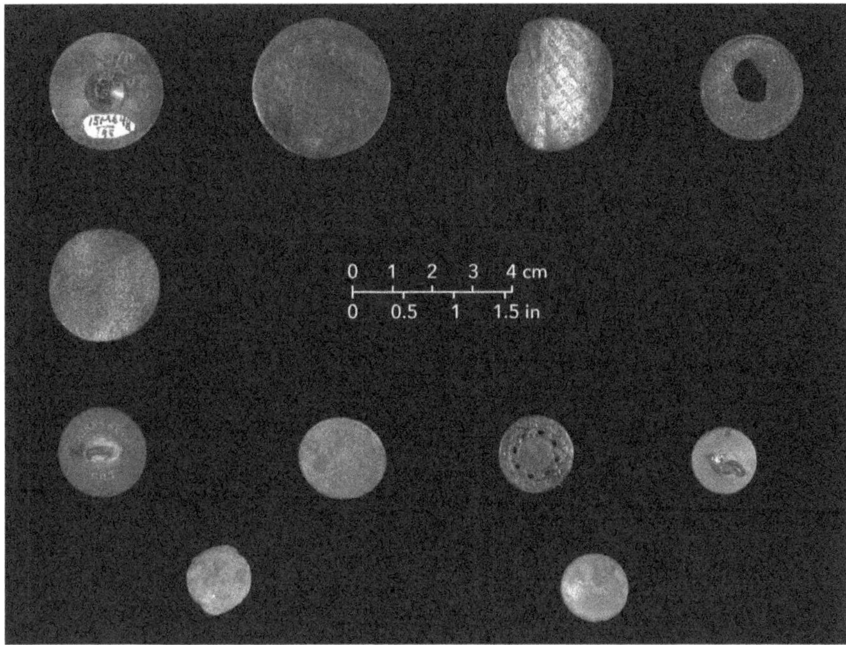

Buttons from McGary's Station (top row, left to right: Type D button, button with sun motif, Type G button with basket weave motif, button missing eyelet; second row: brass breeches button; third row, left to right: button [back and front] marked Cairns & Co., Type D button [perforated design], Type G button; bottom row, left to right: Type A pewter button, Type D button).

Sleeve buttons usually measured between 13 and 17 millimeters. The largest buttons from the site include three brass examples. One is just a fragment, but the other two measure 30 and 33 millimeters in diameter. The larger of the two has a stamped sun or star motif on its exterior face and was sewn to the cloth by means of an eyelet, which is missing. The lack of solder suggests that the eyelet may have been made of bone or wood and glued on. The other button has a stamped basket weave design that covers the entire exterior face. This specimen is bent in half and is missing its metal eyelet. It is classified as a Type G button dating between 1785 and 1800. These buttons are too large to have been used on breeches but would have been appropriate for use on heavier coats or possibly weskits.[4]

Two undecorated brass buttons, one with the remnants of a metal eye, and another whose eye is missing but was probably a glued bone or wood type, measure twenty-two millimeters in diameter. These two buttons may have served to fasten heavier garments such as weskits or coats. A slightly smaller button (25 millimeters in diameter), also made of brass, has an irregular hole in the middle where the eye once was.

Four metal buttons, all with intact metal eyes, and measuring 22 millimeters in diameter, were probably used on breeches. Late colonial breeches usually had a wide buttoned flap in front just below the waistband and a laced opening for adjusting fit in the rear. Technically, breeches ended at the knee, where the cuff was buttoned or buckled. "Overalls" were pants that buttoned at the ankle, and "trousers" were long pants that were buttoned or buckled. Breeches and overalls frequently had a dozen or more buttons per pair. The McGary's Station buttons no longer show evidence of brass plating, but one is stamped with a maker's mark that reads "CAIRNS & CO." and is further marked with the word "GILT," indicating that it was plated or "gilded." Information about Cairns & Co. dates the use of the firm's name between c. 1795 and 1810, which postdates the occupation span of the station as indicated by other data. The source of the date suggests that it is tentative. Although McGary and his family had moved away by 1795, the possibility that the new owner, George Thompson, used the station cabins briefly while he was building his house cannot be eliminated. The button may have been lost at the site during such an occupation.[5]

Six buttons are smaller in diameter. They are all Type D buttons (1760–1785). Two specimens are very similar to the breeches buttons except for their size; they measure only sixteen millimeters in diameter. The eyelet on one of them is made of wire inserted into a metal boss or foot that protrudes from the back of the button.

A small Type G metal button measures nineteen millimeters in diameter, shows traces of gilding, and has a stamped star or sun motif on its face. A circular arrangement of oval holes surrounds the plain center of the button. It was manufactured between 1785 and 1800.

A molded one-piece pewter button, measuring eight millimeters in diameter, was recovered. The button was made in a mold where a square eyelet was formed at the same time as the button face. It is a Type A button dating between 1700 and 1765. All of the smallest buttons could have been affixed to shirt cuffs. Linen shirts or smocks were much more comfortable to wear than buckskin shirts. Tantalizing clues in the historical record suggest that some settlers customized their clothing so that it was recognizable as belonging to a specific person. For instance, McGary is said to have recognized his stepson's shirt being worn by a Shawnee during the skirmish that followed the attack at Shawnee Springs in 1777. The record is silent on how he knew it was his son's shirt, but it is possible that he recognized it because it was made from plain linen or buckskin rather than a printed calico. Nicholas Cresswell learned that Native Americans viewed linen or buckskin hunting shirts as the garb of the backcountry militiaman and interpreted them as hostile symbols. Cresswell had a "Calico shirt made in the Indian fashion" so that he could accompany an English trader on a business trip into Native American territory. McGary was undoubtedly aware of this fashion distinction.[6]

Four button fragments were also recovered. One appears to be the middle of a breeches button that still has an attached eyelet. Two fragments are likely also from breeches buttons but are too incomplete to measure. A thin metal disc from a two-piece button that may have been covered with cloth was also recovered.

Unequivocal evidence of women's clothing is essentially lacking although the smaller buttons may have been from feminine attire. However, colonial women's clothing did not rely heavily on buttons for fastening. The everyday garments probably worn by the women of McGary's Station could have included drawstring petticoats, long-sleeved chemises, aprons, and bodices or weskits. More formal women's wear might have taken the form of a "robe française" worn over an underskirt and supplemented by stays and panniers. Women wore cloaks or coats similar to men's for outerwear, but their typical attire was often fastened by lacing or hooks and eyes with a minimum of buttons.[7]

Another clothing item is a small circular, nonferrous metal hem weight with a central bar. It was sewn into the hem of a woman's dress or skirt. A buckle fragment is part of the chape, specifically the spikes of a double-pronged tongue that help hold the buckle in place. This piece only has two spikes and may have been from a boot or garter buckle. Boot or garter buckles were used to keep tall, close-fitting leather boots from falling. Also recovered was a pin fragment that may have been used to fasten a cloak. This could have been from male or female attire.

Knowing how to sew was an important feminine skill in the days when clothing was all made by hand. Sewing equipment is represented in the assemblage by a fragmentary pair of scissors and two brass thimbles. The scissors are small, similar to embroidery scissors. One of the thimbles is very small

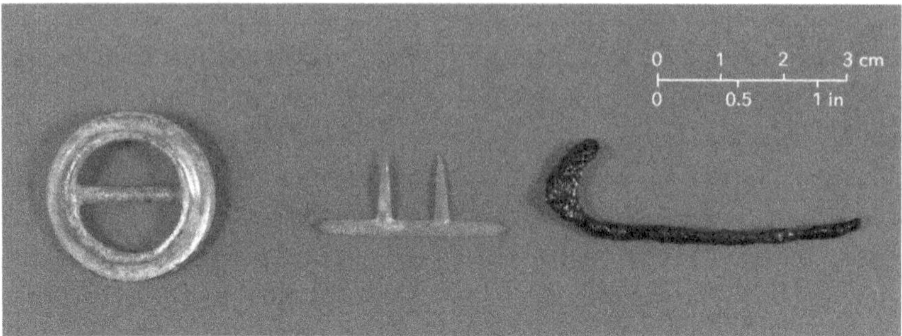

Other clothing-related artifacts from McGary's Station (left to right: hem weight, boot or garter buckle chape, cloak pin).

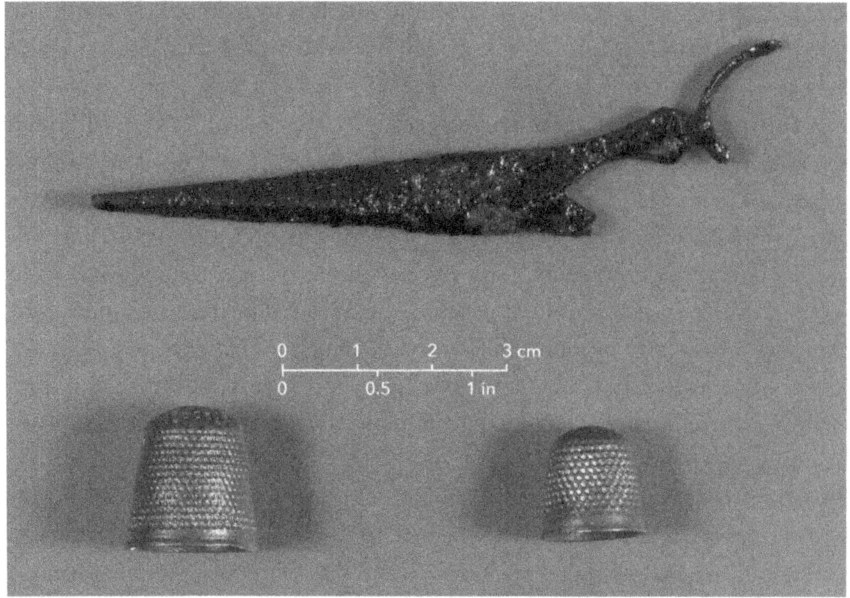

Sewing equipment from McGary's Station (top: small scissors; bottom: adult and child's thimbles).

and was meant for a girl to use. The other fits an adult finger. The diminutive thimble is mute evidence of the training young girls received from their mothers or other female family members so that they became proficient in both creating garments and repairing them when needed.

Two pieces of jewelry were recovered, again reinforcing the conclusion that Kentucky settlers were concerned with their appearance. A brass finger ring,

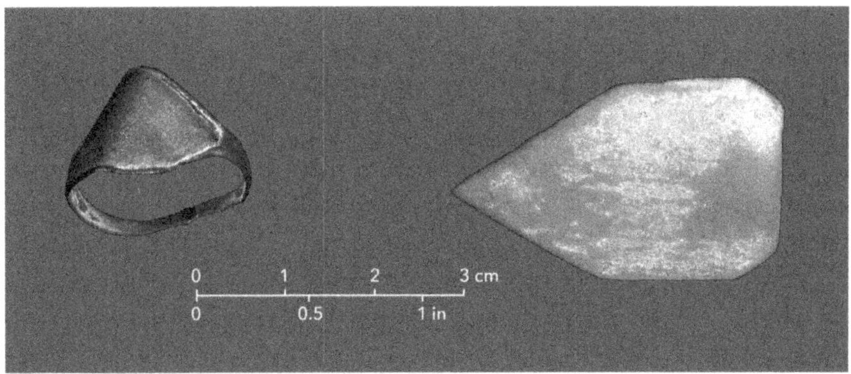

Jewelry from McGary's Station (left to right: finger ring and pin).

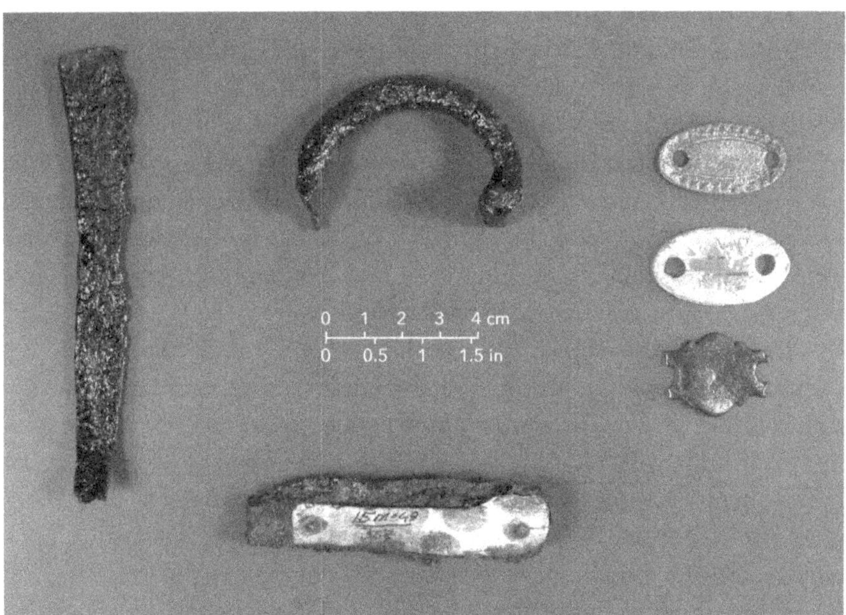

Personal artifacts from McGary's Station (clockwise, left to right: straight razor, padlock shank, box or wallet hardware, and folding knife).

measuring a women's size 7 or 7½, is of the signet type but lacks engraving. This ring could have been worn by a child or a woman but is probably too small for a man's finger. A silver-plated pin, shaped like a trapezoid, was also found.

Although we have no known images of Hugh McGary or any of his family, the three straight razor blades recovered from the site indicate that one or more male occupants of the station shaved. Hugh McGary was described by Henry Wilson as having brown hair, a "fully ruddy countenance and a Romanesque nose." He did not mention facial hair, but a "full, ruddy countenance" may imply that McGary was clean-shaven. The only known sketch of James Ray shows him as clean-shaven, but this drawing was made from a portrait miniature of him as an older man. Beards and mustaches have waxed and waned in popularity for as long as men have been able to choose to wear them or not. Facial hair was unpopular during the eighteenth century. As facial hair scholar Allan Peterkin puts it, "[Beards] were worn only in isolated cases by the old, mad or clueless." Mustaches, however, remained popular in military circles.[8]

As a man with large landholdings, the ownership of enslaved people, and the means for prosperous farming, McGary needed secure storage for his land deeds, currency, and other valuable papers and belongings. Three faceplates, one iron box/chest handle, a small padlock key, and part of a padlock are all artifacts associated with chests or small trunks, which were used for storing clothing, money, important papers, or other personal belongings. Two faceplates are oval with two holes for attachment to the top of a wooden box. One has a reeded edge and a blank center. The other has a hand-engraved design composed of circular and linear elements. This design is rather crude and may have been done by the owner of the box. The third example is made of brass and is more elaborate in shape but has no engraving.

Six fragments of flat glass are most likely from hand mirrors, or "looking glasses," as the pioneers usually called them. Hand mirrors are frequently mentioned in probate inventories of the period and utilized coated flat glass in their manufacture. No trace of a reflective backing was observed on any of the fragments; however, such a backing is only rarely preserved in archaeological contexts. The flat glass fragments were probably not from windows. Windows were not common in station sites since the cabin architecture was designed to be both defensive and residential, and windows did not contribute to defense. Window glass was also very scarce and expensive on the frontier.

The practice of carrying a pocket knife goes back a long way. As the earlier custom of wearing belt knives waned, pocket knives gained universal popularity during the Revolutionary War and were used by a majority of soldiers. Known alternatively as a pocket knife, jackknife, clasp knife, spring knife, and folding knife, the McGary example consists of a single iron blade that folded into a handle mounted with panels (also known as "scales") made of bone that were riveted to each side. The handle has a curved tail and once featured a short bolster adjacent to the base of the blade. The knife is three inches in length when closed. It would have been suitable for tasks such as sharpening a quill pen, cutting a patch to seat a lead ball in a muzzle-loading rifle charge, or other jobs that only required a small blade. The style is dated to c. 1775–1783.[9]

Evidence of the use of tobacco was indicated by the recovery of a single ceramic rim sherd that might have once been part of a pipe bowl. The sherd is composed of buff-colored stoneware clay and exhibits a metallic brown glaze on both the interior and exterior surfaces. Narrow horizontal rouletted bands decorate the exterior surface. The lip is quite thin, but the thickness increases moving down from the rim. The size of the sherd makes its identification as a pipe bowl somewhat conjectural, but the curvature is restricted enough to suggest a small-diameter vessel form. Alternatively, the rim could be from a small mug or a bottle.

Kitchen and Household Artifacts

Historic residential sites dating from the nineteenth century frequently contain more household and kitchen artifacts than any other category because of the quantity of ceramic and glass vessels that were used. This pattern does not hold true for sites occupied during the pioneer era in Kentucky, although material goods became easier to obtain after the Revolutionary War ended. The majority of ceramics, particularly refined earthenware, that American settlers of the late eighteenth century used, were of British manufacture. The glass industry in America developed slowly, and glass containers remained expensive until well into the nineteenth century. Glass bottles were so highly prized in Kentucky during the late eighteenth and early nineteenth centuries that they were inventoried as a separate item in estate settlements and then sold at auction just like any other valued household item. Transportation costs of breakable goods to Kentucky were high, which raised consumer prices. All these factors made acquisition of glass containers expensive for many families.

The kitchen and household assemblage from McGary's Station reflects this trend. A total of 794 household artifacts attributable to the station occupation were recovered from the site. The most numerous category is ceramics although it only numbered 570 fragments, a very low frequency for domestic sites in general. Nevertheless, the fragments are quite varied in type. Despite their low frequency and generally very small size, their presence at a

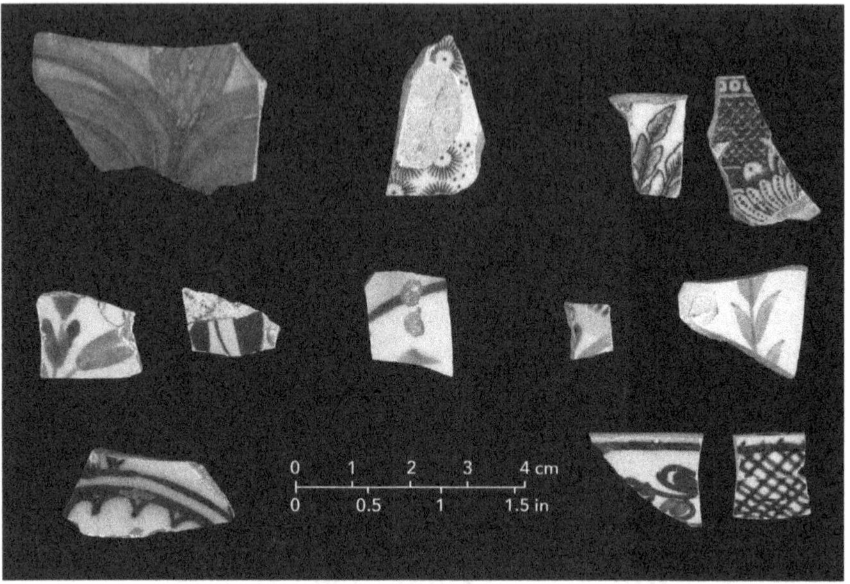

Refined earthenware from McGary's Station (top row, left to right: hand-painted broad-stroke floral pattern, three brown transfer-printed sherds; middle row: hand-painted polychrome floral pattern; bottom row: hand-painted blue patterns).

site dating to the 1780s is significant since it indicates that even the earliest pioneers used ceramics rather than relying solely on wooden trenchers or pewter plates. Ceramics fall into two main categories: refined and unrefined types. Refined earthenware includes ceramics whose clay pastes have particular and unique characteristics. The characteristics are important because they represent technological improvements or changes that are datable, or because they represent a more expensive ware.

Refined earthenware typically has light-colored pastes and glazes that range from cream to white. They were used as serving pieces such as teacups, plates, bowls, tureens, and the like. Technological innovations in the English pottery industry regarding glazes gradually caused refined earthenware to appear whiter. Refined earthenware represented in the McGary ceramic assemblage include delftware, cream-colored ware called "creamware," "Pearl White" or "China Glaze" ware known as "pearlware," and porcelain. The lack of any refined ceramics dating later in time reinforces my conclusion that the station was abandoned shortly after the McGarys sold the property to George Thompson. Refined earthenware sherds from the site are mostly very tiny, often just fragments that chipped off a vessel. At least one plate is represented, but the sherds are mostly too small to identify other vessel forms. In general, many of the dishes that the sherds came from could probably still be used since they were only chipped.

"Delftware" is the common term for a ceramic that was coated with a lead glaze containing tin oxide. When fired, the glaze became opaque white in color. The glaze is also called "tin-enameled" and has a long history on the European continent, dating back to the fourteenth century. The technique was brought to England in the mid-sixteenth century and became very popular by the seventeenth century. It continued to be made through the eighteenth century but declined in production as other, more popular, styles of ceramics developed. Delftware is an uncommon ceramic in Kentucky assemblages because its production had so declined by the time Kentucky was settled that relatively limited quantities were available for purchase. Only two tiny sherds were identified as delftware in the McGary ceramic assemblage. Both sherds exhibit a light-blue narrow band that probably ran below the lip of the vessel and could have come from a single vessel.[10]

Cream-colored ware (commonly called creamware) has a glaze and underlying clay body that produces a cream-colored appearance. It was one of the wares that replaced delftware in the mid- to late eighteenth century and was a common export to the American colonies. A cream-colored ware was developed by Josiah Wedgwood in the 1760s, widely produced by many potters, and imported in great quantities to the American colonies through the early nineteenth century. Potters' price lists prior to the 1820s referred to undecorated creamware as "CC ware," meaning cream-colored ware. The glaze has a greenish or yellowish tint, particularly where it pools in the foot ring of a vessel. Historical archaeologists generally use the term "creamware" for this type of ceramic.[11]

Creamware is represented by 559 fragments, and most of the sherds are undecorated. Of the undecorated creamware sherds, 41 were from the bases of vessels; in at least one case, the vessel form was a plate or saucer. The other sherds are too small for form to be reliably identified but could have come from cups, plates, or saucers. Another 51 undecorated creamware sherds are rims from mostly unidentifiable forms except for 4 sherds from one or more plates or saucers. The remaining 450 undecorated creamware sherds are fragments from the body of vessel forms that cannot be identified more specifically. Decorated sherds are uncommon among the creamware but do occur.

Ten creamware sherds are from at least two dishes that were hand painted with brown bands. Another sherd has yellow banding. Banding generally occurs at the lip or near the rim of a vessel form, forming a border that framed the center in which another design might be executed. Five sherds have hand-painted floral designs in blue, gold/ocher, or polychrome hues. One of these hand-painted sherds also has a brown band, indicating that banding and hand-painted floral designs were combined. One sherd has unpainted molded design detail. Some of the creamware represented by these sherds may have been brought in by the McGarys or other station inhabitants when they first moved to Kentucky, or they obtained them during their earliest years in the commonwealth. They certainly could have obtained ceramics after the war, when mercantile businesses were established in the fledgling towns.

White-bodied earthenware with a blue tint was developed as "China Glaze" by other potters in 1775 and as "Pearl White" by Josiah Wedgwood in 1779 to compete with Chinese porcelain. Cobalt was added to the glaze to mimic the blue tint of Chinese porcelain. The term "pearlware" was coined in the 1960s by ceramics scholars, collectors, and historical archaeologists to describe refined earthenware that had a blue cast to its glaze. Pearlware probably was not easily obtained in Kentucky until after the end of the American Revolution. The presence of pearlware at the site may indicate purchases made from local stores in the latter years of the McGarys' occupation. Pearlware numbered 282 sherds, of which 140 sherds are undecorated. Two unpainted molded sherds have very narrow parallel ribs running along the body of the form and clearly originate from the same vessel. Two other sherds also exhibit molded parallel ribs, but they are wider and are probably from a separate vessel.[12]

Well over half (60 percent) of the pearlware pieces recovered from the McGary Station are decorated in banded, edged, or other hand-painted designs. Although sherd size is also quite small among the pearlware, floral design motifs appear to dominate, with more abstract motifs such as hatching also occurring. Decoration restricted solely to the rim is a common style in pearlware. Rim decoration in the McGary assemblage included six examples of blue banding, six of brown, and two of yellow and brown. Banded wares frequently were accompanied by hand-painted designs on the body of the vessel form. Thirteen rims were edged in green (three specimens) and blue (ten specimens) in a manner resembling feathering strokes along the rim. This rim decoration was very common on pearlware and later ceramics and was generally applied to flatware such as saucers or plates or shallow bowls.

Edged rims sometimes were accompanied by simple or elaborate molded motifs over which the color was applied. Molding was minimal in the McGary edged wares.

Other hand-painted sherds include fifty body sherds with blue, hand-painted designs that included hatching, scallops, and stylized floral motifs or Chinese-inspired designs that were popular at the time. Blue decorated ceramics were and continue to be among the most popular pottery sold. However, the McGary assemblage also includes fifty-one sherds with polychrome, hand-painted floral patterns in earth tones of brown, yellow, and green. Two sherds are coated with a matte amber glaze that is unique among the collection. The polychrome, hand-painted sherds represent at least three different patterns. One pattern employs blue flowers with green leaves and amber-brown stems. Another pattern exhibits gold/amber flowers with amber-brown stems and green leaves. Both patterns are simply executed in an open style so that the underlying white glazed body is not significantly obscured or covered. Finally, a broad-stroke floral pattern that covers much of the vessel body occurs on several sherds. The largest sherd in this pattern exhibits a blue-green flower with broad petals and a gold pistil with amber hatching. The intended flower species is uncertain; except for color, the shape of the flower resembles a magnolia blossom. Six sherds have a brown transfer-printed design.

Another refined ceramic type in use at the time was porcelain, which was made in China and exported to Europe. There were also porcelain factories in Britain and the European continent, although they had not mastered the technology to the same extent as the Chinese had. Porcelain was available to the American colonies although it was quite expensive. The expense of porcelain effectively limited its distribution. The recovery of ten porcelain sherds from McGary's Station supports other evidence that the McGary family was fairly affluent for the time. Eight porcelain sherds are undecorated, including a basal sherd. Two sherds are decorated with a single line of tiny, hand-painted blue dots just below the lip of the rim.

Another type of ceramics found in the station is unrefined in the sense that the clays and glazes are coarser and darker in color and the vessels are utilitarian in nature. Items such as crocks, bottles, churns, milk pans, and mugs fall in this category. Examples of coarse earthenware and stoneware were recovered from the site.

Coarse earthenware (termed "redware") is made of common red clay and fired at relatively low temperatures. Red clay earthenware potteries were in operation in Virginia and North Carolina when the McGarys emigrated and could have been a source for crockery that the family brought with them. Redware was fired either glazed or unglazed. Unglazed redware sherds are rare in the McGary assemblage; only two appear to never have been glazed. A common glaze used powdered galena or some other form of lead as a constituent, an ingredient that posed hazards for potters, who often contracted lead poisoning by absorption through the skin. The lead also could leach out of the vessel into the food being contained, particularly if the food was acidic, and could be absorbed, causing lead poisoning. Most of the seventy-nine redware sherds recovered are quite small and have poorly preserved glazed surfaces. However, an examination of the glaze colors, body decoration (such as incising), and rim shapes indicates that several different vessels are represented.

The most common glaze is reddish brown or amber in color, varying from lighter to darker hues. Much less common is a green glaze, produced by the addition of copper oxide. Only eight sherds have a green glaze. One was probably a mug with a dull olive-green glaze on the interior and exterior. The upper area of the mug was incised with at least two sets of parallel double lines. Four body sherds represent this vessel. One small body sherd has a similar olive-green glaze that is greener than the four sherds just discussed. It may be from a different vessel. Two rims are flat and thickened with an interior reddish-brown glaze that extended over the rim but no farther down the body of the vessel. The thickness of the body of the sherds varies, suggesting that they are not from the same vessel but may be from similar forms, perhaps a wide-mouthed, straight-sided jar. Three sherds (two of which cross mend, forming a large sherd from a globular shaped vessel) share a dark reddish-brown, speckled glaze. Another body sherd may also have the same glaze, but it appears to have been burned and so is difficult to analyze. A rim and rim spall exhibit a shiny, dark-brown glaze that is of higher quality than the other specimens. The larger rim has a rounded lip and exhibits molded ribs that must have run horizontally along the body of the vessel form. Either the remaining sherds have poorly preserved glazed surfaces, or the glaze is a very common medium reddish-brown color that occurs widely in redware assemblages. Minimally, the redware recovered from the site represents perhaps six vessels.

Another type of unrefined ceramic is termed "stoneware." The ten specimens found at McGary's Station were probably made in England. Stoneware is made from clays that can be fired at a higher temperature than redware.

Two basal fragments of unglazed stoneware probably originated from a mug or tankard. Four body sherds exhibit salt-glazed exteriors, only two of which are similar in color (buff) and may be from the same vessel. The other two sherds exhibit an exterior greenish-tan salt glaze with a matte, yellowish-tan glazed interior and a speckled, yellowish-brown salt glaze interior with an unglazed exterior. A single rim has a dark metallic brown exterior glaze that runs over the rim and into the interior of the vessel just below the lip. Parallel molded lines run horizontally around the exterior just below the lip. This sherd is probably from a mug or tankard. The glaze contains large quantities of iron and does not have the "orange peel" texture typical of salt glazes. However, it is consistent in other respects with the brown stoneware that English potters made in the late eighteenth century.[13]

Despite the low ceramic frequency from McGary's Station, considerable variability is present. At least nineteen vessels are represented in the ceramic assemblage from McGary's Station. Elizabeth Perkins's study of late eighteenth-century household possessions in Kentucky, based on documentary records, recorded the presence of ceramics in households falling in what essentially corresponded to the middle and wealthy classes.[14]

Glass container and tableware artifacts were recovered from the site in very small quantities and in very small fragments. Ninety-eight fragments of glass, most identifiable only to color, include thirty clear, five aquamarine, one opaque-white (milk), one "black" (very dark-green), three olive-green, eight dark-green, four light-green, and seven medium-green glass fragments. One of the clear glass fragments is etched but is too small to identify a design. It might have been from tableware. Among the aquamarine glass is a fragment from a tumbler. A "black" glass bottle base with a kickup is probably from a wine bottle. The opaque-white glass fragment may have a painted design on it.

Also relatively numerous are fragments of metal cooking pots. Cast-iron vessel fragments are the most common, although it is difficult to estimate how many vessels are represented. At least one of the vessels is footed. The other fragments may have come from open kettles or Dutch ovens. At least one, possibly two, brass vessels are represented by two riveted handle fragments.

Another common artifact class in the assemblage includes utensils, generally indicated by the remnants of the metal part of the handle or a knife blade. A total of twenty-two utensil fragments, over half of which are blades, were recovered.

Other kitchen artifacts from McGary's Station (top row, left to right: fleam or bleeder for letting blood, copper pot handle; middle row: bone knife scale; bottom row: knife blades).

Three types of handle attachment are identifiable. The most common (at least six fragments) is a flat piece of metal onto which bone or wood scales were riveted, creating a handle where the flat metal was sandwiched between two pieces of wood or bone. Three examples have pointed or blunt-ended tangs that taper from the end of the blade to the termination of the tang. Handles were socketed onto these tangs, which ran nearly the length of the handle. One specimen has a flat, short, triangular tang that is perpendicular to the blade and was riveted to the handle.

Blade fragments cannot, for the most part, be measured for length; however, one appears to have snapped off at the base. The blade is two inches (fifty-one millimeters) in length, or approximately the size of a patch knife. Two small, thin blades may have once been part of the colonial equivalent of penknives. Five specimens are from relatively robust knives, probably suitable for butchering or other heavy-duty cutting tasks. Two possible blade fragments may have been serrated. One blade fragment may have formed part of a scraping tool, like a drawing knife. One problematical specimen is beveled like a blade but is very narrow. Another blade fragment includes a pointed handle tang.

An unusual artifact that served both veterinary and human medical use is a fleam, or bleeder. This tool normally has two or three blades characterized by a protruding point. The blades fold into a brass case. They were used to open a vein for bleeding. This practice was once very common and was based on the belief that blood contained "bad humors" that had to be drained. Its placement in the kitchen/household category is based on its association with bodily health. Bloodletting was also a standard veterinary practice.

A small quantity of animal bone was also recovered from the site. Most of the fifty-seven fragments are unidentifiable as to animal species, but a deer toe bone, a young pig mandible, and at least four pig teeth fragments indicate the consumption of both domestic and wild animals. Numerous contemporary accounts mention the hunting and consumption of wild game as a major part of the pioneer diet and instrumental to survival. Cattle and pigs were brought into Kentucky at an early date and contributed to the diet as well.

Munitions

Life on the frontier, particularly during wartime, required a defensive strategy. For the Kentucky settlers, defense required both the construction of residences that could withstand attack and the ability to use arms and ammunition. Although not all settlers were proficient with guns, possessing one and gaining at least a basic knowledge of how to load and shoot could mean the difference between life and death. The McGarys and Rays were expert marksmen, as witnessed by James Ray's prowess as a hunter and McGary's propensity for generally emerging from battle unscathed. Artifacts falling in the munitions category include a flintlock, two gunflints, four lead bullets, and four lead fragments. The flintlock is particularly interesting though not complete; it lacks several of its component parts. Present are the lock plate, the bolt that held the mainspring in place, and the frizzen spring; missing are the cock assembly, mainspring, and frizzen. The lock plate has three bolt holes, which is characteristic of English-made flintlocks. It did not have a bridle. The pan was a separate piece that was held in place with a screw. A separate bolt held the mainspring in place. A vining leaf pattern is visible on the finial of the frizzen spring. The lock is made for a right-handed shooter. The lock is probably from an English trade gun classified as a Type G that was produced from 1730 to

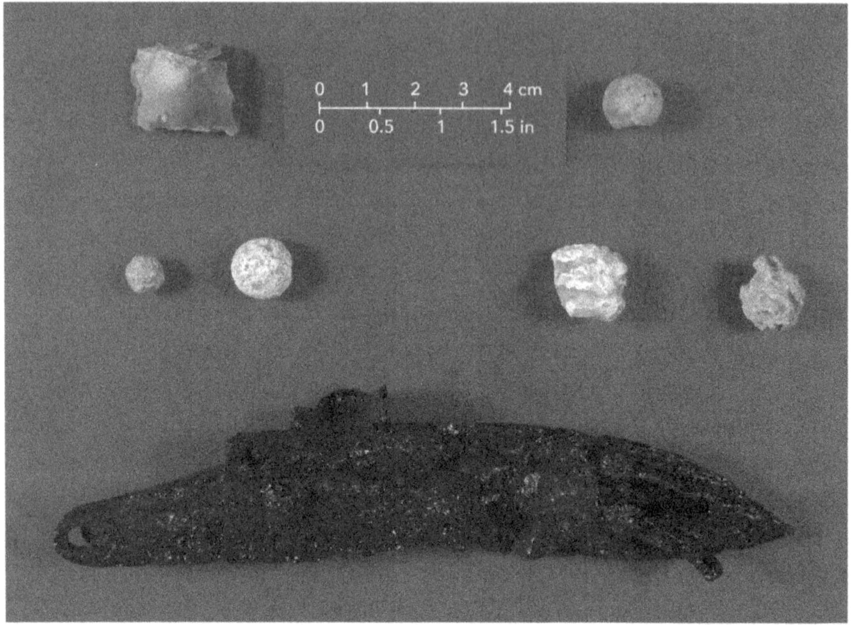

Arms-related artifacts from McGary's Station (top row: English Brandon gunflint, unexpended lead ball; middle row: four expended lead balls; bottom row: flintlock from trade gun).

1760. The lock was found by metal detection at a considerable distance from the main concentration of artifacts and had clearly been discarded.[15]

McGary and James Ray frequently found themselves in situations where they could acquire Native American trade guns. Historian Mann Butler relates an incident that occurred in 1777 at Fort Harrod, when James Ray killed a Native American for the first time. Major George Rogers Clark gave Ray the slain warrior's gun as a reward for his performance. McGary was also involved in many skirmishes with Native warriors.[16]

Lead bullets and scrap are often found on early historic sites where muzzle-loading guns were commonly used. One of the bullets is deformed in such a fashion as to suggest that, when shot, it impacted against a hard surface. Another very small caliber specimen also appears to have been shot. A .48-caliber bullet exhibits a flat facet from the bullet molding process and has never been shot. The final specimen has what appears to be teeth marks, which is often attributable to chewing by animals, most notably pigs. Four fragments may be scraps from the bullet-making process that was carried out by station inhabitants to replenish their bullet supply.[17]

One of the chert gunflints is typical of the British-produced Brandon gunflints that were traded to the American colonies in huge numbers, particularly after the Revolutionary War. The McGary example was very worn down from use. Another possible gunflint was made from a heat-treated chert that might be from a local source. Expendable supplies such as gunpowder, lead, and flints were difficult to obtain in the early years of Kentucky settlement, and settlers were careful not to waste them. This specimen may have been an attempt at making a homemade flint when professionally manufactured ones were not available.

Miscellaneous Artifacts

A variety of miscellaneous artifacts were recovered that can, in some cases, be attributed to agricultural activities that took place on the site after the McGarys moved and the station was no longer standing. Later agricultural artifacts include a whiffletree clip, a harrow point, a ring and snap hook, a hay rake spring, a sheared machine bolt, and a heavy circular ring.

Seven horseshoe fragments and fifteen horseshoe nails might be attributable to the station occupation. Unfortunately, the fragments are rather small. A few exhibit characteristics that represent customization of the shoe to remedy specific gait problems.

Two wrought iron artifacts, a hook, and an unidentified plate with a wrought nail still in the hole drilled through it probably date to either the station occupation or immediately after it ended. Other specimens offer evidence that rudimentary blacksmithing was carried out on the site. As discussed under the section on nails, many of the nailheads are very irregularly made, as they might have been if a person with less skill or practice made them. Two fragments of nailrods (cut iron made specifically for making nails) were found, as well as four fragments of worked iron and seventeen pieces of slag, the latter a common by-product of a forge fire. Another recovered item appears to be an unfinished nail. Two nails with large circular heads are similar to those used in a bellows. These artifacts all hint at the presence of a bellows-equipped forge at the site.

An unusual iron item resembling a harpoon point was also recovered. It was meant to be socketed on a shaft but is not barbed.

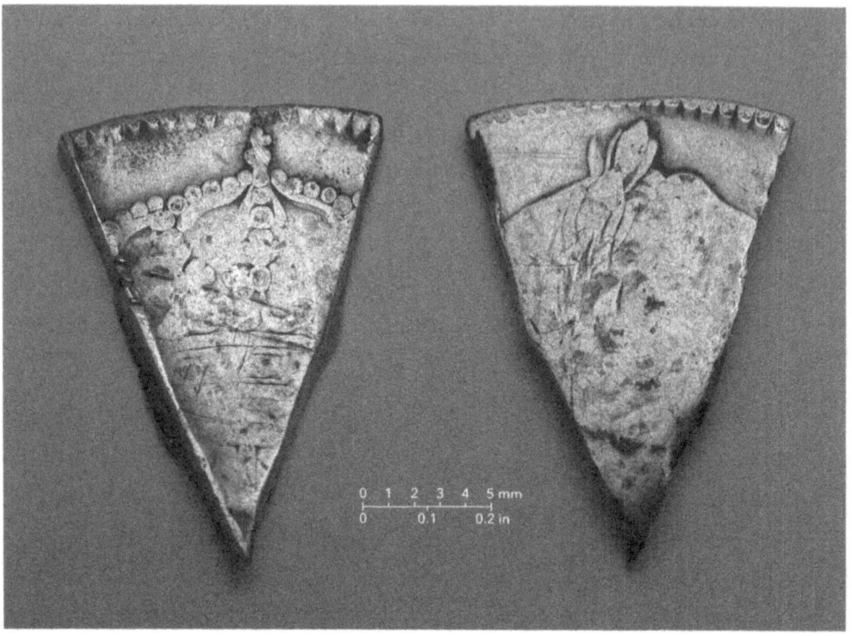

Cut Spanish real (front and back) from McGary's Station.

A single example of coinage was recovered. The coin is a fragment commonly known as a "piece of eight," which was cut from a Spanish real minted between 1772 and 1789. At the time, a full, uncut coin was valued at eight reales. The McGary example represented one-eighth of the coin, hence the term "piece of eight." Money was very scarce in the early years of the republic, and barter was the common form of exchange. Coinage from different countries was commonly in circulation in America. Spanish reales remained legal tender until the US Congress outlawed their use in 1857.[18]

Evidence that precontact Native Americans visited the site was also recovered. Two dartpoint fragments from the Archaic Period were found. One fragment called a Thebes point dating from 8,000 to 6,000 BCE and another stemmed point dating later in the Archaic Period, constitute the earliest precontact artifacts that were recovered. Archaic groups were hunter-gatherers who moved frequently over their home territories, responding to the seasonal availability of the wild, edible plants they gathered and the animals they hunted. Five chert triangular arrowpoint fragments and a single, plain-surfaced ceramic sherd tempered with crushed mussel shell indicate that members of the late precontact culture known as Fort Ancient visited the site. Triangular arrowpoints of various styles were made and used from CE 900 and through historic contact. Late precontact Fort Ancient groups in Kentucky were agriculturalists who grew corn, beans, squash, and a suite of locally domesticated plants. They coupled their agricultural skills with hunting skills to round out their diet. Fort Ancient culture is interpreted by archaeologists to be ancestral to tribes such as the Shawnee, who considered Kentucky part of their territory and opposed the settlement of the area by Euro-American emigrants. A very small shell bead may be of precontact Native American manufacture. A total of 2,655 pieces of chert represent the debris left over from making chert tools. Chert manufacturing debris, or *debitage*, is the most common type of artifact found on precontact sites in Kentucky. Debitage analysis revealed that the Native Americans utilized five locally available cherts to make their tools at this site. Only one flake of a nonlocal chert occurred in the assemblage.[19]

The Status of McGary's Station Inhabitants as Indicated by Their Artifacts

The artifacts people throw away or lose on their residential sites offer mute testimony to the way the inhabitants lived, what they ate or wore, and even how they perceived themselves. Physical artifacts and other aspects of material culture are the tangible clues that archaeologists examine and analyze to discern more intangible aspects of the lives of the people they study.

The McGary's Station research gathered documentary and archaeological data in an attempt to locate the actual site of the station and make inferences about Kentucky life during the Revolutionary War and immediately afterward. Like many other stations, McGary's Station served more than one family in the earliest years of its existence. In 1779 and perhaps part of 1780, the station may have held as many as twelve families plus one or more single men assigned to patrol duty. The blended family of Hugh McGary and his wife, Mary Ray, the large family of Matthias Yocum, the Dentons, and the Corns constituted the largest population the station experienced. Yet this level of occupation was short-lived as families left to establish their own stations in 1780.

From 1780, the station population consisted of McGary's family with his second wife, Catesey, James Ray's small family (wife Milley and eventually two sons), Patrick Jordan and his family, and perhaps one or two single men.

By 1784, the station also probably housed at least seven enslaved persons, acquired by McGary in a land trade. Some of these enslaved persons may have been rented out to others as was common practice.

The archaeological deposits at the site were generated by the occupants of the station, who—unknowingly, as they swept out their cabins, built fires for cooking or laundry, chipped a plate, or lost a button—left evidence of their presence that informs us today. Although the artifacts collected on the site could have been left there by any of the inhabitants, the McGarys and the Rays lived there the longest and probably contributed to the site's archaeology more than other occupants did. Any conclusions that can be drawn, however, must keep in mind the potential contributions that short-term occupants of the site may have made.

The wealth status of the McGarys and their kin can be indirectly investigated by examining their associated artifacts and other historical clues. Available evidence suggests that McGary was relatively affluent. I reached this conclusion in part because he brought forty horses into Kentucky (representing a substantial monetary investment) and because of the numerous land deals in which he was involved. Archaeological artifacts from the site indicate the families living there owned imported ceramics of several types, utensils, possibly a looking glass, guns, and a variety of clothing fastened with plain and decorated buttons and further accessorized with jewelry. The McGarys enslaved and occasionally traded in the sale or purchase of an unknown number of people. Documentary evidence also indicates that McGary was literate and possessed a family Bible. In addition, nearly all of the station families successfully claimed land, often in significant quantity. McGary was involved frequently in transactions with other men, where he acted as security for various sums of money. He also served as a justice of the peace and held relatively high rank in the local militia. All of these characteristics are marks of gentry status. Consulting Elizabeth Perkins's table of selected consumer and capital property for three wealth classes, the McGary's Station inhabitants appear to fall within the middle or upper sections of her socioeconomic divisions.[20]

Despite their social position, the McGarys and their family and friends did not initially live in stylish or pretentious housing. The nature of pioneer stations is that of impermanence, with little or no attention paid to lasting architecture. Like their fellow settlers, the McGarys did not expect to occupy their station for a long period of time. However, had matters transpired differently, they may well have stayed on their land and built a more substantial, fashionable house as James Ray did. Architectural evidence of the station was sparse because the site had been plowed repetitively after it was abandoned and because the log construction materials did not preserve. The excavated hearth feature may be evidence of a fireplace used both for cooking and heating. Such a fireplace would probably have been the major feature in a one-room cabin, possibly with a sleeping loft, that accommodated a family. Since several families stayed at McGary's Station for varying periods, there may have been several cabins. The presence of a stockade was not encountered during excavation, although documentary evidence mentions one. Defensive architecture was a common feature of pioneer stations, taking the form of a rectangular arrangement of cabins connected by stockading—or simply cabins with sturdy, barricadable doors, portholes for shooting at an exterior enemy, and no windows. John Ray referred to McGary's residence as a "cabbin," which was, in the parlance of the time, a temporary log structure with few amenities. By the time the McGarys vacated the property, somewhere between 1788 and 1792, their cabin was a decade or more in age and was probably beginning to deteriorate. The virtual absence of later artifacts associated with residential occupation is a strong indicator that the site was abandoned and not reoccupied after McGary's departure. James Ray had moved to his new house above the Great Blue Spring, and the other station families were in homes on their own land. George Thompson built a much more elaborate house to the east of the station site. At most, he may have housed enslaved persons in the station between 1788 and 1792 while his house and outbuildings were being built. After he completed new quarters for the enslaved, the station site was likely allowed to fall in or may have been purposefully razed to convert the area to agricultural purposes.

12

Locating Archaeological Evidence of Daniel Boone's Station

Unlike Hugh McGary's Station, the general location of Daniel Boone's Station was well known. As detailed in chapter 10, the chain of title for the property was well established by Willard Rouse Jillson and C. Frank Dunn in the 1930s and 1940s. The Boone Station site was part of a larger tract of forty-nine acres that was bequeathed to the Kentucky State Parks Commission in 1991 by Robert Channing Strader, who inherited the land from his mother, Elsie L. Barker Strader. The land transfer took place on March 4, 1992, when Strader's executors deeded the tract to the Kentucky Department of Parks. The Boone's Station site was included in my 1994 publication, *Stockading Up*, which presented my research on pioneer stations in a twelve-county area of the Inner Bluegrass Region of Kentucky. The Department of Parks contracted with the University of Kentucky Program for Cultural Resource Assessment to conduct an archaeological survey of the newly created park under the auspices of the Kentucky Antiquities Act (KRS 164.705–164.735). Additional documentary research was conducted, as well as an archaeological survey that identified several sites on the property, including the station site occupied by Daniel Boone and others.[1]

At the time of the 1993 survey, the exact location of the station site within the larger forty-nine-acre tract was unknown. I used the eight fenced areas on the property to designate survey areas, identified as Fields A through H. Since the tract was entirely covered by pasture, I hired a local farmer to systematically plow strips about ten to fifteen meters apart in each field. My survey crew examined each field after a rainstorm washed away soil and exposed artifacts on the surface. Artifacts found in the plowed field were flagged and collected, and their locations mapped to establish archaeological site boundaries. Field A in the southwest corner of the farm contained a freshwater spring near Gentry Road and three unengraved gravestones at a higher elevation in the north end of the field. Mr. Strader had placed the markers where he believed members of the Boone family were buried. A monument erected by the Daughters of the American Revolution to commemorate the graves stood near the grave markers. Archaeological surveying identified the station site between the spring and the grave markers. Also located was a buried rectangular stone house foundation that a local farmer and close friend of Strader's, Andrew Eades, reported to me. Mr. Eades had previously farmed the property and encountered the foundation when he plowed the field for tobacco cultivation over a period of a few years. The stone foundation was located within the confines of the station site but was later in date. Documentary research established that the stone house was built by Robert Frank prior to 1795. Frank also apparently utilized the station cabins for his own purposes after the site ceased to serve as a defensive sanctuary during the Revolutionary War.

The survey of Field A in the Boone Station State Park identified the precise location of the Boone's Station site by plotting the distribution of late eighteenth- and early nineteenth-century artifacts and excavating nine units to identify possible cultural features and look for undisturbed cultural midden (organically enriched soil containing historic artifacts). The results were encouraging, though not conclusive, that residential midden and structural foundations were present. Also observed was a vegetational anomaly measuring about ten by eleven meters in which the grass was greener and taller. As at Hugh McGary's Station, Dr. R. Berle Clay conducted a limited soil conductivity survey, using an EM38 Geonics conductivity meter. The map of the conductivity readings identified two features of interest. Our investigation of Feature 1 revealed a heavily reddened and burned hearth area that extended below the plow zone (the disturbed soil level that had been mixed by plowing in the past). Feature 2 was a concentration of fragmented limestone that covered a dark brown cultural midden zone that extended to at least forty centimeters below the surface. This feature was interpreted as a filled depression with a possible post mold overlain by stone foundations.[2]

Although preliminary and limited in scope, the archaeological survey and identification of the Boone Station site (designated 15FA218 by the Office of State Archaeology) confirmed the presence of a late eighteenth-century occupation consistent with the date of the station's use as a defensive residence, as well as a later historic occupation that extended into the first half of the nineteenth century. My documentary research included a chain of title, an important and informative court case concerning a dispute over the land, and various secondary references that further confirmed that the site was indeed Daniel Boone's Station. An interview by Reverend John Dabney Shane with David Thompson states that Boone "never owned the land at Athens, Boon's S[tation]. He tho't he did, but it belonged to one Gordon of Spottsylvania Co: Va. Old Robert Frank [married] his [Gordon's] sister, and got the land and settled there." Lyman Copeland Draper's correspondence with Daniel's son, Nathan Boone, related that the station's "locality was on the northeast side of a small stream, a fork of Boone's Creek—about half a mile east or northeast of Athens or the Cross Plains; & on the locality was a large stone mansion previous to 1799."[3]

Further excavations of the Boone Station site were initiated in the summer of 1999, when an archaeological field school was conducted through the Department of Anthropology at the University of Kentucky. Dr. Donald Linebaugh and I, assisted by a graduate research assistant, Jim White, directed thirteen students during an eight-week course. Fieldwork began by imposing a mapping grid over most of Field A, followed by a systematic shovel probe survey, supervised by Dr. Linebaugh. The students excavated 128 screened shovel probes, sifted the soil through quarter-inch mesh screens, and bagged the artifacts found in each probe. Subsequent analysis mapped the frequency and distribution of eighteenth- and nineteenth-century artifacts and pinpointed the station's location in the center of the field about sixty to seventy meters uphill from the station spring. The highest density of artifacts covered an area of approximately thirty (north–south) by fifty (east–west) meters.

Once the location of the site was determined by the artifact distribution, Dr. Clay, who was then the geophysical specialist for Cultural Resource Analysts, Inc., of Lexington, Kentucky, conducted a second, more extensive remote sensing survey. A magnetic and a soil conductivity survey was conducted on an area measuring forty by sixty meters, where the artifact density was highest. The magnetic survey collected readings with a Geoscan Research fluxgate gradiometer. A magnetic survey measures variations over space in the near-surface magnetic field. These variations may signify the presence of cultural features such as stone or brick foundations, storage or privy pits, concentrations of iron objects, or areas of burning.

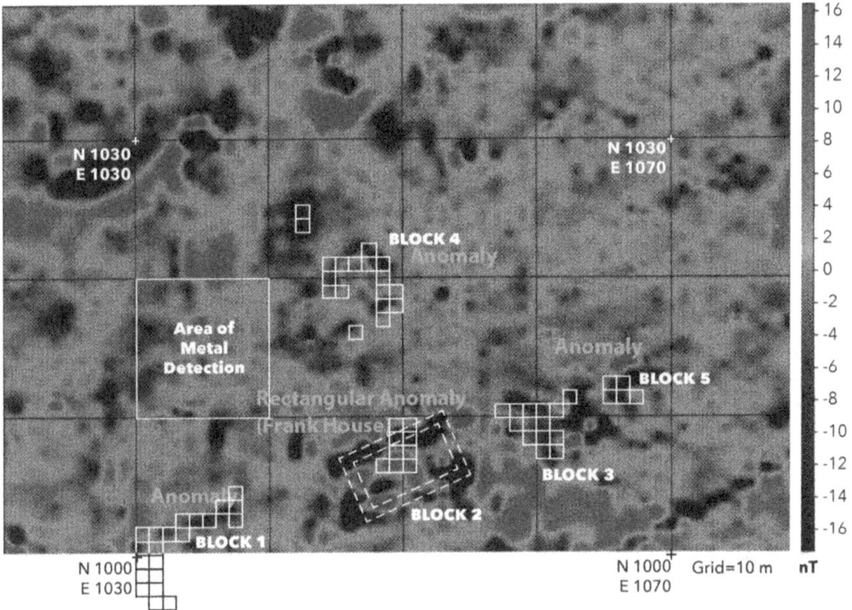

Map of remote sensing survey at Boone's Station.

Dr. Clay again used a Geonics EM38 conductivity meter to identify cultural features such as areas of low conductivity, like a solid house foundation, or pit or trench features that have high conductivity. Another measurement that is taken by a conductivity meter is magnetic susceptibility, which describes the magnetizability of a given material, like cultural features. The results may be hampered by the presence of iron objects such as waterlines, sewer pipes, or cultural midden that contain large quantities of iron.

The results of the two surveys revealed several subsurface features that proved to be structural components of the station architecture and the cellar that was beneath the Frank house. Of the two techniques, the gradiometer survey clearly revealed stone structural foundations as linear features exhibiting high negative values. The conductivity and magnetic survey results depicted the structural features identified by the gradiometer survey in varying detail. Traditional excavation confirmed the presence of a solid limestone foundation associated with the Frank house, as well as continuous shallow limestone foundations associated with two of the station cabins. These three structures formed part of a rectangular enclosure in which the exterior cabin walls, coupled with short intervening sections of log stockade, formed the

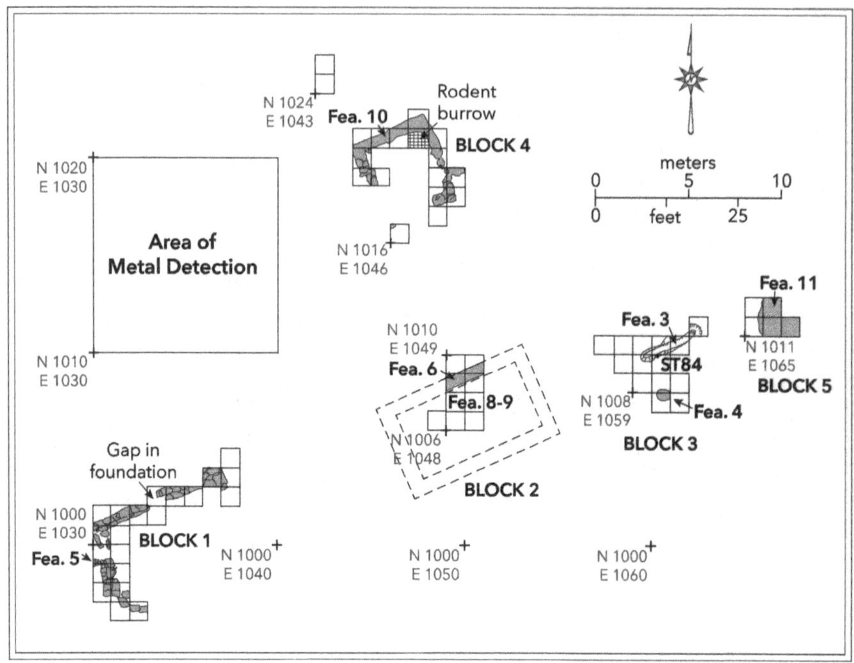

Map of Boone's Station excavations, showing features.

station's architectural footprint. Further excavation following the extrapolated line of the station enclosure revealed a section of the ditch in which stockade logs were vertically placed and a large pit that was probably some type of in-house relatively shallow storage cellar. Although the Frank house was built several years after the original station ceased to function as a defensive residence, it was situated in line with the original log cabins and stockade sections that made up the station enclosure. This unusual juxtaposition of a later house with the rectangular plan of a stockaded station prompted the question: Were the station cabins repurposed for later residential use by the Frank family and other occupants?

A total of five excavation blocks, each composed of contiguous one-by-two meter or one-by-one meter units, exposed the structural remains associated with the station. I numbered excavation blocks from one to five. Block 1 comprised twenty-one square meters in total area. The excavation exposed most of the north and west walls of a continuous dry-laid limestone foundation. Block 2 contained nine square meters and sampled the deep stone cellar foundation that lay beneath the Robert Frank house. Block 3 comprised fourteen square meters and revealed the section of the stockade ditch and a circular pit feature. Block 4 contained fifteen square meters of contiguous units and one square meter unit south of the main block. The entire north wall and partial east and west walls, marked by a continuous dry-laid limestone foundation, were exposed in this block. Block 5 contained five square meters and exposed another cellar feature that was probably inside another cabin.

The distribution of artifacts identified by shovel probes covered approximately fifteen hundred square meters. The remote sensing survey identified anomalies within an area of approximately twenty by forty-five meters. Metal detection in a twenty-by-twenty-meter area yielded additional artifacts that may be associated with another station cabin. Excavation units totaling sixty-five square meters sampled slightly more than 7 percent of the estimated site area. However, since the unit placement was guided by the shovel-probing and remote sensing results and focused on areas where cultural features and artifacts were most likely to be abundant, the most productive areas of the site were sampled.

Block 1 House Foundation

The structure exposed in Block 1 and designated Feature 5 was a log dwelling built on a dry-laid limestone foundation. The structure was oriented east to west along its longest wall. Most of the north wall and the northern section of the west wall were exposed by excavation. This alignment of the north wall appeared as a distinct linear pattern of negative magnetic readings on the remote sensing survey. The west wall was not within the limits of the remote sensing area but was easily located when the inside corner of the building was exposed in one of the excavation units. The foundation stones were laid directly on the ground without a builder's trench. Only the lower courses of the foundation were preserved. Later plowing of the field, after the site was abandoned and the structures were no longer present, undoubtedly encountered foundation stones, and the farmer very likely removed stones that interfered with the plowing. Foundation stones may also have been removed for use elsewhere when the structure was no longer needed. Although I used the metric system for mapping and measurement, I converted measurements that relate to wall length or other architectural features to English standard, since this is the system that was used by the builder. I include rounded-off metric conversions only where it seemed useful to do so. Otherwise, I use the metric system to facilitate comparison with other archaeological analyses. The highest course of foundation stones was encountered approximately ten centimeters below the modern ground surface at the base of the plow zone. The length of the north wall was approximately twenty-six feet (eight meters). There was a gap in the north wall that measured approximately three feet (one meter) in width. The gap was centered on the wall and may have been a doorway that opened into the interior of the station enclosure. The foundation stones forming the west wall were more displaced than the north wall but still sufficiently in place to recognize a chimney and hearth (designated Feature 12) that may have been centrally located along the wall. The estimated length of the west wall was between thirteen (four meters) and sixteen feet (five meters). The estimated dimensions of thirteen feet to sixteen by twenty-six feet are well within the range of dimensions of the rectangular plan common to a cabin in the Scots-Irish tradition, which also featured a chimney on one of the short walls.[4]

Archaeological excavation revealed soil stratigraphy that indicated what happened to the site after it was abandoned as a residential complex. After the houses were abandoned and eventually torn down, or allowed to fall, the field was converted to agricultural use. The foundation stones would have presented an impediment to plowing, and the higher courses of stones were probably removed, leaving the lower courses that lay below the reach of the plow. While the soil stratigraphy clearly indicates that the site was plowed in the past, what is less clear is how often the site was cultivated. Andrew Eades, the local farmer who raised tobacco on the site in the early twentieth century, reported that the site remained mostly in pasture for many years. The presence of the stone foundations across the site may have been a factor in using the site mostly to pasture livestock with only occasional use as a cultivated field because of the labor required to remove the limestone slabs that made up the foundations. In any event, even occasional plowing altered the cultural soil stratigraphy that developed as a consequence of human occupation.

Most of the artifacts associated with the log structure in Block 1 were found in the plow zone, a layer of soil that began at the ground surface and varied in thickness from four to thirty-four centimeters. The variation depended on how much of the underlying stone foundation was preserved and how level the ground was across the site. While the site lay on fairly level ground, there was some variation from north to south that required adjusting the height of the dry-laid stone foundations associated with the structure in

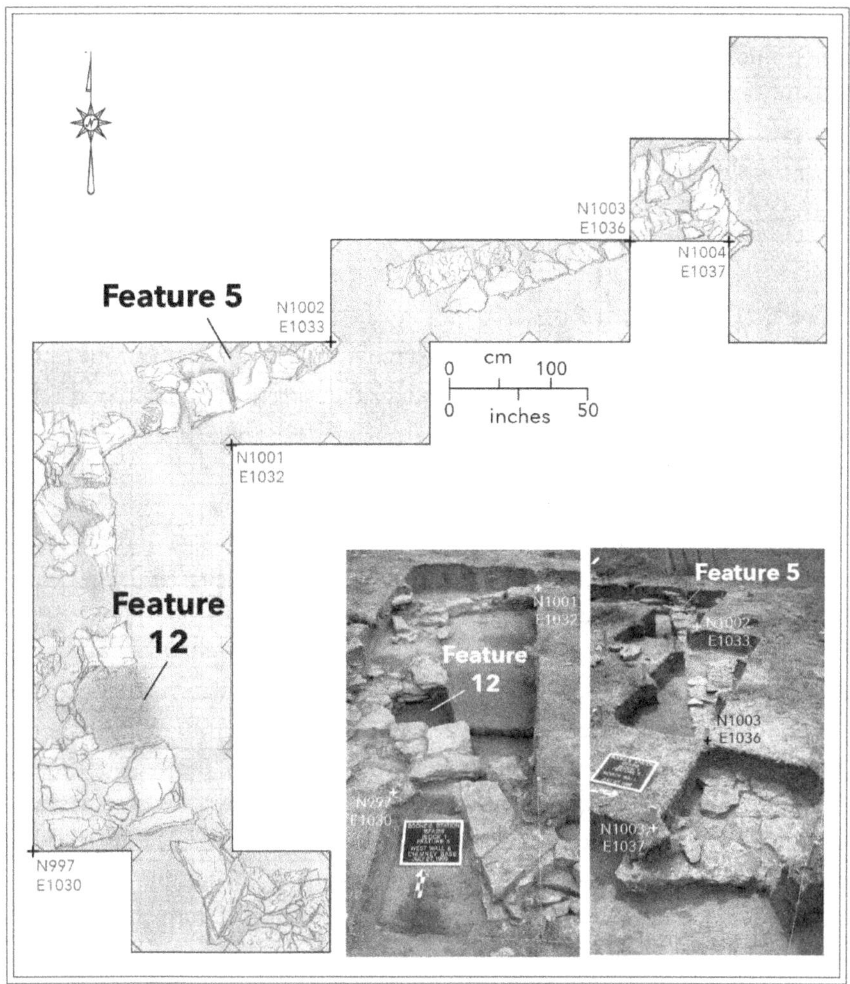

Drawing and photograph of cabin in Block 1 (Boone's Station).

Block 1 so that the interior floor did not slope. The elevational variation was only a few centimeters, but it was enough to affect later plowing. There was a shallow area of plow zone that covered where the foundation stones lay closer to the ground surface. Most of the artifacts were recovered from this disturbed soil layer, but some artifacts lay deeper in the ground and were retrieved from a soil layer, which was generally ten centimeters thick below the plow zone. This layer of soil held the remnants of intact cultural midden that accumulated around and inside the house foundation during its occupation.

If the site had never been plowed, the intact cultural midden would have been much thicker. Excavation focused on exposing the stone foundations of the building rather than targeting the interior living space. Nevertheless, artifacts recovered from the units are primarily from inside the house, near the walls, or in the chimney hearth feature.

Block 2 House Foundation

Block 2 exposed part of the cellar (designated Feature 8) that once lay beneath the stone house built by Robert Frank. The rectangular outline of the entire cellar was clearly indicated by high negative readings on the conductivity map. The orientation of the house lined up with the cardinal directions, with the front and back walls running east–west and the end walls running north–south. The dimensions of the cellar were approximately sixteen by twenty-six feet (five by eight meters). These measurements were very similar to the cabin identified in Block 1. Excavation units were placed in the center of the northerly wall and sampled both inside and outside the foundation.

The house is shown as a drawing on a map of the farm that was produced for a lawsuit in 1814 (as shown in figure 8). Depictions of structures on such documents are quite rare, and this one seems to be an attempt to illustrate the house's actual appearance. The drawing shows a two-story, three-bay structure with end chimneys, a centrally placed front door, and two windows stacked one over one on both floors. No window is shown on the second floor above the door. The end chimneys seem to indicate an internal chimney built flush with the west wall and an external chimney protruding from the east wall. Some of the details are not correct for the late eighteenth-century period of construction. For example, the window sashes are shown as 2/2 panes; stone houses of that era would have been 9/6 or 6/6. A triangle drawn at the roof line and two parallel lines running on either side of the door may indicate a pedimented portico. The pediment is drawn out of scale to the door. Pedimented porticos were not a common feature of late eighteenth-century stone houses but were sometimes added later to update the house's style by altering the porch. Considering the size of the foundation, the three bays, the end chimneys, and the fact that the Franks were from Virginia, their house may have had a hall-parlor plan common to stone houses in that area.[5]

Excavation of the house cellar exposed a sequence of fill zones that explained what caused the house's destruction. Of the nine one-by-one-meter

Photograph of the Frank House cellar in Block 2 (Boone's Station).

units excavated, four units exposed part of the north wall of the foundation. The interior cellar space was documented in five complete units and partially in two of the units that contained the foundation wall. The other two units containing part of the wall exposed a small section outside the foundation. No surface indications of the buried foundations were visible prior to opening the excavation units. The remote sensing survey pinpointed the location of the cellar, which made positioning excavation units more accurate. Excavation revealed a surface plow zone that ranged from approximately twelve to twenty-five centimeters thick. Intact fill zones were located inside the cellar and below the plow zone. The cellar fill was composed of two types of fill: limestone rubble deposited when the house collapsed and a layer of ash that varied in thickness and was distributed primarily in the southern three units of the excavation block. The cellar floor was located approximately one meter below the ground surface, but the height of the cellar was probably greater. The compacted soil at the floor level caused by foot traffic suggests that the cellar was used, and the presumption is that it was at least tall enough to stand up in.

The stratigraphic position of the ash and rubble layers is key to understanding how the house collapsed. In all three units where the ash layer was densest, it was deposited above and below thick deposits of limestone rubble. Ash deposits occurred in some of the other units but largely in patches and not as a continuous layer. Some of the wall collapse had to have occurred

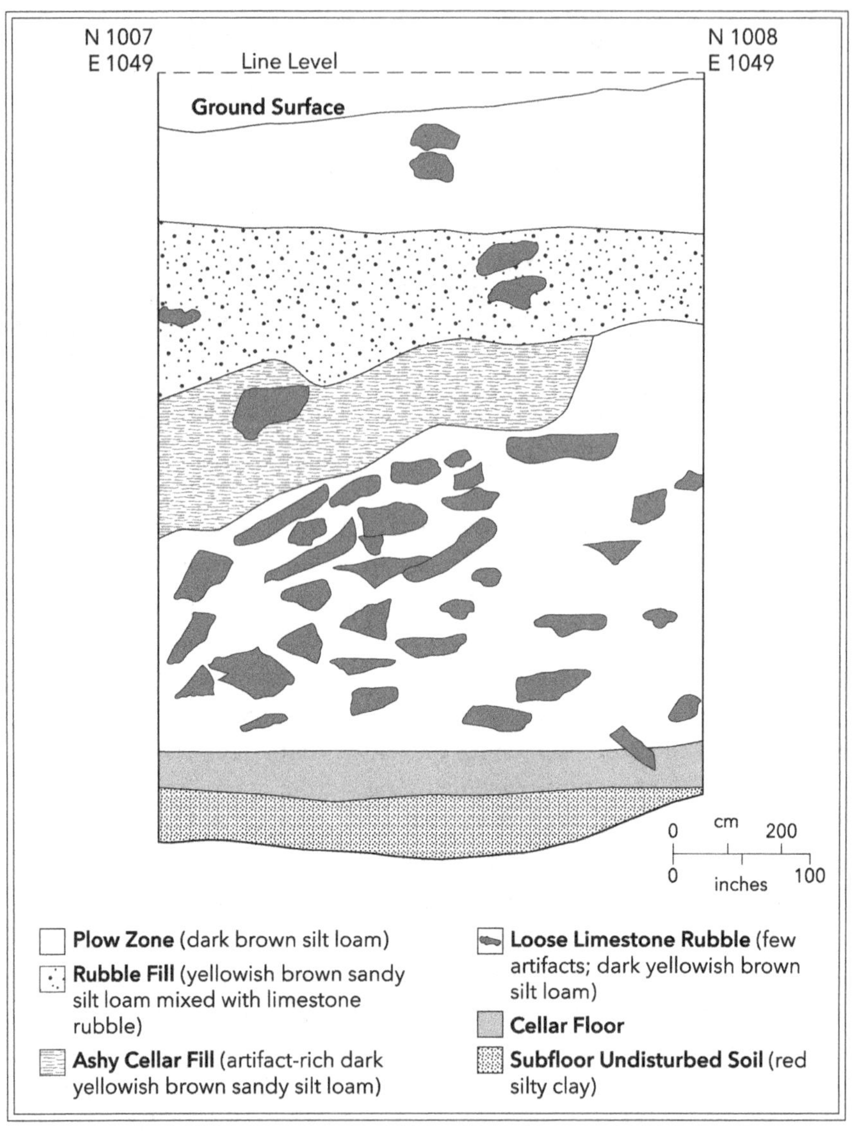

Profile of cellar fill stratigraphy in Block 2 (Boone's Station).

before ash was deposited. If a fire started on an upper floor of the house and was extensive enough, the stone walls might have given way below the fire, particularly if the roof fell in. If the depiction of the house as a two-story structure is accurate, a fire on the second floor could have easily ignited a shake roof and the interior framing that supported it. The weight of the roof falling onto the second floor may have been sufficient to cause the first-floor walls to collapse into the basement and the burning upper story and roof to fall on top. The ash layer was distributed mostly in what would have been the center of the foundation. Its full extent is unknown, but it probably extended to the west and the south of the excavated units. Less ash was documented in the easterly units and very little to the north. A second layer of rubble was documented in two of the units containing large deposits of ash; this layer was stratigraphically above the ash, indicating that a second episode of wall collapse covered some of the ash deposits.

Block 3

Block 3 was placed in an area of high negative readings from the gradiometer survey. High negative readings were associated with stone foundations in other excavation blocks. No evidence of a stone foundation was exposed in Block 3. Two archaeological features, designated 3 and 4, were excavated. Feature 3 was a shallow, linear trench that was narrower at its base and widened in cross section at the top. The trench extended across parts of six 1 by 1 meter units for a total length of 3.4 meters (approximately 11 feet). The orientation of the trench lined up with the east-to-west orientation of the Frank house in Block 2 and the structural foundation in Block 1. The cross section and length of the trench are consistent with a section of stockade that was built to connect the walls of adjacent log cabins that constituted the enclosure of the station.

Feature 4 was a circular stain containing fire-reddened earth located 1.6 meters southeast of Feature 3. This location places the feature outside the station enclosure. Excavation revealed a pit measuring approximately 60 centimeters in diameter that was filled with dark reddish-brown soil that increased in redness with depth. The pit was quite deep, extending 72.5 centimeters from the top of the feature to the bottom. The feature fill contained virtually no artifacts except for very small brick or fired clay fragments that were not collected. Artifacts collected from the soil above the feature and in the four units that contained and surrounded it consisted largely of red clay

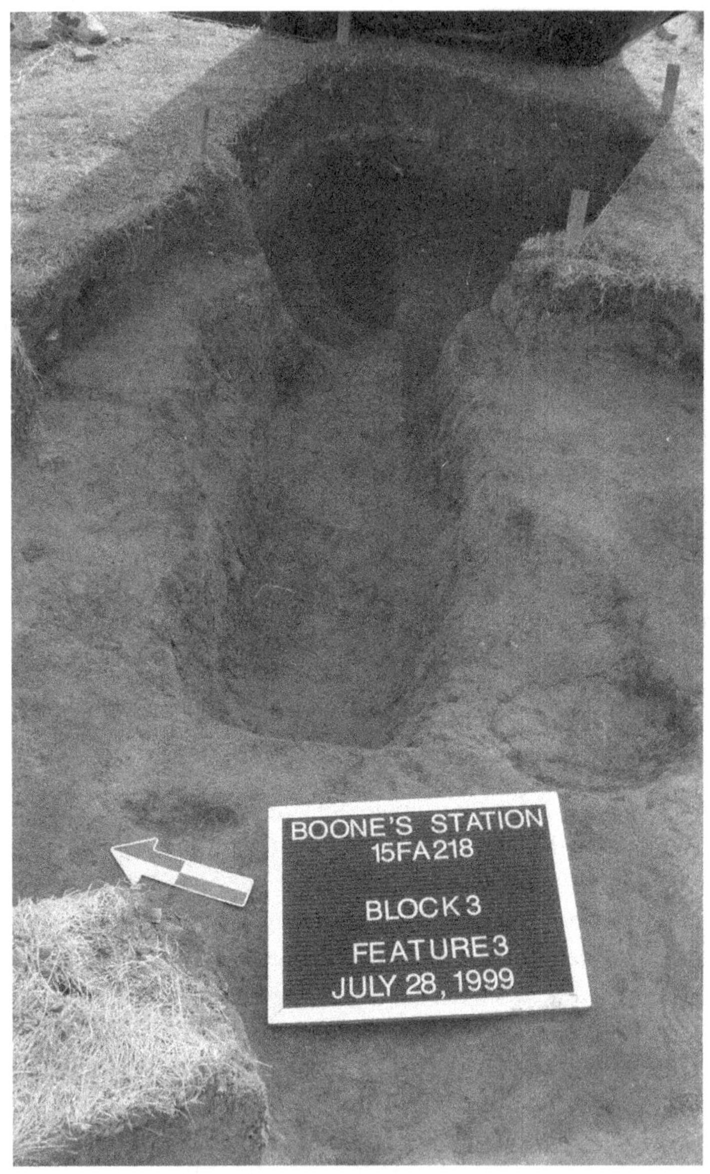

Photograph of the stockade ditch in Block 3 (Boone's Station).

earthenware fragments, most of them small body sherds and spalls. One of the body sherds had an unusual orange glaze on one surface and a dark brown glaze on the other. Also recovered was a rim with a slightly everted, thickened lip. I was unable to identify a cultural function for this feature. It may have been the root hole of a tree or shrub around which some cultural midden containing few artifacts accumulated.

Sections of stockade were built between the cabins that formed the quadrilinear plan of the station. The stockade logs abutted the exterior walls of the cabins. The combination of inwardly facing cabins and a typically ten-foot-high stockade presented a seemingly impenetrable barrier to attackers. While the excavation of Block 3 did not expose evidence of a cabin foundation next to the end of the stockade ditch, the presence of domestic artifacts and nails led me to conclude that a cabin once stood here. An alternative explanation is that the front gate to the station was located here.

Block 4 House Foundation

Block 4 contained another shallow stone foundation (designated Feature 10) that supported one of the log station cabins that stood on the north line of the enclosure. The entire north and west walls and three corners of the structure were exposed by excavation. The west wall was only partially exposed in three units running south from the northwest corner of the structure. A noncontiguous one-by-one-meter unit identified part of the foundation where the southwest corner would have been located. Enough of the foundation remained to determine the cabin's dimensions. The floor plan was rectangular, measuring fourteen by sixteen feet in English standard measurements (four by five meters). The cabin was probably a single pen plan and may have had a loft for sleeping, as was common for cabins of the time. No chimney or hearth was identified. One could have stood on the west or south wall. A central west wall placement is more likely because the front door of the cabin would have logically faced into the station enclosure and so would have been in the south wall.

Block 5 Cellar

Block 5 was opened in the last few days of the field school and offered tantalizing results of yet another cabin that may have had an interior storage cellar

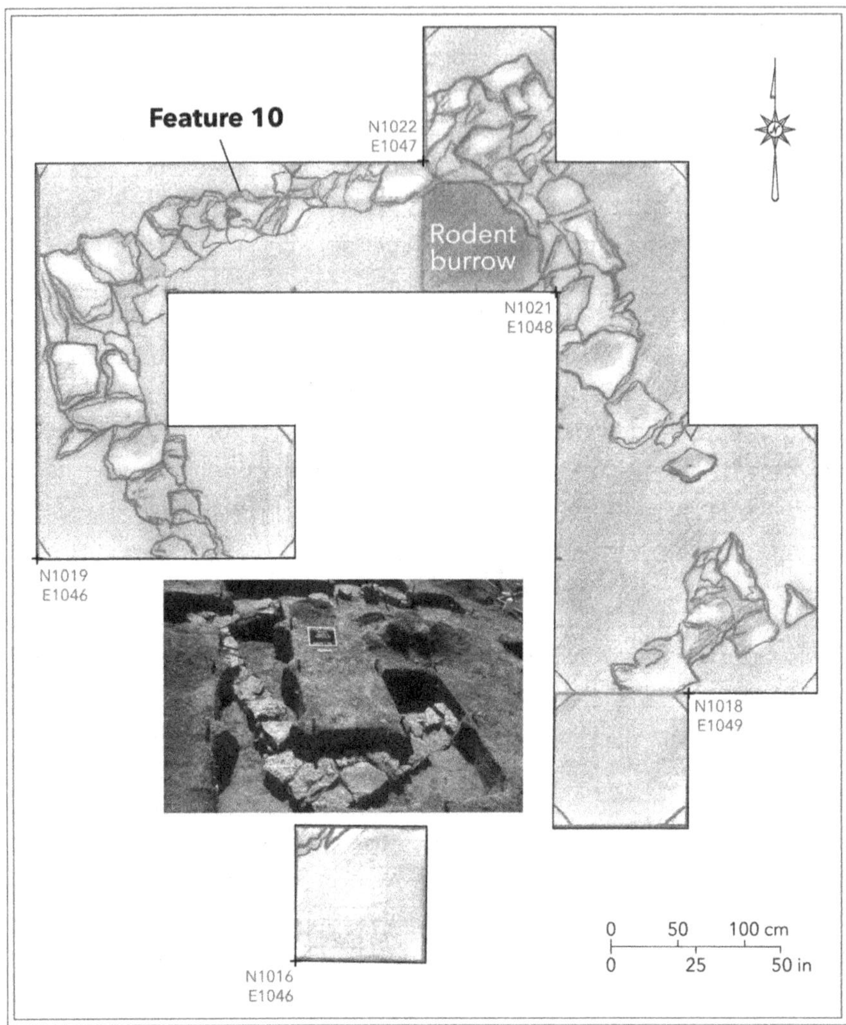

Drawing and photograph of cabin in Block 4 (Boone's Station).

designated Feature 11. Excavation was insufficient to uncover the entire extent of the cellar, but it was roughly circular in shape and was more than seven feet (two meters) in diameter. No structural foundations were identified, but the feature was on the same east-to-west alignment as the Frank house and the cabin in Block 1. The structure was to the east of the Frank house and the stockade ditch feature. The fill within the feature contained many large limestone rocks that could have been part of a foundation but were dislodged and

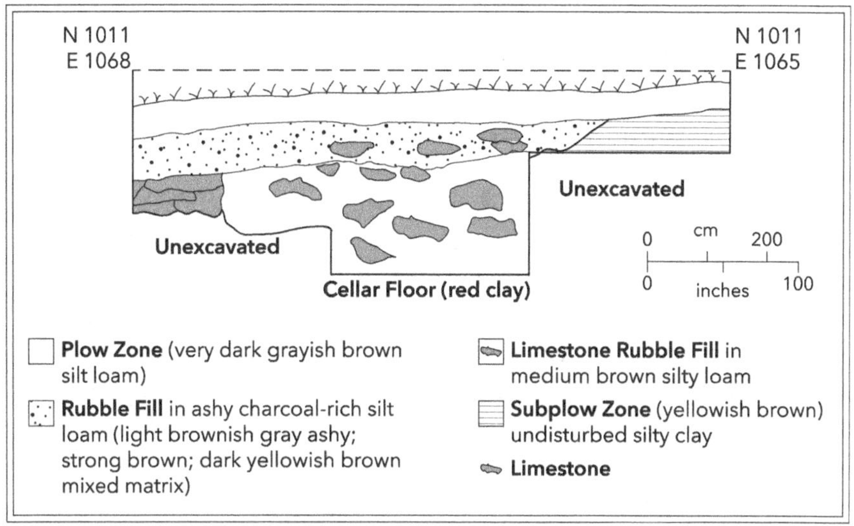

Profile of stratigraphy in Block 5 (Boone's Station).

thrown into the cellar when the cabin was torn down or fell down. The cellar was at least a meter in depth and terminated on a dirt floor.

Metal Detection Area

A metal detector survey was conducted in a ten-by-ten-meter area southwest of Block 4 and north of Block 1 where the remote sensing survey had identified anomalies. While the metal detector identified metal artifacts, each target was hand excavated and screened through a quarter-inch wire screen to recover nonmetallic artifacts. Fifty detection targets yielded a total of 121 artifacts. Forty-three targets contained 4 or fewer artifacts, with thirty targets yielding only the metal artifact identified by the detection equipment. Two of the targets contained much higher artifact frequencies of 14 and 19 specimens. Seventy-eight artifacts were recovered from targets that were concentrated in the south half of the detection area. This concentration lines up with the north wall of the station enclosure as defined by the alignment of the cabin foundation in Block 4. The diversity of artifacts includes coarse and refined ceramics, container glass, utensils, animal bone, an iron pot fragment, flat glass and nails, personal and clothing items, and equine and agricultural specimens. Datable artifacts span the entire occupation of the site, suggesting that the station cabin that probably stood in the area continued to be used by later site inhabitants.

Boone's Station Size and Positioning

The size of a station depended on how many cabins were built, their floor plan dimensions, and how far apart they stood from one another. If the chimney for each cabin stood on a wall perpendicular to the line of the enclosure, as was the case at the larger fort at Boonesborough, then stockade sections that linked the cabins together had to span the distance necessary to accommodate the chimney. While some generalizations can be made about station architecture, there were variations. For example, the cabins at Bryan's Station, located on the Limestone Trace not far from Boone's Station, were farther apart than usual because the families there valued privacy over minimizing the time required to build longer sections of stockade. Henry Wilson and George Rogers Clark both estimated the dimensions at 150 by 600 feet, or about two acres. Joseph Ficklin listed twenty-nine cabins that held families at the station in 1782 and estimated the station enclosure as measuring 250 by 600 feet, or nearly three and a half acres. Both of these sources may be correct, since the station was in the process of being enlarged to include more stockade and cabins at the time of the siege. Four blockhouses anchored the corners and housed single men without families. These dimensions were considerably larger than the dimensions estimated for Fort Boonesborough which was a major defensive site. Fort Boonesborough's dimensions varied slightly according to the observer providing them but measured between 125 and 180 feet in width and 250 and 260 feet in length and enclosed one-half to three-quarters of an acre. The enclosure included four corner blockhouses and twenty-six cabins along the sides.[6]

Sarah Boone Hunter reported that fifteen families lived within a half-acre enclosure of cabins and stockade at Daniel Boone's Station. Assuming the exterior cabin walls formed part of the defensive enclosure of the station, I calculated the width of the station from north to south to be approximately 56 feet. I could not determine the length of the enclosure without more excavation, but based on the excavation data, the length must have been in excess of 130 feet. My calculations based on Hunter's estimate of half an acre and the estimated width suggest that the length may have been as long as 390 feet.

The single section of stockade discovered during excavation measured about 10–11 feet in length.

The positioning of the station on the landscape was influenced by the local topographical elevation. The land on which the station stood slopes from 870 feet above mean sea level at Gentry Road to 920 feet in elevation, over a linear distance of 200 meters. The station was built along the 900-foot contour line, which situated it about 100 meters from Gentry Road and about 60 meters from the station spring (measured from the cabin in Block 1, which was the closest). In order to remain on fairly level ground, the station's lengthwise orientation ran slightly north of an east–west line. This topographic location also avoided the underlying limestone that outcropped near or at the surface at higher elevations. The tradeoff for building on more level ground was the distance to the spring. In practical terms, the trip from the spring carrying heavy buckets of water would have been a strenuous uphill walk.

Estimating the number of cabins is equally problematic in the absence of extensive excavation. Remote sensing provided readings that, when investigated by excavation, revealed three cabins and the later Frank house. The later house probably replaced at least one cabin. I deduced from additional remote sensing readings two possible cabin locations on either side of the cabin in Block 4 along the north line of the station. Metal detection in one of these locations recovered artifacts that were probably associated with a cabin. The cabin in Block 1 was larger than the cabin in Block 4 and may have been a double pen. In any case, it could accommodate a larger family or even two families (such as young married couples with few or no children). Both family types, as well as single men assigned to the station as guards, lived there. The diversity of population and the archaeological data suggest that cabins were built to the size and configuration that were needed for the families who settled there. The earliest families' needs may have dictated the initial size and configuration of the station, but continued occupation by other families, and eventually by the Frank family with their enslaved persons, as well as by later owners, altered the way the station was used. The stockade was most likely eliminated shortly after the end of the Revolutionary War, as it was at Fort Boonesborough and elsewhere when hostilities ceased. The Franks seem to have retained some of the cabins for their own use, perhaps as slave quarters. Later landowners continued to use the station cabins, most likely to house their enslaved workers.[7]

My final observation concerns the inward-looking defensive nature of the original station in which the cabins all faced into the enclosure and presented a united, insular barrier to anyone approaching the station. The height of the stockade posts belied how sturdy they actually were. I found hints in the documentary record of stockade posts that could be removed to allow emergency access, instances when alarmed cattle pushed the posts over, and other indications that the average station stockade may have looked imposing but could have been breached with enough force. However, Native Americans were wary of the shooting skills of the settlers they encountered and rarely tried to use frontal assault and brute force to breach a station's walls. Better to keep a safe distance, shoot flaming arrows onto the cabin roofs, and direct lead balls at every crevice or opening. The settlers, on the other hand, found that holing up in the station and firing accurately at every possible human target often saved the day.[8]

13

The Boone Station Artifact Assemblage

Unlike the artifacts from McGary's Station, the material culture assemblage at Daniel Boone's Station reflects several decades of occupation by numerous families. Daniel Boone's tenure at the site lasted only a few years, although some of his relatives, like Samuel Boone and his family, may have stayed longer. Other unrelated settlers stayed at the station for varying amounts of time after the Revolutionary War ended. These sojourns may have been similar to the arrangements made by proprietors of other station sites who allowed people to live on and work their land, thereby facilitating the clearance of forest and canebrakes for agricultural purposes. John Strode, in present-day Clark County, made such arrangements with settlers who stayed at his station, promising land to settlers who helped him clear his one-thousand-acre preemption if they stayed nine years.[1]

Robert Frank, the first owner to actually reside full time at the site, may have continued a similar pattern of allowing tenants to live in the station cabins for a few years. He also had as many as nine enslaved individuals to house, and some of the cabins may have been used for that purpose. It is likely that the tenancy arrangement was short-lived, as people bought land of their own and moved away. Aside from the cabins needed to house enslaved people, other station cabins may have been removed, and the site would have eventually taken on the appearance of a more conventional farmstead with a main house and ancillary outbuildings.

Analyzing the artifacts as a whole assemblage has the benefit of characterizing the kinds and variety of belongings the site inhabitants acquired. Artifact categories, such as wrought and cut nails and various types of ceramics and glassware, also indicate change over time and offer insights into the lifestyles of the inhabitants over a span of nearly seven decades. Archival information was able to establish, with varying exactitude, the sequence of families that lived on the site and the length of their stay.

1779–c. 1783: Inhabitants of Boone's Station during the Revolutionary War included the Daniel Boone family, several of his siblings, and a reported fifteen other families.

1784–1791: Additional families lived at the site for varying lengths of time while the site was owned by an absentee landowner. Robert Frank and his family were at the site as early as 1788, living there with Samuel Potts Pointer, Richard Chaney, John Henry, John Bledsoe, and George Sharp.

1792–1807: Robert Frank, his wife, three underage children, and possibly two older, unmarried daughters occupied their stone house on the site along with nine enslaved individuals. Robert Frank died in 1798, but his wife continued to live at the site until she died in 1807. At that point, her three youngest children were twenty-one, twenty, and seventeen. The youngest, Thomas, married that year. The older daughters may have already married and moved away.

1807–1809: John S. Cockrell, his wife Catherine, and their son, Thomas, lived briefly at the site. There were apparently no enslaved people living on the site with the Cockrells. Their occupation ended prematurely, with John Cockrell's death.

1809–1815: John Hendley owned the property and may have lived there with his family. In 1810, the Hendley household included an adult male between twenty-six and forty-four years old (Hendley), a woman between sixteen and twenty-five years old (presumably his wife), a male younger than ten, two males aged sixteen to twenty-five years, four females younger than ten, and four enslaved people.

1815–1824: Charles Grimes owned the property but did not live there. He may have rented it to tenants.

1824–1848: Three brothers, Simeon, Harvey, and Robert Bledsoe, bought the property together. Harvey Bledsoe was the only brother who most likely lived on the property until his death in

> 1833. His household in 1830 included two white men, aged twenty to twenty-nine years and thirty to thirty-nine years, and six enslaved individuals. After his death, his surviving brother, Robert, who lived in Georgia, probably rented it out until 1849, when it was sold through an intermediary to Thomas and Joseph Barker. The site was abandoned as a residence after 1849.

The artifact analysis sheds some light on how long the stone house and its associated buildings stood, and it partially reconstructs the household assemblages of specific occupants. I employed functional categories of architectural or construction-related, munitions, clothing, accessory and personal, kitchen and household, furnishings, hardware, equine and agricultural, and mysteries as an organizational framework. A total of 16,482 artifacts were recovered from the site. This total includes all artifacts collected from shovel tests, metal detection, and block excavations. The focus of the artifact analysis is on the block excavations because they contain the best evidence of structures and other cultural features. The block excavations yielded the bulk of the artifacts, a total of 15,227. Artifact frequency within each excavation block reflects several factors: the amount of excavation that took place, the method of artifact retrieval, and actual artifact density. Table 13.1 includes gross artifact frequencies of major artifact categories as well as a gross estimate of artifact frequency per cubic meter of archaeological midden excavated. Artifact frequencies are highest in the kitchen, architecture, and faunal categories, which is driven by the relatively high number of ceramic fragments and nails and the good preservation of animal bone. Block 1 yielded the highest number of artifacts, followed by Blocks 2, 3, 5, and 4. Considering estimated artifact frequency by cubic meter, artifact density is highest in Block 5, followed in descending order by Blocks 2, 3, 1, and 4. The cabin in Block 1 was the larger of the two measurable cabins and seems to have been occupied the longest. Both Blocks 2 and 5 contained cellars with deep midden deposits, which typically contain high artifact frequencies. Block 4, which contained the smaller of the two measurable log station cabins, stands out for its much lower artifact density. It may have been occupied more sporadically than the other structures or not always used for residential purposes.

Block 3 also exhibits an interesting pattern. Its artifact density was the third highest of the five blocks with the highest frequencies in kitchen-related

Table 13.1. Artifact Frequency and Density by Excavation Blocks in Boone's Station

Excavation Block	Kitchen-Related Artifacts	Architecture	Hardware, Arms, Clothing, Personal, Hygiene, Smoking, Activities	Faunal Artifacts	Artifact Frequency per Cubic Meter	Total Artifact Frequency by Excavation Block
1	1,911	2,297	80	673	502	4961
2	2,123	1,782	125	671	736	4701
3	1,200	296	12	996	662	2504
4	598	340	8	92	158	1038
5	1,069	190	25	739	920	2023

and faunal artifacts. Trash disposal was handled in various ways before regular trash pickup and offsite removal began to take place in the modern era. English agricultural reformer William Cobbett observed a particular pattern at Pennsylvania farmhouses in 1818: "A sort of out-of-door slovenliness. . . . You see bits of wood, timber, boards, chips, lying about, here and there, and pigs tramping about in a sort of confusion." Marley Brown documented the use of a particular area as a dump at Mott Farm in Rhode Island, a practice that has also been documented in Kentucky at the Johnson-Bates house site in Jefferson County. Trash was also buried in pits. Bones and food scraps were thrown out for pigs and chickens to consume, but archaeological studies of farmyards document the accumulation of nonfood trash such as broken dishes as observed in Block 3.[2]

Architectural artifacts from Block 3 were substantially lower in frequency, a statistic that could have several explanations. Although no definitive evidence of a cabin foundation was identified in Block 3, a section of stockade ditch that terminated near the center of the block was excavated. Stockade sections typically connected the walls of adjacent cabins to form the station enclosure. A cabin probably stood there as part of the station enclosure but was torn down sometime after the site was converted to a farmstead by the Frank family. Block 3 is between the Frank's stone house and the structure indicated by the cellar in Block 5. The area may have been used as a work area between the two structures or as an area where broken household goods were discarded.

Architectural and Construction-Related Artifacts

This category of artifacts is dominated by flat glass and nails, with small quantities of construction materials (such as brick, plaster, and mortar), other fasteners, such as brads and tacks, and parts of a door latch. The flat glass occurs in sufficient quantities from every excavation block to conclude that most of it is windowpane glass. A few fragments were probably once part of hand mirrors and are classified under the personal category. The stone Frank house was built with windows, while the log houses in Blocks 1 and 3 (and possibly 5) probably did not have paned windows originally—though later occupants likely added them. Windowpane thickness was measured for a sample of the flat glass to help estimate when windows were installed. Window thickness varied over time, according to how it was made and the size of the pane. Karl G. Roenke pioneered the development of a formula for dating window glass by its thickness, and I utilized that formula in my analysis. His measurements were in the English standard system. Estimating date by window thickness works best for nineteenth-century structures because the dominant means of producing windowpanes was the cylinder glass method, which results in a pane of fairly uniform thickness. The method is less useful for late eighteenth-century buildings, like the Frank house, because the dominant means of producing windowpanes was the crown glass method that resulted in panes of varying thickness. However, the fact that flat glass occurred all over the site suggests that windows were present in all of the identified buildings, and some limited conclusions can be drawn from a thickness analysis.[3]

I selected and measured a sample of 368 flat glass fragments with a pair of calipers. Flat glass frequencies varied from block to block. Block 1 had the highest number of fragments (1,748), followed by Block 2 (594), 3 (160), 4 (142), and 5 (98). The sample focused on the larger fragments in order to assess variations in the thickness of a given fragment. The fragments were largely uniform in thickness across the area of an individual fragment. For the entire sample, flat glass thickness ranged from 0.027 to 0.083 inches, with a median measurement of 0.045 inches and two modal values of 0.039 and 0.042 containing nearly equal frequencies. The highest frequency of fragments measured between 0.038 and 0.046 inches, representing 47 percent of the sample. A comparison of samples from each block resulted in similar median values, ranging from 0.042 to 0.047 inches. The fluctuations in glass thickness when viewed graphically are very similar from block to block and reflect flat glass that is quite thin compared to sites dating later in the nineteenth century. The Block 2 sample from the Frank house may be less suitable for this type of analysis because its windows were installed at the time the house was built and so would have had the thinner pane glass associated with the late eighteenth century. Thicker specimens found in Block 2 possibly represent glass replacement due to breakage. The other block samples, however, skew toward relatively thin glass that may indicate windowpane installation in the first few decades of the nineteenth century as part of a process of improving and upgrading the station's log buildings.[4]

Daniel Boone's Station presents an interesting case study regarding the study of nails and how their presence in an archaeological assemblage can be analyzed and interpreted. Nails had been largely ignored in archaeological analysis until research by Charles Faulkner, Amy Young, and Philip Carr at the University of Tennessee opened new avenues of inquiry about these ubiquitous artifacts. Virtually all research on nails focuses on nineteenth-century sites. Daniel Boone's Station predates but overlaps with the nineteenth century, making it suitable for analysis while simultaneously presenting challenges to applying the approach to earlier sites. Young's research focused on nineteenth-century house and dump sites, looking for differing patterns between the two and seeking to find evidence of deterioration in place, demolition, or other forms of building destruction. Daniel Boone's Station offers an interesting contrast to her examples. First, all but one of the excavation blocks exposed evidence of structures. The exception exposed a stockade section that may have utilized nails in its construction. Second, of the four buildings identified by excavation, one is of stone construction, two are early log with stone foundations, and the fourth is probably also one of the original log buildings on the site. Nail use in log construction is less than would be expected for a frame structure.

Settlers building a pioneer station did not usually intend to occupy the site for long, and the perilous conditions at the time sometimes meant that cabins were built without taking the time to cure the logs prior to construction. These "green logs" inevitably warped and bent as they dried in place. My pioneer-station research documented far more stations that were abandoned after a few years than examples that continued to be occupied long after the need for a defensive residence had passed. However, some settlers may have mitigated the warpage problem if it were feasible to do so. Daniel Boone and his settlers initially occupied the station in the winter of 1779 when they built "half-faced camps." The next spring, they built the station. The archival record is silent on this point, but it is plausible that Boone, knowing a good deal about log construction and wanting to stay in the location for an extended period, cut logs to cure over the winter so that he could build a house in the spring that would last longer than a temporary cabin. Granted, this is speculation. But the buildings survived to be used by a later generation. Boone's foresight may have made this conversion more feasible.

Nails that are associated with the historic occupation of the site include both handwrought and machine cut, which were most likely used in window and door framing, flooring, and perhaps some furniture. Since the dwellings revealed by excavation were either of log or of stone construction, the nail assemblage is not as large as it would have been if the buildings were all frame construction.

Table 13.2. Nail Statistics from Daniel Boone's Station

Wrought Nails				
2d pennyweight				
Head type	**Straight**	**Curved/Pulled**	**Clinched**	**Total**
Circular		1		1
Irregular	3	4		7
Recto-ovate	9	1	1	11
Rosehead	1			1
Subtotal	13	6	1	20
3d pennyweight				
Irregular	2	2		4
Recto-ovate	2	1		3
Rosehead		2		2
Subtotal	4	5		9
4d pennyweight				
Circular		1		1
Irregular	4			4
L-head		1		1
Recto-ovate	9	4	1	14
Rosehead	4	2		6
Subtotal	17	8	1	26

(continued)

Table 13.2. Nail Statistics from Daniel Boone's Station (continued)

Wrought Nails				
5d pennyweight				
Irregular	1	3	1	5
Recto-ovate	4	4	1	9
Rosehead	4	2		6
T-head	1			1
Subtotal	10	9	2	21
6d pennyweight				
Broken head		1		1
Circular, large			1	1
Irregular	3	3		6
L-head		1		1
Recto-ovate	5	3		8
Rosehead		2		2
Subtotal	8	10	1	19
7d pennyweight				
Expanded		2		2
Irregular	1	2		3
L-head		1		1
Recto-ovate	2	3	3	8
Rosehead			1	1
T-head		2		2
Undetermined			1	1
Subtotal	3	10	5	18
8d pennyweight				
Circular, off-center		1		1
Headless		2		2
Recto-ovate	2	3	2	7
Rosehead			1	1
T-head		2		2
Subtotal	2	8	3	13

Table 13.2. Nail Statistics from Daniel Boone's Station (continued)

		Wrought Nails		
		9d pennyweight		
Recto-ovate		1		1
10d pennyweight				
Recto-ovate			1	1
20d pennyweight				
Recto-ovate		1		1
Grand total	57	58	14	129
		Cut Nails		
		2d pennyweight		
Head type	Straight	Curved/Pulled	Clinched	Total
Expanded	2			2
L-head	4	1		5
Recto-ovate	102	10	1	113
T-head		1		1
Undetermined	1			1
Subtotal	109	12	1	122
		3d pennyweight		
Expanded	2			2
L-head	3			3
Recto-ovate	167	15	5	187
T-head		1		1
Undetermined		1		1
Subtotal	172	17	5	194
		4d pennyweight		
Circular, off-center		1		1
Headless	1			1
Irregular	2		1	3
L-head	6			6
Recto-ovate	85	22	1	108
T-head	1			1
Undetermined	2			2
Subtotal	97	23	2	122

(continued)

Table 13.2. Nail Statistics from Daniel Boone's Station (continued)

Cut Nails				
5d pennyweight				
Headless		1		1
Irregular	1			1
L-head	1	1		2
Recto-ovate	30	13	5	48
Subtotal	32	15	5	52
6d pennyweight				
Expanded			1	1
Headless	1	1		2
Irregular	1	1		2
L-head		2		2
Recto-ovate	67	33	13	113
T-head	1			1
Subtotal	70	37	14	121
7d pennyweight				
Expanded	1			1
Irregular		2		2
L-head	1		2	3
Recto-ovate	25	23	2	50
Subtotal	27	25	4	56
8d pennyweight				
Expanded	1			1
Headless		1	1	2
Irregular	1			1
L-head		1		1
Recto-ovate	17	12	5	34
Subtotal	19	14	6	39
9d pennyweight				
Headless	1	2		3
L-head	2	2		4
Recto-ovate	4	4	1	9
Subtotal	7	8	1	16

Table 13.2. Nail Statistics from Daniel Boone's Station (continued)

Cut Nails				
10d pennyweight				
L-head			1	1
Recto-ovate	2	4	2	8
Subtotal	2	4	3	9
12d pennyweight				
Recto-ovate			1	1
16d pennyweight				
Headless	1			1
Recto-ovate		1		1
Subtotal	1	1		2
Grand total	537	157	42	736

I classified the nails by their head type, pennyweight (length), and condition (straight, pulled, or clinched). I recorded nail fragments as cut or wrought and tabulated their frequency but did not record their head type. Conclusions drawn from the nail analysis, accordingly, refer only to complete nails. Of the 1,719 nails and nail fragments recovered from the excavations, 148 are wrought, while the remaining 1,571 are cut nails. Complete wrought nails account for 129 specimens; 19 fragments were excluded from detailed analysis. Complete cut nails number 735 specimens, or 47 percent of the total cut nail assemblage. Cut nails generally were more poorly preserved than their wrought counterparts. The corrosion rate is high, and many of the cut nail fragments are small pieces from the shaft. Their poorer preservation is in part due to the way they were made. Early machine-cut nails were sliced from the ends of nail sheets, resulting in a shaft that was cut across the grain of the metal. This method produced a weaker nail that was more likely to break.

Nevertheless, the invention of a machine that could produce large quantities of cut nails ushered in a remarkable transition from 1790 to 1830, when cut nails gradually overtook the market and wrought nails became much less common. The occupation of Boone's Station straddled this period beginning in 1779, when wrought nails were the predominant form available, to the early nineteenth century, when cut nails began to predominate. The Frank house builder would have had access to both wrought and early cut nails for installing doors, windows, flooring, and interior framing.[5]

Cut nails were far more numerous than wrought nails at the site, constituting 86 percent of the nail assemblage. Both types of nails were found in every excavation block. Wrought nails were fairly evenly distributed among the excavation blocks, ranging from 14 and 15 percent of the total number of wrought nails in Blocks 4 and 5, respectively, to 22 percent in Blocks 1 and 2. Interestingly, wrought nails in Block 3—where no building foundations were found, but a stockade ditch occurred—accounted for 26 percent of the total number of wrought nails. Only 11 percent of the cut nails were recovered from Block 3. Cut nails were recovered in the highest frequency from Block 2, where the Frank stone house stood, amounting to 53 percent of the cut nail assemblage. The remainder of the cut nails were recovered from Blocks 1, 4, 3, and 5, in order of high to low frequency. The frequency of cut nails from Block 1 was quite high considering that the building was of log construction.

Nailhead types for wrought nails include, in order of frequency from high to low, recto-ovate, irregular, rosehead, T-head, circular, L-head, and expanded. The first three types account for 86 percent of the intact wrought nails. All three types are versatile nails that can be used in many contexts. Recto-ovate heads dominate the nail assemblage regardless of how a nail was produced. Rosehead nails are much more likely to be wrought rather than cut. Irregular nailheads probably occurred due to deformations that were made as the nail was being driven into wood. The less common nailhead forms (T-head, circular, L-head, and expanded) could have been used in contexts such as flooring or paneling that required that the nails be driven flush with or countersunk into the wood.

Cut nailhead types mirrored wrought nails in variety but were dominated by the recto-ovate type. The order from next highest to lowest frequency is L-head, headless, irregular, expanded, T-head, circular, and rosehead.

The size, or pennyweight, of a nail also offers some hints about how it was used. An anonymous writer for the *American Architect and Building News* wrote, "The sizes of nails used for specific purposes is largely a matter of judgment on the part of the builder, but the common custom is to use four-penny nails for shingling and slating, six-penny for clapboarding, sixes and eights for finishing, eights and nines for flooring, nines and tens for boarding, and forty-penny and upwards for framing." The wrought nails range in pennyweight from 2d to 20d, with most nails measuring 2d to 8d in nearly equal quantities. The larger nails (9d, 10d, and 20d) only numbered four in total. Among the cut nails, the pennyweights range from 2d to 16d, with most nails falling in the 2d to 8d range. The highest frequencies of nails measure 2d, 3d, 4d, and 6d. Since log structures do not require nails for the house walls, nail use would have been for doors, windows, possibly flooring (in lieu of pegging), and roofing. Similar nail usage is likely for the Frank stone house, along with some internal framing for stairs to the second floor or partitions between rooms.[6]

The condition of the nail can offer insights on whether the building of which it was a part was dismantled, was burned, or simply fell down. The distribution of nails in an archaeological site is often referred to as "nail rain." A distribution dominated by straight, unaltered nails may indicate a building that simply fell and disintegrated over time. If the nails show evidence of having been subjected to extreme heat, the building may have burned. Pulled or curved nails may be an indicator of a building that was dismantled. Clinched nails generally are associated with a functional context, such as window or door frames. Wrought nails for the site as a whole are unaltered or pulled in nearly equivalent frequencies with many fewer clinched nails. Unaltered nails account for 45 percent, while pulled nails form 44 percent of the wrought nail assemblage. The proportion of unaltered cut nails compared to pulled nails is 74 to 20 percent. Clinched nails are uncommon, regardless of nail type or size. Of particular note in Block 2, where the Frank stone house stood, the sediments that filled the cellar contained large quantities of ash, and many of the artifacts show evidence of having been burned. The archaeological evidence clearly indicates that the house caught fire and the stories likely collapsed into the cellar, where they were consumed by fire. This left a thick ash layer with a high density of artifacts.[7]

Construction materials like brick fragments, mortar, and plaster were recovered in small quantities. Brick fragments were recovered from all excavation blocks. Blocks 1 and 2 contained the highest frequencies of brick, with most of the fragments coming from Block 2 (the Frank house cellar). A single larger fragment is measurable; it is 3.9 inches wide by 2 inches thick. Bricks may have been used inside the structures to form the chimney hearth. No evidence of a brick chimney was associated with the log houses in Blocks 1 and 4. The base of the chimney in Block 1 was built of dry-laid stone. The Frank house chimney was not excavated, but most stone houses of the time had chimneys also made of stone. Mortar and plaster fragments were recovered from Blocks 1 and 2 with most of the fragments coming from the Frank house cellar. The fragments were usually too small to distinguish between mortar and plaster. Some of the fragments have smoothed surfaces and are generally considered to be from an interior plastered wall.

Munitions

The Boone's Station assemblage contains several artifacts related to muzzle-loading firearms. Its establishment during the Revolutionary War, when Kentucky was involved in armed conflict with British-backed Native American tribes, and the need for hunting to provide wild meat for the table meant that most households owned at least one gun. Daniel Boone was well known as a commercial hunter who owned several guns. His fellow settlers were also armed, and gun ownership remained common after the war for sport hunting and the eradication of pests that threatened crops.

Artifacts included under this category include gunflints, lead bullets, receptacles for holding gunpowder or shot, and a rifling tool. The artifacts were recovered only from Blocks 1 and 2. Guns used during the late eighteenth century were either smoothbore or rifled firearms. A musket barrel has a smooth interior wall, while a rifle barrel has grooves cut into the interior wall. There were many types of muskets and rifles in use during the Revolutionary War and afterward.

The American colonies were prevented by English law from developing a gun manufacturing industry and therefore received substandard weapons from England that were often damaged, surplus, or obsolete. With the onset of war, the colonists raided local arsenals and took guns from Loyalists, and they then began local production that seldom followed consistent specifications. "The result was a broad mixture of doglocks, fowlers, rifles, muskets, trade or commercial guns, as well as shiploads of European castoffs purchased through independent agents." Fowlers were commonly used by civilians for hunting. Men who served in county militias during the war had to provide their own firearm, and fowlers fitted the bill.[8]

Regardless of the type of gun, all employed lead balls as projectiles, gunflints to produce a spark, and gunpowder ignited by a spark to propel the ball. The diameter (or caliber) of the lead ball is related to the diameter of the barrel. Muskets tended to use larger caliber lead balls, often combined with smaller caliber balls and gunpowder in a paper wrapper to form a combo known as a buck-and-ball load, while rifles generally used a single lead ball

Arms-related artifacts from Boone's Station (top row: rifling button, brass shot pouch snake; bottom row: French honey gunflint, antler powder horn neck fragment).

and a cloth patch that was wrapped around the ball so that it fitted snugly in the barrel when a ramrod was used to push it down the length of the barrel.

At least two gunflints are represented, including a French honey flint (which shows evidence of hard use) and two flakes from a flint made of English Brandon chert. Both flints were recovered from Block 1; the French honey flint was recovered from a level below the plow zone, while the English Brandon flint flakes came from the plow zone in an adjoining excavation unit. They were found in front of and adjacent to the chimney hearth on the west wall of the house. French honey gunflints were imported by the thousands and were the most commonly available type in the American colonies during the Revolutionary War. English gunflints made from Brandon flint quarried from the cliffs of Dover became dominant after 1790, although they were available earlier. The Brandon flint flakes may have resulted from resharpening of the flint after repeated use caused its edge to dull. The stratigraphic position of the French honey flint may indicate it was used by an earlier occupant, possibly while the station was in use as a defensive site. The English flint probably dates slightly later.[9]

Four lead bullets were recovered from both Blocks 1 and 2. The two bullets from Block 1 were from the same unit north of the hearth along the west wall of the cabin. A .32 caliber bullet was recovered from the plow zone. It has a flattened area where the casting sprue (excess lead in the bullet mold inlet channel) was trimmed away and does not appear to have been fired. It may have been intended for use in a buck-and-ball load shot from a smoothbore musket. The other bullet is .50 caliber and slightly distorted; it was recovered from below the plow zone. It may have been fired and hit a soft target. It was probably used in a rifle. Both smoothbore and rifled firearms used lead bullets and gunpowder to propel the bullet. A rifling button (a tube made of nonferrous metal with exterior facets used to cut the grooves into the interior of a barrel) was recovered from a level below the plow zone in the same unit that contained the chimney hearth. This tool confirms that a rifle was in use in the earlier years of the station occupation and that a gunsmith lived at the site, presumably in the cabin in Block 1. Daniel Boone was capable of some gun repair such as restocking barrels and repairing locks and barrels, which he demonstrated when he was a captive in 1778. Other men with gunsmithing skills may have lived at the site as well, but the archival record is mute on that possibility. Also recovered from Block 1 was a neck fragment from a powder horn made of antler. It is a turned cylinder with interior threads and exterior bands. The spout is not present and would have been a separate piece inserted into the neck of the powder horn.[10]

The cellar fill of the stone house built by the Franks in the early 1790s yielded one bullet and a brass closure tube called a shot snake that was probably once part of a shot pouch or powder flask. A second bullet was found in a unit adjacent to, but outside of, the stone foundation wall of the cellar. The two bullets are both small caliber. One pitted example is approximately .36 or .37 caliber, while the other ball is flattened and had obviously been shot. Both would have been suitable for use in a buck-and-ball load. The shot snake and the pitted bullet were both recovered from a thick layer of ash below a zone of limestone rubble. The brass tube is flattened and measures about two inches in length and an inch in diameter. One end is plain with a folded rim. The other end has a slotted flat lip with a channel cut into it. This end of the closure probably was attached to the pouch itself and may have had an interior spring mechanism that opened and closed the tube so that the chamber (the opposite end being covered with a thumb) filled with the appropriate amount of shot. Given the fairly large (one-inch diameter) of the tube, I interpreted this artifact as part of a shot pouch rather than a powder flask, since shot has larger particles than powder has.

Clothing, Accessory, and Personal Artifacts

Clothing, accessories, and other personal artifacts from Boone's Station reflect the decades-long occupation of the site by various families, their types of garments, and specific personal habits they had. Most of the 141 artifacts in this category are fasteners and accessories for clothing. Sixteen buckles, one brass aglet, sixty-nine buttons or button fragments, an iron snap, an iron corset loop, three eyes and two hooks from hook/eye fasteners, two suspender/overall fasteners, a parasol stretcher or rib, and jewelry constitute the clothing and accessories category. Included within the personal category are sewing equipment, glass from hand mirrors, marbles, a mouth harp, folding knife parts, and coinage.

Buckles

Buckles were first used to fasten clothing elements such as shoes, breeches, stocks, hats, girdles, and collars in the seventeenth century. They remained the most common form of fastener until the late eighteenth century when buttons, ribbons, and shoestrings superseded most of their functions—except for belt buckles. Changes in fashion also contributed to the demise of buckles. An example is the shift from knee breeches, which used buckles to tighten the knee strap, to long pants (often tucked into high boots) that did not need a buckle. Buckles had other uses as well, including harness, arms-related accessories like cartridge boxes, and other items that were not clothing but were worn on the body. All but one of the twenty-one buckles recovered from the site are assumed to be related to clothing or accessories rather than harness or other functions because most of them were recovered from residential contexts. However, harness buckles vary in size, and distinguishing the smaller ones from similarly sized buckles used for clothing or accessories is difficult.

Every buckle from the station site dates after 1779, and the seven examples from Block 2 date after c. 1792–1795. Every excavation block yielded at least one buckle. Three buckles, one from a shoe, one frame fragment, and one rectangular frame with a separate tube enclosing one side, were located by a metal detector. One additional buckle is classified as a harness buckle because of its size and is described under equine and agricultural artifacts.

Buckles from Boone's Station (first row: small frame buckles, fourth from left has center tongue attachment; second row: large rectangular buckles; third row: large rectangular buckle and shoe buckle).

The shoe buckle was recovered from a metal detector target near or along the north wall of the station. Only half of the buckle frame is preserved. Using Merry Abbitt's typology for shoe buckles, the Boone Station example falls within Type 5: openwork high copper alloy buckles. The frame design consists of three parallel narrow bars that are connected by a perpendicular bar in the middle of each side and by a diagonal bar at the corners. The exterior of the buckle frame has decorative stamping along the inner and outer bands and at the cross bars. The buckle was probably square in shape, measuring two and one-half inches per side. No evidence of the fastening mechanism that held the buckle in place on the shoe remains. Notably, the holes holding the pin terminal are also lacking, but this might be due to where the frame broke in half. Owing to its fragmentary state, dating the buckle is difficult, but it probably is late eighteenth century.[11]

Determining the function of individual buckles other than shoe buckles based on their characteristics is more difficult because of both the way the fastening mechanism was made and the lack of analytical studies. Unlike eighteenth-century examples that generally had a two-pronged tongue, all the intact buckles from the station were held in place by a narrow bar forming the tongue that attached to either the short or long axis of a rectangular frame or along the straight side of several round-cornered square frames. Only one example has the tongue attached to a bar that extends across the center of the frame. These buckles essentially have the same form as in use today. Excepting the shoe buckle, all the buckles are made of iron or an iron alloy and were not elaborate, suggesting that their use was entirely utilitarian and practical, with no intent to signal high social class or elaborate dress.

Twelve buckles are intact, retaining the entire frame and the tongue. Five of these buckles have fairly large rectangular frames, ranging from 1.36 (34.5 mm) to 1.67 inches (42.4 mm) in length and 1 (25.4 mm) to 1.35 inches (34.3 mm) in width. The tongue is attached on the longer side of the frame in four examples. A single example shows the tongue attached on the short side. A nearly square example has a tongue attached on the slightly longer side but also has a separate rolled tube encircling the side opposite the tongue. The roll moved freely around the frame and facilitated the movement of a strap, most likely of leather, as the wearer tightened or loosened to adjust the length. These buckles could have been used on a belt at the waist (e.g., to hold a coat or hunting shirt closed) or for adjusting a leather strap in other contexts such as cartridge boxes for carrying paper-wrapped buck-and-ball loads used in muskets, rifle straps, holsters, and hunting bags. Two of the buckles were recovered from Block 1 while single examples were recovered from Blocks 3, 4, and 5.

Eight smaller buckles measure 1.4 inches (35.6 mm) or less in length or width. They are square or slightly rectangular with rounded corners on two sides. All but two have a tongue on the straight side of the buckle; the exceptions have a tongue attached to a bar running across the center of the buckle. The placement of the tongue dictates how the buckle was placed on the strap it fastened. All the small buckles would have been placed so that the rounded corners would be visible on the buckled garment or strap. Small buckles were used to hold a stock or neckcloth in place and to tighten a strap on the knee cuff of breeches. They may also have fastened the narrow straps used on saddlebags, knapsacks, and spurs. The small buckles were recovered from Blocks 1, 2, and 3.[12]

Clothing Fasteners

Buttons are ubiquitous and common artifacts on residential sites from any era. Numerous buttons, totaling seventy intact and fragmentary examples, were recovered from the excavations. Diagnostic characteristics date the majority of the buttons to the late eighteenth century and early nineteenth century—confirming the occupation span of the site buttressed by the documentary evidence and other chronological indicators of material culture. I considered the variation in the materials composing the buttons, their size, and other features to draw conclusions on the type of clothing they fastened and who wore the garments. Buttons were used mostly on men's clothing in the late eighteenth and early nineteenth centuries. Women's clothing utilized ties, hooks and eyes, straight pins, and lacings to hold the garment to the body—although riding habits designed similarly to men's had buttons. Buttons increased in use for women's clothing as fashions changed during the nineteenth century, but they did not become ubiquitous on female attire until later in the century. Most of the buttons recovered from the site were probably sewn to men's garments.

The families that occupied Boone's Station varied in status, occupation, and class, and their clothing reflected these differences. Daniel Boone, for example, was a commercial hunter and surveyor who spent much of his time away from home in the woods, canebrakes, and other wild Kentucky settings. His clothing was utilitarian and sturdy, befitting the practical necessities for a life spent outdoors. The hallmark of the hunter was the hunting shirt: a garment that opened down the front, had fringe decoration, and was held shut with a belt or sash. Generally made of linen or other sturdy cloth, the hunting shirt was paired with a cloth breechclout or buckskin breeches and leggings that laced around the lower legs and ended about midthigh. Stockings provided additional warmth beneath the leggings. Footwear might be moccasins, shoes with buckles or ties, or harder soled shoe packs cut from half-dressed hides. Daniel Boone preferred a brimmed hat for headgear; others wore fur caps (including the iconic coonskin), head kerchiefs, tricorn hats, or other head coverings fashioned from available materials. An engraving by James O. Lewis based on artist Chester Harding's full-length painting of Boone shows him dressed in a near knee-length coat that wrapped across the body and was held in place by a buckled belt that also secured a knife. The coat has a stand-up collar and an attached capelet. It covered a collared shirt. His lower garment is probably leggings, and he has moccasins on his feet. He holds a narrow-brimmed hat and a flintlock rifle. Another depiction of Boone adapted by Alonzo Chappel from Chester Harding's painting shows a bearskin-trimmed coat covering a shirt that appears to have a stock tied at the neck. This image includes a fur cap, possibly made from raccoon fur, which is inaccurate, according to his son Nathan, who said Boone "despised" such caps and "always had a hat."[13]

When Boone attended the Virginia General Assembly, he wore a "common jeans suit" with beaded buckskin leggings. Jeans fabric was a linen and cotton blend that was a variety of fustian (a sturdy cloth made in England and Europe). Jeans fabric was twilled so that the finished cloth weave had a diagonal appearance. The "common jeans suit" included a pair of knee breeches, a long-sleeved shirt, a closely fitted, sleeveless waistcoat that covered the hips and buttoned below the waist, and a long coat with sleeves. Waistcoats had buttons that closed the front of the garment and decorative buttons on the lower sections. Coats had slightly larger buttons to close the front—as well as buttons at the vents in the back, at the pockets, and on the sleeves. Like the waistcoat, some of the buttons were simply included for decoration. Buttons featured prominently on breeches too, fastening the "fall," a flap of fabric at the waist that required from two to five buttons to hold it securely. The flap, when unbuttoned, allowed the wearer to urinate or disrobe. Either buttons or buckles were used to fasten the knee cuff.[14]

Other men who lived at Boone's Station were farmers and wore the appropriate attire. One probable resident, Harvey Bledsoe, likely owned more formal attire, in keeping with his status as a businessman and merchant. The Franks, the Hendleys, and Harvey Bledsoe owned enslaved persons and had to provide clothing for them to wear as they worked in the fields, barnyard, garden, and house. The need for practical, utilitarian clothing worn daily is reflected in the predominance of simple, mostly plain buttons recovered from the excavations. The sixty-eight buttons and button fragments recovered from the excavations are made from a variety of materials, including bone, brass, iron, shell, white metal or other nonferrous metal, pewter, porcelain, glass, and celluloid or plastic. The single celluloid or plastic button, as well as the porcelain button, were probably lost on the site at a much later date after the site was converted to agricultural use. The buttons represent several different methods of production, ranging from buttons with drilled holes to those featuring eyelets soldered or otherwise attached to the back. Two-piece buttons also were found.

Buttons were often reused on other garments and may be found in archaeological contexts that date later than the period in which the button was manufactured. At Boone's Station, all the buttons were deposited at the site no earlier than 1779, even though they may have been manufactured earlier and brought

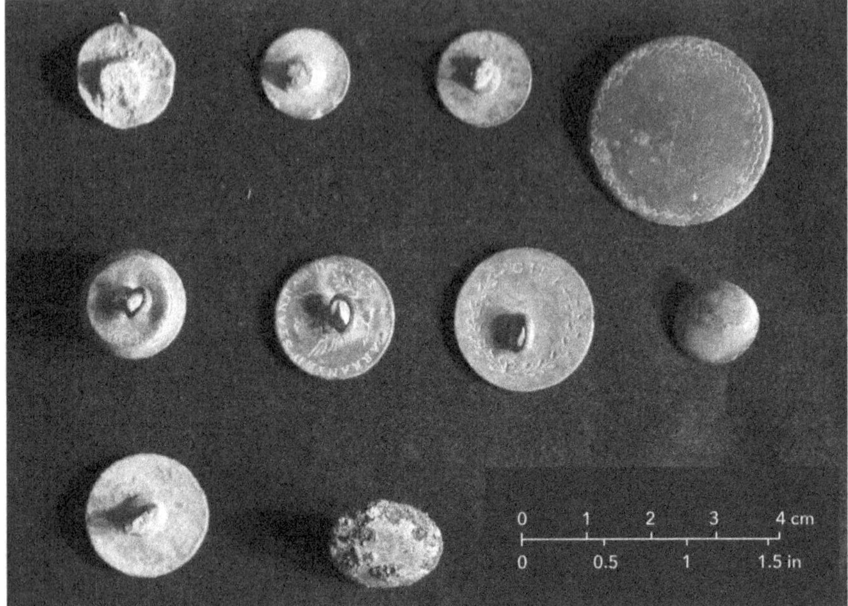

Metal buttons from Boone's Station (top row, left to right: Type A pewter button, two Type D buttons, large Type D button with zigzag decoration; middle row, left to right: brass Type F button, brass Type G button marked WARRANTED STANDARD GILT with spread eagle; brass Type G with laurel wreath; slightly domed brass Type G button; bottom row, left to right: white metal Type D button, degraded Type C or D button).

to the site attached to clothing. Olsen types identified in the Boone's Station assemblage include two Type A (1700–1765), one Type C (1760–1790), fifteen Type D (1760–1785), one Type F (1812–1830), twelve Type G (1785–1800), one Type H (1812–1830), and two Type I (1830 to present).[15]

The Type A buttons are the earliest datable buttons in the assemblage. An intact example was recovered from the floor of the cellar beneath the Frank house in Block 2. It was roughly cast as one piece, including the eyelet, from a nonferrous metal that is probably pewter. The shank is diamond-shaped. Its seventeen-millimeter diameter places it in White's medium-sized button category. This type of button was typically sewed to men's waistcoats or breeches. Another molded pewter button retains the base of the shank but is missing the eye, which may have broken or sheared off. Slightly smaller at fifteen millimeters in diameter, the smaller button may have been sewn to either a waistcoat or breeches. It also was recovered from the cellar of the Frank house in Block 2 but at a higher level in the fill.

Olsen's terminal date of 1765 suggests that the buttons were over ten years old when they were brought to the site. Carolyn White's research on eighteenth-century buttons associates mold-cast pewter buttons with people of lower socioeconomic means. The two buttons may have been brought to the site as part of old pieces of clothing or reused on a newer garment. Inexpensive buttons may have been common on clothing for the enslaved. The Frank family held ten people in servitude. One or more of them may have worked and/or lived in the cellar where the buttons were lost.[16]

The Type C button was recovered from a plow zone context next to, but outside of, the house cellar and could have been lost any time after 1779 but more likely was lost after 1790. It is a white metal button with the remnants of an iron eyelet soldered to the button face. Its diameter of fourteen millimeters places it in the smaller end of the medium-size range. It may have been attached to a sleeve, perhaps as part of a pair of linked buttons. The range of its manufacturing date, and its proximity to the Frank house foundation, suggests that it, too, was brought to the site as part of an older garment, possibly by the Frank family.

The Type D category contains the greatest frequency of buttons from the site. Fifteen buttons, ranging in diameter from thirteen to twenty-eight millimeters, were recovered from all five excavation blocks. This button type features a wire eyelet that was affixed to the button face by one of two methods. Two of the buttons from Blocks 4 and 5 have eyelets that were inserted in a small piece of metal that was then soldered to the button back. The drawback to this method of attachment is that the metal holding the eyelet can become detached from the button face, as occurred to the two specimens from the site. Another variation features a wire eyelet set into a metal cone that was molded as part of the button face. This method was used to make most of the Type D buttons. Similarly, the disadvantage to this method of attachment is that the eyelet can detach from the metal cone. Five of the specimens are missing the eyelets. The remaining eight Type D buttons are intact. Both variations date to the same period: 1760–1785. All but four of the Type D buttons are made from white metal or a similar alloy; the exceptions are brass. One of the brass buttons has the term LONDON SUPERFINE on the back, indicating it was made in London, England.

The size range of the Type D buttons falls within Carolyn White's medium and large categories. Of the fifteen measurable buttons, nine are medium

Table 13.3. Characteristics of Type D Buttons from Boone's Station

Context	Diameter (mm)	Eyelet Present	Gilt	Plated	London Superfine	Laurel Wreath / Other Modification	Remnant Silverplating
Block 1	13 (medium)	no	no	no	yes	no	no
Block 1	15 (medium)	yes	no	no	no	no	no
Block 1	c. 25.4 (large)	yes	no	no	no	no	no
Block 1	14 (medium)	yes	no	no	no	no	no
Block 1	18 (medium)	no	no	no	no	no	no
Block 1	17 (medium)	yes	no	no	no	no	no
Block 2	13 (medium)	yes	no	no	no	no	no
Block 2	21 (large)	no	no	no	no	no	no
Block 3	15 (medium)	yes	no	no	no	no	no
Block 3	28 (large)	no	no	no	no	zigzag motif on front	no
Block 4	Eyelet only	yes	no	no	no	no	no
Block 4	16 (medium)	no	no	no	no	no	no
Block 5	Eyelet only	yes	no	no	no	no	no
Block 5	14 (medium)	yes	no	no	no	no	no
Block 5	21 (large)	yes	no	no	no	no	no

sized, measuring from thirteen to eighteen millimeters in diameter. Four of the buttons are within the size range commonly associated with waistcoats and breeches, while five smaller buttons may have been attached to sleeves. Four buttons are large, measuring from twenty-one to twenty-eight millimeters in diameter. These buttons probably were attached to coats. The largest coat button has a decorative stamped zigzag edge on its face.

A single button is a two-piece, pressed, dome-shaped button, similar to Olsen's Type F, and dated between 1812 and 1830. The brass eye is soldered to the back of the button, and the button face is pressed into a spherical shape commonly referred to as a "bullet button" and used on military uniforms during the War of 1812 and afterward. It was recovered as a metal detection target in an area of the site that was not excavated but was probably once occupied by a cabin. This button may be the only button from the site that was sewn to a military uniform although none of the known site occupants fought in the War of 1812. However, the button could have been sewn to a militia uniform, as all able-bodied adult men were required to serve in the county militia. Fayette County was part of the Third Brigade. Boone's Station was part of the Eighth Regiment. Site occupants after 1812 who would have been militia members include John Hendley and probably Harvey Bledsoe.[17]

Olsen's Type G buttons constitute the second most numerous category. I classified thirteen brass buttons as Type G because the eyelet was soldered directly to the brass button back without being inserted into a metal foot. An additional button made of nonferrous metal that is missing its eye and has no remnant solder on the back may also be a Type G button. Eight of the buttons are missing the eye, but the method of attachment can still be discerned by the remnant of solder on the button back. This type dates between 1785 and 1800, well within the range of occupation at the site. The Type G buttons have more decorative elements and back stamps than any other category. Two of the buttons retain remnants of silver plating, and both have a laurel wreath motif and the word "PLATED" on the back. One of these buttons also has a stamped spread-eagle motif on the back. Another large button has a laurel wreath stamped on the back. One button is stamped WARRANTED STANDARD GILT, indicating that it was plated to resemble a gold button; its large size suggests that it was sewn to a coat.

The size of the Type G buttons ranges from ten to twenty-four millimeters, conforming to White's small, medium, and large categories. The size range is slightly smaller than the Type D buttons, but the median size is the

Table 13.4. Characteristics of Type G Buttons from Boone's Station

Context	Diameter (mm)	Eyelet Present	Stamped GILT	Stamped Warranted Standard Gilt	Stamped Plated	Stamped Motif / Other Modification	Remnant Silver-Plated Face
Block 1	14 (medium)	no	no	no	no	no	no
Block 1	13 (medium)	no	no	no	no	no	no
Block 1	10 (small)	yes	no	no	no	raised floral motif; raised rim	no
Block 1	13 (medium)	yes	no	no	no	slightly domed	yes
Block 1	15 (medium)	no	no	no	no	laurel wreath	yes
Block 1	17 (medium)	no	no	no	yes	laurel wreath	no
Block 2	19 (large)	no	no	no	no	laurel wreath on back	no
Block 3	15 (medium)	no	no	no	no	no	no
Block 4	12 (medium)	no	no	no	no	dots/stars on face; illegible letters on back	no
Block 4	24 (large; bent and pitted)	no	no	no	no	no	no
Block 5	19 (large)	yes	no	yes	yes	laurel wreath / eagle motif on back	no
Block 5	20 (large)	yes	no	no	no	slightly domed	no
Block 5	22 (large)	yes	yes	no	no	laurel wreath on back	no
Block 5	20 (large)	no	no	no	no	dots on back	no

same for both; half of the buttons in each category are fifteen millimeters or smaller. Both types of buttons were probably sewn to similar garments.

A single button classified as Olsen's Type I is a two-part silver-plated example to which a brass eye is soldered to the back. This type was made from 1830 and for many decades afterward. The button was found in the cellar of the Frank house in Block 2 and has burned material adhering to it. Its diameter of eighteen millimeters places it in the high end of the medium-size range. It is a suitable size for a waistcoat or a pair of breeches. Another two-piece button that has a slightly concave, possibly brass face affixed to an iron back and a brass eye is probably also a Type I button. It was recovered from Block 1. Its diameter of seventeen millimeters suggests that it was used on a waistcoat or a pair of breeches. A brass button face that has detached from its back and been crushed into a distorted shape may also be a Type I button. It is larger than the other Type I buttons at approximately 0.8 inch and may have been sewn to a coat.

Other metal buttons include three four-holed, sew-through iron buttons measuring thirteen, eighteen, and nineteen millimeters, and two examples of a two-part stamped metal button measuring fourteen millimeters in diameter. The sew-through iron buttons were probably sewn to work garments. Both stamped metal buttons are made from an iron alloy and are missing the shank. The better-preserved example has a thin metal button cover that is crimped over a button core. The button core has a central hole where a shank was once attached. All three of the sew-through buttons, and one of the stamped metal–covered buttons, were recovered from the Frank house in Block 2. The other stamped metal–covered button was found in Block 1.

Eighteen buttons or button fragments are made of animal bone. All but three are sew-through buttons; the exceptions are a fragment and two complete buttons that functioned as the base for a covered button. The single central hole is a product of button manufacture and is not functional. The button served as a mold and base for the fabric cover. A thread shank was used to sew the button to the garment. The number of holes in the sew-through buttons varies from four to five. Five-holed buttons also have a nonfunctional central hole where the button blank was held in place by one of three points on a rotating tool that cut the circular blank from cow shinbones. Of the ten intact and fragmentary buttons that can be analyzed for the number of holes, seven have five holes and three have four holes. All the four- and five-holed buttons have a recessed center within which the holes are drilled. One

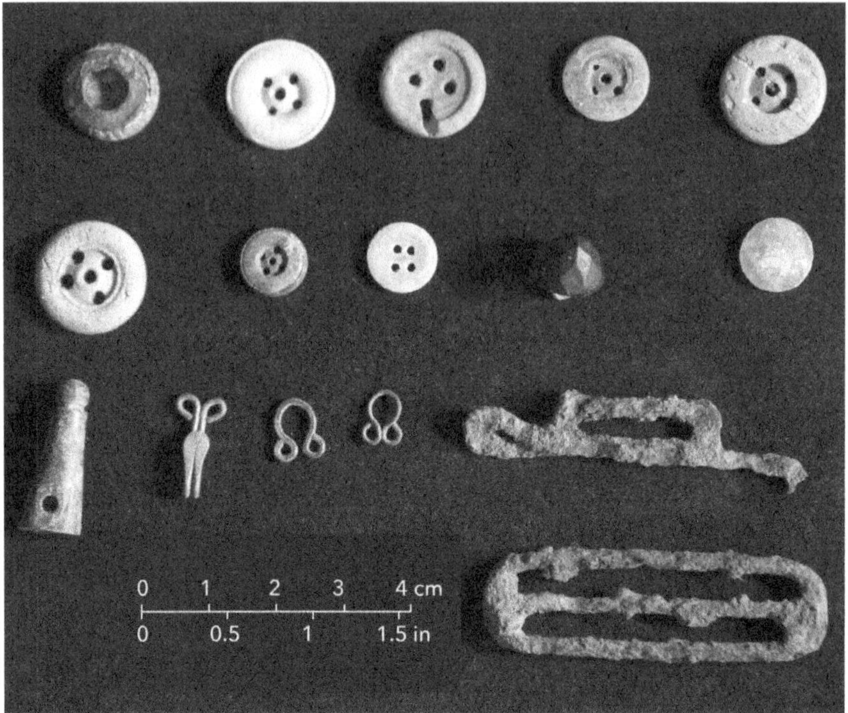

Bone buttons and other clothing fasteners from Boone's Station (top row, left to right: two-part iron button, five-holed bone button, four-holed bone button, incompletely drilled bone button, five-holed bone button; middle row, left to right: two five-holed bone buttons, four-holed shell button, faceted black glass button with eyelet, possible linked glass button missing attachment; bottom row, left to right: brass aglet, hook and two eyes, two iron overall fasteners).

example is a small button in which the holes are incompletely drilled, creating a button that was intended to be five-holed but one of the sew-through holes is missing. The buttons range in diameter from ten to twenty-two millimeters for eight measurable buttons. Four of the eight measure between fifteen and seventeen millimeters, placing them in the medium-size category used on waistcoats, breeches, and sleeves. A button fragment that measured no larger than twenty-two millimeters was probably sewn to a work coat. Bone buttons were less expensive to produce and were used on men's work garments and underwear in the eighteenth century. They also were used on women's garments, particularly undergarments, as button use became more common for women's clothing in the nineteenth century.[18]

Table 13.5. Characteristics of Bone Buttons from Boone's Station

Context	Condition	Number of holes	Diameter (mm)	Recessed Center
Block 1	fragment	5	not measured	yes
Block 1	fragment	indeterminate	not measured	yes
Block 1	complete	4	15	yes
Block 1	covered button base fragment	indeterminate	not measured	no
Block 1	complete	5	15	yes
Block 1	complete	5	10	yes
Block 1	complete	5	17	yes
Block 1	fragment	5	not measured	slight
Block 2	complete	5	16	yes
Block 2	fragments, burned (2)	indeterminate	not measured	yes
Block 2	fragments (2)	indeterminate	not measured	yes
Block 2	fragment	indeterminate	<22	yes
Block 2	complete (incompletely drilled)	5	12	yes
Block 2	complete	4	16	yes
Block 2	fragment	indeterminate	not measured	yes
Block 3	fragment	indeterminate	not measured	yes

Two shell and two glass buttons were recovered from Blocks 2 and 3. The two shell sew-through buttons are four-holed and small, measuring only ten millimeters in diameter. Shell buttons were made from mother-of-pearl and were expensive in the eighteenth century because each shell produced only a small quantity of usable material. Neither button has any decorative design. They probably date in the later years of the site's occupation and may have been lost even later when the site was cultivated.

The two glass buttons were recovered from Blocks 2 and 3. The button from Block 2 is a cone-shaped, faceted button made of black glass with a brass eye set into a metal base. Its diameter is eleven millimeters. It is very similar to dress buttons found on women's wear. Its location within the cellar of the Frank stone house dates it after the construction of the house in the early 1790s. It is likely from the last years that the house was occupied. The other glass button is a small slightly domed button measuring eleven millimeters and lacking an eye or other form of attachment. It may have been inserted into a setting that held the method of attachment. Glass paste buttons set into metal settings were often part of linked sleeve buttons. The glass is translucent, and the button face is smooth. It was recovered from the plow zone of a unit in Block 3 that was adjacent to Feature 4 in an area that was outside the station enclosure. It may have been lost after the station stockade was dismantled and the area around the cabins was used as a house yard.[19]

Other clothing fasteners include five examples of the metal hook and eye combination that was often used to hold garments closed in an edge-to-edge fashion. They were used on both women's and men's garments. Hooks and eyes were often used in pairs, but a hook could also be used singly with a thread eye. Three eyes and two hooks were recovered from Blocks 1 and 2. The eyes share a common form of a circular loop that terminates in two small loops that anchored the thread used to sew the eye onto the fabric. Two examples have small loops that close completely, while the other eye has loops that do not close. One of the eyes is slightly larger than the other two. The two hooks also share a similar basic shape, formed by wire bent into a very narrow loop that was folded over to form the hook. The terminus of the hook is flattened in one example. The two small loops, used to sew the hook onto the fabric, close in one example and are not closed in the other. Both hooks are longer than modern machine-made hooks and eyes.[20]

A single aglet was recovered from Block 1. An aglet is a cone that is attached to the end of a lacing or string to prevent it from unraveling. An aglet-tipped lacing was easier to thread through eyelets on clothing. The Boone Station example is made of a copper alloy and has two holes near the open end of the aglet where small iron rivets could be inserted to hold the aglet onto the lacing or where it could be sewn on. The end of the aglet is finished with a round ball.[21]

Two iron artifacts may have been used to adjust the straps of suspenders or overalls. Both artifacts were recovered from a building context, in Blocks 1 and 2, respectively. Overalls and suspenders both have their origins in the eighteenth century. The Boone Station examples are two inches (fifty-one millimeters) wide and are more likely to be part of overalls rather than suspenders. One of the artifacts is an elongated oval with a central parallel bar; a fabric strap could be threaded over and under the bars to allow the strap to be adjusted. The other artifact once had an elongated oval shape with an open rectangular section along one side where a fabric strap could be threaded through.

Jewelry from Boone's Station (top row, left to right: blue-green oval bead, blue faceted bead, two translucent faceted beads; bottom row, left to right: turquoise brilliant cut paste glass stone, gold paste glass stone with molded facets).

Jewelry

Several artifacts associated with jewelry were recovered from Blocks 1, 2, 3, and 4. Four glass beads and two gemstones made of gold and turquoise paste glass were recovered from Blocks 1, 2, and 3. The Block 1 specimens include two blue glass beads. One of the beads is a faceted cylinder measuring 0.17 inch (4 millimeters) in length and 0.23 inch (6 millimeters) in diameter. The other bead is an oval blue-green glass bead that has an abraded surface and measures 0.5 inch (13 millimeters) in length. A translucent, faceted glass bead measuring 0.2 inch (5 millimeters) in length and 0.28 inch (7 millimeters) in diameter was also recovered from Block 1. Block 2 yielded a similar translucent, faceted bead that was slightly smaller than the example in Block 1.

The gold and turquoise paste glass gemstones were both found in Block 3. The turquoise gemstone is circular, is brilliant cut, and measures 0.47 inch (12 millimeters) in diameter. The base or pavilion of the stone is faceted to a point called a culet. The face or crown of the stone that is visible when it is arranged in a setting has a large central facet called a table facet that covers approximately 40 percent of the crown surface. The table is surrounded by crown main facets interspersed with star facets around the table and break facets adjacent to the edge or girdle of the stone. Although made of glass, its faceting is very finely executed, and it refracts light well in spite of its having become weathered from being buried in soil for many years. It could have been arranged into a ring or brooch setting. The stone was recovered from the stockade ditch fill below the overlying, plow-disturbed soil. This stratigraphic location suggests that the stone belonged to a person in residence at the time the station was occupied as a fortified site.

The gold stone is rectangular in shape, measures 0.51 (13 millimeters) by 0.44 inch (11 millimeters), and appears to have been molded into an emerald cut. The facets do not have sharp edges, and the pavilion is flat. It does not refract light as well as the turquoise example. It could have been set into a ring, a brooch, or a necklace. The stone was recovered from a unit that was adjacent to the stockade ditch and outside the station enclosure.

An unusual artifact found in the plow zone of a unit near but outside the house in Block 4 may have been a precontact Native American ornament or a "found" object that was suspended as a pendant. A roughly oblong limestone pebble with a chalky surface has a perforation near one edge. The hole may be a product of water erosion rather than purposefully drilled.

Accessories

Accessories that were carried either in a pocket or in hand include an iron folding knife handle, parasol frame parts, glass from hand mirrors, and fragments of three smoking pipes.

About half of the folding knife is preserved. It is a double bolster knife that was popular during the French and Indian and Revolutionary Wars and continued to be made until c. 1840. Still present is a metal bolster on one end, remnants of the iron handle to which bone, wood, or antler scales were riveted, and the spine that stopped the blade when it was folded. The blade and scales that attached to the handle are missing. The knife is a medium-sized utility type measuring more than four inches in length but probably no greater than about six inches. Folding knives had many uses; the larger examples were used for butchering, fighting, or other heavy-duty cutting, while smaller knives were used for such tasks as sharpening quill pens, cutting patches for a lead ball and gunpowder charge, and numerous other cutting tasks. It was recovered from a unit in the Frank house cellar in Block 2, dating it to the 1790s or later.[22]

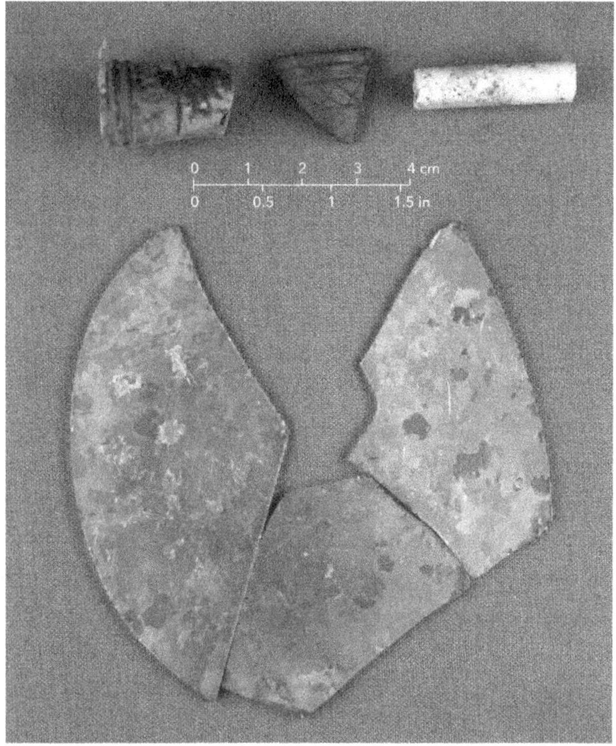

Personal artifacts from Boone's Station (clockwise: two tobacco pipebowl rims with molded decoration, ball clay pipestem fragment, mirror fragments).

Four pieces of a narrow, cut-iron rod are probably from a parasol or umbrella frame. The rods formed the spines of the parasol that were attached to the fabric cover of the parasol and formed its shape when it was unfurled. One of the rods has a perforated, rounded end. Another has a split end with a rivet holding the ends together. These artifacts were recovered from the house cellar in Block 2. They may date to the later years of the occupation since the spines are made of metal rather than whalebone as was the case for earlier parasols. However, there is scant historical information on umbrellas and parasols, their manufacture, and details of their construction. Umbrellas and parasols were considered fashionable accessories and were expensive. Margaret Patton inherited an umbrella valued at four dollars from her husband's estate in 1816. The item was twice as valuable as a spinning wheel and equivalent to a collection of pot hooks, pot rack, spider skillet, wooden bowl, and tea kettle stand in the same inventory.[23]

Archaeological evidence of mirrors, either as part of furniture or in the form of hand mirrors, is difficult to identify in absence of a reflective backing. The thickness range is similar to the thickness of flat glass used in windowpanes and distinguishing between the two is difficult if none of the reflective surface is preserved. The reflective surface of mirrors of the late eighteenth and early nineteenth centuries was produced by fire gilding, a process that resulted in an even and highly reflective tin amalgam coating. First developed in Venice, Italy, at the beginning of the European Renaissance, the French eventually learned the technique by the end of the seventeenth century and became mass producers of more affordable mirrors. Mirrors were occasionally listed in estate inventories as "looking glasses" and their value varied, perhaps according to their size and condition. In 1816, Margaret Patton's mirror was valued at $1.25. Eleven years later, Martha Wright's mirror sold for 37½¢. Elizabeth Allentharp's estate inventory listed two "old looking glasses" at an estimated value of 25¢ in 1841. The estimated value of the mirrors was equivalent to that of an old fire shovel and tongs. They both sold at auction at a higher price to the same man. Hannah Fisher's two mirrors were valued at $2.50 in 1845; the intact mirror brought $2.00 at auction, while the broken mirror fetched 68¾¢. All the women were affluent and had many other household goods, including such personal items as dressing tables, formal apparel, and side saddles, as well as fancy accoutrements for taking tea.[24]

Eleven fragments of flat glass identified as mirrors were recovered from the house cellar in Block 5. Four of the fragments form an oval hand mirror, estimated to measure 4 by 5 inches. It was likely set into a backing with a handle. The glass measures from 0.39 to 0.052 inch in thickness, with an average thickness of 0.043 inch. The four fragments were found together and had remnants of a coating, and two fragments retained a curved edge of the oval form. The other six fragments range in thickness from 0.042 to 0.067 inch, with an average of 0.052 inch, and have remnants of a weathered coating.

Three smoking pipe fragments, representing three different pipes, were recovered from Blocks 1 and 2. Two of the sherds are from pipestems. A clay pipestem fragment measuring 3/64 inch in bore diameter and 0.29 inch in stem diameter was recovered from the house floor in Block 2. Its provenience dates it to after the construction of the house in the 1790s. The stem was once part of a single-unit, molded, white ball clay pipe. A stem fragment from a two-unit pipe, consisting of a molded bowl and shank that was designed to hold a separate stem, was recovered from the ashy soil layer that was deposited when the house caught on fire. It is made from an unglazed gray clay. The pipestem retains the lip and 0.95 inch of the stem and is molded with abstract geometric designs consisting of two narrow bands at the lip, followed by a band of circular motifs and another narrow band. The stem fragment is too short to determine how long it originally was, and no evidence of the base of the pipe bowl where it joins the stem remains. The borehole in the stem is off-center and measures 0.2 inch (5 millimeters) in diameter. The bore of the pipe would have held a reed stem; such pipes are often called stubstem pipes. Stubstem pipes were produced by Moravian settlers who settled in Bethabara, North Carolina, in the early 1750s. Similar pipes were produced in the Bucks County area of Pennsylvania and the Pamplin area of Virginia in the eighteenth century. Potteries in Ohio also produced thousands of stubstem pipes in the nineteenth century. The origin of the Boone's Station pipe is unknown. A rim sherd from a pipebowl was recovered from the plow zone of the house in Block 1. It is made from a brownish-gray stoneware clay and has a band of X motifs just below the lip. The thickness of the bowl is 0.1 inch (3 millimeters). The estimated diameter of the bowl is approximately 0.5 inch (13 millimeters). The thinness of the bowl and its relatively small diameter suggests that it may have had a long narrow shape exceeding 1.25 inches (32 millimeters) in height.[25]

Toys and Entertainment

Artifacts classified as toys and entertainment include marbles, a mouth harp, and two late precontact triangular arrowpoints. Marbles are generally associated with children's play, but adults occasionally played with them as well. Marble games have a long antiquity, having been found in precontact contexts and even in Egyptian graves and in many European contexts. An early primer on child rearing published in 1770 contained a verse and moral about marble playing.

Marbles.
Knuckle down to your Taw,
Aim well, shoot away;
Keep out of the Ring,
And you'll soon learn to play.

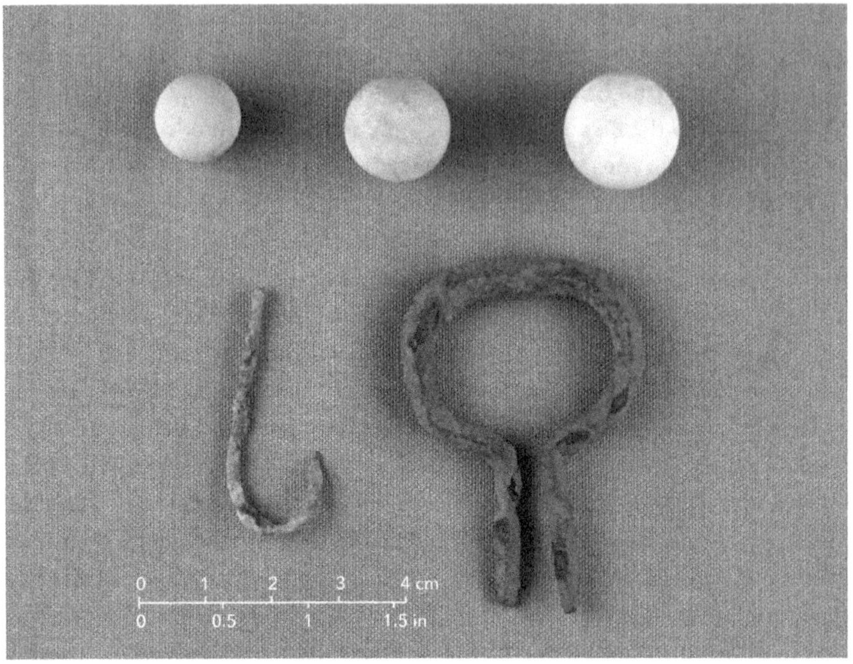

Marbles, fishhook, and mouth harp from Boone's Station.

Moral.
Time rolls like a Marble.
And awes ev'ry State;
Then husband each Moment,
Before 'tis too late.[26]

Eleven complete and two fragmentary marbles were recovered from Boone's Station. All of them are made of limestone and were probably produced in Germany, which dominated the market for marbles in the eighteenth century. The marbles range in color from a buff white to light gray to light or mottled brown. Four marbles have a flat plane resulting from the manufacturing process. Marbles are sized by passing them through sieves that had holes in 1/16 inch increments. The smallest hole that the marble could pass through was its size. This method resulted in a range of error of 3/64 inch. The marbles from Boone's Station range from 0.5 to 0.68 inches (8/16–11/16 inch). This size range encompasses the average size for most marbles and excludes the larger marbles (known as taws or shooters, among many other colloquial names) that were used to take aim at smaller marbles known as "ducks."[27]

Ten of the intact marbles were recovered from the house in Block 1. One marble was found in a metal detection target in an area along the north line of the station enclosure west of Block 4. The two fragments came from the ashy soil zone associated with the Frank house in Block 2. Both are darkened in color and may have been altered and/or fractured by the heat of the house fire. The marbles from Block 1 were recovered from the plow zone except for one that was in a sub-plow-zone level. They were not concentrated spatially, and some may have been just outside the house foundation.

The mouth or jaw harp (also called a Jew's harp by English speakers) is another artifact that has a long history of use. The instrument occurs in various forms all over the world. Typically, only the frame survives archaeologically. The mouth harp is a simple lamellophone (an instrument that produces sound by plucking) that has a metal frame shaped like an open-ended keyhole to which a flexible metal or bamboo reed, or tongue, is attached so that it extends down the middle of the frame. The harp is held firmly between the teeth, and the tongue is plucked by a finger. The instrument uses the mouth as a resonator to increase volume. The pitch of the sound remains the same, but the note or tone can be modified by changing the shape of the mouth and the amount of air contained in it. The mouth harp from Boone's Station is made of iron and consists of the frame. It was recovered as a metal detector target and is probably associated with an unexcavated house on the north line of the station enclosure and west of Block 4.[28]

Precontact Native American artifacts are frequently found on historically occupied sites. Their presence is due to two factors: the site was originally occupied, and artifacts were deposited during precontact times, and/or historic occupants collected Native American artifacts as novelties. The presence of precontact artifacts at Boone's Station is likely the result of both factors. The site's location near a freshwater spring would have been very attractive to precontact people, and they very likely camped there. Most of the 167 precontact artifacts recovered from the site are flakes and chips that are manufacturing debris from the process of forming tools from pieces of chert. The shovel testing yielded twelve chert flakes from ten locations across the field, and the remainder of the chert manufacturing debris was scattered through the block excavations, mostly in plow zone contexts. Most of these artifacts probably were deposited by Native Americans who occupied the site many years before settlers built the station. Chert manufacturing debris does not generally attract the attention of most collectors, who focus their efforts on finding tools.

Eight artifacts are precontact chert tools made by Native Americans. These include two biface fragments, two scraper fragments, an end scraper, and two arrowpoints. All but one of the tools (a biface fragment) were recovered from inside the houses in Blocks 1, 2, and 5 and may have been collected from either the Native American occupation that preceded the station or another nearby. The arrowpoints and end scraper are from the late precontact period. They could have been found in a plowed field after a rain, a common setting in which such artifacts are collected. Triangular arrowpoints and end scrapers date from 900–1600 CE and are associated with ancestral Native American groups related to the Shawnee and other Ohio valley tribes that were encountered by settlers when they moved to Kentucky in the late eighteenth century. The two arrowpoints from Boone's Station are made from local cherts and measure 1 inch (25 millimeters) and 1.3 inches (33 millimeters) in length. All of the precontact Native American tools found within the site's historic structures are complete and are included in this section because their presence implies the hobby of "relic collecting" as a means of entertainment.[29]

Currency

Two coins were recovered from Boone's Station during the initial 1993 survey and the 1999 archaeological field school. The coin found during the 1993 survey is an English large cent with an image of King George II and a date of either 1741 or 1747. George II's reign lasted from 1727 to 1760. He was a popular king among the American colonists, particularly in contrast to his successor, George III, who ruled the British empire during the American Revolution.

This particular coin is not only pierced but also heavily worn as if it had been rubbed and handled often—so much so that the images and the date on either side are nearly indistinguishable. The coin has a crudely drilled hole along the edge that gives the appearance of perforating King George's forehead. Clearly meant for suspension, this artifact is arguably the most unusual specimen in the assemblage. Coins remain in circulation for long periods of time as legal tender. Coins of British and foreign mintage were used in the colonies and in the United States as legal tender until 1857. Large cent coins were not popular and, given the piercing and wear on the Boone's Station

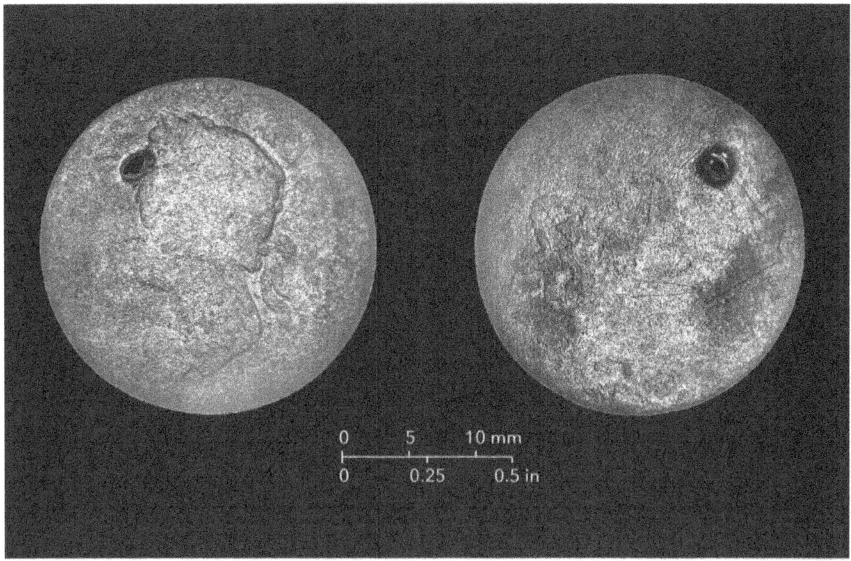

Large English cent, perforated, from Boone's Station.

example, it is likely that it was repurposed and used as an ornament or charm by one of the site's inhabitants.

Drilled coins are not common but occasionally are found archaeologically. The significance of wearing a drilled coin has been much debated. Reported cases of pierced coins found archaeologically date from the late eighteenth to early twentieth centuries and are distributed over a broad spatial area in the United States. Many of the finds were in sites associated with African Americans in the South, including enslaved persons' housing contexts in middle Tennessee, Georgia, Mississippi, South Carolina, Thomas Jefferson's Monticello and other sites in Virginia, and Oakley Plantation in Louisiana. Enslaved individuals lived on the site from the time of the Frank family's occupation to the end of the site as a residence. However, pierced coins have also been documented in the Pacific Northwest and in Native American sites in the Great Plains and Michigan. The coins may have been worn as charms to ward off evil, used as medicinal prophylactics (e.g., to relieve teething pain), or, when worn in multiples on an anklet, to scare off snakes.[30]

The coin found during the 1999 archaeological field school is a large American Matron Head penny minted in 1822 and made of copper. First minted in 1816, over two million Matron Head pennies were minted in

1822. The Matron Head is struck in profile facing to the left. The head is surrounded by stars along the edge of the coin, with the mint year below the head. The obverse of the coin reads "UNITED STATES OF AMERICA" along the edge, and "ONE CENT" encircled by a laurel wreath in the center. Large cent pieces were not popular because of their bulky size relative to their value. They were also more expensive to produce, and fluctuations in the price of copper made production in numbers adequate to meet demand difficult. The Matron Head cent was discontinued in 1835. Large cents continued to be minted until 1857 when they were reduced in size to that of the modern penny. The Boone's Station penny was recovered from the house in Block 1 and would have been deposited between 1822 and the abandonment of the site in the 1840s.

Sewing Equipment

Before the advent of ready-to-wear clothing, garments were made to order by either home seamstresses or professional tailors and dressmakers. Other than male tailors, much of the clothing construction was done by women and girls. Clothes were not the only items that were sewn. Bed linens, tablecloths and napkins, towels, and many other household textiles were also produced. Girls were trained to sew from an early age while also learning to spin and weave. Textile production, clothing construction, and mending were time-consuming undertakings in a busy household.

Archaeological assemblages frequently contain sewing equipment. Boone's Station yielded scissors, seven straight pins, and a thimble as evidence of sewing. Scissors have a long history, dating as far back as 150 BCE in France and Germany. England had a brisk scissors industry from the twelfth century on, with Sheffield dominating scissors production. Sheffield scissors were exported all over the world and particularly to the British colonies and to the American market. The scissors from Boone's Station likely originated from Sheffield, England. Only one-half of the pair of scissors was recovered from Boone's Station. The scissors consist of the right side of the pair with an iron blade and arm or shank with a terminating finger ring, also known as a loop or bow. The sides of the original tool obviously became unriveted, rendering the tool useless. The tip of the blade is broken and was either a flat or bodkin (round) type, referring to its shape and termination. The total length of the scissors is in excess of six inches but probably not much longer. The bow and arm account for three inches of length. The bow style was called

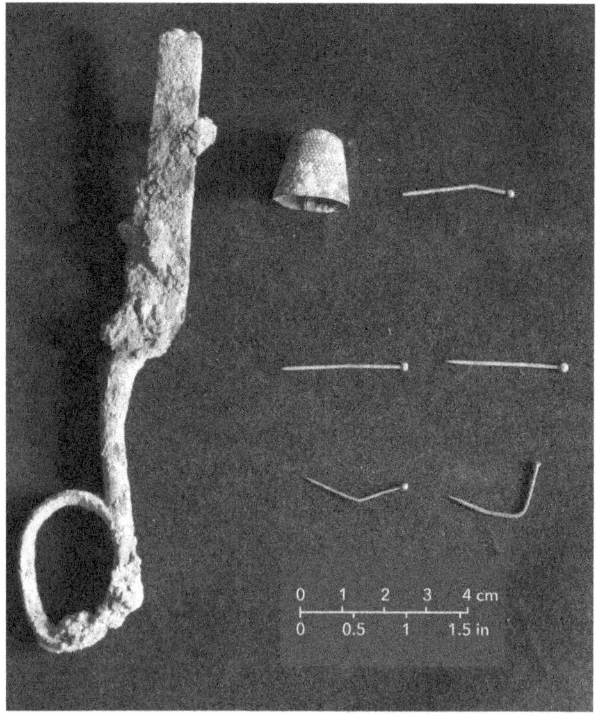

Sewing equipment from Boone's Station (Sheffield flat bow–style scissors, adult thimble, five straight pins with wound heads).

a "flat bow" by Sheffield scissor smiths. The shank was called a "round tup" type by Sheffield scissor smiths—meaning the shank bowed outwardly, like a comma, between the blade and the bow. The tool was probably intended mostly for utility sewing but, obviously, could have been utilized for other cutting purposes. It was found in the rubble zone beneath the ash layer of the house cellar in Block 2 and therefore dates to after the construction of the house in the 1790s.[31]

An important part of a sewing kit was "the ubiquitous and occasionally ordinary thimble." From the earliest times, when precontact peoples used small pieces of wood or a drilled rock to help them push a needle through a leather hide, a tool was needed to protect the finger and thumb during sewing. The brass thimble from Boone's Station is intended for an adult and was probably imported from Birmingham, England. It is 0.7 inch in height and has an estimated base diameter of 0.6 inch. It appears to have been made by the deep-drawn process or an improvement called "thimble spinning." The mechanically applied indentations, or "knurlings," cover the top and sides of the thimble. The thimble was recovered from the ash layer of the house cellar in Block 2.[32]

Seven wound-head straight pins were recovered from Blocks 1, 2, and 5. Five of the pins are classified as "long whites" and vary in length from 1.125 (two examples) to 1.2 (one example), 1.25 (one example) to 2 inches (one example). Long whites were also called "middling pins" and were commonly used for sewing. The other two pins are classified as "short whites" and measure an inch in length. Straight pins were used not only for sewing but also to fasten parts of women's clothing in the late eighteenth century or to hold the pages of a document together. The long whites were recovered from Blocks 1 (two pins), 2 (two pins), and 5 (one pin). One of the Block 2 pins, a short white, was found on the floor of the cellar, while the other two, both long whites, came from the ash layer. One short white and two long whites were recovered from Block 1 while a long white came from the cellar fill in Block 5.[33]

Pharmaceutical and Personal Hygiene Artifacts

A small number of artifacts are classified under the category of pharmaceutical and personal hygiene. Included are the remnants of hair combs, a toothbrush, glass vials, a glass stopper, and ceramic containers that might have held ointments or other pharmaceutical products. The category is small because most of the site's occupation dates prior to the advent of proprietary medicines packaged in glass bottles that dominated the medical products market in the mid-nineteenth century and later.

Five fragments of two fine-toothed bone combs were recovered from Blocks 1 and 3. Four fragments from Block 1 cross-mend to two fragments of the same comb. This comb once had teeth on both edges of a flat rectangular piece of thin bone. All the teeth on the fragments have broken off, but the remnants of the bases of the teeth indicate that the comb had approximately thirty-six teeth in an inch. The close spacing and the configuration of the teeth on both sides identify this artifact as a head lice comb. A much smaller example of a second comb was recovered from Block 3. This comb also has teeth distributed on both sides of the bone plate, but one side had more closely spaced teeth (now missing) while the opposite side has approximately twenty-two teeth to the inch. Six of the teeth are still preserved and measure ¼ inch

Pharmaceutical and personal hygiene artifacts from Boone's Station (top row: three bone lice comb fragments; bottom row, left to right: glass vial base, glass vial neck and rim, glass stopper).

in length. Fine-tooth combs have a long history of use to remove head lice. Similar examples are documented in Copenhagen, Denmark, in 1750.[34]

Slim evidence in the form of a sliver of bone with holes arranged in rows suggests that an inhabitant of the house in Block 1 owned a toothbrush. Toothbrushes, like lice combs, also have a long antiquity, dating back to 1498 in China. Toothbrushes in the eighteenth and nineteenth centuries had boar bristles set in rows in a bone backing very similar to modern toothbrushes. A book titled *The Compleat Housewife*, published in 1741 in London, admonished the reader to use a toothbrush moderately so that the teeth would not become "long and deformed." Toothbrushes were offered for sale by local dentists, who placed advertisements in local newspapers. One example is Charles B. Pelton, who practiced dentistry and sold toothbrushes in Lexington in 1829.[35]

Small glass vials, generally classified as "apothecary bottles," contained medical products either prescribed by a doctor or compounded by pharmacists and sold as cures for various medical ailments. Glass packaging was expensive in the eighteenth and early nineteenth centuries because of the scarcity of glass factories in the colonies and, later, the United States, and because of the time-consuming process of producing them. Glass bottles and vials were considered valuable enough to be mentioned in probate inventories. When she died in 1823, Elizabeth Ward, of Bourbon County, Kentucky, gave "about a dozen vials" to her daughter, Malinda. Margaret Kenney's inventory mentioned bottles in association with a mortar and pestle in 1829.[36]

Two vials, represented by a base and a neck and rim, were recovered from Blocks 1 and 2. The vial neck and rim are made of thin, heavily patinated aquamarine glass and probably had a circular cross section. The bottle's height is not measurable, but its body is only 0.05 inch thick. The rim is everted, and the orifice diameter is 3/10 of an inch. The body of the vial has an estimated diameter of approximately 8/10 of an inch. It was recovered from Block 2. The vial base from Block 1 is made of heavily patinated, dark-aquamarine glass and has an empontilled mark, indicating it was handblown into a mold. Lack of mold seams may indicate it was blown into a dip mold. Its cross section is square, measuring approximately 3/4 of an inch per side. The base of the vial is approximately 4/10 of an inch thick, which is quite thick for a relatively small form. The walls of the vial are slightly less than 1/10 of an inch thick. The shank or plug of a glass stopper was recovered from Block 1. It is made of clear glass and is missing the finial that was grasped to pull the stopper out of the bottle orifice. The stopper section, measuring 3/5 of an inch in length and having a tapered width of 2/5 to 3/10 of an inch from top to bottom, has a ground surface that increased the tightness of the seal when inserted into the neck of a bottle.

Two ceramic sherds from two vessel forms were recovered from Blocks 2 and 5. A porcelain bisque jar base from Block 5 may have been used to hold ointment, cosmetics, or other hygiene products. It was probably from a globular jar. A burned refined earthenware rim, recovered from the cellar in Block 2, is from a vessel form that had an orifice diameter of 1.6 inches. The rim is slightly everted with a rounded lip. The rim height is only 0.4 inch. It may have also been from a vessel that held ointment or a cosmetic.

Eleven gray, salt-glazed stoneware sherds may be from a chamber pot. The vessel is a slightly ovoid form with an unrestricted orifice that has a flat rolled rim. The calculated orifice diameter is 8.8 inches with a basal diameter of 5.8 inches. The base is flat and was cut off the wheel with a single plain wire. The vessel height is estimated to be approximately seven inches. A single line is incised along the circumference of the vessel body about one inch below the rim. All the sherds have an unidentified white residue adhering to the interior surface. The reconstructed vessel form does not fit well within the jar or bowl form classification suggested by stoneware expert Georgeanna Greer. The closest match is to a chamber pot form. Chamber pots typically have a flat, wide lip and a handle, but some archaeological examples with rims similar to the sherds from Boone's Station were recovered from the "lunatic asylum" in Colonial Williamsburg and date from 1790 to 1810. The sherds were recovered from the ash layer and the rubble in the cellar. Their provenience suggests that the pot was located on a floor above the cellar, a location that makes a chamber pot identification more plausible.[37]

Kitchen and Household Artifacts

Artifacts related to cooking, serving, and storage of food are abundant in residential sites. The Boone's Station assemblage is particularly interesting because it spans the time from the Revolutionary War to the first half of the nineteenth century just prior to technological advances in glass containers and bottle production, changes in dining habits, increased production of commercially processed foods, and other changes that markedly altered the composition, diversity, and size of typical kitchen and household artifact assemblages.

For instance, locally made utilitarian food processing and storage crockery was commonly made of red clay earthenware (redware) from the 1790s to the 1840s in Kentucky and elsewhere. Redware is abundant in the Boone's Station assemblage. The ware was supplanted by more durable stonewares, often salt glazed, that dominated the market by the mid-nineteenth century. Small quantities of stoneware compared to more numerous redware in the assemblage reflect this shift.

Another example is the production of glass bottles, containers, and tableware. In the late eighteenth and early nineteenth centuries, glass was expensive to produce. Before the Revolutionary War, the American colonies were restricted by English laws that regulated the establishment of glassmaking factories to discourage competition. Liquor and wine bottles, glass tableware, and other glass products could be purchased, but they were imported from England and Europe and were expensive. More "glasshouses" were established in the newly created United States, but the process was still expensive because each piece had to be blown by hand. Technological advances in glassmaking gradually automated the process so that more containers could be produced in less time, increasing supply and lowering costs to the consumer.

Innovations in the production of refined dinnerware also ushered in a proliferation of new decorative patterns, vessel forms, and clay paste formulations that are chronologically significant for dating ceramic sherds. The potteries in Staffordshire, England, were in the vanguard of technological innovations that produced white wares that were exported all over the world. The American market became the Staffordshire potters' most important customer by the early nineteenth century. The refined ceramics from Boone's Station reflect the importance of the English export trade. In addition, refined tea- and tableware became less expensive over time, which meant that even consumers of modest means could purchase decorated ceramics in greater quantities.

Refined Tea- and Tableware

The refined tea- and tableware in the Boone's Station assemblage include ceramic types that were manufactured from the early eighteenth to the mid-nineteenth centuries. Technological innovations produced new types of ceramic wares that gradually supplanted earlier ones, allowing the recognition of chronological markers in the ceramic assemblage. Dates derived from the site's history allow some further fine-tuning of the ceramic chronology. All the ceramics at the site were deposited after 1779 when the station was first built. Ceramics excavated from the Frank house cellar were not deposited until after the house was built (1788–1792). The buildings excavated in Blocks 1, 4, and 5 were part of the original stockaded station plan of log cabins forming a rectangular enclosure. Early ceramic wares from these features could date as early as 1779. Wares that were manufactured in the early nineteenth century or later must have been deposited by later occupants.

Identification of ceramic wares in the assemblage is somewhat hampered by the very small size of most of the sherds and the proportion of burned sherds. If sherd size or condition made identification of the ware type unreliable or impossible, the sherd was classified as "refined earthenware." In some instances, decoration could be discerned and recorded, but sherd size was too small to distinguish the ware type. This was particularly difficult in the case of spalls that only retained one intact surface. Of the 4,266 refined ceramic sherds in the assemblage, 1,007 sherds (24 percent) were identified only as refined earthenware. Of the 1,007 sherds, 471 sherds (47 percent) are burned (table 13.6). Despite the limitations placed on the analysis because of sherd size and condition, a sizable sample of sherds is classifiable by ware type and decoration.

Table 13.6. Refined Tea- and Tableware Types from Boone's Station

Ware type	Block 1	Block 2	Block 3	Block 4	Block 5	Total
Delftware	0	0	1	0	0	1
White salt-glazed whiteware	2	0	0	0	0	2
Blackware	0	1	0	0	0	1
Red-bodied ware	0	0	1	0	0	1
Chinese export porcelain	3	16	4	2	5	30
Creamware, undecorated	148	68	83	45	111	455
Creamware, annular/Mocha decorated	0	4	1	2	8	15
Creamware, hand painted	0	5	0	0	2	7
Creamware, transfer printed	0	1	0	0	1	2
Pearlware, undecorated	181	190	170	52	103	696
Pearlware, edged (may also have molding)	7	36	7	3	10	63
Pearlware, hand painted	48	69	23	13	13	166
Pearlware, transfer printed (blue)	48	62	26	5	5	146
Pearlware, transfer printed (brown and black)	2	1	1	1	1	6
Whiteware, undecorated	460	375	152	103	124	1,214
Whiteware, edged (may also have molding)	23	35	10	8	21	97
Whiteware, annular/Mocha	1	2	3	1	0	7
Whiteware, hand painted / sponged	41	47	23	9	21	141
Whiteware, transfer printed (blue)	34	40	15	13	21	123
Whiteware, transfer printed (black, red, pink, purple, green, orange, green/yellow)	58	58	7	1	1	125
Ironstone, undecorated	44	49	2	6	0	101
Ironstone, hand painted	1	5	0	0	0	6
Ironstone, transfer printed (red)	0	2	0	0	0	2
Ironstone, decaled	8	1	0	0	0	9
Porcelain, undecorated	32	41	5	5	8	91

(continued)

Table 13.6. Refined Tea- and Tableware Types from Boone's Station (continued)

Ware type	Block 1	Block 2	Block 3	Block 4	Block 5	Total
Porcelain, hand painted	1	18	0	1	1	21
Porcelain, decaled	1	2	0	0	0	3
Refined earthenware, undecorated	19	37	5	5	19	85
Refined earthenware, hand painted	68	49	44	21	21	203
Refined earthenware, annular/Mocha	6	2	4	7	4	23
Refined earthenware, transfer printed	56	20	34	27	18	155
Refined earthenware, burned (includes undecorated and decorated sherds)	82	220	67	55	103	527

The following wares were identified in the Boone's Station refined ceramic assemblage:

Delftware. Tin-enameled earthenware of the same type as recovered from McGary's Station.

English White Salt-Glazed Stoneware. The typical English tableware of the mid-eighteenth century, generally undecorated except for border designs along the edges of vessels, particularly plates. The white glaze surface has a very subtle pitted texture. This ware replaced much of the tableware imported from the European continent in the eighteenth century and was itself supplanted by the development of creamware in the 1760s. For the same reasons as delftware, English white salt-glazed stoneware is rare in Kentucky sites because it ceased to be commonly exported after the 1760s.

Unidentified Red-Bodied Ware. This dark-red clay-bodied ware with dark-brown and white glazed surfaces is distinguishable from the coarser, red clay earthenware that was used for utilitarian vessels such as chamber pots, milk pans, crocks, and other storage and processing forms. Like delftware and English white salt-glazed stoneware, it is present in very low frequency in the assemblage.

Basalt Ware. A dark gray stoneware with a matte black glazed surface that was popular from the mid-eighteenth century to the 1820s. It was also known as Egyptian Black. A single tiny rim was classified as Basalt ware.

Chinese Export Porcelain. Also recovered from McGary's Station. By the time Boone's Station was established, the Chinese export porcelain trade was in serious decline. The ware not only was suffering competition from European and English porcelains but was also more expensive to purchase, and the quality declined toward the end of the eighteenth century. Overglaze hand-painted patterns made solely for the export trade consisted of squiggly lines, swags, dashes, and dots in various colors along the rims of cups and saucers. Small floral sprays were painted on the bodies of the cups or in the center of the saucers.

Porcelain. A very fine, high-fired ware that was developed in England in the 1740s to compete with Chinese porcelain. Hard-paste porcelain resembles Chinese porcelain in appearance, while soft-paste porcelain (also called artificial porcelain) was originally made of ground glass stiffened with white clay. Around 1790, the Spode factory introduced a bone china body that became the standard porcelain body.

Cream-Colored Ware (creamware). Also represented in the McGary's Station ceramics, most of the creamware found in American assemblages is undecorated. This was true for the Boone's Station assemblage as well, but a few decorated sherds were recovered.

"China Glaze" and "Pearl White" Wares (pearlware). Also recovered from McGary's Station, this blue-tinted ware reached its peak of popularity from the late 1790s to the 1820s. As the blue-tinted ware became more popular, cream-colored ware was increasingly used for utilitarian vessels such as chamber pots and inexpensive mugs, bowls, and plates. Underglaze transfer-printed designs were introduced around 1784 and often displayed Chinese themes. Cobalt blue was the most popular color, but black and brown transfer-printed designs were also produced. Other decoration included molded and painted edges on plates, saucers, and bowls, and hand-painted floral and Chinese-inspired designs. The development of a blue-tinted glaze to impart a whiter appearance was less important than the shift to colored decoration, and the new ware became known by its decoration. Thus potters and their customers used terms like "painted," "edged," "printed," or "dip't" to describe pearlware.[38]

White-Bodied Earthenware. A white-bodied ware that lacks the green or yellow tint of creamware and the blue tint of pearlware and appears whiter than the earlier wares. Historical archaeologists use the term "whiteware" to describe this type of refined earthenware. White-bodied earthenware lacking a blue tint was developed as early as 1805 and became increasingly popular after the War of 1812. The development by John Rose of Coalport in 1820 of a lead-free glaze that utilized borax oxide also produced a whiter ware, but the high cost of borax precluded widespread production until the 1830s. Potters experimented with many glaze formulas in a search for a whiter ware. Accompanying the glaze formulas that produced a whiter earthenware was the use of bright colors like pink, purple, and green for transfer-printed and hand-painted designs. The term "CC ware" used in potters' price lists from the 1820s forward refers to undecorated, white-bodied ware.[39]

Ironstone. A hard, dense earthenware body that combined traits of porcelain and pottery to produce a very durable ware. Charles James Mason patented his ironstone composition in 1813, and other potters produced similar wares. Also known as "Stone China" and "New Stone," most pottery manufacturers made their own version of ironstone in the 1810–1830 period.[40]

Delftware, White Salt-Glazed Stoneware, Basaltware, and Red-Bodied Ware

The earliest refined ceramics in the assemblage include two delftware sherds; a small rim and a basal sherd of white salt-glazed stoneware; a very small, black-glazed rim with a line of molded beading just below the lip that might be Basaltware; and a body sherd of an unidentified, red-bodied ware with a dark brown and white glaze. The delftware sherds have a simple hand-painted floral design on the interior. The white salt-glazed stoneware is undecorated.

Creamware, delftware, and Chinese export porcelain from Boone's Station (first row, left to right: delftware and Chinese export porcelain; second and third rows: Chinese export porcelain; fourth row: Mocha and annular banded creamware).

One of the delftware sherds, the white salt-glazed stoneware base, and the red-bodied sherd were recovered from Block 3, which contained a section of stockade ditch. A larger, red-bodied sherd with the same glaze combination was recovered during the 1993 survey of the site in a general surface context. The white salt-glazed stoneware rim and the delftware spall were found in association with the house in Block 1. The black-glazed rim came from the stone house cellar in Block 2, so it must have been deposited in the late 1780s or later. All of these wares were being replaced in popularity by creamware and pearlware by the time the site was settled. The sherds from Blocks 1 and 3 may have been from vessels brought to the site by some of the station inhabitants.

Chinese Export Porcelain

Chinese export porcelain was introduced into England in the sixteenth century and was immediately popular. The British East India Company had a monopoly on the importation of Chinese porcelain, and it persisted until the 1780s, when conflicts arose between the company and London wholesale buyers who typically bought their chinaware at public auction. Bowing to these market pressures, the British East India Company stopped importing Chinese porcelain in 1791 for the general market. A customs duty higher than 100 percent was placed on Chinese porcelain in 1799 as a revenue measure, which effectively killed the trade. Nevertheless, Chinese porcelain enjoyed a long period of popularity among English and American consumers who could afford to buy it.[41]

Chinese export porcelain is represented by thirty-one sherds, of which eighteen are decorated. The decoration is all hand-painted overglaze motifs that required very little skill to execute. The porcelain was probably made in the late eighteenth century, when the export trade was waning. Most of the sherds are quite small and vessel form is difficult to determine, but several sherds appear to be from a bowl or a cup. At least two patterns include motifs painted along the exterior edge of the rim. The simplest is two parallel narrow orange bands with a line of orange dots between them observed on three sherds that probably were part of a bowl. The decoration is executed on both the interior and the exterior. All the sherds were recovered from Block 5.

Five rim sherds have a pattern consisting of a narrow brown band at the lip followed by a wider orange band that is bordered by an orange swag interspersed with blue dots that gives the appearance of pom-pom fringe. A basal sherd also has an orange swag line that may be part of this pattern. Blocks 1 and 2 yielded examples of this pattern.

A floral pattern is represented on six sherds from Block 2. This pattern utilizes dark-pink, light-pink, light-purple, greenish-blue, and moss-green colors to produce floral sprays of a daisylike flower with ovate leaves. A sherd with a narrow line consisting of a swag and dots may also be part of this pattern, which was probably executed on a cup.

Three sherds, also from Block 2, exhibit a pinkish-red floral motif and lines of tiny dots that are arranged in a spoke pattern. A fourth pattern may be represented by a base with a faded gray wavy line and a body sherd that has a similar faded gray motif that was not identifiable. These two sherds, also from Block 2, are thicker than the other sherds and may be from a larger bowl.

Chinese export porcelain was recovered from all five excavation blocks in very small quantities. The sherds recovered from Blocks 3 and 4 are all undecorated and only number four and three sherds, respectively. The Chinese export porcelain was most likely owned by the Frank family and only represents five or six different dishes.

Porcelain

The introduction of Chinese porcelain into England spurred English potters to discover its secrets and produce their own versions. Porcelain is more translucent than earthenware and has a completely vitrified paste. A soft-paste version of porcelain was developed by the 1750s. In 1768, William Cookworthy received a patent for a true hard-paste porcelain that utilized English clay and china stone from Cornwall. The English porcelain types developed in the eighteenth century were mostly replaced by bone china, introduced by Josiah Spode around 1794. Bone china remains the most common English porcelain manufactured today. European potteries focused on producing hard-paste porcelain. Porcelain was more expensive, and it was not exported to America in large quantities, which limited its distribution.[42]

I identified only ninety sherds of porcelain that were not of Chinese export from the Boone's Station excavation blocks. Seventy-six sherds are hard-paste porcelain. All but seven are undecorated. Undecorated hard-paste porcelain sherds were recovered from all five excavation blocks. Blocks 1 and 2 yielded the greatest number of undecorated sherds (thirty and twenty-two sherds, respectively). Blocks 3, 4, and 5 contained very small quantities of undecorated porcelain.

Most of the decorated porcelain and bone china was recovered from Block 2. Overglaze hand-painted floral decoration is present on six sherds. Two of the hand-painted, hard-paste sherds are from Block 2 and have faint designs that have mostly worn off. Single sherds from Blocks 4 and 5 are hand-painted with a blue floral design that includes berries as a design element. One sherd is from a plate; the other may be from a cup. One sherd from Block 1 has a fugitive overglaze design that may have been a stencil. Fourteen sherds are made of English bone china. Sherds from a handled teacup and a vessel with a spout exhibited a floral purple luster design. A possibly related pattern has purple and red hand-painted floral elements. All the decorated bone china sherds were recovered from Block 2.

Cream-Colored Ware

Cream-colored ware, commonly termed "creamware," includes 451 sherds of which 250 (55 percent) are spalls. All but 25 sherds are undecorated. The small size of most of the sherds makes identification of vessel form very difficult. Two sherds are from a plate or shallow bowl (such as a soup bowl). Five sherds are from the shoulder of a holloware form, while a wide handle fragment is from a form larger than a teacup, perhaps a tea- or coffeepot.

Twenty creamware sherds are decorated in what English potters called "dipped" or "dip't" and what archaeologists usually call "annular ware" because of the horizontal banding that frequently was applied to the exterior. Jonathan Rickard defines the ware as "factory-made, lathe-turned, refined utilitarian earthenwares whose principal decoration is manipulated slip." Another common term is "Mocha," which refers to a particular decorative technique. Mocha refers to mocho stone, an agate with dendritic or tree-like markings that inspired the reproduction of similar markings on pottery. Decorative techniques include annular banding, dendritic motifs that resembled branching trees (Mocha), marbled and combed slipped surfaces, and a variety of other slip manipulations that produced motifs known as cats-eye, cable, bull's eye, twigging, and fanning. Engine-turned pieces have designs formed by cutting away the slip, leaving slip-filled depressions. The dipped creamware sherds from Boone's Station are decorated with horizontal annular bands, Mocha motifs, and an inlaid slip design. Annular banding is the most common decorative technique, accounting for fifteen sherds that only show banding and a rim with a black band bordering a panel that has a Mocha dendritic motif.[43]

The largest banded sherd is from a bowl and exhibits two parallel dark-brown bands just below the lip, followed by two wide rust bands separated by another set of dark-brown bands. A wider dark-brown band runs below the narrow/wide-band sequence. The vessel was turned to remove slip between the bands, leaving white linear depressions. The edges of the bands are fuzzy and were probably applied with a slip bottle or blowing pot that used two quills to apply the dark-brown bands. The wide rust bands may have been brushed on or formed by applying a simple band in a continuous spiral. Eleven sherds from Blocks 2, 3, 4, and 5 display this annular pattern, with one sherd showing a variation in the width of the space between the dark-brown bands. Several similar vessels may be represented, since the pattern occurs in four different parts of the site.[44]

A single small rim exhibits a different banded pattern consisting of four slip-trailed bands of dark brown and gold applied below the rim that were not separated by white bands. This pattern came from a different vessel and was found in Block 5. Another very small sherd from the same block exhibits the lower part of the band sequence and also has remnants of a rust band. The sherds are too small to determine vessel form, but they were probably part of a bowl or other holloware form.

Mocha decoration was identified on a rim and a body sherd from Block 2 and a small body sherd from Block 3. The rim is from a straight-sided vessel form. A crisply defined black band applied by dipping and turning the vessel runs horizontally just below the lip. Below the band, a wide band of gold slip was laid to form the background. A brush loaded with an acidic solution was touched to the wet surface, causing the solution to spread and form intricate fernlike motifs. Only a portion of the dendritic motif is visible; it was probably intended to resemble a tree.[45]

A single body sherd from Block 5 has parallel bands of interrupted lines running horizontally around the vessel. The bands were applied by cutting the pattern into the clay body with a dicing lathe, dipping the piece into dark-brown slip, and then mounting it on a regular lathe and scraping all the slip off except for what remained in the depressed lines.

Hand-painted creamware was identified on only six sherds. The specimens were all very small, and little can be said about their decoration. One rim has linear blue bands and lines that crisscross on the interior of the vessel form. Two body sherds are covered in a brown glaze. Two sherds may have a floral design with rusty red and brown elements. A small rim has a medium blue band below the lip.

Two black, transfer-printed creamware sherds were identified from Blocks 2 and 5. The very small spall from Block 2 is similar to the larger sherd from Block 5 in the execution of the pattern but is too small for a definitive association. The pattern illustrates a man wearing knee breeches, a weskit, a stock at his neck, a frock coat, and a tall hat that is shaped like a truncated cone. He is standing outside in front of two buildings with steeply pitched roofs and end chimneys. The hat suggests a Puritan theme. Trees and shrubby vegetation are visible in front of and behind the buildings.

Creamware was recovered from all five of the excavation blocks and could have been used by station inhabitants or any of the families that lived at the site after the Revolutionary War to the end of the eighteenth century as creamware manufacture waned and was supplanted by pearlware. The largest quantities of creamware were recovered from Blocks 1 (148 sherds) and 5 (122), with smaller frequencies from Blocks 3 (84 sherds), 2 (79 sherds), and 4 (45 sherds), in decreasing order. The relatively high frequency of sherds from Blocks 1 and 5 may be indicative of creamware being part of the household goods of the earliest occupants of the site; however, creamware was clearly also used by the Frank family.

"China Glaze" or "Pearl White" Ware

The blue-tinted, refined earthenware (pearlware) at Boone's Station is most likely associated with families that lived at the site after the Revolutionary War, when trade with England resumed. A single plate base from the stone house cellar in Block 2 has a poorly impressed maker's mark that is attributed to William Adams & Sons. The mark is circular with a crown in the center and STAFFORDSHIRE/ADAMS/WARRANTED in a band around the edge. This mark was used from 1810 to 1825. Pearlware sherds were recovered from all five excavation blocks but were more common in Blocks 2, 1, and 3 (in decreasing order) than in 4 and 5. As with other ceramic ware categories, many of the pearlware specimens are spalls or very small sherds. Of the 1,171 pearlware sherds, 407 fragments (35 percent) are spalls that have only one intact surface. While the fragmentation of pearlware is lower than creamware's, many of the intact sherds are also relatively small, hampering recognition of decorative patterns and vessel forms.

Extrapolating from a small number of sherds, I identified plates, soup plates, cups, bowls, a heavy form with a spout (probably a pitcher), and a handled form. These forms are likely from tableware and teaware that were purchased separately. Large, matched sets of refined ceramics that combined table- and teaware were not manufactured until the late nineteenth century. Thus it is not unusual to encounter different decorative patterns for teaware compared to tableware like plates and bowls. Research on refined ceramic assemblages from American sites by George Miller, Ann Smart Martin, and Nancy S. Dickinson concluded that "one of the most common table assemblages for the last two decades of the eighteenth century consisted of creamware plates, painted pearlware or porcelain teas, and dipt or delft bowls."[46]

Changes in decorative treatments also occurred as styles succeeded one another. Thus from the late 1790s to the 1820s, blue- and green-edged plates replaced creamware plates, combining them with painted or printed teas and dipped or painted bowls. Printed plates became more common from the 1820s in combination with printed or painted teas. Printed tea- and tableware predominated in the 1840s but exhibited different patterns.[47]

Another important development in the marketing of refined ceramics to American buyers was the drop in prices of table- and teaware after the War of 1812, which made decorated wares more affordable for people of modest means. More expensive decorated tea- and tableware were purchased by affluent families, but even enslaved and tenant household assemblages contain some decorated wares, either purchased new or used or received as castoffs from owners or employers.[48]

The pearlware from Boone's Station follows trends elsewhere in having a wide variety of decorative styles. While the majority of sherds are undecorated when measured by frequency, the lack of decoration is probably due to the fragments having originated from undecorated portions of vessels. This is particularly true for decorative styles like edged plates that only have color along the rim or simple hand-painted designs in the center of the plate's well. The high degree of fragmentation in the assemblage artificially inflates the sherd count by creating very small fragments. Thus, of the 479 sherds that exhibit decoration, 83 (17 percent) are spalls. Spalls account for 37 percent of the pearlware sherds. Decoration among the pearlware includes blue or green edging with or without molding, hand painting, banding (often combined with hand-painted motifs), dipped annular, marbled and Mocha decorating, and transfer printing in blue, brown, and black.

Blue and green shell-edged pearlware plates and platters were widely produced by many English potters and exported in large quantities to the American market. They were second in popularity after plain creamware from the 1780s to the end of the War of 1812. However, they became the most popular option from 1815 to the early 1830s. These simply decorated tableware most commonly have scalloped rims with shallow molding that has been painted blue or green. Variations on the theme include more elaborate molding

Shell-edged pearlware from Boone's Station (top, clockwise: simple scalloped, green shell-edged, elaborate green-edged with feathers and wreath motif, simple scalloped, blue shell-edged, elaborate green-edged with fleur-de-lis motif).

that employs ropy borders along the lip, interspersed fleur-de-lis motifs, and wreaths topped with feathers. All the sherds that are large enough to determine vessel form are from plates or shallow bowls such as soup bowls.[49]

Of the sixty-four edged pearlware rims, forty are painted blue and twenty-four green. Four molding patterns are represented. The most numerous, with nineteen blue-painted and seven green-painted sherds, exhibit simple molded straight lines on the rim, generally combined with a regularly scalloped lip. This rim style dates from 1810 to 1835 and could have been used by the Hendley family, Harvey Bledsoe, or unidentified tenants who may have lived on the property in the early nineteenth century. Two elaborate rim styles are recognizable, and both date from 1820 to 1835. Neither of the styles has the straight or slightly curved molded lines typical of the simpler rim style. Both styles use an element that looks somewhat like an elongated stylized pine cone as a repetitive motif, interspersed with other design elements. One of the styles employs a two-ply twist border at the lip with pine-cone elements interspersed with fleur-de-lis motifs along the rim. Only two blue-painted rim spalls, probably from the same plate, exhibit this pattern, while at least five green-painted sherds from the same plate show it. The other style employs shorter pine-cone elements along the rim. At intervals along the circumference of the rim is a wreath topped by two feathers. This pattern is identifiable only for four green-painted sherds recovered from Blocks 2, 4, and 5 and probably represents three different plates. A single sherd combines simple curved molded lines along the lip with an unpainted molded design on the adjacent rim area. This pattern may date to 1820–1835 since it combines elements of both simple and elaborate patterns. The more elaborate patterns may have been used by Harvey Bledsoe or unidentified tenants.

Edged pearlware sherds were recovered from all five excavation blocks but are most numerous from Block 2. Block 1 yielded six sherds, with one representing a blue-painted plate with simple molding and scalloped lip. The greatest diversity of rim patterns is seen in the sherds from Block 2. Twelve blue-painted sherds exhibit simple molding and scalloped rims. Six sherds are decorated with the elaborate fleur-de-lis variation in green, and two exhibit the wreath variation, also in green. Block 3 yielded six sherds, representing the simple, scalloped style in green, the fleur-de-lis style in blue, and the hybrid simple painted molding with an unidentified unpainted motif. Examples of the simple, scalloped, and elaborate wreath patterns were recovered from Block 4. Block 5 contained examples of all three of the dominant rim patterns: simple, scalloped blue; simple, scalloped green; and elaborate wreath in green.

Hand-painted designs are executed on 190 pearlware sherds and include a variety of patterns. Most of the sherds are too small to discern anything other than color and isolated design elements. Generally, the patterns tend to be floral designs in either a broad-stroke style that consists of monochromatic blue elements or a fine/medium-line style that incorporates polychrome flowers, often with banding at the lip. One of the more discernible medium-line patterns occurs on three sherds that are probably from a teacup. The decoration is on the exterior of the cup and includes molded beads encircling the base and a stylized floral design that features an orange and blue circular motif and green leaves. The handle is missing, but brown outlining is visible where it attached to the cup. This style was popular between 1795 and 1815. All the sherds were recovered from Block 5. The Frank family may have owned this cup originally. Its presence in the pit or cellar feature in Block 5 may be due to

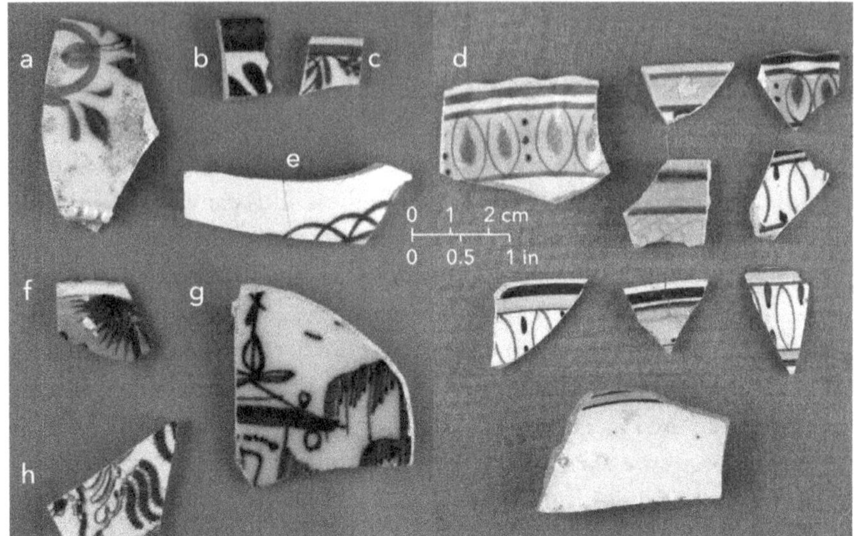

Hand-painted pearlware from Boone's Station (a. polychrome floral design with molded beading on cup sherd; b. broad-stroke blue design on rim; c. polychrome blue/brown floral design on rim; d. nine sherds with yellow, brown, and green pattern variations with banding and curvilinear motifs; e. blue, curvilinear design on body sherd; f. blue floral design on rim; g. blue "Chinese TV House" pattern on plate base; h. blue willow pattern on base).

the cup being given to an enslaved family working for the Franks or another family that lived at the site after them.[50]

Broad-stroke, blue, hand-painted floral patterns occur on the exterior of holloware forms that probably include cups and bowls. Two sherds from Block 1 are from forms with an angled body. These may be London-style cups. Broad-stroke, blue floral patterns were popular from 1815 to 1830. This period corresponds to a period of absentee ownership and the early years of Harvey Bledsoe's occupation of the site.[51]

A large sherd from the base of a plate exhibits a Chinese-inspired design that Colonial Williamsburg archaeologist Audrey Noël Hume dubbed the "Chinese TV House" because of a design element coming out of the roof of the house that looked like a television antenna. The underglaze decoration is executed in blue. The sherd was recovered from Block 5. Chinoiserie patterns were popular from 1775 to 1810.[52]

Table 13.7. Hand-Painted Pearlware from Boone's Station Excavation Blocks

Style	Block 1	Block 2	Block 3	Block 4	Block 5	Total
China Glaze cobalt blue pattern (1795–1810)	0	0	0	0	3	3
Polychrome floral with minimal use of cobalt (1795–1815)	0	4	2	0	15	21
Broad-stroke blue floral (1815–1830)	10	5	2	0	0	17
Polychrome fine-line floral sprig (1835–1870s)	17	8	9	3	14	51
Undetermined floral / too small to determine	34	48	20	8	10	120

Another distinctive pattern occurs in at least two variations applied either on the exterior or the interior of bowls. One of the patterns applied to the interior of a bowl exhibits two rather casually painted brown bands at the rim edge followed below by a wide band of yellow with brown, outlined ovate shapes that all have a green leaf painted inside. Each pair of ovate shapes is separated by a vertical line of three brown dots. The bottom of the band is bordered by a single brown band. The body of the bowl is slightly fluted. The same pattern was identified on the exterior of another rim sherd. The other pattern also was identified on either the interior or exterior of six sherds. The pattern has crisply painted, dark-brown and yellow bands at the rim edge followed below by a white band containing brown, outlined ovate shapes without any interior motifs. A line of two or three ovate dots separates each ovate element. A yellow and brown band borders the band holding the elements. Four rims have brown and yellow bands at the rim edge that may be yet another variation. The sherds were recovered from Blocks 2, 3, and 5 and were probably manufactured between 1795 and 1810. The site was occupied by the Frank family and their enslaved workers for most of this time span and very briefly by John Cockrell and his family.

Polychrome, fine-line, floral sprig patterns were the most commonly identified style at the site. Patterns of this type required less skill and time to execute and were less expensive. The pearlware examples from Boone's Station

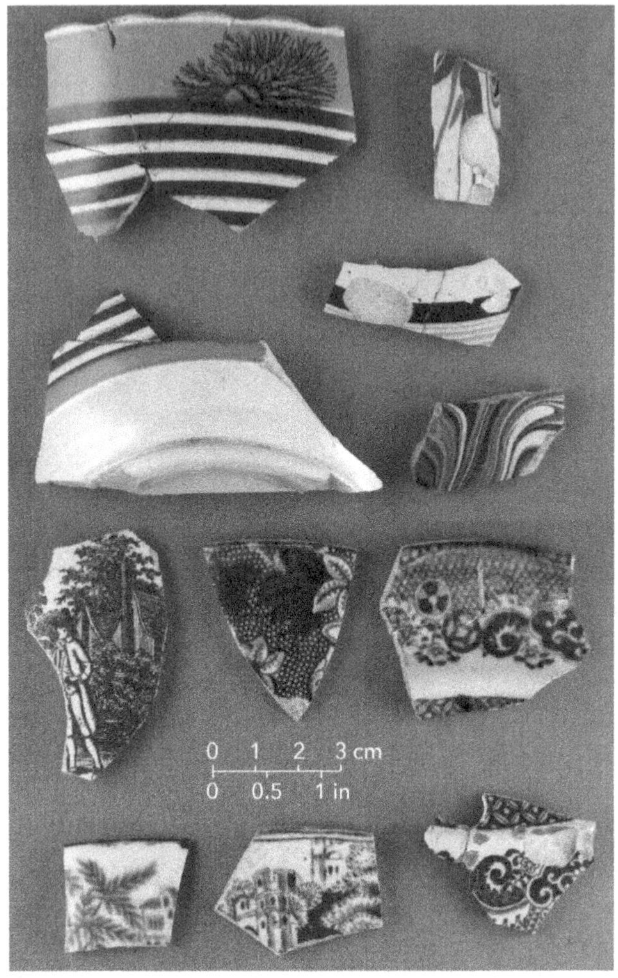

Mocha, annular, and transfer-printed pearlware from Boone's Station (top five sherds, left to right: bowl rim and base with dendritic Mocha motif and orange, brown, and white annular bands; right side, top to bottom: polychrome blue, rust swirl design, brown and white banding with rouletted green bands, rust, dark brown, white, and blue marbled design; bottom six transfer-printed sherds, clockwise from top left: black landscape design on body sherd; blue floral design on rim, two sherds with similar blue geometric design, blue landscape design with crenellated building; blue willow pattern on base).

utilized blue and orange for the flowers, brown for the stems, and green or brown for the leaves. Although fine-line floral sprig patterns became common around 1835, the pearlware examples from the site may date slightly earlier. Every block excavation yielded examples of this type of decoration. Their higher frequency compared to other styles may be due to lower prices that encouraged consumers to buy more refined ceramics.

Purchase of dipped, annular, and Mocha decorated ceramics by Boone's Station inhabitants continued as the shift to pearlware occurred in the first two decades of the nineteenth century. Twenty-three pearlware sherds exhibit rouletted or slip banding, marbling, Mocha, and lathe cut designs—sometimes in combination. Many of the sherds are quite small, and only a portion of the design can be determined. A few of the spalls that are classified as refined earthenware could be associated with the patterns by the elements they displayed.

The largest sherd is the base of a bowl with a foot ring that features an orange band at the base followed by engine-turned white and dark-brown narrow bands toward the rim. A large rim sherd that is from the same bowl has a shallowly scalloped lip, below which a wide orange band displays a dendritic element. Below the band is a series of nine dark-brown and white bands. A remnant of orange slip indicates that the middle area of the bowl had another panel of orange slip before changing to brown and white bands at the base. All the sherds were recovered from the cellar in the stone house in Block 2.

At least one, possibly two vessels are represented by marbled decoration composed of rust, dark-brown, white, and blue slips that were applied while the leather hard pot turned slowly on a lathe. The first slip was applied through a goose quill attached to a specially designed slip pot. Subsequent colors were added by dropping small quantities on the wet slip and allowing gravity to cause some of the color to run. The process created a marbled appearance on the surface of the vessel. Five body sherds and several spalls show the marbled pattern. Sherds displaying this pattern were recovered from Blocks 2, 3, 4, and 5. The distribution may be indicative of how many vessels with this pattern are represented or where the vessel was broken and the sherds disposed of. The largest sherds were recovered from Block 2, which may have been where the pot broke. The smallest sherds were recovered from Block 3, which may have been open space between the house in Block 2 and the house in Block 5. The large spall from Block 4 may have been from a second vessel with the same pattern.

Another marbled and banded pattern is suggested by several elements that combine narrow, rouletted, green horizontal and vertical lines, a wider dark-brown band, and a row of connected concentric circles with triangular projections on the outside edge. Only six sherds from Blocks 2, 3, and 5 exhibit this pattern. The distribution between three adjacent excavation blocks containing at least two buildings and an open space between them reinforces the possibility of a functional relationship between these areas.

The use of underglaze, transfer-printed patterns on tea- and tableware is one of the most common forms of refined ceramic decoration. The most popular color for transfer-printed patterns is blue, produced by the addition of cobalt and used on many types of earthenware and porcelains. Other colors that were used on pearlware are black and brown. Transfer-printed pearlware have a limited color palette because of the high firing temperatures necessary for underglaze decoration. The process begins with a design engraved on a copper plate. Cobalt, or another inorganic metal oxide mixed with oils, is rubbed into a heated, engraved plate, and the excess scraped off. After the copper plate cools, tissue paper sized with soap is placed on the plate and run through a press to force contact with every line of the drawing. The plate is reheated to dry the paper and soften the color. Then the paper is carefully peeled away, bringing the image with it. Sections of the transfer are cut out and applied to the ceramic vessel. On plates and bowls, the center is positioned first, then the border. The print is rubbed down with a brush lubricated with soft soap. The tissue is removed by immersing the piece in water. After firing at a low temperature to "harden on" the print, the potter dips the piece in glaze that appears white before firing and covers the entire vessel form. The piece is then fired at 1,070 degrees centigrade (1,958 degrees Fahrenheit).[53]

Blue transfer-printed pearlware numbers 178 sherds from the site as a whole and were recovered from all five of the excavation blocks. Most of the sherds are too small to identify a particular pattern and, for many sherds, even specific elements are difficult to specify. Vessel forms represented in the assemblage include plates, a tureen, cups, and possibly bowls. The patterns include floral designs and landscape scenes.

A few sherds from holloware forms have patterns on both the inside and outside surfaces. One rim from Block 2 has a landscape with palm trees and architectural elements on the exterior and abstract, curvilinear elements on the interior. Another rim from the same block has a floral pattern on the exterior and what appears to be an ornate planter sitting on a pedestal on the interior. The same planter element occurs on a large spall from Block 3 that was probably printed on the interior of a saucer, perhaps meant to accompany the cup rim. A cup base exhibits what may be the roof of a Chinese pagoda on the interior and possibly floral elements on the exterior.

Landscape patterns include the famous "Willow" design, a popular pattern that was printed on pearlware from the 1780s to the early nineteenth century and is still produced on modern tableware today. Ten sherds from at least two different pieces of flatware were recovered from Blocks 2 and 5. The sherd from Block 2 is probably from a plate base. Its design is well defined and crisply printed. The classic willow tree element is discernible on this sherd, along with the foundation corner of a pagoda and possibly a fisherman. The standard version of the Willow pattern has three fishermen who are casting their lines from a bridge. The sherds from Block 5 are much smaller but are also probably from a plate. Two bases exhibit a Chinese boat called a junk, a zigzag fence, a bridge, and a willow tree. All of the Willow-patterned sherds from Block 5 appear slightly blurry, in contrast to the well-defined edges of the pattern from Block 2.

Other landscape patterns include a rim from Block 2 that exhibits a large castle and another large building in the background. The castle has a crenellated tower. Such patterns are termed "Gothic Revival," and they began to replace earlier Classical themes in the 1840s. This sherd probably dates to the final years of occupation at the site. Another sherd from Block 1 also exhibits a building element, but it is too small to identify more specifically.

Four plate rims from Block 2 and one plate rim from Block 1 exhibit the same continuous running geometric pattern on the marly (flat rim area between the well and lip) of the plate. At least two, probably three, plates are represented by the sherds. The pattern on one of the rims from Block 2 is blurry along the edge, as if the transfer tissue shifted slightly when it was positioned. This produced a flawed pattern that may have consigned this plate to the seconds shelf, to be sold at a reduced price. Continuous geometric marly patterns were commonly produced between 1818 and 1829, a period when Charles Grimes was probably renting to tenants; however, Harvey Bledsoe could also have been the owner of these plates.

Eighteen sherds exhibit very dark-blue patterns that are called "Old Blue" and were popular from around 1818 through the 1820s. Ten sherds were recovered from Block 1 and eight from Block 2. The patterns are so dark, and most of the sherds so small, that no elements are identifiable. A single large rim with a scalloped lip from Block 2 is probably from a tureen. The Old Blue sherds are probably associated with either Harvey Bledsoe or one of Charles Grimes's tenants.[54]

A single very small body sherd exhibits an unidentifiable brown transfer-printed pattern. It was recovered from Block 3.

Whiteware

Archaeological use of the term "whiteware" refers to refined earthenware that are white in appearance but lack the yellowish tint of creamware or the bluish tint of pearlware. The whiteness of the ware is attributed by ceramic expert George L. Miller to the use of kaolin clay in the paste. Other authors attribute the whiter appearance to the use of borax in an alkaline glaze. Borax was too expensive for general use until about 1830, and the older lead glazes continued to be used throughout the nineteenth century. There were many other glaze formulas that were used by the dozens of English potters who were the main source of imported refined ceramics to the United States. Concurrent with the development of a whiter earthenware in the 1820s was the use of a wider palette of colors for transfer printing. "Printed wares in red, brown, green, and purple are common in potters' invoices to the United States from 1829 to the 1840s, and excavated assemblages from 1830 to 1850 are distinctive because of the great variety of colors used to decorate the vessels." Undecorated sherds classified as whiteware can generally be dated from the 1820s on, but decoration is more important as a chronological indicator.[55]

Vessel forms are similar to the forms identified for earlier wares. Plates, shallow bowls, teacups, and sparse evidence of larger, heavier serving pieces are documented for whiteware. Large matched sets of dinner services common in late nineteenth-century assemblages are not evident, and the practice of buying tea- and tableware separately continued. Decoration is common and includes all the types identified for creamware and pearlware: edged, hand-painted, annular/Mocha, banded, and transfer-printed, with the addition of more colors within the transfer-printed sherds. The whiteware is attributable to Harvey Bledsoe or the unidentified tenants that lived at the site after Bledsoe died and up to 1849, when it ceased to serve a residential purpose.

As with the creamware and pearlware, many of the fragments are spalls with only one intact surface. Just under one-third of the sherds are spalls. This is a lower percentage than the pearlware or creamware but still fairly high. However, the whiteware sherds with both interior and exterior surfaces are

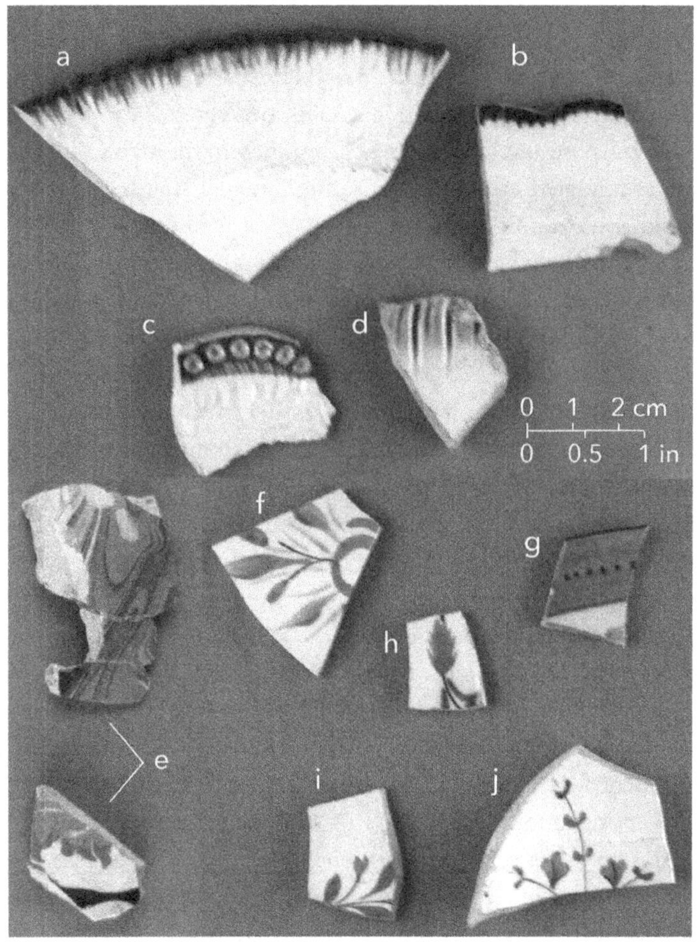

Shell-edged, annular, and hand-painted whiteware from Boone's Station (first and second rows, clockwise: (a) simple, scalloped, blue shell-edged plate rim; (b) poorly executed, simple, blue-edged, and scalloped rim; (d) simple, scalloped, green-edged rim; (c) elaborate blue shell and beaded-edge rim; third row, left to right: (e) marbled and swirled rust, blue and brown Mocha body sherd; (f–h) polychrome hand-painted floral and rim design; fourth row: (e) marbled and swirled rust, blue, and brown Mocha body sherd; (i–j) two sherds with polychrome, hand-painted sprig floral designs).

generally larger than the older wares. This may simply be due to their having been subjected to adverse preservation conditions, such as fragmentation by plowing, or environmental forces, such as freeze/thaw cycles that caused splitting and spalling for a shorter time. Another explanation pertains to human behavior that creates broken ceramics. A chipped ceramic form can still serve its intended purpose and may never be consigned to the archaeological record unless it was rendered useless by shattering. Smaller sherds and spalls might be overlooked in cleaning up and disposing of broken ceramics, leaving them distributed through archaeological deposits at higher rates than larger sherds.

Edged whiteware is painted in blue and green, with blue predominating. Seventy-six rims are blue edged while only nineteen rims have green edging. Edged whiteware was the second most common tableware from the 1830s to around the Civil War, when ironstone or white granite ware supplanted it. It was the least expensive decorated tableware, which made it readily affordable even to households of limited means. The larger sherds in the Boone's Station assemblage were once part of dinner plates and shallow soup bowls. No holloware forms having edged decoration were identified in the assemblage.

Variations in the shape of the rim, the extent and type of molded edge, and the care with which the colored glaze was applied are apparent in the edged whiteware from the site. Even-scalloped edges vary from, most commonly, small regular scallops to large scallops; molding is most often shallow. One style employs shallow molding with a molded "bud" that originated in the earlier rococo-style edging. The colored glaze on this style is usually feathered with varying amounts of skill. This style was widely produced until the 1840s. Only one blue-edged rim exhibits elaborate molding that consists of beads just below the lip and flame-like molding interspersed with molded tassels. The colored glaze on this rim was swiped across the bead molding with no attempt to feather the glaze, as is common on more simply molded rims. This style may date between 1820 and 1830. Several sherds, probably from a single shallow soup bowl, have broad scallops along the edge and a narrow line of colored glaze that is barely feathered. Molding below the lip is also very minimal. This piece was probably made in the 1840s.[56]

Notable among the green-edged rims is one with straight molded lines and colored glaze that was swiped across the molding without feathering. This rim also has glaze that dripped below the molding accidentally; this mistake would have consigned the piece to the seconds shelf. Another green-edged rim has more deeply molded and longer lines than other examples.

Eighty-nine sherds exhibit hand-painted designs. Most of the sherds are very small and retain very limited evidence of the design. Only one rim has a broad-stroke blue design on the interior. The sherd is probably from a bowl. A wide band of blue glaze was painted below the lip, and darker blue dots were added to the middle of the band. All the other hand-painted designs are floral. A distinctive design on two sherds from Block 5 is executed on the interior of one sherd and the exterior of the other. Burnt-orange floral elements with green leaves constitute the design. The flowers are painted in an exuberant style.

Sprig floral designs are also evident. One pattern has small blue flowers on brown stems with green leaves that are arranged in pairs along the stem. Another pattern has dark-pink flowers. These designs date to the 1830s and 1840s at the site.

Another form of hand-painted decoration involves the use of a sponge to apply colored glaze to the surface of a vessel. Fifty-two sponged sherds

Table 13.8. Distribution of Whiteware in Excavation Blocks and Metal Detection Area

Decoration	**Block 1**	**Block 2**	**Block 3**	**Block 4**	**Block 5**	**Metal Detection**	**Total**
Undecorated	299	199	96	70	66	5	735
Edged	22	36	10	8	21	0	97
Hand painted	19	34	17	3	19	0	92
Annular/Mocha	5	5	9	4	8	1	32
Sponged	25	15	6	6	0	1	53
Blue transfer print	34	39	12	13	25	2	125
			Other transfer print				
Black	4	0	0	0	0	0	4
Red	2	40	5	1	0	2	50
Pink	39	9	0	0	1	0	49
Purple	5	1	0	0	0	0	6
Orange	1	0	1	0	0	0	2
Green	1	7	1	0	0	0	9
Green/Yellow	1	0	0	0	0	0	1
Green/Brown	1	0	0	0	0	0	1
Total	458	385	157	105	140	11	1,256

were recovered from Blocks 1, 2, 3, and 4. The majority of sponged sherds came from Blocks 1 (twenty-five sherds) and 2 (fifteen sherds). The remaining twelve sherds were recovered in equal frequency from Blocks 3 and 4. All the sherds are sponged in blue. Sponged decoration often is paired with hand-painted representational designs, although no evidence of such a combination was observed in the Boone's Station assemblage. Sponge decoration has been identified as a fill technique on pearlware but is much more common on later ware. Ceramics expert George Miller suggests that sponged ware lacking hand-painted designs was uncommon until Staffordshire potters introduced simple patterns made by cut sponges in the 1840s. Sponge-decorated ceramics were as inexpensive as edged wares.[57]

Three very small rims have narrow overglaze pink bands at the rim that are most likely from a luster-decorated vessel. Luster decoration utilizes thin films of metal to produce the design. The technique dates to the early nineteenth century and was popular for many decades.[58]

Annular, marbled, and Mocha ware is represented among the whiteware by thirty-four sherds. The small size of the sherds only allows for the recognition of specific design elements rather than entire patterns of decoration. Annular banding occurs in several color combinations. One body sherd has medium-width blue and white bands that may combine with wide bands of the same blue hue seen on two other body sherds. Two small rims exhibit a medium-width blue band just below the lip, bordered by a pale-yellow band. One of the rims has a tiny remnant of brown that may be part of a Mocha dendritic element within the pale-yellow band. A remnant of blue slip is also combined with gold banding on another small sherd.

Six sherds have blurred dark-brown and gold bands at the rim bordered by a white ground. This annular pattern may have also included a rust-colored band, observed as a tiny remnant on one small sherd. One large body sherd from a holloware form has narrow dark brown bands bracketing wide gold bands. The vessel was poorly fired, leaving a dull, granular surface. The vessel, while functional, would have been sold at a discount because of its flawed appearance. A more elaborate pattern has narrow, green-slipped horizontal reeding, a light-brown slip band, and white horizontal reeding. The reeding is inlaid into the vessel surface, possibly by using a rouletting tool or employing rilling (use of a sharp-toothed tool to produce narrow, turned grooves). A variation on a small sherd shows a narrow green band bordered by inlaid green, closely spaced, narrow vertical lines, possibly applied with a rouletting tool. Three very small sherds have inlaid dashed and continuous black lines on a white ground. These elements were produced by using a dicing lathe to cut the pattern, then dipping the piece in slip and mounting it on a turning lathe to scrape the slip from the surface, leaving the slip-filled design elements filled with color.[59]

Marbling is identifiable on nine sherds. Color combinations include rust, white, and brown; blue, white, and black; dark brown, light blue-gray, and orange. Most of the marbled sherds were recovered from Block 3, with single examples found in Blocks 2, and 4 and in an area of metal detection. Blocks 3 and 5 yielded the largest number of annular, marbled, or Mocha sherds, with smaller quantities recovered from the other excavation blocks.

Transfer-printed, white-bodied earthenware became the most popular tea- and tableware by the 1830s. The decrease in price allowed more consumers to purchase a greater variety and more vessels than they had earlier. Printed wares saw a fivefold increase in availability from 1814 to 1846, based on potters' price-fixing lists. Blue remained the most popular color on the market, but other colors such as pink, purple, green, and polychrome combinations also were sold. The Boone's Station assemblage includes, in descending order of frequency, blue, pink/red, green, light-orange and green/light-orange, purple, and black transfer printing on the whiteware.[60]

Blue transfer-printed designs were identified on 126 whiteware sherds from the five excavation blocks. Most of the sherds are very small, hampering the determination of pattern design elements and vessel form. Floral, geometric, and landscape design elements are notable, and most of the sherds have patterns that cover the entire surface with little white space. However, one plate rim exhibits a more open light-blue floral pattern with a scalloped lip bordered by molded hatch marks. Several sherds have patterns on both the interior and the exterior. A bowl rim exhibits curvilinear elements in a wide band on the interior and a landscape scene employing architecture and vegetation on the exterior. Another rim has a floral element on the exterior and curvilinear elements on the interior. Geometric elements are combined with diaper patterns of diamonds, dots, or lozenges to form borders around the central pattern, as seen on a shallow bowl sherd.

Blue transfer-printed whiteware was recovered from every excavation block, with the greatest quantities from Blocks 1, 2, and 5. Block 2 yielded the plate with the scalloped and molded rim and open floral pattern as well as the bowl rim with an exterior landscape pattern and an interior band of

Blue, green, and green/orange transfer-printed whiteware from Boone's Station (top six sherds, clockwise from left: blue geometric design, blue landscape design, blue floral design with scalloped lip, blue geometric design on plate rim and body sherd [same design as on first sherd], blue floral design; bottom four sherds: green floral designs with light-orange overlay motifs).

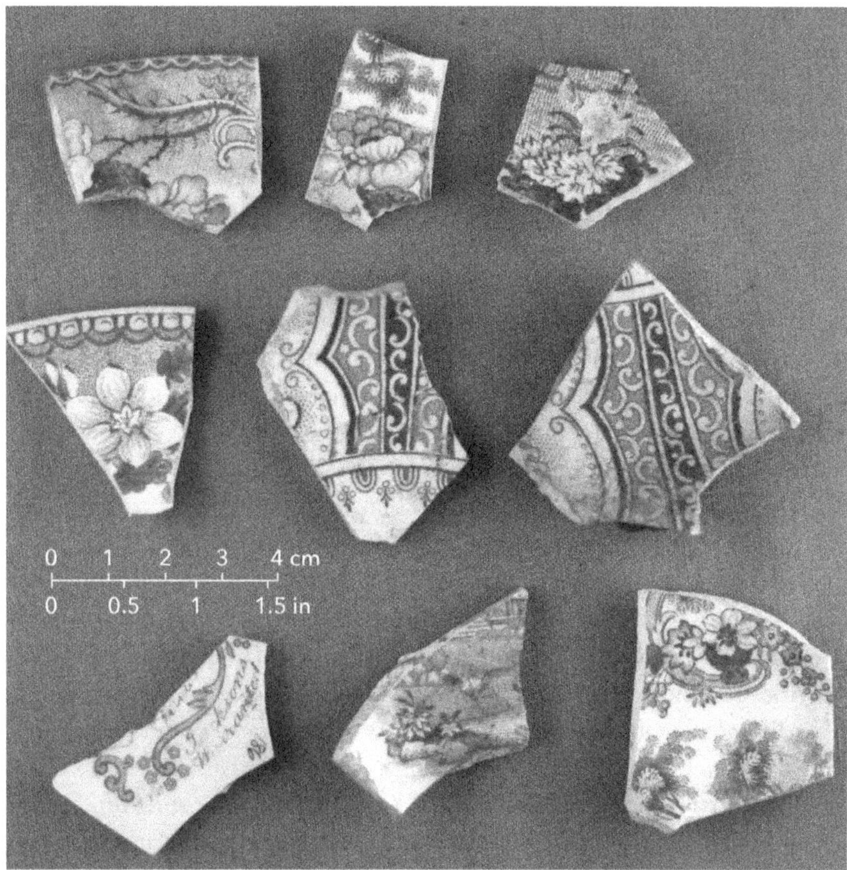

Red/pink transfer-printed whiteware from Boone's Station (top row: floral patterns; middle row: one floral patterned rim, two bases with curvilinear "comma" motifs; bottom row: base marked with stamped mark of John and Job Jackson, Staffordshire, England, 1831–1835, landscape pattern, floral pattern).

curvilinear elements. The sherds from Blocks 1 and 5 are mostly very small in size. Recognizable vessel forms include plates, bowls, and soup plates, but no teaware.

Pink or red transfer-printed whiteware occurs on ninety-one sherds. The red is closer to a dark-pink or burgundy color, and frequently both hues occur on the same sherd. Ninety-one percent (eighty-three specimens) of the sherds were recovered from Blocks 1 and 2, with very few sherds from the other blocks or the metal detection area. Most of the sherds were too small for complete patterns to be recognized, but partial patterns that appeared on more than one sherd allowed some identification of vessels that shared particular motifs. Design elements include floral, landscape, and geometric motifs. Eleven sherds have patterns on both their interior and exterior surfaces; floral elements are recognizable on three sherds, including a sherd from a London-style cup.

A partial geometric pattern recognized on nine sherds distributed between Blocks 1 and 2 with a single example in Block 3 exhibits bands of comma-shaped elements against a red background or a pink, stippled background. On a plate base, the bands radiate out like spokes from an unidentified design in the center of the plate well. This pattern is present on at least one plate from Block 2. Its presence in Block 1 suggests that there was more than one vessel form of this pattern and that they were used by occupants of the stone house in Block 2 and the log house in Block 1. Harvey Bledsoe, or an unidentified tenant who lived at the site after Bledsoe's death, are the most likely owners. The sherds from Block 1 may have been from a dish that was given to enslaved people by an inhabitant of the stone house in Block 2.

Another landscape pattern appears on two bases with partial manufacturer's marks attributable to John and Job Jackson, who ran a pottery at Church Yard Works in Burslem, Staffordshire, England, between 1831 and 1835. They used several printed marks of differing designs; the one appearing on the two sherds from Boone's Station has a curvilinear cartouche with "Jackson's Warranted" printed on the outside edge. The interior of the sherd exhibits an urn within a landscape. The pattern is called Florentine Villas and was commonly produced in the 1830s. The pattern name was usually printed inside the cartouche. Another base bearing a portion of the same mark exhibits flowers in the foreground and architectural features in the background that are also part of the Florentine Villas pattern. Both sherds were recovered from the stone house in Block 2. These dishes were probably owned by Harvey Bledsoe.[61]

John and Job Jackson were the nephews of Ralph and James Clews, who operated a pottery in Cobridge, Staffordshire, England, from 1818 to 1834. The Clews taught their nephews the business of pottery manufacturing only to have them leave to start their own company in 1830. John Jackson came to the United States to establish business relationships with American customers and was successful, much to the dismay of his uncles. An invoice from the firm in 1834 indicates that they shipped thirty-one crates, the equivalent of approximately 14,460 pieces of pottery, to Philadelphia, which was a major source of manufactured goods for Kentucky merchants who made yearly trips to replenish their inventory for sale in their stores. Despite their early success, the Staffordshire potteries suffered from work stoppages and disagreements with the Union of Operative Potters about pay and working conditions, which led to the bankruptcy of Ralph and James Clews and John and Job Jackson by 1835. The Jacksons left the pottery manufacturing business, but their experience with the American trade inspired them to move to the United States and set themselves up as retailers in earthenware and china in New York.[62]

Several other partial landscape and floral patterns are observable, but the sherds are too small to recognize the overall design. A floral design was identified on a cup sherd made in the London style, and other floral elements were noted on saucer sherds. A London cup style has an angled shoulder toward the base of the cup; it is also known as a Grecian cup. The form was very common among transfer-printed wares in the 1830s and 1840s. The single red transfer-printed sherd from Block 4 is also from a London-style cup, but design elements are not identifiable. While floral elements appear on many vessel forms in tableware and teaware, patterns in which floral elements are dominant and landscape features are absent seem to have been common on teaware.[63]

The nearly equal distribution of red/pink transfer-printed sherds between Blocks 1 and 2 and the fact that the same or similar patterns were recovered from both blocks suggest a relationship between the two houses. Harvey Bledsoe co-owned and probably lived at the site from 1824 to 1833. In 1830, the federal census listed two young white men and six enslaved individuals. Bledsoe was the head of the household and probably was the older man of thirty to thirty-nine years listed. The younger man, twenty to twenty-nine years of age, was not identified by name, and his identity is unknown. Bledsoe and the unidentified white man would have lived in the stone house. The enslaved individuals, who included two women between twenty-four and thirty-five years of age, one male between ten and twenty-three years of age, and two girls and a boy under the age of ten, may have lived in the log house in Block 1. In 1833, Bledsoe's estate was appraised in preparation to be sold. Five enslaved people are identified by name: a woman named Esther with her child, Israel; two boys, named Jackson and Moses; and a girl named Letha Jane. While the ages and sexes of the enslaved individuals do not match up exactly between 1830 and 1833, there may be some overlap between the two tabulations. Perhaps the other adult woman and one of the girls in the census were enslaved by Bledsoe's unidentified housemate. A similar household arrangement may have been in place for unidentified tenants and enslaved people who probably lived at the site after Bledsoe died. Giving enslaved persons cast-off household items was a common practice. Enslaved women who worked as house servants and cooks would have been well situated to receive such goods.[64]

Fifteen sherds exhibit green, light orange, or a combination of the two in designs that represent two different patterns—probably each on a single vessel. A green transfer-printed floral pattern that includes some curvilinear filigree elements is identified on a holloware form that has a rim treatment that resembles a zipper and a shallowly scalloped lip. The design continues over the lip to cover the top of the rim on the interior. The vessel diameter expands from the orifice to a prominent shoulder. The form may be a vase. All but one of the six sherds showing this pattern are from Block 2. A single very small rim spall is from Block 3.

Another pattern, represented by six sherds, combines green and light-orange transfer-printed elements and is embellished with some hand painting. The design is printed on both sides of two of the sherds. The sherds are too small to determine vessel form with certainty, but it was probably a holloware form. As with the green and red/pink transfer-printed sherds, this pattern was recovered mostly from Blocks 1 and 2, with only one small sherd recovered from Block 3.

Additional evidence of other types of decorated whitewares that were recovered in very small quantities may indicate the acquisition of single pieces of china that have different decorations. Such dishes could have been purchased secondhand, given as a castoff or a gift, or by some other means. Most of these sherds are from Block 1. Nine small sherds mostly from Block 1 with single examples from Block 2 and 3 have purple transfer printing. The identifiable design elements are floral, and one of the sherds is from a shouldered form. More than one pattern is probably present, and they may all be from teaware. Four very small sherds, probably from a single vessel, have a polychrome floral pattern that includes pink flowers and green leaves and is discernible on both surfaces of one of the sherds. All the polychrome transfer-printed sherds are from Block 1. Also from Block 1 are three black, transfer-printed whiteware sherds that include one with the printed letters "—u wuld." "Wuld" is an archaic form of the word "would" and may have formed part of a phrase or sentence beginning or including "You wuld."

Ironstone

The hard white vitrified or semivitrified wares that are commonly classified by archaeologists as ironstone have been described by ceramics expert George L. Miller as "one of the most confusing terms to describe the 19th century ceramics." The term is taken from "Mason's Patent Ironstone China," patented in 1813, but other potters produced similar ware, such as William Turner's Stone China (patented in 1800), John Davenport's Stone China (ca. 1805–1820), and Josiah Spode's Stone China, which he introduced around 1814. The early ironstone ware was usually heavily decorated. Later stone china became known as "white granite" and was exported to the United States by the 1840s. It was often undecorated or had simple, decaled overglaze, hand-painted, or transfer-printed decoration. The ironstone from Boone's Station is the "white granite" type and dates from the last years of the site's occupation in the 1840s.

Ironstone accounts for 119 sherds, recovered mostly from Blocks 1 and 2. Most of the sherds are undecorated. Only 16 sherds exhibit some form of decoration. Vessel forms include bowls, plates, and teacups. Decoration is very limited. Two sherds have a dark-pink design that may be luster; another is pink transfer printed. These sherds were recovered from Block 2. Nine sherds have overglaze decoration that has mostly worn off, leaving fugitive shadows of the floral elements. Overglaze decoration was identified on at least one teacup, a plate, and a bowl, all from Block 1. The design may have been applied by using a stencil or a decal. A single bowl rim exhibits a hand-painted floral sprig design of a blue flower with green leaves on the interior surface. A handle has a brown stripe running its length, and two body sherds exhibit brown, hand-painted elements. These sherds indicate single examples of ironstone ceramics that have a limited range of decoration executed on tea- and tableware. All the decorated sherds were recovered from Blocks 1 and 2. Blocks 3 and 4 yielded only 8 undecorated sherds; no ironstone was found in Block 5.

Unrefined Earthen- and Stoneware

Utilitarian crockery used in the kitchen for processing and storing various foodstuffs included a wide range of vessel forms and was made from specific types of clay. What archaeologists call "redware" is a relatively low-fired ceramic made from common clays. Earthenware clays are less resistant to heat and will slump in the kiln if the temperature is too high. For redware, a firing temperature between 1,000 and 1,100 degrees centigrade is necessary for low-firing clays, while clays in the upper earthenware range require 1,100–1,200 degrees to mature. The clay does not completely fuse and remains water permeable after firing. Redware must be glazed to hold liquids. The most practical glaze that melts at earthenware kiln temperatures contains lead in the form of lead oxides that are added to the glaze formula. Red clay earthenware was the first unrefined ceramic to be produced in many regions because the clays were abundant and the firing temperatures were easier to reach and maintain.[65]

A more durable and dense unrefined ceramic is called stoneware. Stoneware is made from clay that can withstand very high kiln temperatures—in excess of 1,200 degrees centigrade. Such clays are called fire clays or potter's clays. Greer describes a good stoneware clay as having "plasticity, good wet and dry tensile strength, a moderate or very small amount of iron, minimal shrinkage, suitable vitrification point, and adequate silica content if it is to be salt glazed." Stoneware will vitrify or fuse at high temperatures without slumping and becomes impermeable as a result. Although stoneware does not need a glaze if it is properly vitrified, the ware was usually glazed on one or both surfaces to ensure its impermeability and make it easy to clean.[66]

Yellow ware is a utilitarian ceramic that is made from pale yellow clay and often glazed with a clear lead glaze that allows the yellow or gold hues of the clay to color the glazed surface. East Liverpool, Ohio, potteries began manufacturing yellow ware as early as 1839, when an English potter named James Bennett established the first pottery in the city. Yellow ware became much more common later in the nineteenth and early twentieth centuries.

The earliest settlers in Kentucky had to transport unrefined ceramic vessels from elsewhere until a local pottery industry could be established. For the Boone's Station settlers, the source was most likely North Carolina or Virginia—both of which had established redware pottery industries by the late eighteenth century. Local redware potteries were established in Kentucky as early as the 1790s, and several potters were plying their trade in Lexington and nearby counties by the early nineteenth century. James Jeffs opened a pottery business in Lexington in 1794, where he encouraged the wholesale trade. Robert Campbell opened a pottery in 1805 and was advertising for potters to hire in 1807. John Carty and Richard Metheny were in business in Lexington by 1818. In neighboring Bourbon County, only a few miles from

Boone's Station, John Huffman and James Ingels were producing redware as early as 1810 and possibly earlier.[67]

Clays suitable for stoneware must be fired in a kiln that can produce the necessary high temperatures required for vitrification. These clays occur less frequently in nature than redware clays, and their distribution influences the establishment and success of stoneware production in a given area. Stoneware industries developed later than redware and in more restricted distribution as a result. In 1820, only two potters, George Swingle and Thomas Linebaugh, were listed in the federal manufacturing census as manufacturing stoneware. Their potteries were located in Lewis and Russell Counties, respectively, which are quite distant from Fayette County and Lexington. While the presence of stoneware in the Boone's Station assemblage indicates that it was in use, it is far less numerous than the redware and represents only a few vessels, which probably date to the later years of occupations.[68]

Another potential source of stoneware was England, where potters began to imitate Rhenish salt-glazed stoneware in the seventeenth century and were producing large quantities by the mid-eighteenth century. However, they focused on the use of stoneware for fancy tableware with a white glaze. Its use for utilitarian wares such as mugs and beer bottles became more common after white salt-glazed stoneware tables were supplanted by cream-colored earthenware. Only one body sherd in the Boone's Station assemblage was identified as possibly English brown, salt-glazed stoneware. Alternatively, it may have been from an American-made vessel that mimicked the English style.

Redware

Like McGary's Station, redware dominated the unrefined ceramics from Boone's Station. Most of the redware found is from processing and storage vessels, such as milk pans and crocks. However, plates, pitchers, and mugs suitable for use at the table were also made. The majority of unrefined ceramics from Boone's Station are made of red clay earthenware, totaling 1,739 sherds. Sherds with no glazing on either the interior or the exterior surface account for 212 specimens, many of which are spalls. Glazing occurs on either the interior or the exterior or on both surfaces. Small sherd size made it difficult to distinguish between sherds glazed only on the interior or only on the exterior. Where identification was possible, 598 sherds are glazed on both

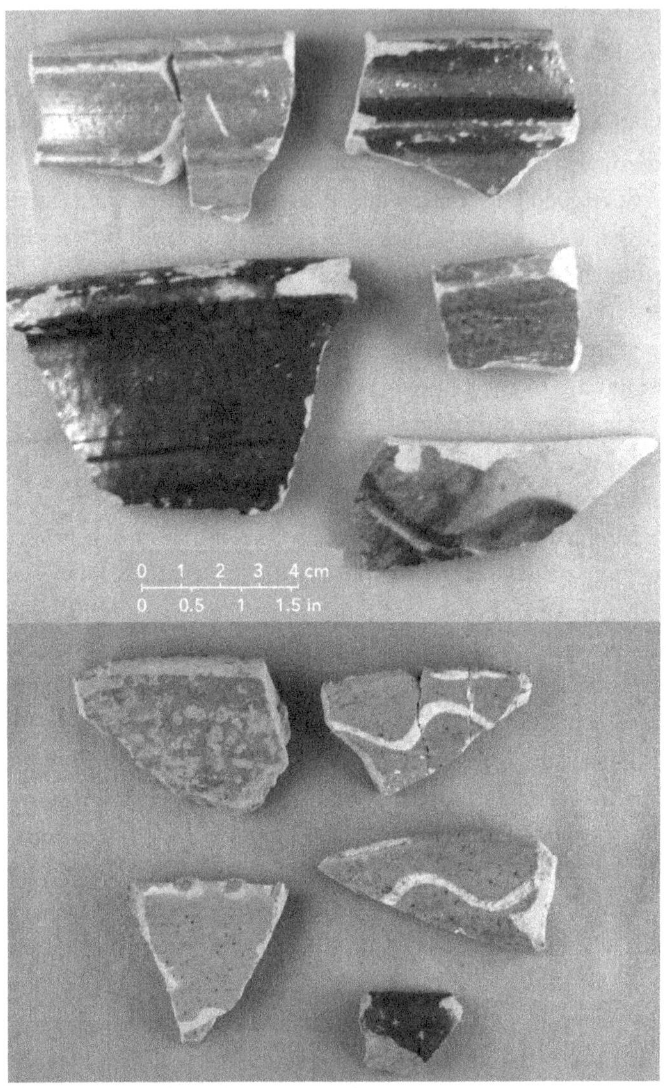

Redware from Boone's Station (first row: two collared rims; second row: two thickened, everted rims and cobalt blue decorated body sherd; third row, left to right: plain plate rim, yellow slip-trailed plate rim; fourth row, clockwise: notched plate rim, yellow slip-trailed plate rim, jug rim).

surfaces, 11 sherds are glazed only on the exterior, and 184 sherds are glazed only on the interior. Ninety-five sherds are glazed on one surface but were too small to identify whether the glaze was on the interior or exterior. The remaining 618 sherds are spalls, generally with remnants of glaze. Glazing only the interior lowered the price of the vessel while still making it impermeable. Glazing only the exterior made the vessel less versatile in its use, being suitable only for dry storage or processing. However, such vessels may have been used for storing salt, herbs, or spices that simply needed a dry environment.

Lead glazes on redware generally appear amber to reddish brown in color. They may vary in how light or dark they are but generally are fairly uniform across the pot. There has not been sufficient archaeological investigation of individual pottery manufacturing sites in Kentucky to determine if glaze or other variations distinguished specific potters. Most redware analyses do not identify distinctive glazes, in large part because the sample size is frequently relatively small. The Boone's Station redware assemblage is large enough to attempt to recognize distinctive glazes that may eventually be associated with specific potters as research continues. Most of the sherds exhibit the common medium to dark-amber or reddish-brown glaze that is ubiquitous among locally produced redware in the Central Kentucky area. However, I identified seven glaze variations that suggest to me that the variation was intended by the potter, who introduced specific mineral oxides to create specific colors.

The most common glaze variation is a dark-brown glaze that often has a metallic sheen. This glaze may have involved the use of manganese oxide to produce the dark-brown color and metallic sheen. The dark-brown glaze is also observed in combination with a mottled/speckled glaze that occurs as another glaze variation. A dark-orange glaze is present on fifty sherds. A particularly distinctive glaze is bright orange that is exclusively used with yellow slip trailing as well as alone. Finally, a green glaze also observed in a few examples at other early historic sites was possibly produced by adding copper salts. It occurs often enough in other assemblages to be considered a glaze that many potters produced. The green color varies from a bright, vivid hue to a duller lighter green.

Vessel forms include plates, globular and straight-sided crocks, collared rim forms in which the rim is shaped in an ogee curve, small orifice forms such as jugs or bottles, a handled form, and thin-walled forms with straight rims that may be drinking vessels. The 1993 survey recovered two sherds with pouring spouts that may be from pitchers.

Table 13.9. Distribution of Redware Glaze Types from Boone's Station

Glaze Variations	Block 1	Block 2	Block 3	Block 4	Block 5	Total
Common amber glaze	219	218	308	104	292	1,141
Dark-brown/metallic glaze	16	102	64	30	26	238
Dark-brown glaze exterior and common amber glaze interior	1	17	9	0	0	27
Dark-brown glaze exterior and mottled/speckled glaze interior	0	62	2	0	0	64
Unglazed	69	19	78	17	29	212
Mottled, speckled glaze	17	53	20	10	25	125
Mottled, speckled/dark-brown glaze	0	51	0	8	1	60
Dark-orange glaze	4	15	17	5	9	50
Dark-orange glaze exterior and dark-brown glaze interior	0	1	0	0	0	1
Bright-orange glaze	0	0	8	2	7	17
Bright-orange glaze with slip trailing	0	0	0	0	2	2
Green glaze	3	0	4	1	2	10

I examined the redware rims and bases associated with the excavation blocks containing remains of structures to determine the types of vessels used in each house. The redware from Block 1 totals 323 sherds of which 24 sherds are rims, bases, or appendages. At least four thickened, everted rims, with either flattened or rounded lips, may have been wide-mouthed jars with either ovoid or straight-sided bodies. These vessels are glazed with the common amber, mottled/speckled, and dark-brown glazes. A thin, straight rim may indicate a mug. Two collared rim sherds glazed with common amber and dark-brown glazes may indicate the use of bowls or straight-sided pots. The common amber glazed rim is only glazed on the interior and incompletely in the curve of the collar, which is one inch in height. The single strap handle was also recovered from this block. Its dark-brown metallic glaze could not be associated with other sherds to infer its vessel form definitively. The handle fragment is nearly flat and is from either the top or bottom end of the handle where it attaches to the pot. It may have once been part of a jug. Dark-orange, bright-orange, and green glazed sherds, numbering only 5 sherds total, were also identified, but no vessel form was identifiable.

Block 1 yielded a single sherd from a large diameter crock that has a light-amber exterior glaze with a blue decoration; the interior is unglazed. This is the only evidence of applied blue decorative elements to a redware vessel from the site. Another possible decorative treatment includes a glaze squiggle on the unglazed exterior of a single body sherd.

An estimated sixteen or seventeen vessels were identified among the Block 2 sherds, which, at 433 fragments, is the highest number of sherds recovered from any of the blocks. However, the sherd count per cubic meter of excavated cultural midden is only 33 sherds. This low density is partly due to the amount of stone rubble, which did not yield very many artifacts of any kind. The vessels fall into five forms, including collared rim vessels that are either ovoid or straight sided in form; relatively small vessels with thin, straight rims, such as mugs; heavy-duty pans or jars with thickened, everted rims and flat or rounded lips; and one possible bowl with a rounded rim and a plate. Glazes include, in order by decreasing frequency, common amber, dark brown, mottled/speckled, dark orange, and three combinations of two glazes (dark-brown glaze exterior, and mottled/speckled glaze interior; dark-brown glaze exterior and common-amber glaze interior; and dark-orange glaze exterior and dark-brown glaze interior). No green or bright-orange glazed sherds were identified.

Three or four vessels have collared rims that measure 1.2 inches from the lip to the bottom of the rim. This rim type would have facilitated the use of fabric covers that were tied around the top of the vessel, because of the indentation of the curve from the lip. Two heavily spalled, dark-brown glazed rim sherds from the same pot were recovered from the floor of the cellar in two different units. Another very similar rim was recovered from the same unit as one of the rims on the floor but stratigraphically at a much higher level within the ash layer above stone rubble fill. It may have been from a different pot that had the same type of rim since it was not found at the floor level. Glaze spalling was common on redware from the ash layer and may have been caused by the fire that ignited in the house. However, spalling also seems to be related to the thinness of the glaze.

Another pot is represented by two collared rims that have a dark-brown glazed exterior and a common amber glazed interior. The potter slopped some dark-brown glaze over the rim on the interior. The rims are slightly more than a half-inch thick at the lip and were part of a heavy-duty pot that was likely fairly large. One was found on the cellar floor, while the other was slightly higher in the rubble fill in an adjacent unit.

A collared rim glazed with common amber glaze was recovered from outside the cellar next to the foundation. Like the other collared rims, the lip is more than a half-inch thick, indicative of a heavy-duty pot. Its location outside the house suggests another use that was not related to food storage or processing.

Four sherds with thin, straight rims and rounded lips indicate smaller, lighter vessels that may have been from mugs or tankards. Three of the rims have dark-brown glaze, and the remaining rim has common amber glaze. They were distributed outside the foundation, in the plow zone on top of the cellar fill, and on the cellar floor.

Three pot bases, representing two vessels, have an ovoid form with a tooled foot flange at the base of the pot. The calculated diameter of the two of the sherds from the same pot is approximately 3.75 inches. It is glazed dark brown on both surfaces. Another pot base, glazed dark brown, has a calculated diameter of six and one-half inches. It was recovered from the floor of the cellar. They may have been from ovoid vessel forms.

Evidence of four vessels with thin, straight rims suggests that they were from smaller, lightweight form such as mugs or jars. Three of them exhibit dark brown glaze; the fourth vessel has common amber glaze. They were distributed similarly to the collared rim vessels, with one on the cellar floor, another in the ash layer, and a third outside the cellar next to the foundation. The fourth rim was recovered from the plow zone inside the cellar. This distribution suggests that redware vessels were kept in several places in the house, including the cellar and on an upper floor, as well as outside.

Three vessels indicated by rims recovered from the ash layer may have been kept on the first or second floor of the house. One of the rims is glazed with heavily spalled, common amber glaze and has a thickened flat lip and a pair of lines scored on the lip. It appears to be from a plate. Two rims from two different vessels, both with a mottled/speckled glaze, are everted with rounded lips. One of the rims is very similar to a larger rim sherd found in the rubble layer that may be from a bowl. It has two raised bands encircling the vessel body 1.5 inches below the lip.

The redware from Block 2 represents a variety of food storage and processing forms as well as tableware. The vessels with collared rims are particularly interesting because they are a common form in the assemblage but seem to be uncommon among redware in general. They may be associated with a particular potter. I identified collared rims among the pottery produced by James Ingels in Bourbon County during the early nineteenth century. A collared rim is also illustrated in the technical report on Constant's Station, in Clark County. The distribution of sherds on the cellar floor suggests that the cellar was used to store and use some of the pots, possibly in a kitchen setting. Sherds from higher in the cellar fill stratigraphy may be from pots that were kept on upper floors. The single plate rim, for example, was recovered from ashy fill, as was a collared rim vessel and two vessels with everted rims. The bowl rim came from the rubble zone that underlay the ash layer. Plates, bowls, mugs, and pitchers were used on the table and may have been stored near a dining area. While redware is normally associated with cooking, processing, and storage of food, the vessels could have been used for other, nonculinary purposes. Some examples are slop jars, chamber pots, water dishes for pets, or storage of personal items.[69]

Block 4 has the lowest frequency of redware of the blocks with verified structures and the lowest number of sherds per cubic meter at twenty-five sherds. However, eight glazes or glaze combinations were recovered, dominated by the common amber glaze (seventy sherds), dark-brown glaze (thirty-three sherds), and mottled/speckled glaze (sixteen sherds). All the minor glazes (bright orange, dark orange, and green) are also present but in very small quantities (less than four sherds). Glaze combinations include single examples of dark brown and common amber, as well as dark orange and dark brown. Minimally, eleven vessels are represented by the glazes, although some only have one representative sherd. Vessel forms include a thin-walled, mottled/speckled glazed vessel, a dark-brown and common amber glazed form with a straight rim and slightly thickened lip, and a common amber glazed form with a slightly everted, thickened rim with a flat lip. No collared rims or plates were recovered.

Block 5, containing the cellar of a fourth structure at the site, yielded 335 sherds. Proportionally, based on a gross calculation of sherd frequency per cubic meter of cultural midden excavated, the redware sherd count from Block 5 was the highest, at 152 sherds per cubic meter. The redware from Block 5 was also quite diverse, both in the glazes represented and the vessel forms, including unique occurrence of plates that were not found in any of the other blocks. The minimum number of vessels represented by sherds from

Block 5 is estimated to be fifteen. At least five plates are represented. One of them has a bright-orange glaze with yellow slip-trailed wavy lines encircling the inside edge of the rim. This plate is very similar to plates that have been identified in a site from Lexington and may have been made by a Lexington potter. Possibilities include James Jeffs, Robert Campbell, John Carty, or Richard Metheny. Another plate with a bright-orange glaze has a notched rim. Three plates have amber, mottled/speckled, and dark-orange glazes with simple, unembellished rims. The only evidence of a bottle or jug also came from Block 5. The two rims have a dark-brown, shiny glaze. Straight rims with rounded lips may have been from two mugs glazed in green and amber. An amber glazed vessel with a wide-collared rim, another large cylindrical form with a mottled/speckled glaze, as well as two vessels (glazed in amber and dark brown) with slightly thickened rims and rounded or flat lips probably represent food storage and processing crocks.

In addition to the common glazes (amber, dark brown, and mottled/speckled), all the minor glazes (bright orange, dark orange, and green) occur, as well as five glaze combinations. These include bright orange and amber, dark brown exterior and orange interior, dark orange and amber, dark orange and dark brown, and dark orange and mottled/speckled. Each of these glaze combinations probably represents a separate vessel.

Although Block 3 did not have definitive evidence of a structural foundation or feature as found in the other blocks, there may have been a station cabin next to the stockade ditch, as was the norm for stockaded stations. It may not have stood or been occupied as long as the other structures, as suggested by the low frequencies of nails and windowpane. The relatively large quantities of kitchen-related and faunal artifacts, however, suggest that Block 3 was a common work area between the stone house and the structure in Block 5 or that it served as a place for disposal of broken or discarded household goods. The frequency of redware in Block 3 is nearly as high as Block 2. Common amber glaze is the most frequent, followed by dark brown, mottled/speckled, bright orange, green, and five-glaze combinations (amber and mottled/speckled, dark brown and amber, dark brown and dark orange, dark brown and mottled/speckled, and mottled/speckled and dark orange). Two bases with a bright-orange interior glaze and a mottled/speckled glaze on the interior and exterior are from globular or ovoid forms. The latter has a slight foot flange. Other vessels are represented by dark-brown glazed bases, one on only the interior and one on both surfaces. Another base has an interior common amber glaze, and one is unglazed. Two common amber glazed rims are from two vessels with an everted, thickened lip and a thickened rim with a rounded lip. A simple plate rim without embellishments has a dark-orange glaze. Most of the sherds are from the vessel body or are spalls. The body sherds include specimens that are glazed on just one side and on both. The small size of most of the body sherds precludes an accurate minimum vessel count, but based on the rims and bases, at least eight vessels are represented as well as five vessels that have various glaze combinations.

Stoneware

Although stoneware was being produced in Kentucky as early as 1820, it did not become the most common utilitarian ceramic in use until the mid- to late nineteenth century. The Boone's Station excavation recovered only one hundred sherds. Brown and gray exterior salt glazes are the only two recognizable types. Twenty-six sherds are burned, or their glaze is too debased to identify. The stoneware probably dates to the 1840s and represents a small number of vessels.

Several vessels are identifiable when the sherds are segregated by excavation block. Nine sherds were recovered from Block 1, all of which are basal or body sherds; no rims were recovered. A minimum number of four vessels are identifiable. Two sherds with gray salt-glazed exteriors and slip-glazed interiors are from a vessel that had a thick, heavy base with a diameter of 3.6 inches. The vessel was probably straight sided. Two body sherds that crossmend to a single sherd have a gray, salt-glazed exterior and an unglazed interior. The interior paste of the sherds is unusually yellow for stoneware, which generally has a gray paste. Another base has a grayish-brown glazed exterior and a brown slip interior, but the extant basal curve is too small to measure. The interior section of a base represents a fourth vessel, but no other sherds are associated with it.

Block 2 has the highest frequency of stoneware with fifty-two sherds. Eleven of the sherds are from a single vessel that is tentatively identified as a chamber pot and described under pharmaceutical and personal hygiene artifacts. Seventeen are burned or the glaze is unidentifiable. However, the six rim sherds in this group indicate that vessels featuring flattened or everted rounded lips are represented.

Nineteen sherds have brown salt-glazed exteriors. A minimum of three vessels are identifiable. One sherd is from a vessel with a thick, heavy base with an unglazed or lightly slipped interior. Two sherds from the same vessel have a calculated basal diameter of 4.8 inches. Seven sherds are from a cylindrical vessel with a calculated basal diameter of 14.8 inches. The brown salt glaze on the exterior has some precipitate adhering to its surface; the interior is a brown slip.

Gray, salt-glazed sherds that may have been from vessels used in the kitchen include only four examples. Two are underfired. Underfired vessels are still functional but may have been sold at a reduced price. A single sherd has an unusual dark-gray slip interior accompanying a well-vitrified, gray, salt-glazed exterior. It is unique in its glaze characteristics. Another unique sherd has a brownish-gray salt-glazed exterior and a brown-slipped interior. A narrow, incised line runs horizontally across the sherd.

Only ten stoneware sherds were recovered from Block 3. Two sherds are brown salt glazed, six are gray salt glazed, and two have indeterminate glazes. Two gray, salt-glazed rims may represent a single vessel with a narrow-collared rim and a lug handle. The stoneware from Block 3 probably was broken elsewhere on the site and discarded here as trash.

Block 4 yielded fourteen stoneware sherds that include one brown, salt-glazed sherd from a thick-walled vessel, two sherds that are burned, and eleven gray, salt-glazed sherds that likely all came from the same vessel. The gray, salt-glazed vessel has a calculated basal diameter of 7.4 inches, which is fairly large. The rim, based on two spalls, may have been a type of rolled rim. The body sherds do not have much curvature, suggesting a cylindrical form. The base is flat and footless. It may have been a wide-mouthed jar with an unrestricted orifice.

Only nine stoneware sherds were recovered from Block 5. Four sherds are too burned to identify glaze or other characteristics. Three sherds fit together and represent a gray, salt-glazed vessel with an unglazed interior with a similar yellow paste found on sherds from Block 1. Two sherds are gray salt glazed but appear to be from different vessels. One is a thick-walled vessel; the other is from a thinner-walled vessel.

Yellow Ware

Five sherds of yellow ware were recovered from Block 1. The sherds are probably from the same vessel, which was thin walled with an everted rim and narrow brown banding on the exterior. The surface color of the sherds is a warm gold. The sherds are too small to determine vessel form. Although yellow ware was made in the 1840s, it became more common later in the century. However, some of the early yellow ware must have been available, given its presence at Boone's Station.[70]

Glass Tableware and Containers

The laborious process of early glass container production by hand blowing each piece made glass bottles, containers, and tableware expensive compared to containers of other materials. Glassmaking in the American colonies began as early as Jamestown in the seventeenth century, but this and other attempts were largely unsuccessful through the eighteenth century. The glass industry only began to thrive when immigrants, many of German origin, brought European glass technology to the United States in the early nineteenth century. A federal manufacturing census in 1820 listed six American firms making glassware and bottles. The early nineteenth century was a period of technological innovation in the production of glassware that culminated in highly efficient, high-volume production of glass packaging and tableware by the last half of the century. However, during the time Boone's Station was occupied, glass bottles, containers, and tableware remained relatively expensive to acquire.[71]

Glass bottles and tableware were considered important enough to be listed separately in estate inventories and resold. John Floyd's inventory, taken in 1783, listed a large bottle valued at three shillings—$27.66 today. While the buying power of currency was greater than it is today because of inflation, the relative cost of glass tableware and bottles meant that a consumer had to have enough discretionary income to afford them. Jonathan Clark's estate sale of 1812 listed eleven glass mugs at $2.50, twenty tumblers at $3.75, wine glasses at $2.00, eleven jelly glasses at $1.83, three glass salts at $1.25, a five-gallon demijohn, and twenty-five quart bottles at $5.12½, as well as many other glass bottles and containers. Judging by the items offered for sale and the $4,589.00 that they brought, Clark was an affluent man. Bourbon County resident Winney Webb was an affluent woman with many assets. By 1823, when her personal estate was sold, Isaac Webb Jr. bought her eight used wine glasses for $2.00, and his father, Isaac Sr., bought eight mugs and fourteen tumblers for $5.37½.[72]

Glass bottles, containers, and tableware artifacts number 962 specimens for the site as a whole. Most of the fragments (879 pieces) were recovered from the excavation blocks. Most of the fragments are too small to be identified by their function and do not have other characteristics that are informative. Most of them are probably from bottles. The remaining 86 fragments are classified as bottles, flasks, general tableware, tumblers, and stemware. In addition to clear and translucent colorless glass, colored glass includes amber, aquamarine, light green, dark green (including "black" glass, which is a very dark green), olive green, medium green, light blue, and cobalt blue.

Glass tableware was recovered from every excavation block but is most frequent from Blocks 1 and 2. Tumblers, faceted body forms, stemmed goblets, and holloware are represented. Pressed, etched, and a single example of cut glass indicate more elaborate glass tableware—the translucent cut glass rim from Block 2 is particularly elaborate. It features a serrated edge consisting of scalloped and pointed elements, and circular medallions with a daisy-like flower in the center. When viewed in cross section, the rim flares slightly from the body of what may have been a bowl. Pressed designs include a large checkered pattern consisting of 5/8-inch squares separated by pressed ribs. Two clear fragments from Block 1 and one clear fragment from Block 2 share this pattern. A tighter check pattern occurs on another clear glass fragment from Block 1. Pressed vertical ribs running parallel to each other, or on a slight diagonal, and possible circular or oval hobnail elements form other designs, but the fragments are too small to discern the patterns more completely.

The most common vessel forms in the glass tableware are tumblers and stemware. Tumblers are the most common form. At least three tumblers and two stemmed vessels are represented, with ten rims indicating either tumblers or stemware. All fragments are clear or translucent glass.

Block 1 contained the highest frequency of glass tableware with thirty-two fragments. Block 2 yielded eight fragments while Block 5 had seven fragments—including the two stemmed goblet bases. Four fragments were recovered from Block 4 and a single fragment from Block 3. The single cut glass rim is from the ash layer of the cellar in Block 2. All the tableware from Block 2 was recovered from the ash layer, the stone rubble, or, in one case, the plow zone, indicating that they were stored in an upper story of the house, mostly likely on the first floor.

Container glass that served as commercial packaging accounts for the largest proportion of the glass assemblage. Where rims and bases retain diagnostic traits regarding their date of manufacture, as well as specific features like body shape or rim finish, they exhibit traits associated with early bottle-making techniques: for example, hand blowing with a blowpipe, which leaves a jagged, empontilled scar on the base of the bottle, and later innovations such as using a lipping tool to produce a more uniform finish. None of the container glass has any of the characteristics of machine-blown glass. Body shapes include a small number of panel bottles with evidence of embossed labels on three fragments. Cylindrical bottle shape is the most common form. Rim types include bead, sheared ring, prescription, flanged, straight with fire-polished lip, Packer, and oil finishes that are either applied by adding glass or manipulating the glass at the end of the neck or by using a lipping tool to produce a more uniform finish. Lipping tools gained popularity in the 1840s. One small, translucent rim from Block 4 has a very small orifice diameter that would have dispensed its product in very small amounts. It may have been part of a cologne bottle.[73]

A very specific type of bottle, the flask, was produced to hold alcoholic beverages. Sixty-one fragments are identifiable as coming from flasks. All but one olive-green fragment from Block 1 are aquamarine in color. All fragments, save two, were recovered from the ash and stone rubble layers and plow zone in Block 2. A single aquamarine fragment was recovered from Block 4. Two flask bases are empontilled, indicating they were handblown in a mold with a blowpipe. One rim has a bead finish. The body type of the flasks is what is commonly called a violin or scroll shape. The capacity of the flasks represented in the assemblage was probably a pint or less. The flask style suggests manufacturing dates in the 1830s or 1840s.[74]

Iron Cooking Ware

Cast-iron cooking pots, skillets, Dutch ovens, and the like were commonly used to prepare food over open fires or on cookstoves. During the time the site was occupied as a defensive station, the inhabitants would have cooked over open fires in the small fireplaces typical of station cabins. The Frank house would have had much larger chimney hearths common to early houses. The depiction of the house on a map from a lawsuit shows two end chimneys; depending on how many flues the chimneys had, there could have been as many as six hearths (two on each floor and two in the basement), but it is more likely that there were fewer—at least two on the first floor at a minimum and perhaps one on the second floor. The fireplace used for cooking would have been furnished with hooks and a trammel for suspending pots over the fire and moving them to various areas as a means of controlling the amount of heat.

Estate inventories often mention cooking equipment because of their value. When John Cockrell died on the site in 1809, his inventory listed a "large iron kettle," two ovens (most likely Dutch ovens), two iron pots, an iron griddle, and a frying pan. Elizabeth Frank's inventory listed one pot and hooks, a small pot, a skillet, an old bake oven, and a griddle. She also had a kettle and a frying pan that were probably metal but may not have been cast iron. The mention of the hooks suggests that she or an enslaved cook prepared food over an open fire in a fireplace. The "old bake oven" was probably a Dutch oven with a lid. Food such as bread could be baked by nestling the pot in coals and piling additional coals on top of the lid to surround the food with consistent heat.[75]

Cast iron is durable and long-lasting if taken care of properly. It does not break easily and, as a result, is not commonly found in archaeological assemblages. Only six fragments of cast-iron cookware were recovered from Boone's Station. Four are remnants from unidentified pots. Two are lid fragments. One of the lids is from the lower levels of the cellar fill in Block 5. It has a lid ledge and a raised, one-inch rim, and its calculated diameter is 12.4 inches. The other lid fragment is from the stone rubble layer in Block 2; it, too, has a lid ledge and a one-inch raised rim. It may have been from a larger Dutch oven, perhaps as large as eighteen to twenty inches in diameter. A pot of this size may have had short legs. Both lids could have been used with a Dutch oven. A single pot fragment was found in the metal detection area and in Block 4, and two fragments are from Block 5.

Utensils

Forty-two utensils are represented in the Boone's Station assemblage. They include forks, knives, and spoons made of ferrous metal that is probably steel in most cases, and nonferrous metal that was used only for spoons. The utensils are not high-quality silverware but rather cheaper-quality table cutlery with handles made of less expensive materials such as bone, generally termed "composite cutlery." As with other household goods discussed previously, utensils are often listed in estate inventories. Knives and forks are generally mentioned together, as the appraisers for Elizabeth Frank's did in 1807. There is no mention of spoons in her inventory, but they may have been claimed

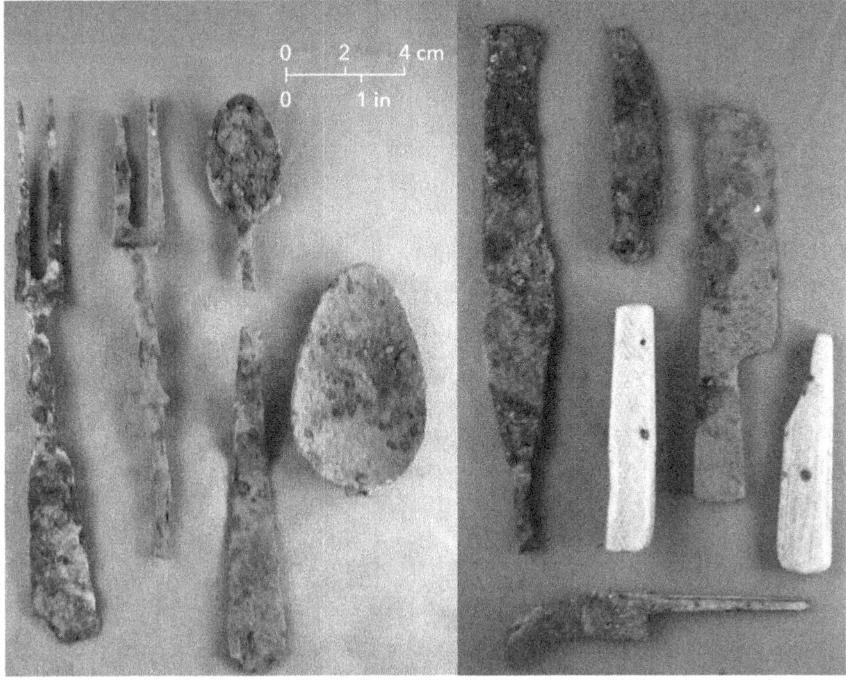

Utensils from Boone's Station (left: two tined forks, teaspoon bowl, spoon handle, and serving spoon bowl; right: three iron knife blades, two bone riveted handle scales, iron folding knife handle, missing blade).

by a family member, particularly if they were silver or pewter. Similarly, John Cockrell's estate also included a set of knives and forks, valued the same as Mrs. Frank's at six shillings.

The features of composite knives and forks have their own terminology. Knife features include the blade; the bolster, which may be present where the blade joins the handle; the scale, which is the nonmetal part that is riveted to each side of a flat tang that forms the base of the handle; and pins, a term for rivets. Tangs could be flat or of the "rat-tail" or "through" variety, for use with socketed handles. A through tang runs the length of the handle and is terminated with a butt cap. Knife blades are straight, curved, or humpbacked. Another feature of a knife blade is the choil, or heel, which occurs at the bolster. The business end of a fork is its tines, or prongs, which connect to a shoulder and shank. The shank is attached to the handle by either flat, rat-tail, or through tangs.[76]

Table 13.10. Distribution of Utensils in Excavation Blocks and Metal Detection Area

Utensil Type	Block 1	Block 2	Block 3	Block 4	Block 5	Metal Detection	Total
Handles							
Bone scale	1	2	0	0	0	0	3
Flat tang	1	2	0	0	0	0	3
Knife Blades							
Flat tang	0	2	1	0	3	1	7
Rat-tail tang	0	2	1	0	1	1	5
Tang missing	1	2	2	2	1	0	8
Forks	1	1	0	1	4	0	7
Spoons	1	2	1	2	1	1	8
Total	5	13	5	5	10	3	41

Spoons were often made of pewter, a soft metal that was easily melted, and people could make their own spoons in molds. Pewter was commonly used and recycled for many household objects like spoons, plates, and basins. As a result, it is uncommon in the archaeological record. Spoons were also made of steel or nonferrous metal like brass or silver. They usually were cast as a single piece. The spoons from Boone's Station are made from steel or a nonferrous metal that is not pewter and are either teaspoon or serving size. The forks from the site are two-pronged. Knives are more numerous and more varied in length and style than forks and spoons are. Utensils were recovered from every block excavation and from the metal detection area.

The utensils vary in type and specific features, suggesting that they were discarded or lost at various times and by various people over the history of the site. Although the knives shared characteristics such as having a choil and a bolster, no two knives are identical, and the straight, curved, or humpbacked variety of knife blade can be seen throughout. All three types occur at Boone's Station; six straight, four humpbacked, and two curved blades, as well as a heavily resharpened blade, are identifiable. The humpbacked type of blade came into use between 1720 and 1760 and continued to be available until about 1820. Knife technology changed relatively slowly during the late eighteenth and early nineteenth centuries. Knives could be used for decades if they were properly cared for. Even if broken, a blade could be resharpened, which changed its original shape. At least two blades, both from Block 5, show evidence of resharpening to the point where the choil is gone. One of the blades is straight, the other is humpbacked, and both are bolstered.[77]

Knife handles exhibit two methods of attachment. The older style has a rat-tail tang to which a bone, an antler, or a wooden handle was attached. By the 1720s, use of a flat tang allowed the attachment of two scales to be riveted to either side. The technique allowed the use of thinner pieces of material. The scales are wedge-shaped and taper toward the blade. Two bone scales of this type are present in the Boone's Station assemblage. Both are from Block 2. One of the scales is faceted and has cross-hatching on the side facets and diagonal slashes on the top. The end of the scale retains unpolished bone showing the interior spongy marrow of the material. The other scale is flat and has narrow ribs running its length. Two rivets that extend through the tang hold the scales in place.[78]

Another feature that developed during the 1760s is the addition of a choil or heel to the blade at its juncture with the bolster. Of the ten blades with intact blade/bolster junctures, six have a choil and four do not. Two other blades may have had choils, but resharpening may have removed them. On the other end of the blade, the three blade tips have a bulbous termination that is often associated with English knives.[79]

Thirteen bolstered and two nonbolstered blades are identifiable. All the bolsters appear to be integral to the blade and not applied separately. Where the full length of the blade is measurable, examples of two-and-a-half-, four-, and six-inch blades occur. Partial lengths suggest that most of the blades are over four inches in length. Both bone scales are three inches in length, as is one of the flat-tanged blades, suggesting that a three-inch handle is a common handle length. The majority of the knives are probably meant for use as eating utensils rather than as carving or slicing knives. An exception is a small blade from Block 2 that is the size of a paring knife or perhaps a patch knife (used to cut patch material for a muzzle-loading rifle charge).

Seven two-pronged forks include three examples with mostly intact prongs measuring two or two-and-a-half inches in length. Four forks have flat tangs, and one has a rat-tail tang or possibly a through tang for attaching the handle. Two of the flat tang handles are missing the prongs but retain the circular shank typical of a fork. Block 5 yielded the highest number of forks at four specimens; single examples were recovered from Blocks 1, 2, and 4.

Eight spoons are represented by either the bowl or a handle with characteristics typical of a spoon. All but two are probably made of steel; the other two are of a nonferrous metal. Three are serving size, and two are teaspoons. The three handles were cast as a single piece that included the spoon bowls. The weakest part of the utensil is the narrow neck at the junction with the spoon bowl. Two of the serving spoons, one of the teaspoons, and two handles broke off at this point. The other teaspoon broke along the neck of the handle one inch below the spoon bowl. One of the serving spoons is represented by half of the bowl, including the bowl tip. The break is jagged and must have required considerable force to break the metal. One spoon was recovered from Blocks 1, 3, 5, and the metal detection area. Two spoons each were recovered from Blocks 2 and 4.

Foodways and Diet

Evidence of the diet consumed by the inhabitants of Boone's Station is comprised of animal bone, a few fish scales, a corn cob fragment, and a fruit pit. The bulk of the evidence pertains to the meat portion of the diet. The assemblage contains 3,008 animal bones. These range from complete, or mostly complete, bone elements that can be identified to the level of family or species to small fragments that could not be identified. The animal bone identification and analysis were completed by students in a University of Kentucky Department of Anthropology class (ANT 580) taught by Dr. Tanya Peres in the spring semester of 2003.

The first occupants of Boone's Station, when it served as a defensive residence, brought domesticated animals with them. Horses were essential for transportation and beasts of burden. Cows, pigs, sheep, and poultry were also brought to Kentucky. Domestic dogs accompanied settlers as well.

The settlers' diet was augmented by wild game until their domestic livestock was well enough established to provide all the meat they needed. Large game animals such as bison, white-tailed deer, and elk provided the largest quantities of meat as well as hides for making leather; bone and antler were manufactured into various articles such as utensil handles, buttons, and powder horns. As the population grew, some of the wild species, like bison and deer, became scarce as their numbers dwindled from overhunting and habitat alteration. The bison were the first to disappear. Their herds were essentially decimated long before the last sighting of a bison in 1820. Deer decreased in numbers at a lower rate because of their adaptability to forest edge environments created by the humans who cleared forests for farmland, leaving patches of woodlands across the landscape. John James Audubon observed around 1810 that the vast number of deer that once thrived in the Ohio valley had "ceased to exist." As wild game became harder to procure, domestic animals grew in number, essentially making up for the loss of wild game. This process of replacement was well underway by the 1790s.[80]

Once the frontier period had passed, the occupants of Boone's Station focused on developing the property for farming and raising livestock. The consumption of wild game diminished except for sport hunting as an occasional pastime. Robert Frank raised pigs, horses, and cattle. By the time his wife died in 1807, her estate appraisal listed eleven shoats, three sows, five young pigs, and twelve "fatt Hogs," a bay colt with white feet, a "sorrell" (sorrel) horse, a brown mare, a pair of oxen, two "pided" (marked with two or more colors) steers, two pided cows, two red and white steers, a red "Muley Cow & pided Calf," a pided heifer calf, a red steer yearling, and two bull calves. John Cockrell's estate appraisal lists a ten-year-old dark-brown mare, a one-year-old brown filly, a four-year-old brown mare, a seven-year-old bay mare, a four-year-old gray horse, a three-year-old sorrel colt, seven sheep, a black cow, a red and white cow, a red and white heifer, three red heifers and two red calves, three other calves, sixteen hogs, a sow, a sow with pigs, and eight geese. The cattle may have been from red and white Dutch cattle, red Devon, or mixes of these breeds, which were common in Virginia. Cockrell seems to have been more engaged in raising horses than the Franks were, and he was more diverse generally in his stock.

Horse bone is relatively rare in archaeological assemblages because horses were rarely eaten. Exceptions occurred—for example, consumption under conditions of food shortages. During the siege of Fort Boonesborough in 1778, the settlers were forced to stay in the fort for nine days while a large army of Native Americans besieged the site. During the exchange of gunfire, a gray mare belonging to Richard Callaway was killed. The animal was butchered and eaten because food was getting scarce, and the settlers did not know when or if the siege would be lifted. A pit filled with the remains of a mare that had been butchered was discovered inside the fort during archaeological excavations.

Not surprisingly, only two horse bones were identified in the Boone's Station sample. Both were recovered from Block 2, and one exhibits cut marks, indicating butchering. Modern American cultural practices do not consider horse meat as a food source, but that was not always the case. Nevertheless, the value of a live horse outweighed its value as a meat source in the late eighteenth and early nineteenth centuries.[81]

Other domesticated animals entered the food chain in different ways and for different reasons. Cows were raised for their milk (which encouraged the retention of females), meat, hides (for leather), and bone, as well as for their horns and hooves for powder horns, utensil handles, and other products. Bulls were needed for reproductive purposes, but the average farm did not need more than one. Cattle required more pasturage than pigs or poultry did, but they were valuable because they could be sold. Cattle breeding became a major agricultural practice in Kentucky, beginning in the late eighteenth century. The Kentucky Bluegrass became a cattle-feeding area by the 1790s, which provided the impetus for improving the cattle breeds. English breeds were imported by farmers on the Eastern Seaboard, and some of these cattle, or their offspring, were brought into Kentucky. Later in the early nineteenth century, Kentucky breeders imported English cattle directly as part of a breed improvement initiative. The Central Kentucky area became famous for its Shorthorn cattle.[82]

Sheep were brought to Kentucky as early as 1775, when Fort Boonesborough was settled, but they were difficult to raise on the frontier because of their need for shelter during inclement weather and their vulnerability against predators. Raising sheep for their wool and meat never became a major agricultural activity in the Central Kentucky area, though large-scale farmers did some breed experimentation. Nor is mutton and lamb prominent in Kentucky foodways even today. No evidence of sheep was identified in the faunal assemblage at Boone's Station.

Pigs were perhaps the most successful livestock raised by the settlers and, later, farmers. They are the most common domesticated animal represented in the site faunal assemblage. When Kentucky was first settled, pigs were turned out into the woods to forage and fatten on acorns and other forest resources. They were rounded up in the fall, slaughtered, and preserved as hams, jowl, bacon, souse, sausage, and lard. Later, as the area became more settled, pigs were kept confined. They were useful for consuming food scraps and had large litters of piglets, making them a reliable, sustainable source of meat. Pigs are well represented in the Boone's Station assemblage.

Poultry, such as chickens, were commonly raised, mostly by women, who sold or traded surplus eggs to local merchants as well as for personal consumption. Although vulnerable to predation, both by wild animals like coyotes or wolves and domestic pets like dogs, they were easy to shelter and useful for cleaning up food scraps. However, their presence in archaeological assemblages is usually limited because their lightweight bones, easily consumed by scavengers, do not preserve well. This seems to be the case at Boone's Station.

Domestic dogs came to Kentucky with the earliest settlers and have remained faithful members of many Kentucky families since. They were used for hunting, companionship, and protection. Dogs were present at Boone's Station, though it is impossible to determine how common they were.

Wild animals represented in the Boone's Station faunal assemblage include species that contributed to the diet as well as animals that were attracted to the food resources of human groups and simply extended their habitats to include human residences. The principal large animals taken for their meat were white-tailed deer, elk, and bison. Smaller animals included wild turkeys, birds (such as quail), various fishes, and possibly turtles, rabbits, and squirrels. The assemblage also includes fish bones, including those of drum, catfish, and bony fish of unidentified species that were probably taken from nearby Boone or Baughman Creeks or the Kentucky River, located only a few miles away. Eleven of the twelve fish bones were recovered from Block 5. A single bone from a drum was recovered from Block 2. A fishhook from Block 2 is further evidence that some of the occupants enjoyed fishing. Animals that were probably not part of the diet but were present on the site include mole, raccoon, chipmunk, opossum, and rat. A single bone from a bobcat was also identified. Bobcats shun human contact, and it is safe to assume that this incidence was a rare event, perhaps a onetime encounter.

The frequency of animal bone is highest in Block 3, followed by 5, 1, 2, and 4, in descending order (table 13.11). The scarcity of wild meat sources in the Frank house cellar in Block 2 suggests that the abandonment of large game as a significant source of meat was underway by the time Robert Frank built his house. Of the small wild animals represented in Block 2, all are species that continued to flourish in Kentucky, and some of them, such as the rabbit and squirrel, may have been consumed, while raccoon and chipmunk were not. The relatively high number of pig and cow bones relative to the other blocks where houses stood further reinforces this conclusion. Unidentified bird bones suggest that more poultry is represented here.

Block 3 stands out as having the greatest diversity and the largest quantity of animal bone. While it is likely that a cabin once stood next to the

Table 13.11.Identified Animal Species by Excavation Block

Animal Species	Block 1	Block 2	Block 3	Block 4	Block 5	Total
Domestic Species						
Pig (*Sus scrofa*)	64	81	62	5	43	255
Cow (*Bos taurus*)	1	15	18	2	2	38
Chicken (*Gallus gallus domesticus*)	5	0	0	0	1	6
Horse (*Equus caballus*)	0	2	0	0	0	2
Dog (*Canis familiaris*)	2	0	0	0	1	3
Wild Species						
White-tailed deer (*Odocoileus virginianus*)	8	6	41	2	3	60
Elk (*Cervus canadensis*)	0	0	3	0	1	4
Wild turkey (*Meleagus gallopavo*)	1	0	0	0	0	1
Quail (*Phasianidae*)	0	0	0	0	1	1
Gray squirrel (*Sciurus carolensis or Sciurus sp.*)	1	1	0	0	4	6
Mole (*Scalopus aquatica*)	3	0	0	0	0	3
Raccoon (*Procyon lotor*)	0	1	0	0	0	1
Eastern cottontail rabbit (*Sylvilagus floridanus*)	0	2	1	0	0	3
Eastern chipmunk (*Tamias striatus*)	0	2	0	0	0	2
Virginia opossum (*Didelphis virginiana*)	0	0	1	0	0	1
Bobcat (*Lynx rufus*)	0	0	1	0	0	1
Turtle (*Testudines*)	0	0	0	0	1	1
Drumfish (*Aplodinotus grunniens*)	0	1	0	0	1	2
Catfish (*Ictaluridae*)	0	0	0	0	1	1
Bony fish (*Osteichthyes*)	0	0	0	0	9	9
Rat (*Cricetidae*)	0	0	0	0	1	1
Subtotal	85	111	127	9	69	401
Unidentified Mammal	395	296	801	66	284	1,842
Unidentified Bird	23	22	9	2	47	103
Grand Total	503	429	937	77	400	2,346

stockade section in Block 3, the artifact patterns noted elsewhere in this chapter suggest that this area became a work and/or disposal area. Household trash, including food scraps and discarded bones, is abundant in Block 3. The block yielded the highest quantity of deer bone and most of the elk bone.

While the raw numbers for large game animal bone are relatively small, its presence in areas where the early station cabins stood does confirm that the site's first inhabitants were consuming a mixed meat diet from domestic and wild sources. One wild species that was commonly hunted and consumed by Kentuckian settlers, the bison, is absent from the assemblage. Daniel Boone was a market hunter, and he and his family were most assuredly eating bison while they lived there. However, the large size of bison dictated the practice of butchering most of the meat at the site of the kill and leaving the larger bones behind. The exception is the hump, where the meat was considered a delicacy. The hump is composed of a series of thoracic vertebra. It was generally butchered as a single piece with the vertebra retained within the meat. The meat was generally roasted and consumed by gnawing the bone. Disposal for dogs and other animals to eat typically results in breaking long, thin bones like ribs, long bones, and thoracic vertebra into small pieces that are difficult to identify. Other diagnostic parts of the bison, such as the large, bony skull, were not usually brought back by the hunter. Bison and cows share many anatomical similarities, and distinguishing between them is difficult if diagnostic bones are not present. Given these factors, and the short period that the station was occupied when bison were more plentiful, it is not surprising that it was not identified, even though the archival record confirms that bison was an important part of the pioneer diet.

Furnishings

Artifacts classified as furnishings cover a potentially wide range of types, from furniture to decorative items to fireplace equipment and the like. However, artifacts in this category are usually uncommon in archaeological assemblages. Only seventeen artifacts are classified as furnishings. Not all artifacts are definitively identified because of their fragmentary condition.

Block 1 yielded four artifacts. A narrow flat iron strip with a rectangular perforation near a rounded end may be related to door hardware. The artifact is six inches in length and a half-inch wide. It may be missing either or both ends. Speculatively, it may have been part of a door hinge strap or a latch

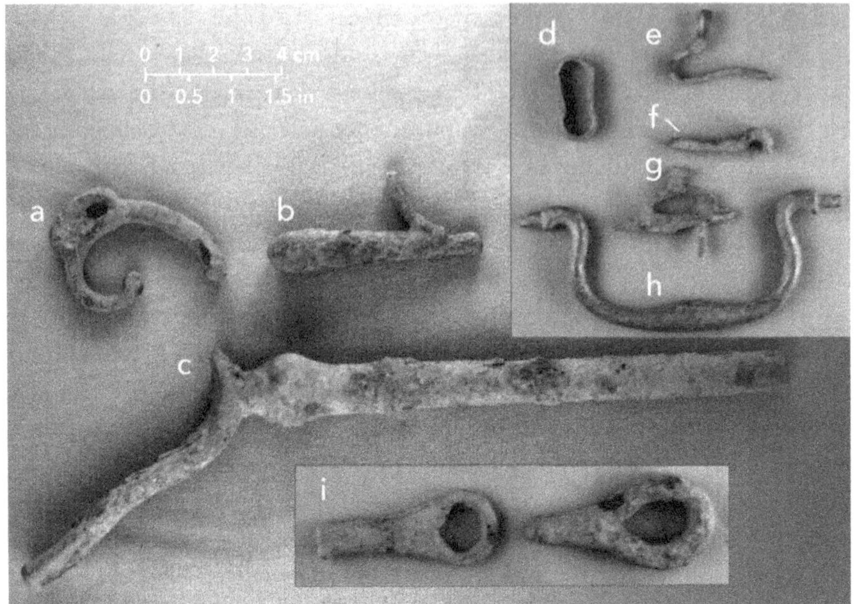

Furnishings from Boone's Station (a–c. cast-iron bracket and finial fragments; d. brass keyhole escutcheon; e, f. iron closure hooks; g. possible iron latch part; h. Chippendale style handle; i. iron closure eyes).

mechanism. Two artifacts are both made of brass. A brass bail handle for a drawer is curved and has a bulging midsection that dates it after 1750 but before 1785. It may have been attached to a piece of furniture in the Chippendale style. A small brass hook was also recovered from Block 1. The hook has a small ring attached perpendicular to the vertical shaft that attaches to the hook. The orientation of the ring attached to the back of the hook suggests that the hook was suspended from a small eye so that it could pivot from left to right to engage the catch. It could have been attached to a box lid that had a lip extending slightly beyond the walls of the box so that the hook could hang freely from the eye. Possibly related to the hook and the bail handle are two handmade screws. The screws have threads that vary in the angle or pitch of the thread to the shaft, which does not taper like modern screws. Handmade screws were time consuming to make, requiring a file to cut the threads. A machine for cutting the screw threads on a lathe was invented around the time of the War of 1812. The timing of its invention delayed its distribution and development until after the war. It produced screws with sharp, even threads but the slot in the screw head still was hand cut with a hacksaw and was often off-center. The slots on the screws from Block 1 are both slightly off-center.

Block 2 yielded four carpet or furniture tacks, two handmade screws, one brass lock escutcheon, two small iron latch parts, and two cross-mended, clear glass fragments from the rim of a lamp chimney. The tacks have cut shafts. One of the screws in Block 2 appears to have an off-center slot and is similar to the screw in Block 1. The other screw is very worn, and diagnostic features are difficult to identify. However, it is very similar to the other handmade screws from the site. The lock escutcheon could have been part of many different items that are fitted with locks, including many types of storage boxes (for documents, jewelry, and other valuables) or a piece of furniture that had locking doors or drawers—to give only two examples. The escutcheon is nearly one inch in length and is the same size as escutcheons I have observed on an antique chest of drawers and desk. The latch parts include a small hook and a part that is only tentatively identified as a latch. The lamp chimney identification is based on the roughened exterior of the fragments, which cross mend to form part of a rim. Lamp chimney rims were roughened to achieve a tighter fit within the lamp collar that surrounded the wick holder. The chimney has pressed decorative ribbing. The fragments were recovered from the ash and rubble zones of the cellar in Block 2, indicating that the lamp was on an upper floor when the house collapsed.[83]

Block 3 yielded four artifacts that are tentatively classified under furnishings. A very small iron eye with a cut shaft may be the catch for a latch hook mechanism. The other three artifacts are cast iron. A curvilinear decorative fragment may have been part of a trivet or perhaps a decorative railing or grillwork. Another artifact is more difficult to identify definitively. It has a circular shaft that is 4.5 inches long, at which point the casting forms some type of pronged armature. The object is fairly heavy but retains decorative elements. The remaining artifact is a short iron shaft with an expanded circular loop on one end. The other end is broken. This artifact is similar to the eye used in a hook-and-eye door closure. Eyes used in this fashion are also called pintles. The eye was driven into the wood of the door frame, and a hook was attached to the door with a staple so that the eye served as a catch to hold the hook.

Block 4 yielded a handmade screw similar to the other screws from the site and a single cast-iron fragment that may be some type of finial or perhaps the end of a fireplace poker. Its identification is tentative.

An oval plate made of incised metal that once attached to a document or storage box and a curved piece of clear glass, which may have been part of a picture frame, were recovered from Block 5. The glass has a rounded, smooth edge and was either circular or oval. It was probably used with a frame for a miniature portrait. Block 5 also yielded an iron loop similar to but slightly larger and heavier than the artifact from Block 3, tentatively identified as an eye for a hook-and-eye door closure.

Hardware

Hardware is a diverse category that contains many different types of artifacts that can be used in multiple contexts. Tools, chains and chain links, staples, and hooks are examples of artifacts classified as general hardware. Among the tools recovered from the site are a whetstone fragment for sharpening edged tools, a serrated blade that may have been from a hacksaw, a bipointed tool that may be an awl or punch, and a heavy iron wedge for splitting wood. Other hardware includes four iron staples, three iron hooks, four iron chain segments, an iron horn cleat for securing rope, and a large threaded iron bolt.

The four staples may have been architectural in function. All of them appear to be made by a blacksmith. Two of them are similarly made of cut strips of iron that were bent into a squared-off staple with pointed, flattened ends to facilitate driving them into wood. They are heavy-duty and could have been used to hold heavy wooden structural members together. One of them is clinched, so it must have been driven completely through the wood and the protruding ends hammered back against the wood. It measures 1.9 inches in width, and the clinched side is 2.8 inches in total length. The other side is broken off. The other staple has straight, pointed ends that are not the same length. This staple is 1.6 inches wide with ends that measure 1.9 and 2.4 inches, respectively.

The other two staples are bent into a U-shape and have flattened ends. The larger of the two, measuring 1.3 inches wide and 2.1 inches in length, has a circular cross section at the top of the staple. The smaller staple appears to be made from a square-cut iron strip. It measures 0.7 inch in width, and its measurable prong is 2.1 inches in length. These staples could have been used to secure a hasp to a wooden frame, such as a door, or to hold heavy wooden structural members together. Three of the staples were recovered from the ash layer in the cellar of the house in Block 2. The clinched staple is from the metal detection area.[84]

Every hook recovered came from the ash layer in Block 2. Two are similar in size, about 3.5 inches in length, but they are made differently. One of them has a circular cross section and was bent into an elongated "U" that has a pointed termination on one side. The other hook is flat and was made by welding two flat pieces of iron together. The hook is shaped like a "U," but the termination on one side ends in a right angle. The other termination is broken. The third hook is a curved piece of heavy bar iron. The hook termination is squared off; the other end of the hook is broken. It is more heavy-duty than the other hooks. Hooks had many uses around a farm when connected to a chain, or attached to a whiffletree—a horizontal crossbar with hooks on each end to which animal harness traces were attached (also called a singletree). The harness traces fit around the horse and attach to a cart, wagon, or other farm implement. Hooks were also used in fireplaces to lift hot cooking pots or in tandem with a fireplace crane that had a hook to suspend pots over a fire.[85]

Three chain segments, three broken chain link fragments, and an intact link were recovered from Blocks 1, 2, and 5. All the chain and links are made of iron and appear to be handmade. Two fragments of the same lightweight link were recovered from Block 1. An identical intact link was recovered from Block 2. The links are 1.4 inches long, oblong in shape, and less than 0.1 inch in link diameter. A heavy-duty chain segment comprised of three links, a lighter weight chain segment comprised of three links, a broken link, and an intact link all were recovered from the rubble and ash layers of Block 2. A chain segment of two oblong links that are pinched to meet in the middle (forming a figure eight) was recovered from Block 5. The lighter-weight chains and broken links are similar in size; however, because the links were handmade, their diameter varies slightly. The smaller chains average around 0.24–0.25 inches in diameter while the heavier chain has a link diameter of approximately 0.4 inch. Like hooks, chains have many diverse uses. The provenience of the Block 2 chains suggests that they were on an upper floor of the stone house.

Iron horn cleats are usually associated with boats and used for securing mooring ropes, but they can be used in any context where rope needs to be secured. The cleat is from Block 5 and differs from boat cleats in that it has a ring for attachment rather than a flat base with two holes for attachment.

The ring hole is oval and approximately 0.5 inch at its longest dimension. The ring is suggestive of a specific type of attachment, perhaps on a shaft or rope.

The large bolt is either handmade or early machine cut. It is 4.5 inches in length, and the large circular head was attached by hand. The threads are cut along two inches of the shaft, which is square cut where there is no threading. The bolt was recovered from the ash layer in the cellar in Block 2.

Equine and Agricultural Artifacts

The families that lived at Boone's Station were mostly engaged in farming as either a principal occupation, like the Frank family, or supplemental, like John Hendley, who ran a tavern, and Harvey Bledsoe, who was involved in business affairs in Athens. Horses were essential for transportation as well as farmwork. The artifact assemblage from the site contains ample evidence of farming tools as well as the presence of horses.

Tools associated with farming include an axe head, three hoe blades, an iron tooth from a rake or similar implement, and a blade fragment from a tool like a spade or a trowel. The axe head was recovered from the rubble layer of Block 2 and has a square poll with ears. It is known as a broad, felling, or camp axe. It is quite heavy at five pounds and has seen extensive use. The three hoe blades are two different sizes. The smallest one is approximately six inches wide and lighter weight than the other two. The other two hoes are comparably sized at eight inches wide. The larger hoes are massive implements that required considerable strength to use. All three hoes show heavy use wear, and one of the blades is broken off. Large, heavy hoes are associated with field labor generally carried out by enslaved workers. The rake tooth was recovered from Block 1 and the spade or trowel blade from Block 4.

Equine artifacts refer to items associated with horses like harness tacks, horseshoes, and horseshoe nails. Archival information about the livestock owned by some of the site inhabitants mentions only horses and excludes any evidence of mules. However, horses and mules were both used in agriculture. Oxen are mentioned in one estate appraisal; it is possible that the artifacts discussed in this section were used with them. Equine artifacts include one possible harness buckle, sixteen horse- or oxen-shoe nails, and a nonferrous metal guide used to hold a leather strap in place on a saddle or harness trace. The buckle is the largest buckle recovered from the site. It has a rectangular frame measuring 1.8 by 2.4 inches. The tongue is attached to a long side. It

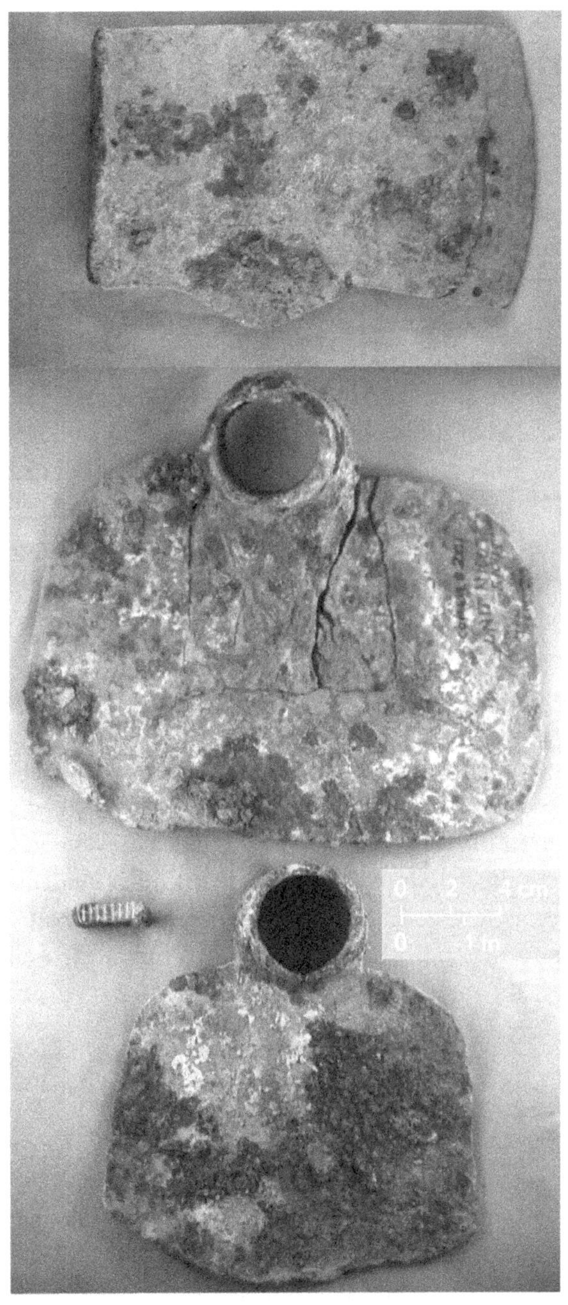

Equine and agricultural artifacts from Boone's Station (axe, two hoes, and a saddle strap guide).

was recovered from the metal detection area. It is similar in form to a buckle shown in a catalog issued in 1900 by J. H. & F. A. Sells Company, but it probably dates earlier in the nineteenth century.

Nails for horse, mule, or oxen shoes are specialized nails that required higher-quality iron and were handmade until machine-made processes were sufficiently improved in the middle to late 1860s. Preservation quality of the nails from Boone's Station is not optimal, and the difference between handmade and machine-made specimens was not easily recognizable. However, other features of the nails identify them as animal shoe nails. These characteristics are a function of how the nail was driven into the animal's hoof to attach the horseshoe. The nail is driven through the hole and through the outer edge of the hoof no higher than an inch or an inch and a half on the wall of the foot to avoid injury. The protruding end of the nail is bent over, and the end of the nail is clipped off. Then the nail is clinched by squeezing it with a clinching tool. This step produces a very tight bend or "pigtail" termination to the nail. If a horse "throws" a shoe (detaching the shoe from its hoof), the shoe often will be found with some of the nails still in their holes. This was not the case at Boone's Station. Five nails were recovered from Block 1, two each from Blocks 2 and 3, one from Block 5, and three from the metal detection area and two shovel tests.

The guide is a nonferrous metal strip slightly more than an inch long that was attached to a leather saddle to hold a one-inch leather strap in place. This example from Block 5 has parallel decorative grooves that have been cut perpendicular to the length of the guide. Two similar guides were found at Fort Boonesborough. One is plain without engraving; the other has X's and circles. The engraving on the Boone's Station example and the ones from Fort Boonesborough are not precise or well executed.[86]

Mysteries

The processes by which artifacts become part of the archaeological record are many and varied. The most common process is that an item breaks or becomes unusable and is discarded. The fragments of the broken item may be discarded in a specific trash disposal facility, scattered, or even taken offsite. Another process is loss, as when a button falls off a garment or an item is accidentally dropped. Artifacts like animal bone may be purposefully thrown out for domestic animals to scavenge, and, in so doing, they may consume them completely or simply fragment them further. Preservation factors such as soil acidity, moisture, heat, oxidation, and other processes affect artifacts once they are consigned to the soil. A bone button in acidic soil may not survive, while a porcelain button will be unaffected. Soil moisture causes iron objects to rust but has less effect on nonferrous metal. The effect of the many processes that influence what artifacts are deposited, their condition at the time of deposition, and what happens to them over time as preservation factors affect them, combine to produce an assemblage that is an incomplete picture. The preceding sections of this chapter presented information on many identifiable artifacts from Boone's Station, despite the factors that mitigate against artifact identification.

However, archaeologists inevitably encounter artifacts that have been so altered from their original functional state that little or no information or identification can be made. This category includes sheet and scrap metal (particularly iron) that is deteriorated beyond recognition, nondescript fragments of various materials, slag, melted glass, and the like. The Boone's Station assemblage contains examples that could not be identified, and they were eliminated from the analysis. This section describes four artifacts for which a definitive identification was not reached, in the hopes that they will be identified sometime in the future, and for comparative purposes in the event that a similar object is found elsewhere.

Two artifacts are identical except that one is made of iron and the other is made of steel. The iron specimen was recovered from the plow zone of Block 4. The steel specimen was recovered from Feature 7 of Block 2. Feature 7 was assigned to an ashy feature that was encountered in the subsoil along the west wall of Unit N1006E1049 at a depth of forty-three to fifty-four centimeters below datum. This feature, when further explored by excavation to the west of the unit, became part of the ash layer that was deposited between two layers of limestone rubble. The upper layer of limestone rubble just below the plow zone was only about seventeen centimeters thick, and the ash layer was intermingled. The artifact could have been deposited at a higher level and migrated downward as a result of plowing—the effects of bioturbation and the lack of consolidation of the soil because of air pockets in the rubble zone. The location of these artifacts relatively close to the surface suggests that they may have been deposited on the site after it was converted to farmland and possibly while it was being cultivated.

The artifacts are cut out of sheet iron or steel into a curvilinear form that is oval on one end, circular on the other, and joined by a neck. Two rivets are

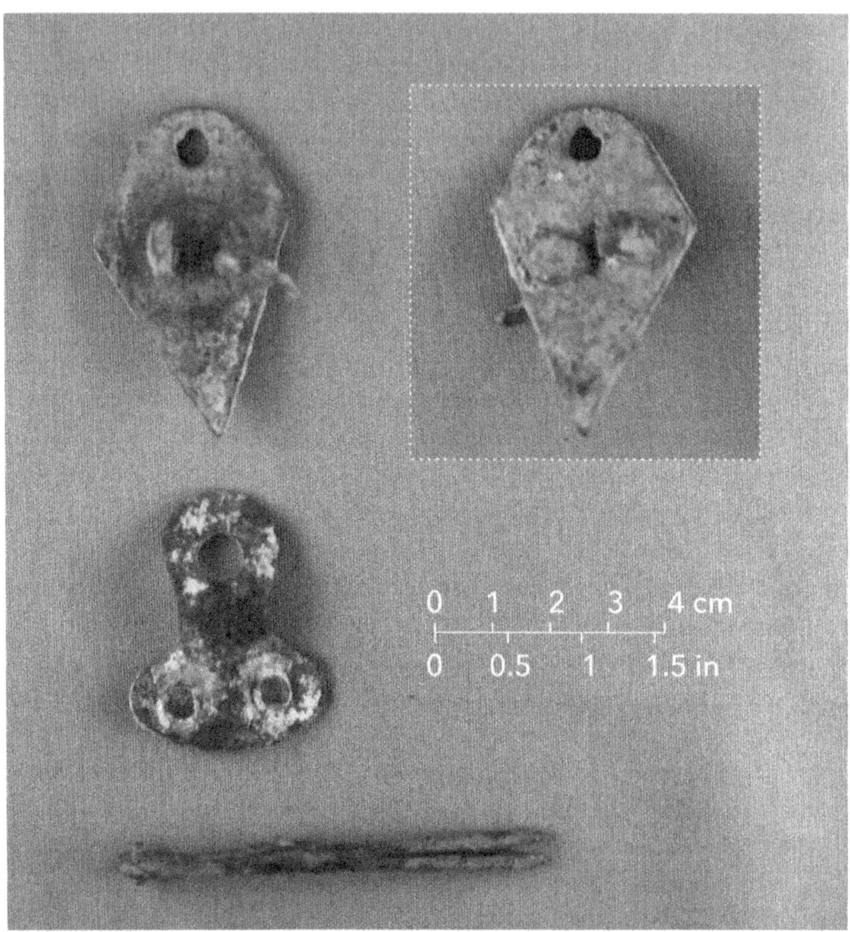

Mystery artifacts from Boone's Station.

present in the larger oval end, and a circular hole is centered on the circular end. The rivets attached the artifact to an unknown material. Its dimensions are 1.7 inches long, 1.3 inches wide at the oval end, and 0.8 inch wide at the circular end. The hole may have been intended to accept some type of hook or possibly a rope.

Another mystery artifact was recovered from the same unit as the two artifacts described above but at a much deeper location, 1.3 meters below the datum, which places it at the cellar floor. This artifact is clearly handmade from a ferrous metal that may be a steel alloy. The artifact was cut from a sheet and is triangular on one end and rounded on the other. The two sides of the triangular end form a forty-five-degree angle and are one and a half inches in length. Two wrought nails pierce the center of the artifact and protrude from the back, where their ends are clinched. The rivets are not perfectly centered, which conveys an asymmetrical appearance even though the metal backplate is symmetrical. A circular hole is at the rounded end. Maximum length is approximately two inches. The clinched ends of the nails resemble the clinching observed on a brass bridle rosette found at Fort Boonesborough. Bridle rosettes connected the horizontal browband that ran across the forehead of the horse just below its ears to the throat lash strap that ran vertically under its neck. The Boone's Station artifact is about twice the size of the Fort Boonesborough specimen, and its pointed end does not seem practical for use on a harness that has contact with an animal's head. However, the means of attachment appears similar. The hole at the rounded end remains a mystery.

A final mystery artifact was recovered from Block 1 in the plow zone. The iron artifact is just under three inches in length and features two square cut prongs 1.5 inches in length that are attached to a narrow handle with rivets similar to those seen on utensil handles that have bone scales. The underside of the handle is missing. The line of the prongs continues straight along the top of the handle, which seems to have had a curved end. The prongs are oriented next to each other if viewed from above, looking at the top of the artifact. The author's imagination has failed to come up with a plausible explanation of this artifact's function.

Conclusions

Kentucky's historic settlement period originated in conflict. The larger dispute was between the American colonies and England, their mother country. To the settlers who ventured across the Appalachians to the land known to the Wyandots as Kentucke (meaning the "land of tomorrow"), the conflict was instead with Native American tribes, who at first viewed them as trespassers and then as dangerous interlopers intent on appropriating Native American territory. The Native American alliance with England cemented this antagonism during the Revolutionary War. Both sides suffered great losses. This is not a book about settler-Native conflict, but that adversarial relationship underpins the origins of the two sites discussed here.[1]

The years defined by Daniel Boone's and Hugh McGary's Station sites, 1779–1849, was a pivotal time in American history. McGary's Station epitomizes the Revolutionary War period, when Kentucky was being settled amid dangerous and violent wartime conditions that led to defensive stations being built all over Central Kentucky. Constructed expediently and abandoned when more peaceful conditions prevailed, McGary's Station represents an archaeological time capsule of a pioneer occupation spanning at least nine years. The settlers who lived here endured primitive living conditions, deprivation, and the prospect of sudden, often fatal, Native American attacks. The artifacts they left behind are a testament to life under wartime conditions.

Boone's Station shares a common origin but takes the story of Kentucky's history further into its emergence as the fourteenth state, its adoption of slavery, its embrace of a capitalist economic system, and its place in antebellum

Upland South culture. During its occupation of seventy years, the American colonies won their independence and "created a new national government and a distinct party system and culture of democratic politics." Nationwide, the population nearly quadrupled between 1790 and 1840, and westward expansion enlarged the country almost threefold. A national transportation system was put in place, and an enslaved labor economy expanded in the South, while the North embraced industry.[2]

The families that lived at Boone's Station after the Revolutionary War were of the "middling" sort whose lifestyles were considerably different from the wealthy elite who were building wealth and large estates, influencing politics and maintaining lavish households. As Catherine Hutchins explained, "We can now say with some surety that most people had discretionary income or at the very least a choice about which essential goods to purchase or where to buy them. This ability to choose changed the quality of people's lives." The archaeological artifacts and features at Boone's and McGary's Stations offer important insights into the transition from frontier life through the early republic period of political unification and economics that terminated in the middle of the nineteenth century, only a dozen years before our cataclysmic Civil War brought the antebellum period to a close.[3]

The frontier period of the two sites, according to archival and archaeological evidence, is represented by the construction of a "station" using a standard template: log cabins arranged in a quadrilinear plan and connected by short sections of log stockade. The erection of a defensive residential complex that housed numerous families was a hybrid version that drew from classic military fort features such as stockades, and "house-forts" like Jarrett's Fort in the Greenbrier River valley of present-day West Virginia. The "community frontier defense system" in the Greenbrier valley utilized militia, spies, and the construction of forts that served as operational bases for militiamen and as "places of refuge for settlers in time of danger." Some of the forts consisted of stockaded enclosures with corner bastions and internal log buildings, while others were fortified houses. Living in the forts was seasonal for most settlers, who preferred to remain on their own land until an alarm compelled them to take refuge in the nearest fort.[4]

The Kentucky station model differed from fortified models further east—in that stations were occupied year-round rather than serving as seasonal places of sanctuary. They did not generally include corner bastions built in the classic military architectural style common to militia forts, although the military feature known as a "blockhouse," with an overhanging second story and gunports, was sometimes substituted. Families that lived in the stations still ventured out to their land claims to clear timber and plant crops, but they retreated at night to the station with which they were affiliated.

A commonality among fortified sites is the insular, protective stance the stockaded enclosures embodied. Cabin doors opened into the enclosure interior, and external walls lacked windows. The log walls of the cabins, the upright log puncheons that formed the stockade, gunports through which settlers could fire, and, in some sites, corner blockhouses that allowed for raking fire presented a strong, unassailable appearance that was intended to discourage attack. So unique and particular to purpose were these sites that they were usually abandoned or dismantled when the defensive need subsided. McGary's Station followed this pattern. Its artifact assemblage indicates that the occupants were affluent for the times but constrained by frontier conditions that affected the acquisition of material goods. Thus, while the inhabitants used wrought nails for construction and other purposes, the assemblage contains artifacts that suggest that someone at the site had blacksmithing skills to make many of the nails. This skill was not in evidence at Daniel Boone's Station.

Both assemblages contain clothing artifacts that were used on similar garments such as men's knee breeches, weskits, coats, and shirts. McGary's Station artifacts suggest greater attention to fashion through the use of decorative weskit or coat buttons, high leather boots held in place by buckles, and jewelry. The presence of straight razors also indicates the settler's prioritization of personal appearance. (Cultural proscriptions against facial hair prevailed among American men from the late seventeenth century until the late 1820s.) In contrast, clothing-related artifacts at Boone's Station that date early suggest simpler, unembellished clothing, perhaps a response to less concern about fashion.[5]

Early refined ceramics include delft, creamware, pearlware, and Chinese porcelain, indicating a level of refinement in dining and access to market sources, even if limited. Both McGary and Boone traveled back and forth between Kentucky and more easterly Virginia counties, where they could replenish their household goods if necessary.

Another parallel is the presence of artifacts relating to the safe storage of important documents, such as land grants and money, in locked document boxes. Although coinage was scarce on the frontier, a fragment of a Spanish reale, cut into a "piece of eight," from McGary's Station indicates that coins did circulate. Two oval box plates, a small medallion with a more ornate shape, a padlock hasp, and a box key were recovered from that site. The two plates probably were attached to two different boxes. A similar box plate was recovered from Boone's Station. The box plates were attached to the top of document boxes that were closed with a hasp that accepted a padlock or had an internal locking mechanism. These artifacts are indicative of the business affairs of men who were active in acquiring and selling land for themselves and for other men, requiring close attention to keeping transaction records secure.

Artifacts related to arms and ammunition also find parallels between the two sites. Unique to Boone's Station is the evidence of gunsmithing, a skill that Daniel Boone possessed. The use of muzzle-loading rifles or smoothbore guns was common for defense and hunting, and both sites contain evidence of these activities. The trade gun lock found at McGary's Station is particularly interesting because of his enmity against Native Americans. While trade guns were in circulation among the settlers and were not exclusive to Native Americans, the lock from McGary's was stripped of many of its parts and was discarded at some distance from the site. One can only speculate how it came to be there and wonder if McGary took an old trade gun from a Native American he killed. James Ray may also be the source of the lock as archival sources relate that he was given a trade gun belonging to a warrior he had killed.

The archaeological and archival data from the two stations form a picture of necessary or desirable goods to include when preparing to settle in Kentucky. The means by which to transport household and personal belongings varied, as did the individual resources of the settlers. McGary's forty horses would have served not only as transportation for the incoming settlers but also as beasts of burden to carry material goods. The artifact assemblages confirm that wrought nails, blacksmithing tools, imported refined ceramics, unrefined crockery, iron cookware and utensils, work and formal clothing and jewelry, sewing equipment, storage boxes for important documents and valuables, personal items (such as straight razors, hand mirrors, and smoking pipes), money, guns and ammunition, gunsmithing tools, and horse tack were considered important enough to include.

Architectural features in Boone's Station provide important information on how the station was constructed for residence and defense. Stockade construction was minimized to short sections between the cabins. The log cabins in Blocks 1 and 4 indicate that one was smaller than the other and that both had stacked limestone foundations that underpinned the entire structure.

The presence of foundations indicates that the cabins were floored. The cellar in Block 5 was probably an internal storage feature in another cabin. Variations in cabin size may be due to the individual family that built it. Archival evidence states that the Boones moved to the site in the winter but did not build the cabins and stockade until the following spring. The family may have cut the timber ahead of time to allow it to season (lose moisture). If the logs were hewn and stacked properly, the drying process would result in a station construction that would have lasted longer. This precaution, in turn, may have been a decisive factor in retaining some of the cabins for reuse. A similar pattern of continued use of a station is documented at John Constant's Station in Clark County. The Constant family built an unstockaded station consisting of three cabins that they occupied from 1783 to the late 1820s or early 1830s. The artifact assemblage and architectural features such as cellars and limestone foundations share similarities to, and duplicate, some of the patterns identified for Boone's and McGary's Stations. In contrast, McGary's Station did not have a long period of occupation, which seems to be more common among stations that originated during the Revolutionary War.[6]

The transition to the early republic and antebellum periods is represented by changes in the site architecture and artifacts at Boone's Station. The station was unusual because it was repurposed to become part of a late eighteenth- to mid-nineteenth-century farmstead that retained some of the frontier era cabins, minus their flanking stockade, that housed enslaved persons or had other uses. The conversion reversed the insular quality of the station and reoriented the residential complex to an outward-facing posture. The stone house built by the Frank family probably faced Gentry Road, while the removal of the stockade and, most likely, some of the cabins, produced an orderly farmstead arrangement of a main house flanked by auxiliary buildings. The new site organization reflects the late eighteenth- to early nineteenth-century adoption of Georgian-style architecture, with its emphasis on order and balance. The conversion of the site from a defensive residence to a prosperous farm underscores the development of a settled society that was uniquely Kentuckian as well as American. The dangerous conditions of living under the threat of Native American attack were extinguished by the decisive defeat of the Shawnee at the Battle of Fallen Timbers in 1794 and the signing of the Treaty of Greenville in 1795.[7]

The adaptive reuse of Boone's Station entailed some modifications of the original stockaded enclosure. The stockade was torn down soon after the end of the Revolutionary War, since it was no longer needed for defense. Archaeological evidence from Block 3, where a stockade section was located, suggests that the cabin adjacent to the stockade was not retained for reuse. After the Frank family built their stone house on the south line of the station, they retained two cabins on either side of the house and at least one along the former north line. Artifacts such as small quantities of brick and windowpane glass suggest that the cabins were upgraded to include windows, possibly with improvements to their chimneys, and kept in repair so that they were suitable for occupation over several decades. Remote sensing, shovel probe, and metal detection data identified at least two other possible cabin locations that were not further investigated but were part of the original station plan. They may have also been torn down.

Samuel Potts Pointer mentioned five men, including himself, who may have lived with the Franks and occupied some of the cabins in 1788, but this was a short-term arrangement. Pointer said, "I made my home at Crossplains, Boon's [*sic*] old station. John Henry, [John] Bledsoe (Butcher, we called him), old [Robert] Frank . . . , [Richard] Chaney, and [George] Sharp (a son in law of old R. Frank), a one handed man—were in that neighbourhood. . . . The station was evacuated, but these men I have named, kept arms. There was no station there any more."[8]

The artifact assemblage from the stone house in Block 2 offers insights into the wealth status and social class of its white inhabitants. The Frank family built a fashionable house and owned enslaved persons—two indicators of a relatively high social class. Robert Frank's original land purchase of five hundred acres was large enough to divide among his children, which amounted to a generous legacy. His household goods included imported English and Chinese dinnerware, among the more expensive items to acquire. The family probably updated the house by adding a fashionable porch portico. Subsequent families who lived in the house were similarly affluent and upheld their middle-class social status embodied in tableware embellished with decorative ceramic and pressed glass patterns, and evidence of stylish attire. Yet the artifact assemblage does not suggest that the families at Boone's Station functioned on the same social level as, for example, Senator Henry Clay, who lived at his Ashland estate in Lexington around the same time. One of the privies excavated at Ashland dated between 1809 and 1852 and contained many examples of expensive ceramic and glass tableware that testified to Clay's wealth, social and political prominence, and upper-class position.

By comparison, the ceramic tableware from Block 2 have a wide diversity of refined wares and decorative types, ranging from edged and hand painted to transfer printed, but most of the sherds either are undecorated or have simply executed, hand-painted or edged decoration. Even among the more expensive transfer-printed wares, there are examples of manufacturing errors in transferring the pattern that resulted in lower priced "seconds." Undecorated sherds account for 63 percent of the refined ceramic ware types, excluding creamware, which is nearly all undecorated. The least expensive decoration, edged, hand painted, and annular/Mocha, comprises 20 percent of the assemblage, while the more expensive transfer printing accounts for 17 percent. The same calculations for the other block excavation yield very similar percentages.[9]

Glass tableware is even less embellished and much lower in frequency. A single fragment from a cut glass vessel in Block 2 is the most elaborate example. The pressed glass tableware only represents four possible patterns on ten fragments. One of the patterns, a simple pressed check, was recovered from both Blocks 1 and 2, representing another instance of shared patterns between houses. Most of the glass tableware fragments are from drinking vessels (tumblers and stemware). Some of the tumbler fragments have ribbed body molding blown in a contact mold. Both stemware fragments were recovered from Block 5. They are too small to determine the style, but the stem of one of them is attached rather sloppily to the base that has remnants of an empontilled mark, suggesting that it was made quickly and without much attention to detail.[10]

Archaeological evidence confirms that the three cabins in Blocks 1, 4, and 5 were used either continuously or sporadically after the station period ended until the 1840s, when the site ceased to be residential. One of the cabins may have served as a detached kitchen. Others were probably occupied by the enslaved persons associated with the white families known to have lived at the site.

The number of enslaved people living at the site at any given time is known only for the Frank family, John Hendley, and Hiram Bledsoe. Robert Frank enslaved at least nine individuals in 1792 when he wrote his will. They included one adult man, two adult women, four boys, and two girls (including one who was probably biracial). Although familial relationships are not stated in the will, the man, Will, and one of the women, most likely Dinah, may have been parents to some of the children. The other adult woman, Jenny, may have been the mother of the biracial girl, Aggy, and perhaps other children. Each family may have occupied two of the station cabins, leaving a third to serve as a kitchen. Frank's death in 1798 would have disrupted the familial relationships of his enslaved persons when five of the children (Cozer, Ben, Suckey, George, and Aggy) he willed to his grown children were claimed by their new owners. Remaining with Frank's wife Elizabeth were the three adults and a boy named Tom. By the time of Elizabeth's death in 1807, she still owned Tom, Will, Dinah, and a boy named Jefry, who was probably Dinah's child. Jenny was not listed and may have died or been sold. The four individuals were all to be sold upon Elizabeth's death, and the property was sold as well.[11]

The new owners, John Cockrell and his wife, did not own any enslaved persons, though they could have rented their labor, as was common practice. It should be noted that they lived at the site for such a short period that they probably did not contribute much to the archaeological record.[12]

The next owner, John Hendley, was censused with four enslaved individuals in 1810, when he was probably living at the site. Their ages and sex are not known, but they may have only occupied one cabin. Hendley owned a tavern and may have used the house and cabins for his business until he lost the property in 1815.[13]

Following a nine-year period when the site was owned by an absentee landowner, Charles Grimes, the Bledsoe brothers purchased the property in 1824. One of the brothers, Harvey, probably lived at the site. A woman and four children were enslaved by Bledsoe at the time of his death in 1833. Presumably, they would have lived in only one of the houses, but a detached kitchen may have still been in use. Of the three cabins, the one in Block 4 is the best candidate for sporadic occupation because of its low frequency of artifacts. The cabin in Block 5 may have been the detached kitchen, leaving the building in Block 1 to house enslaved families.

The association of enslaved people with the occupation of Boone's Station offers interesting insights into the lives of individuals held in bondage. The archaeology of life among the enslaved developed as a new research field in the 1960s, with the excavation of quarters for enslaved people on Southern plantations. One of the initial objectives was to identify material elements that represented African heritage or cultural practices. The elements may be "recreations of African-styled or African-influenced objects" or "mass-produced objects and other Euro-American materials reinterpreted by slaves for African American meaning." Of particular interest are one translucent and three blue beads found in Blocks 1 and 2, a pierced stone pebble near Block 4, and the pierced King Charles II coin found during the 1993 survey. Both pierced coins and beads have been archaeologically documented in the context of the enslaved persons' cabin at President Andrew Jackson's Hermitage plantation in Tennessee as well as other sites in the southern United States. Blue is the predominant color of beads found in the enslaved peoples' sites from Virginia to Texas, but translucent beads were also documented at Hermitage. Blue beads may represent a vestige of Muslim belief that a single blue bead worn or sewn on clothing warded off "the evil eye." Likewise, bead use has African antecedents for decorative, medicinal, religious, and economic purposes.[14]

Folklorists have documented many instances of pierced coins used for good luck, protection from "conjuration," and to promote health. Pierced coins have been recovered from many enslaved persons' contexts, including the Hermitage, Andrew Jefferson's Monticello, and Harmony Hall in Georgia. Odd smooth stones have also been found in enslaved contexts. These artifacts may have had a role in traditional medicine and ritual, which have roots in African cultural practices.[15]

Other interactions between the enslaved inhabitants of Boone's Station and the white families that enslaved them concern household goods. Enslaved people had few opportunities to acquire material belongings on their own and were mostly dependent on what their owners supplied them. One means of supply was to give them cast-off refined ceramics or other household goods. The refined ceramics from Block 2 that date to the tenure of the Frank family include Chinese export porcelain as well as undecorated and decorated creamware and pearlware. All the excavation blocks containing houses held sherds from these wares, suggesting that enslaved people at the site were provided a variety of dishes in different patterns and ware types. In some cases, sherds with the same decorative pattern were recovered from the stone house where the Franks lived, as well as one or more of the enslaved's houses. These include: examples of Chinese porcelain from Blocks 1 and 2; a creamware annular ware pattern in Blocks 2, 4, and 5; a distinctive pearlware pattern in Blocks 2 and 5; and two marbled pearlware patterns from Blocks 2, 4, and 5. Block 3 contained several instances of sherd patterns that were duplicated in Blocks 2 and 5, suggesting that Block 3 was used as a common work and trash disposal area between the houses. Similar examples of shared ceramic patterns occur in the whiteware, notably in red/pink and green/light-orange transfer-printed sherds in Blocks 1 and 2, when Harvey Bledsoe was living at the site. His enslaved persons may have been living in the house in Block 1.

Other similarities are documented between the excavation blocks for the unrefined ceramics category. All the households were using redware in similar forms and similar glazes. Likewise, small quantities of stoneware with similar glazes occurred in the houses.

An interesting exception to the pattern of shared household goods is the presence of flasks that held alcoholic beverages in Block 2 but have very little representation elsewhere. While it was possible for enslaved people to obtain alcohol by various means, alcohol consumption was likely to have been prohibited by owners of the enslaved, which might account for the limited evidence. Another exception is the lack of evidence for the use of guns in enslaved contexts. The arms-related artifacts in Block 1 are mostly associated with the station occupation. The only other arms-related artifacts were recovered from the house cellar in Block 2, where the white landowners lived.

Enslaved people at the site also used eating utensils similar to those used by their owners and were eating mostly pork for their meat diet. They may have enhanced their diet with wild animals such as turkey, quail, turtle, and fish, which occur in small quantities in enslaved contexts.

The possible pit cellar identified in Block 5 is an intriguing feature that was not encountered in either Blocks 1, 3, or 4. Pit cellars are underground storage facilities that are not part of the foundation of a house as the cellar in Block 2 is. They have been documented in eighteenth-century houses occupied by enslaved people in Virginia and Kentucky. Internal storage cellars are not exclusive to housing for the enslaved, but they seem to be part of a pattern that is common enough to deserve consideration of its meaning at Boone's Station. Archaeologists have speculated that they were used to store root crops, household belongings, or contraband goods stolen from the owners of enslaved persons.[16]

Comparisons between the houses at Boone's Station reveal other contrasts. Blocks 1 and 2 have a much higher incidence of diverse ceramic wares with different glazes and decorative techniques. Both blocks have thirty-three combinations of ceramic ware types and decorative techniques (excluding undecorated creamware, pearlware, and whiteware, which occur in every excavation block). If the house in Block 1 was occupied by the enslaved after the station was converted to a farm, and white landowners or tenants lived in the stone house in Block 2, the presence of diverse ceramics may be due to a closer relationship between the two groups that manifested in frequent transfer of cooking and serving wares. This might have been the case if enslaved house servants were living in the house in Block 1. The occupants may also have had the means to acquire household goods in other ways, such as being allowed to work for pay outside of their normal duties.

In contrast, Blocks 4 and 5 exhibit much lower diversity of ceramic ware and decorative combinations, having twenty-one and twenty-three combinations respectively. The Block 4 assemblage is particularly impoverished, compared to other excavation blocks, in artifact density per cubic meter and in ceramic diversity. Its occupants were not completely excluded from receiving or acquiring decorated ceramics, but they do not seem to have participated to the extent that other enslaved people living on the site did. The house in Block 4 is smaller than either of the houses in Blocks 1 and 2; an alternative explanation is that fewer people lived there and simply did not own as many household goods. Another possibility is that the house may have been periodically vacant or served another purpose.

The archaeology of Boone's and McGary's Stations revealed many details about how early settlers and the Kentucky citizens that followed them went about their everyday lives. From tense years of warfare to the establishment of a more settled society, the artifacts and cultural features at the site evoke the gritty conditions of frontier life, the accommodations and resistance that enslaved people made to their forced servitude, the striving for middle-class respectability, and "the reshaping of everyday life" in the context of a changing world—or what Harriett Beecher Stowe recognized as "a transition period of society." Francis Underwood wrote that "the life of every community is made up of infinite details." So, too, is the life of an archaeological site. Archaeology provides many details at a granular scale, from the child-size thimble that a young girl used while sewing at McGary's Station to the pierced coin and beads that enslaved people may have worn as protection against evil spirits. The brightly patterned plates and bowls that women used to set a fashionable table, and the heavy hoes that field workers wielded to put food on that table—all these "infinite details" make up the tapestry of daily life.[17]

Acknowledgments

No one who conducts research of any kind operates in a vacuum. Archaeologists in particular rack up many names of people who helped with field and lab work, archival research, financial backing, support services like copyediting and manuscript review, and myriad other forms of assistance. My debts are many because the research for this book took place over many years and involved a large cast of helpful people. I tried my best to keep track of all the wonderful people who took an interest in my research and offered their assistance. I am also indebted to the staff at my former place of employment, the archaeological units in the Department of Anthropology at the University of Kentucky. These included the Program for Archaeological Research (formerly the Program for Cultural Resource Assessment) and the William S. Webb Museum of Anthropology.

The many students who cheerfully wielded shovels and trowels, pushed dirt through screens in hot, dry weather, and spent hours washing and cataloging artifacts deserve the first accolade. Each site was excavated during an archaeological field school offered by the University of Kentucky in 1999 at Daniel Boone's Station and by Transylvania University at Hugh McGary's Station in 2005.

Students who attended the 1999 field school at Boone's Station included Benjamin Baggett, Katie Bales, Jenna Cardwell, Alice Carver, Melissa Coomer, April Farmer, Will Goodman, John Hunter, Elizabeth Mills, Stephanie Tharp, Jodi Treadway, and David Turner. Graduate student Jim White served as crew chief, and Dr. Donald Linebaugh directed the students during the site-mapping and shovel-testing phases. I supervised the subsequent excavation. Artifact washing and cataloging was performed primarily by April Farmer, D. B. House, and Sara Gaines.

Students who attended the 2005 field school at McGary's Station included Shayden Bathon, Corey Clatterbuck, Michael Cruikshank, Stephanie Hart, Amanda Kerley, Gabe Montgomery, Austin Price, Monica Rowlett, Beth Smith, Lauren Strain, Rachel Wallace, and Andrew Wood. Transylvania University professor Dr. Chris Begley cotaught the class. Lab processing of the artifacts was performed by A. Goes and D. B. House. Metal conservation of some of the artifacts was conducted by Clifford Smith, Randy Fouts, and Carl Shields.

Other volunteers that helped with the fieldwork at McGary's Station included Mary Elizabeth Barrington, Susan Barrington, Marian Bauer, Austin Carter, John Carter, Dan Davis, Tanya Day, Ray Dexter, Jed Duffy, Pat Duffy, Wayne Estes, Becca Hebrock, Casey Lahndorff, David Nicholson, Deborah Peckler, Paul Ritchie, Lee Russell, Betsy Sale, Michael Sims, Tom Sussenbach, Bridget Tyler, Brittany Tyler, Will Updike, Tyler Walton, Diane White, Jennifer White, Travis White, and Aaron Ziebart. Stanley Felix, metal detectorist extraordinaire, was instrumental in locating the exact location of McGary's Station by identifying metal targets.

Dr. R. Berle Clay donated his time to perform remote-sensing surveys at both sites. His first survey at McGary's Station was conducted while he was director of the Office of State Archaeology at the University of Kentucky. His survey of Boone's Station was done while he was the geophysical specialist at Cultural Resource Analysts in Lexington. His employer, Chuck Niquette, graciously allowed the use of his firm's remote-sensing equipment at Boone's Station.

Financial assistance was provided by the Kentucky Department of Parks and the University of Kentucky Department of Anthropology, for survey and excavation of Boone's Station, and by the late Ralph Anderson of Belcan Corporation and Anderson Circle Farm and Transylvania University, for McGary's Station.

Over the many years that my research spanned, some of the people who helped have unfortunately died and did not have the chance to learn how it all came out. Nevertheless, I offer my gratitude in their memory. Frances Keightley introduced me to her childhood friend, Ralph Anderson, who owned McGary's Station, and shared her prodigious historic knowledge of Mercer County. My dear friend Neal Hammon exchanged emails with me, provided information and ideas, debated the interpretation of my data, and was a great sounding board over our long friendship. Rochelle Cochran of the

Boone Society was very supportive of my research and provided assistance in various ways.

Genealogical information on the Frank and Cockrell families was provided by Eleanor Marcotte and Tom Cockerel. Kathryn Weiss provided information on the Boone family. Architectural historian Karen Hudson worked with me on the initial survey of Boone's Station and analyzed the drawing of the Frank house for this book. Clary Estes copyedited my draft before I sent it to the press and served as a thoughtful lay reader. Dr. Mary Powell, my friend and colleague, read the draft and made useful and encouraging comments. Donna Gilbreath and Hayward Wilkirson prepared many of the book's figures. George Kissick provided photographic aid for a last-minute change to one of the figures. The Wisconsin Historical Society gave permission for the use of James Ray's portrait in figure 5 (WIH-Name File). The two George Thompsons in figure 8 were from the Rafinesque Manuscript Collection, and their use was permitted by the Transylvania University Library. Barbara Gortman and Ed Winkle made sure the bills got paid and provided the unsung but necessary support services that every researcher needs. We worked together for decades, and they never missed a beat.

Notes

Introduction

1. Stephen Aron, "Putting Kentucky in Its Place," in *Bluegrass Renaissance: The History and Culture of Central Kentucky, 1792–1852*, ed. James C. Klotter and Daniel Rowland (Lexington: University Press of Kentucky, 2012), 38.

1. Daniel Boone and Hugh McGary

1. John Mack Faragher, *Daniel Boone: The Life and Legend of an American Pioneer* (New York: Henry Holt, 1992), 80–84.

2. Faragher, *Daniel Boone*, 85–87.

3. Andrea L. Smalley, "'They Steal Our Deer and Land': Contested Hunting Grounds in the Trans-Appalachian West," *Register of the Kentucky Historical Society* 114, nos. 3 and 4 (2016): 303–39.

4. Faragher, *Daniel Boone*, 88; John Bakeless, *Daniel Boone: Master of the Wilderness* (New York: William Morrow, 1939), 67; Mary Powell Hammersmith, *Hugh McGary, Senior: Pioneer of Virginia, North Carolina, Kentucky and Indiana* (Wheaton, IL: Nodus Press, 2000), 117; Kathryn H. Weiss, *Daniel Bryan, Nephew of Daniel Boone: His Narrative and Other Stories* (Forbestown, CA: Privately Printed, 2008), 88.

5. Hammersmith, *Hugh McGary*, 88, 114. McGary eventually was the head of a blended family composed of his wife, Mary Buntin Ray McGary; her three sons, James, William, and John, by her first husband, John Ray; and her sons, Robert (born in 1767), Daniel (born in 1770), and William R. (born after 1772 but before 1775), by McGary.

6. Faragher, *Daniel Boone*, 89–96.

7. Hammersmith, *Hugh McGary*, 114–15, 118.

8. Weiss, *Daniel Bryan*, 88; Julian P. Boyd, "The Sheriff in Colonial North Carolina," in *Essays on American Colonial History*, ed. Paul Goodman (New York: Holt, Rinehart and Winston, 1972), 313.

9. Boyd, "Sheriff," 314.

10. Hammersmith, *Hugh McGary*, 137.

11. Faragher, *Daniel Boone*, 100–101; Nancy O'Malley, *Boonesborough Unearthed: Frontier Archaeology at a Revolutionary Fort* (Lexington: University Press of Kentucky, 2019), 5.

12. Colin G. Calloway, "'We Have Always Been the Frontier': The American Revolution in Shawnee Country," *American Indian Quarterly* 16, no. 1 (1992): 39–41.

13. O'Malley, *Boonesborough Unearthed*, 13–14.

14. Daniel Boone returned to North Carolina in June, where his wife Rebecca was nearly ready to give birth to a son, named William, who did not live long. After a few brief weeks of recuperation, Rebecca packed her household goods and prepared to move to Kentucky with her husband and children. Bakeless, *Daniel Boone*, 107. McGary's association and presumed friendship with Daniel Boone is intriguing given the very different reputations of the two men. Boone was not prone to criticize people, but he did prize honesty and forthrightness in all his personal relationships. It seems unlikely that he would have allowed McGary to accompany him on a journey that required the cooperation of all involved if he did not trust him to be a reliable and capable companion. A series of three letters (Draper MSS 12C16, WHS) from Dr. John Ray, son of James Ray, to Lyman C. Draper, constitute the major source of information on James Ray's activities during the early settlement period of Kentucky. Mann Butler's notes from a conversation with James Ray, Hugh McGary's stepson, state that McGary brought forty horses with him when he came to Kentucky (Draper MSS 12C15, WHS). This is a sizable herd of animals that were very valuable on the Kentucky frontier. Horses were often stolen by Native Americans or were killed in skirmishes. McGary was unfortunate enough to lose all but one of his horses by these means. His stepson, James Ray, retained the remaining horse and used it when he hunted for game to feed the inhabitants of Fort Harrod.

2. The McGarys Settle in Harrodsburg

1. Notes by Mann Butler, Draper MSS 12C15, WHS.

2. Sarah Graham told Reverend Shane that "McGary's Station" was at the present location of the Mercer County Courthouse; Lucien Beckner, "Rev. John Dabney Shane's Interview with Mrs. Sarah Graham of Bath County," *Filson Club History Quarterly* 9 (1935): 225.

3. George Morgan Chinn, *Kentucky Settlement and Statehood 1750–1800* (Frankfort: Kentucky Historical Society, 1975), 117–18; Mary Powell Hammersmith, *Hugh McGary, Senior: Pioneer of Virginia, North Carolina, Kentucky and Indiana* (Wheaton, IL: Nodus Press, 2000), 125–26.

4. Hammersmith, *Hugh McGary*, 126–28; John Cowan's Journal, Draper MSS 4CC30, WHS.

5. John Ray's letter dated February 23, 1843, to Lyman C. Draper, Draper MSS 12C15, WHS. John Ray is not as specific in his letter, but Mann Butler's notes from

an 1833 interview with James Ray indicate that William was boiling sap while the others were chopping down trees.

6. While the petition sent by McGary's committee seemingly recognized acute danger in their situation, James Ray's son later described the settlers' attitude differently. "From the time of their arrival in the County up to 6th March 1777, they had remained unmolested—they had not seen a foe the yellow man. They ware entirely ungarded in all their intercourse & transactions for they did not even dream of Indians being in the Country." Draper MSS 12C16(4), WHS; 7J43–45, WHS; 16J11, WHS; Kathryn Harrod Mason, "The Career of General James Ray, Kentucky Pioneer," *Filson Club History Quarterly* 19 (1945): 86–114. James Ray related an anecdote to Mann Butler about meeting George Rogers Clark at the Shawnee Springs. Clark expressed concern at seeing such a young man out on his own, and Ray was surprised to learn that Clark considered his situation dangerous. Colonel William Whitley, who came to Kentucky in 1775 and settled on the Wilderness Road between present Stanton and Crab Orchard, Kentucky, also expressed the general view that it was considered safe to settle in 1775. The change in attitude was largely a function of increased Native American hostilities in 1776. The capture of the Boone and Callaway girls at Fort Boonesborough in the spring of 1776, the attack against John G. Jones and others on Christmas Day, and the strike against McClelland's Station heightened awareness of the Native American threat. Nevertheless, the need to clear land and raise a corn crop both for sustenance and to prove their land claims drove settlers to take risks. Bayless Hardin, "Whitley Papers, Volume 9—Draper Manuscripts—Kentucky Papers," *Register of the Kentucky Historical Society* 36 (1938): 189–209. Draper MSS 12C16(2). According to John Ray, the incident took place on March 6, 1777. This day was William Ray's fourteenth birthday, according to the McGary family bible. Draper MSS 12C20, WHS; Mann Butler, 12C15, WHS.

7. John Ray's letter to Lyman C. Draper, Draper MSS 12C16, WHS.

8. Bakeless, *Daniel Boone*, 146–47; Draper MSS 12C16, WHS.

9. Letter from Dr. John Ray to Lyman C. Draper, February 20, 1843.

10. The comment about William's shirt is a curious detail. What was so distinctive about William's shirt that it was recognizable? One may speculate that it must have been badly bloodstained if William received a chest wound. But if William's fate was not yet fully known, what other features of the shirt tipped off McGary? Accounts of clothing with distinguishing characteristics that enabled an association with a particular owner occur sporadically in the settlement literature—usually as a casual comment with little elaboration. Other documentary information, however, describe how settlers from different areas were distinguishable from one another by their dress, their speech, or other characteristics. Perhaps William's shirt had some distinctive ornamentation such as a ruffled collar. Another possibility, suggested to me by reenactor Jon Hagee, was that clothing was identifiable by distinctive patchwork to repair holes and worn places in the fabric. Clothing received hard use on the Kentucky frontier and was difficult to replace; patched clothing was undoubtedly common. Draper MSS 12C16(4), WHS.

11. Thomas Shores was captured and eventually was taken to Detroit in January 1778 where he testified that he was kindly treated by the British. Draper MSS 12O30, WHS; 14S127, WHS; Jacob Stevens interview, Draper MSS 12CC133–138, WHS.

12. Draper MSS 12C17(2), WHS. Hardin, "Whitley Papers," 190; Draper MSS 12CC136, WHS. Jacob Stevens did not name the older man but simply referred to him inaccurately as an "Irishman." The Irish were also victims of prejudicial attitudes, and such attitudes may have contributed to McGary's reputation as well. He may have retained an Irish brogue learned from his parents who probably emigrated to America from Ireland. He certainly has been quoted as using colorful, colloquial language that may have had its origins in Irish expressions.

13. Letter from Dr. John Ray to Lyman C. Draper, July 4, 1843.

14. Draper MSS 12C16.

15. Draper MSS 12C17(2)–17(3), WHS. Martin John Spalding, *Sketches of the Early Catholic Missions in Kentucky* (Louisville, KY: B.J. Webb and Brothers, 1844). William Coomes and his family were one of the first Catholic families to emigrate to Kentucky. Coomes was originally from Charles County, Maryland, but moved to the South Branch of the Potomac River in Virginia. He came to Kentucky with Abraham and Isaac Hite. Mrs. Coomes reportedly opened a school in Fort Harrod.

16. The attack is reported in Spalding, "Sketches," 39 and Thomas D. Clark, ed. *The Voice of the Frontier: John Bradford's Notes on Kentucky* (Lexington: University Press of Kentucky, 1993).

17. Mason, "General James Ray," note 4.

18. Draper MSS 12C16(13), WHS. John Ray related an incident in which a woman was at the Fort Harrod spring, and James Ray saw a Native warrior crawling toward her. Ray waited until he was within gunshot and fired, killing him.

19. Robert McAfee quote, Draper MSS 1OO142, WHS. Information from C. Columbus Graham, Draper 12C16(6)-16(7), WHS. The use of the term "little" for Ray apparently refers more to his build than his size. His physician, C. Columbus Graham, described him as 5 feet, 9 inches in height, with finely developed muscles and weighing 165 pounds. This description was of Ray as an older man when he may have weighed more than he did as a younger man, but the inference is that he had a compact, wiry frame.

20. William G. Carter, "The McGary Frontier Family" Manuscript on file, Harrodsburg Historical Society: Harrodsburg, Kentucky, undated. Carter mentions two incidents: one in which McGary retrieved the body of a man named Hinton and another in which he brought Mrs. John Haggin and her two children to safety. William McBride related the rescue of Mrs. Haggin and her children to John Dabney Shane (Draper MSS 11CC259, WHS). The reference to the retrieval of Hinton's body is rather ambiguous but may be from John Dabney Shane's interview with Josiah Collins in the Draper MSS 12CC64–78, 97–110, WHS. Deposition of Joseph Kennedy who served under Hugh McGary on the Vincennes campaign, Draper MSS 1O O46, WHS.

3. The McGary Family Settles at Shawnee Springs

1. *Kentucky Doomsday Book, 1779–1780*, 27, accessed February 10, 2025, https://www.sos.ky.gov/land/non-military/settlements_preemptions/Pages/Kentucky-Doomsday-Book.aspx.

2. David Williams vs. Samuel Taylor et al., Mercer Circuit Court case files, Box S-20; Deposition of John Haggin, August 18, 1806.

3. Virginia Survey Book 4, March 19, 1781, 319–20; Virginia Grant Book 8, December 20, 1785, 45–47 (Frankfort: Kentucky Land Office, Office of the Secretary of State, online database).

4. Clerk of Court, Jefferson County Entry Book A, November 3, 1779, 1; Clerk of Court, Jefferson County Entry Book A, April 26, 1780, 27; Clerk of Court, Lincoln County Entry Book 1, April 16, 1781, 116.

5. Lyman C. Draper's Notes on Henry Wilson interview, Draper MSS 9J48; Depositions of Peter Jordan and John Ray. David Williams vs. Samuel Taylor et al., filed in Box S-20 with papers of Slaughter et ux. vs. Taylor Heirs, Mercer County Circuit Court Records, Harrodsburg, Kentucky. The Williams vs. Taylor et al. case was filed in Lincoln County Circuit Court, but the original depositions taken in this case were apparently transferred to Mercer County to be used as evidence and never returned to Lincoln County. Various depositions filed in these cases indicate that several different springs were referred to as the Shawnee Springs, but the deponents make a distinction between the spring nearest to James Ray's house and the one nearest to McGary's Station. The depositions were originally filed with a plat showing the land in dispute and also the various springs on Shawnee Run in Lincoln County. Although the case files in the Lincoln County Circuit Court were searched exhaustively, the plat was not found with other papers of the case between David Williams and Samuel Taylor et al. The plat eventually came to light in case files housed in the Kentucky Department for Libraries and Archives in Frankfort. The plat showed the relationship of the springs nearest to James Ray's and Hugh McGary's houses but did not pinpoint either house site, nor did it show the exact location of the "old mill." Nevertheless, verifying the locations of the two springs made it possible to confirm the location of Ray's house (which now exists as a stone cellar foundation) and narrow down the probable location of McGary's house, verified later by archaeological field investigation.

6. Clerk of Court, Lincoln County Entry Book 1:116, 116; Clerk of Court, Mercer County Order Book 1:5, 138.

7. David Williams vs. Samuel Taylor et al., Mercer County Circuit Court case file S-20.

8. Draper MSS 11CC237-238.

9. James Ray's pension application, Draper MSS 1OO142, WHS. James Ray supplied details of his military service in his pension declaration. His application was supported by depositions by various people. See also Mason, "The Career of General James Ray, Kentucky Pioneer"; and James Alton James, *George Rogers Clark*

Papers 1771–1781, Collection of Illinois State Historical Library 8, Virginia Series 3 (Springfield: Illinois State Historical Library, 1912).

10. Beckner, "Mrs. Sarah Graham," 225–26.

11. Among the limited evidence concerning McGary's attitude toward women, he wrote a petition to Virginia concerning the plight of Fort Harrod, which was supporting widows and orphans of male settlers who had been killed. He also rescued John Haggins's family from an exposed situation and refused to allow a party of settlers, including women, on their way to the Falls of the Ohio for a frolic, to continue when warriors were discovered to be present and patrolling. These clues are suggestive of a protective attitude about women although it is difficult to extrapolate from this evidence how he might have reacted to his marital situation. John Dabney Shane memorandum on Hugh McGary, Draper MSS 14CC192.

12. John Ray's letter to Lyman C. Draper, July 4, 1843, Draper MSS 12C17(5), WHS.

13. Deposition of Hugh McGary, Alexander Robertson vs. Ambrose Gordon, Heir-at-Law to John Gordon. Lincoln County Circuit Court Records, Stanton, Kentucky; Will of Hugh McGary, Clerk of Court, Knox County (Indiana) Will Book A, 3–5; Will of James Ray, Clerk of Court, Mercer County (Kentucky) Will Book 9, 544; Hammersmith, *Hugh McGary*, 154.

14. Rebecca Wilson Conover, *James Harrod: The Man and His Family* (Harrodsburg, KY: Harrodsburg Herald, 1972), 7. Conover states that Nathaniel Hart was a student at Harrod's Latin school but provides no source for this claim. The school closed after Harrod's stepson, James McDonald Jr., was killed by Native Americans in November 1787. Marriage record for Sarah Hart and George C. Thompson, *Kentucky U.S., County Marriage Records*, online database (Lehi, UT: Ancestry.com Operations, 2016).

15. Patricia Watlington, *The Partisan Spirit: Kentucky Politics, 1779–1792* (New York: Atheneum, 1972).

16. In a curious coincidence, a man of the same name married Mary Thompson, daughter of George C. Thompson who had inherited Shawnee Springs from his father, Col. George Thompson. This John Kinkead was probably related in some way (perhaps a son) to the John Kinkead who aroused McGary's wrath. Letters from John Cowan and James Ray in Mrs. Robert S. Todd's papers, Draper MSS 16CC39-49.

17. Humphrey Marshall, *The History of Kentucky* (Frankfort: George S. Robinson, 1824); Mann Butler, *A History of the Commonwealth of Kentucky* (Louisville: Wilcox, Dickerson, 1834); John Mason Peck, *Life of Daniel Boone: The Pioneer of Kentucky* (New York: University Society, 1904 reprint of 1847 printing).

18. Hammersmith, *Hugh McGary*, xix.

4. The Boone Family Settles at Fort Boonesborough

1. Harry G. Enoch and Anne Crabb, *Crisis in the Wilderness: The Capture and Rescue of the Boone and Callaway Girls, 1776* (Monee, IL: Fort Boonesborough

Foundation, 2021); George Washington Ranck, *Boonesborough: Its Founding, Pioneer Struggles, Indian Experiences, Transylvania Days, and Revolutionary Annals* (Louisville, KY: John P. Morton, 1901).

2. Ranck, *Boonesborough*, 64–66.

3. Anne Crabb, *And the Battle Began Like Claps of Thunder: The Siege of Boonesboro—1778—As Told by the Pioneers* (Richmond, KY: Privately Printed, 1998); Nancy O'Malley, *Drawing Battle Lines at Fort Boonesborough: The Siege of 1778* (Report prepared for the American Battlefield Protection Program, Lexington, KY, 2012); Faragher, *Daniel Boone*, 200–202; John Filson, *The Adventures of Daniel Boon, Formerly a Hunter: Containing a Narrative of the Wars of Kentucky, with the Discovery, Purchase, and Settlement of Kentucky, and the Piankashaw Council, 1784, and Territory of North American Indians, and the Rights of Land in Kentucky* (Old Chillicothe, OH: Privately Printed, 1967), 16; Neal O. Hammon, *My Father, Daniel Boone: The Draper Interviews with Nathan Boone* (Lexington: University Press of Kentucky, 1999), 70.

5. Daniel Boone Builds a Station on Boone's Creek

1. William Waller Hening, ed., *The Statues at Large; Being a Collection of All the Laws of Virginia, From the First Session of the Legislature, in the Year 1619, Volume X* (Richmond, VA: George Cochran, Printer, 1822), 35–51; Faragher, *Daniel Boone*, 203–204.

2. Faragher, *Daniel Boone*, 205; Neal Hammon to Nancy O'Malley, unpublished article via email, "Daniel Boone's Land Problems," July 8, 2002; Virginia Survey Book 4: 313–14; Virginia Grant Book 3: 311.

3. Hazel Atterbury Straker, *The Boone Family: A Genealogical History of the Descendants of George and Mary Boone Who Came to America in 1717* (Rutland, VT: Tuttle, 1922); Boone Family Tree, accessed October 29, 2021, http://www.booneassociation.com/genealogy.html; Deposition of Peter Scholl, Case 1120, Bourbon County Circuit Court; Information from Mrs. Rachel Denton, Draper MSS 23C104, WHS; Nancy O'Malley, *"Stockading Up": A Study of Pioneer Stations in the Inner Bluegrass Region Of Kentucky*, Archaeological Report 127 (Lexington: Program for Cultural Resource Assessment, Department of Anthropology, University of Kentucky, 1994 revised), 159–60.

4. Peter Scholl deposition, Fletcher vs. Piper; Mrs. Rachel Denton interview, 23C104, WHS; E. B. Scholl to Lyman C. Draper, Draper MSS 23C104, WHS; Sarah Boone Hunter to Lyman C. Draper, Draper MSS 22C67 (60), WHS.

5. Mrs. Rachel Denton Interview, 23C104, WHS; Interview with Mrs. Rachel Henton by Lyman C. Draper, Draper MSS 31C2, WHS.

6. Faragher, *Daniel Boone*, 208; Neal O. Hammon and James Russell Harris, "Daniel Boone the Businessman: Revising the Myth of Failure," *Register of the Kentucky Historical Society* 36 (1938): 5–50; "Memorandum of Certificates of Which Daniel Boone Was Robbed on the Night of the 20th of March 1780," accessed May 4, 2023, https://web.sos.ky.gov/land/imageviewer/jukeboximage.aspx?imgctr=62243.

7. Maude Ward Lafferty, "Destruction of Ruddle's and Martin's Forts in the Revolutionary War," *Register of the Kentucky Historical Society* 54, no. 189 (October 1956): 297–338; website of the Ruddell's and Martin's Stations Historical Association, accessed January 17, 2025, https://ramsha1780.org.

8. Clark, *Voice of the Frontier*, 35–36; Historical sources vary on the number and type of heavy artillery that Byrd transported. Capt. Henry Byrd mentioned in a letter to Maj. Arnet S. De Peyster on May 21, 1780, that he kept "the little gun for quick transportation from one [station] to the other": Michigan Pioneer and Historical Society, *Historical Collections of the Michigan Pioneer and Historical Society 19* (Lansing, MI: Robert Smith, 1892), 524–25. A subsequent letter written by Byrd to De Peyster on July 1 after the attack mentioned a three pounder (the "small gun" previously mentioned) and a six pounder: Michigan Pioneer and Historical Society, *Historical Collections*, 538–39.

9. Clark, *Voice of the Frontier*, 39–42; Charles G. Talbert, "Kentucky Invades Ohio—1780," *Register of the Kentucky Historical Society* 52, no. 181 (October 1954): 291–300; Ephraim Sodowsky interview, Draper MSS 11CC143, WHS.

10. Letter from Sarah Boone Hunter, 22C67 (60), WHS; information from Col. James Davidson, Draper MSS 19C138–139, WHS; letter from Daniel Bryan to Lyman C. Draper, Draper MSS 22C9 (2–3), WHS; Bakeless, *Daniel Boone*, 257. Bakeless used Daniel Bryan's information as his source of Ned Boone's death and the treatment of his body. Michael Lofaro also believed that Edward was beheaded. His source for the information was Peter Houston, whose memoir contains many errors and omissions that render it a highly unreliable source: Michael A. Lofaro, *Daniel Boone: An American Life* (Lexington: University Press of Kentucky, 2003), 114–15; Ted Franklin Belue, ed., *A Sketch of the Life and Character of Daniel Boone: A Memoir of Peter Houston* (Mechanicsburg, PA: Stackpole Books, 1997). While Daniel Bryan knew Daniel Boone and was a generally credible source of information, he was the only contemporary source to state that Ned was beheaded; others who were eyewitnesses or told of the event immediately afterward mentioned scalping. Interview of Josiah Collins, 12CC96–97, WHS.

11. Hammon, *My Father, Daniel Boone*, 71–72; Deposition of John McIntire, Mason County Circuit Court, Bruce's Heirs vs. Barbour's Heirs, 1817, in Hattie Marshall Scott, *Scott's Papers: Kentucky Court and Other Records* (Frankfort: Kentucky Historical Society, 1953); Deposition of James Ray, October 24, 1817, Draper MSS 7C82, WHS. James Ray lived at Shawnee Springs in present Mercer County, about five miles northeast of Harrodsburg. As a single man, he served as a "spy" and sometimes was assigned to stations away from his stepfather's station. He may have been serving this capacity at Bryan's Station or another station near Lexington when he joined Boone's burial party. Deposition of John Stephenson, May 5, 1816, Draper MSS 7C83, WHS; Deposition of Peter Scholl, Draper MSS 7C84–87, WHS.

12. Pension statement of Charles Gatliff, Ancestry.com, accessed January 28, 2025, https://www.ancestry.com/mediaui-viewer/tree/69843481/person/32206558491/media/8c6ad097-f61c-4aae-94ea-1289fd6089a9.

13. Thomas Speed, *The Wilderness Road: A Description of the Routes of Travel by Which the Pioneers and Early Settlers First Came to Kentucky* (New York: Lenox Hill Publishing and Distribution Company, 1886), 18–20.

14. Lofaro, *Daniel Boone*, 118; O'Malley, *"Stockading Up,"* 161–62; Lucien Beckner, "Reverend John D. Shane's Interview with Pioneer William Clinkenbeard," *Filson Club History Quarterly* 2, no. 3 (April 1928): 106–107; Joan E. Brookes-Smith, *Master Index Virginia Surveys and Grants* (Frankfort: Kentucky Historical Society, 1976), 205–206.

15. *Journal of the House of Delegates of the Commonwealth of Virginia*, Session of 1781–1782, Internet Archive, accessed February 4, 2022, https://archive.org/details/journalofhouseof178186virg/page/4/mode/1up; Attendance Book for the House of Delegates of the Commonwealth of Virginia, Accession #35171, BC #1078198, Library of Virginia, Richmond.

16. Lofaro, *Daniel Boone*, 117; Lieutenant-General Banastre Tarleton, *A History of the Campaigns of 1780 and 1781, in the Southern Provinces of North* America (London: Printed for T. Cadell, 1787), accessed December 15, 2021, Internet Archive, https://archive.org/details/historyofcampaig00tarl; Hammon, *My Father, Daniel Boone*, 73; Ken Kamper, "An Accurate Summary of the Life of Daniel Boone," *Daniel Boone History Research Newsletter* 6 (2021): 1–14.

17. Boone's son, Nathan, told Lyman Draper a family story about how his father correctly distinguished him from his two nephews born around the same time, the sons of his sisters, Susannah and Jemima, implying that Boone had been absent at his birth. While an amusing family story, Nathan may not have gotten the details correct. His sister, Susannah Hays, had a son, William Hays Jr., who, according to descendants, was born in 1780 at the station. This birth year would have made William at least three months older than Nathan. Jemima Callaway's son, John Boone Callaway, was born in 1781, according to the same source, so could have been closer to Nathan's age. Faragher states that Daniel Boone left in April to travel to Virginia for the spring session of the House of Delegates. Lofaro states that he was in Richmond in April when Cornwallis's troop advanced and caused the Assembly to reconvene in Charlottesville on May 7. Boone was sworn in as a delegate on May 24, indicating that he did not attend the first four days of the session, when an insufficient number of delegates attended and the session was adjourned. Faragher, *Daniel Boone*, 213; Lofaro, *Daniel Boone*, 117; Hammon, *My Father, Daniel Boone*, 72–73; Bakeless, *Daniel Boone*, 258–59; O'Malley, *Boonesborough Unearthed*, 110; *Journal of the House of Delegates of the Commonwealth of Virginia*, accessed December 14, 2021, Internet Archive, https://ia800206.us.archive.org/7/items/journalofhouseof178186virg/journalofhouseof178186virg.pdf; Tarleton, *A History of the Campaigns of 1780 and 1781*.

18. *Journal of the House of Delegates* (Spring), 4–7, 13, 16, 19–20, 27, 29.

19. Bakeless, *Daniel Boone*, 260; *Journal of the House of Delegates* (Fall), 4–6.

20. *Journal of the House of Delegates* (Fall), 7, 20, 29, 39, 40, 46.

21. *Journal of the House of Delegates* (Fall), 19, 74.

6. Kentucky's "Year of Blood"

1. R. S. Cotterill, *History of Pioneer Kentucky* (Cincinnati, OH: Johnson & Hardin, 1917), 178–79; Samuel M. Wilson, *Battle of Blue Licks, August 19, 1782* (Lexington, KY: Privately Printed, 1927), 10.

2. Neal O. Hammon and Richard Taylor, *Virginia's Western War: 1775–1786* (Mechanicsburg, PA: Stackpole Books, 2002), 150–51; Cotterill, *Pioneer Kentucky*, 179–80.

3. Bakeless, *Daniel Boone*, 273–74; Hammon and Taylor, *Virginia's Western War*, 155; Cotterill, *Pioneer Kentucky*, 182.

4. George Washington Ranck, *The Story of Bryan's Station* (Lexington, KY: Transylvania Printing Company, 1896); Hammon and Taylor, *Virginia's Western War*, 155–56.

5. Bakeless, *Daniel Boone*, 269, 272; Lofaro, *Daniel Boone*, 121; Hammon, *My Father, Daniel Boone*, 75; Nancy O'Malley, *Searching for Boonesborough*, Archaeological Report 193 (Lexington: University of Kentucky Program for Cultural Resource Assessment, 1989), 28; Letter from Joseph Ficklin to Lyman C. Draper, June 26, 1845, Draper MSS 13C74; Notes by Lyman C. Draper on information received from Joseph Ficklin, Draper MSS 13C79(4–5).

6. Bakeless, *Daniel Boone*, 280; Clark, *Voice of the Frontier*, 51; Draper's notes on Joseph Ficklin, 13C79.4.

7. Bakeless, *Daniel Boone*, 274–75; Doyle, George F., Excerpts from the Boone Papers. MSS on file, n.d., Special Collections, M. I. King Library, University of Kentucky, Lexington; Letters from Mrs. Elizabeth Payne to Lyman C. Draper, Draper MSS 13C116–117; Clark, *Voice of the Frontier*, 51.

8. Joseph Ficklin, Draper MSS 13C79.1.

9. Lyman C. Draper's notes on John Gatewood's memory of the Bryan's Station siege, Draper MSS 22C10; Interview of Mrs. John Arnold by John Dabney Shane, Draper MSS 11CC241–245; Charles Cist, *The Cincinnati Miscellany or Antiquities of the West and Pioneer History and General and Local Statistics Compiled from the* Western General Advertiser *from October 1st, 1844, to April 1st, 1845*, vol. 1 (Cincinnati, OH: Caleb Clark, Printer, 1845), 236–39; Bessie Taul Conkwright, "A Historical Error," *Lexington Herald*, August 1916. Historian R. S. Cotterill characterized the courageous water-gathering story as "pure fiction" unsupported by contemporary accounts. Bessie Conkwright blamed Rev. John Alexander McClung for originating and embellishing the story.

10. Clark, *Voice of the Frontier*, 51–52.

11. Cotterill, *Pioneer Kentucky*, 187–88; Hammon and Taylor, *Virginia's Western War*, 156–58.

12. Cotterill, *Pioneer Kentucky*, 188.

7. Daniel Boone and Hugh McGary Meet Again

1. "Battle of Blue Licks," *Register of the Kentucky Historical Society* 47, no. 160 (1949): 247–49; Neal O. Hammon, *Daniel Boone and Defeat at Blue Licks* (Minneapolis, MN: Boone Society, 2005), 21, 40. Information from Mrs. Rachel Denton, Draper MSS 23C104. Mrs. Denton said that "some twenty men" accompanied Capt. William Hays from Boone's Station to aid Bryan's Station, but this number seems too high and is not in agreement with other sources. She also said that five men from the station were killed at the Battle of Blue Licks but only named Israel Boone and Samuel Brannon. Joseph Scholl told Lyman C. Draper (MSS 24S205–22) that James was taken in by the Boone family when he was orphaned and that he accompanied them to Kentucky in 1775.

2. Hammon, *Defeat at Blue Licks*, 33, 38.

3. Hammon, *Defeat at Blue Licks*, 39.

4. Richard W. Stewart, *The United States Army and the Forging of a Nation, 1775–1917*, American Military History 1 (Washington, DC: Center of Military United States Army, 2005), 30–31.

5. Wilson, *Battle of Blue Licks*, 38; Hammon, *Defeat at Blue Licks*, 39.

6. Butler, *A History*, 129.

7. Hammon, *Defeat at Blue Licks*, 45–47.

8. Marshall, *The History of Kentucky*; Bennett H. Young, *History of the Battle of the Blue Licks* (Louisville, KY: John P. Morton, 1897); John A. McClung, *Sketches of Western Adventure* (Philadelphia: Grigg & Elliot, 1832); Richard H. Collins, *History of Kentucky* (Covington, KY: Collins, 1874). Henry Wilson interview, Draper MSS 9J54–64. Henry Wilson named several of the men who composed Harlan's advance guard, which he said was formed at Bryan's Station. Jacob Stevens named the five men who were sent ahead to scout. Interview of Jacob Stevens by John Dabney Shane, Draper MSS 12CC134.

9. Hammon, *Defeat at Blue Licks*, 50–51; Hammon, *My Father, Daniel Boone*, 76; Letter from Hugh McGary to Benjamin Logan, Draper MSS 52J35(1)-36.

10. Wilson, *Battle of Blue Licks*, 57–58.

11. Wilson, *Battle of Blue Licks*, 115–16; Hammon, *Defeat at Blue Licks*, 64.

12. Hammon, *Defeat at Blue Licks*, 58, 62, 64.

13. Young, *History of the Battle*, 199, 206, 201, 202, 211.

14. Wilson, *Battle of Blue Licks*, 66; James Alton James, "George Rogers Clark Papers 1781–1784," in *Collections of the Illinois State Historical Library*, vol. 19, Virginia Series, vol. 4 (Springfield, IL: Illinois State Historical Library, 1926), 91–92.

15. Lincoln County Order Book 1, various entries.

16. Young, *History of the Battle*, 221–22; Hammersmith, *Hugh McGary*, 209–11.

17. Wilson, *Battle of Blue Licks*, 13; Marshall, *History of Kentucky*, 138–39.

18. Hammon, *Defeat at Blue Licks*, 73.

19. Hammon, *Defeat at Blue Licks*, 77; Jacob Stevens, Draper MSS 12CC133–138.

20. Wilson, *Battle of Blue Licks*, 56.

21. Wilson, *Battle of Blue Licks*, 57–58.

22. Wilson, *Battle of Blue Licks*, 72; Hammon, *Defeat at Blue Licks*, 82–83.

23. Young, *History of the Battle*, 216, 220, 224; Hammon, *My Father, Daniel Boone*, 78; Henry Wilson's account, Draper MSS 9J54–64; Beckner, "William Clinkenbeard," 98.

24. Bakeless, *Daniel Boone*, 309; Hammon, *Defeat at Blue Licks*, 67–70; Cotterill, *Pioneer Kentucky*, 197.

25. Hammersmith, *Hugh McGary*, 201.

8. Postwar Life at McGary's Station

1. Michael L. Cook, *Lincoln County Kentucky Records, Volume C* (Evansville, IN: Cook, 1988); Hammersmith, *Hugh McGary*, 147; "An act to suppress excessive gaming," in Hening, *The Statues at Large*, 205–206; Estate Inventory of John Floyd, Reuben Durrett Collection, University of Chicago; Eric W. Nye, "Pounds Sterling to Dollars: Historical Conversion of Currency," accessed February 10, 2025, https://www.uwyo.edu/numimage/currency.htm. George Washington's account ledger for 1783 listed items such as 8 barrels of flour, 25 yards of Irish linen, and 48 gallons of taffia rum that cost approximately five pounds. For approximately twelve pounds, a buyer could purchase 60 bushels of wheat, 396 pounds of sugar, or 280 pounds of white lead. Kentucky prices were higher because of increased transportation costs; regardless, McGary's winnings were substantial for the time. George Washington Financial Papers Project, accessed April 17, 2022, http://financial.gwpapers.org.

2. Hammersmith, *Hugh McGary*, 146; Cook, *Lincoln County Kentucky Records*.

3. Hammon and Taylor, *Virginia's Western War*, 192, 194–96, 198–99.

4. Hammon and Taylor, *Virginia's Western War*, 199–200.

5. William P. Palmer, *Calendar of Virginia State Papers and Other Manuscripts from January 1, 1785, to July 2, 1789*, vol. IV (originally published by Richmond, VA: Sherwin McRae, 1884; New York: Kraus Reprint Corporation, 1968), 258–60; Interview of William Sudduth by John Dabney Shane, Draper MSS 12CC82–83, WHS; Hammon and Taylor, *Virginia's Western War*, 200.

6. Palmer, *Calendar*, 258–60.

7. McClung, *Sketches*, 86–88; Hammon, *Defeat at Blue Licks*, 75.

8. T. Henry Coleman, "Early Marriage Records of Mercer County," *Register of the Kentucky Historical Society* 20 (1922): 9–20; Virginia Grant Book 1, 508–509; Virginia Survey Book 1, 170; Clerk of Court, Mercer County Deed Book 2, 282; Clerk of Court, Mercer County Deed Book 1, 36.

9. Mercer County Deed Book 1, 63; Interview with Isaac Clinkenbeard, Draper MSS. 11CC3, WHS; Interview with William Sudduth, Draper MSS 12CC82–83, WHS; Clerk of Court, Mercer County Deed Book 1, 59; Mercer County Deed Book

2, 304, 329, 409; see also Book 3, 471–75, 479. Jacob Stevens indicated that the McGarys moved to Shelbyville before opening their tavern in Harrodsburg, but their deed transactions indicate a Mercer County residence, so they could not have lived there long if at all: Clerk of Court, Mercer County Deed Book 2, 381, 383–85, 387, 533. Mrs. Sarah Graham said that the tavern was near where the courthouse stood. A brick house of the appropriate age still stands on Out-Lot 47 of Harrodsburg, a lot owned by McGary. Various sources in the Draper MSS indicate that McGary had a predilection for trouble even toward the end of his life. John Ray referred to a charge of robbery in which public sentiment was against McGary. This charge may have been the one that caused him to move to Indiana. Even his sons did not escape censure. Robert Stockwell of LaFayette, Indiana (Draper MSS 36J7, WHS), reported to Lyman C. Draper in 1863 that he knew all but one of McGary's six sons "and can only say without prejudice, that take them altogether, they were the worst men I ever knew. All dead many years since by beastly drunkenness." He went on to accuse three of the sons (unnamed) who remained in Indiana of "stealing free negroes, moving them off South & selling them as slaves." He concluded his criticism with "I will say no more about them, as paper should not be defiled with their names." Mary Hammersmith's research indicated that at least one charge leveled against one of his sons was not proved, but, unjustly or not, for many people, even unproven charges suggest that some impropriety occurred.

10. Letter from Dr. Christopher Columbus Graham to Lyman Draper, Draper MSS 12C20, WHS; Letter from John Ray to Lyman C. Draper, Draper MSS 12C16, WHS; John Dabney Shane's notes on James Ray, 14CC192, WHS; James Ray's Inventory, Clerk of Court, Mercer County Will Book 10, 313.

11. Draper MSS 12C16, WHS; Draper MSS 14CC192, WHS.

12. Mason, "The Career of General James Ray," 105–106.

13. Draper MSS 12C16, WHS; Clerk of Court, Mercer County Will Book 9, 544; Mercer County Deed Book 26, 33.

14. Clerk of Court, Mercer County Will Book 10, 313.

15. Deposition of Colonel George Thompson; David Williams vs. Samuel Taylor et al., Box S-20, Mercer County Circuit Court, Harrodsburg.

16. Thompson family data on file at Kentucky Historical Society, Frankfort, Kentucky; Thompson vs. Vance, &c., Kentucky Court of Appeals, 58 Ky. 669; 1858 Ky. Legislature 85; 1 Met. 669; Clerk of Court, Mercer County Will Book 9, 538–39.

17. W. L. Vance vs. M. Vance and wife, Kentucky Court of Appeals, 1 Ky. Op. 262; 1866 Ky. Lexis 300.

18. Clerk of Court, Mercer County Will Book 15, 232.

19. Vance vs. Vance.

20. Mercer County Circuit Court case files, T-54, T-56, T-59, V-15, V-18; Clerk of Court, Mercer County Deed Book 39, 8; 40, 409; 41, p. 126, 134; 43, p. 322; U.S. Federal population census for 1860, ancestry.com.

21. Clerk of Court, Mercer County Deed Book 43, 322; U.S. Census Bureau, population census for 1880, 1st Ward, New Albany, Floyd County, Indiana, 256B;

Clerk of Court, Mercer County Deed Book 43, 238; Clerk of Court, Mercer County Deed Book 54, 87. Morgan Vance was buried in the New Albany National Cemetery. His wife, Susan, died on June 6, 1915, and was cremated and buried with her mother, Sarah Simpson Hart Thompson, in New Albany; Susan Preston Thompson Vance's obituary, *Kentucky Advocate*, June 8, 1915, Danville, Kentucky; Findagrave.com, accessed June 13, 2022.

22. The chain of title for the area containing the two springs near where McGary's Station is located is quite complex. The tract was traced back from the present to W. W. Goddard, who sold it to M. and Ollie Phillips in 1898 (Clerk of Court, Mercer County Deed Book 66, 324). There is a break in the chain of title that has not been resolved yet, but this tract appears to be part of a larger amount of land (including Ray's land) that was part of an article of agreement between Joseph A. Thompson and Beriah Magoffin in 1845 (Clerk of Court, Mercer County Deed Book 29, 270). Beriah Magoffin had acquired the land that Jefferson Ray inherited from his father, James Ray. Goddard probably purchased the property from a Thompson descendant. Clerk of Court, Mercer County Deed Book 93, 198.

9. Postwar Life at Boone's Station

1. Neal Hammon (email communication, December 29, 2008) suggested that Boone may have erroneously believed, as did the McConnell family and other settlers around Lexington, that the settlement claims awarded by the 1779 land court would take precedence over the old military surveys of 1774 and 1775. In 1781, William Madison (who lived in Botetourt County) sold his grant to John Gordon of Lincoln County (now Mercer County). The title was witnessed by six men, two of whom, along with the purchaser John Gordon, were killed at the Battle of Blue Licks a little more than a year later. The sale was proved again by one of the original witnesses, Benjamin Netherland, on December 10, 1782, so that Gordon's estate could be settled. This evidence of clear title effectively extinguished any claim Daniel Boone's son might have had. C. Frank Dunn, "Boone Station Site," *Register of the Kentucky Historical Society* 41 (1943): 304–309; Willard Rouse Jillson, "Boone's Station," *Filson Club History Quarterly* 8 (1934): 213–16.

2. Draper MSS 23C104, 6S59, WHS; Boofman's Heirs vs. James Hickman, Complete Record Book A, 604–42. In Charles R. Staples, "History in Circuit Court Records, Fayette County," *Register of the Kentucky Historical Society* 30, no. 93 (1932): 344–61; Hickman vs. Boffman, Court of Appeals of Kentucky, 3 Ky 356; 1808 Ky. Lexis 70; 1 Hard. 356. Lexis Nexis database accessed October 10, 2003, http://web.lexis-nexis.com/universe/document?_m=8147fdb2dc15b. Daniel Bryan told Lyman C. Draper that he visited Daniel Boone at the Marble Creek farm in the fall of 1783 and thought he had moved there in 1782. He could have moved in September or October after the Battle of Blue Licks. He spent most of November on a retaliatory raid against the Native American towns. Weiss, *Daniel Bryan*, 34; Faragher, *Daniel*

Boone, 224. He may also have moved in December after all the crops were harvested. Interview with Samuel Potts Pointer by John Dabney Shane, Draper MSS 12CC247, WHS.

3. Nancy O'Malley and Karen Hudson, *Cultural Resource Assessment of Boone Station State Park, Fayette County, Kentucky*, Archaeological Report 316 (Lexington: Program for Cultural Resource Assessment, University of Kentucky, 1993): 10–11; Jillson, "Boone's Station"; Dunn, "Boone Station Site."

4. Will of Robert Frank, John Hendley vs. Edmund Bullock, John S. Cockrell (deceased), Hamilton Jenkins and Thomas Franks, Fayette County Land Trial Book F, 184–86.

5. Hendley vs. Bullock et al., *Kentucky Gazette* 21, no. 1179 (May 31, 1808); Will of John S. Cockrell, Fayette County Will Book B, 58.

6. Hendley vs. Bullock et al., 180; Dunn, "Boone Station Site," 306–307; Jillson, "Boone's Station," 215; John Hendley to Charles Grimes, Fayette County Deed Book N: 233 (1815); Fayette County Sheriff to Simeon Bledsoe & Co., Fayette County Deed Book X: 444–46 (1824).

7. John Bledsoe to Harvey and Robert Bledsoe, Fayette County Deed Book 3: 365 (December 14, 1827); Robert Bledsoe to Simeon Bledsoe, Power of Attorney, Fayette County Deed Book R: 442 (April 15, 1818); Appraisal of Harvey Bledsoe estate, Fayette County Will Book L: 243–44 (September 1833); Sales of Harvey Bledsoe Estate, Fayette County Will Book M: 75.

8. Robert Bledsoe to Garrett Watts, Power of Attorney, Fayette County Deed Book 20: 424 (August 29, 1842); Will of Robert Bledsoe, Fayette County Will Book U: 318–20 (July, 1854); Garrett Watts to Thomas F. and James R. Barker, Fayette County Deed Book 26: 26 (January 24, 1849); Division between Thomas F. and James R. Barker, Fayette County Deed Book 35: 217; Dunn, "Boone Station Site"; Jillson, "Boone's Station."

10. Locating Archaeological Evidence of Hugh McGary's Station

1. W. Stephen McBride and Kim A. McBride, *An Archaeological Survey of Frontier Forts in the Greenbrier and Middle New River Valleys of West Virginia*, Archaeological Report 252 (Lexington: University of Kentucky Program for Cultural Resource Assessment, 1991); Site survey form for Aquilla Whitaker's Station (15SH75), on file, Office of State Archaeology, University of Kentucky, Lexington. Drs. W. Stephen McBride and Kimberly Arbogast McBride have investigated pioneer station sites in West Virginia with the use of a metal detector as well as through other, more traditional methods. They concluded that a metal detector can be very useful, perhaps critical, in locating station sites. I have reaffirmed the efficacy of metal detection at Kentucky station sites that experienced short occupations, such as McGary's Station and Aquilla Whitaker's Station.

2. Lyman C. Draper's Notes on his interview with Henry Wilson, Draper MSS 9J48, WHS. Henry Wilson lived in Mercer County before he moved to Bourbon County, where he built a substantial house near the community of Little Rock in the 1790s. His comments about McGary's Station may have been based on personal experience, but some of his information undoubtedly was secondhand. He knew McGary well enough to describe him as "a straight, well made man, a little short of six feet high, with brown hair & a dark bright eye, full ruddy countenance, a nose [a] little inclining to the Roman." Wilson came to Kentucky by the fall of 1779 with his family and had perhaps made an earlier trip in the spring. He and his family established a station in Mercer County in the fall of 1779 when he was only nineteen years old, making him the contemporary of McGary's stepsons. He would have had several opportunities to meet McGary. He volunteered for several tours of duty that usually lasted two or three months and took him to several different stations for guard duty and on several expeditions. He frequently served as a spy and was away from home for much of 1780, 1781, and 1782. Wilson certainly knew James Ray and served with him at Bryan's Station in the fall of 1780. He also participated in the Battle of Blue Licks, as did McGary and Ray. His interview described how McGary and other men he assembled from the Shawnee Run stations rode to McAfee's Station in the spring of 1781 when Native Americans attacked it. Wilson was on duty as a spy in the Lexington area at the time and was not an eyewitness to McGary's actions but learned about the battle later from the station inhabitants. His view of McGary echoed other settlers' attitudes in that he hinted at McGary's unpopularity and questionable character, but he did not directly accuse him. Speaking of McGary's tenure at Henderson, Kentucky in the 1790s, he said, "McGary . . . opened a house of entertainment. He went on swimmingly for a few years, with a few friends and more enemies. He contrived somehow to gain property; & some, perhaps envious of his success, used to throw an occasional hint that McGary was not exactly the man he ought to be." Then he related a clearly secondhand story about McGary stealing gold from a lodger at his tavern and being forced to leave Henderson or be tried for robbery. Of McGary's character, Wilson concluded, "& thus passed away the brave, impetuous, unprincipled Hugh McGary, leaving behind him a doubtful balance whether his good or evil deeds preponderated."

11. The McGary Station Artifact Assemblage

1. Inventory and Appraisal of John Floyd's Estate, Jefferson County Virginia Court Commissioners, June 7, 1783, Reuben T. Durrett Collections, Perkins Special Collections Research Center, University of Chicago; Eric W. Nye, "Pounds Sterling to Dollars: Historical Conversion of Currency," accessed February 2, 2025, https://www.uwyo.edu/numimage/currency.htm.

2. Ivor Noël Hume, *A Guide to Artifacts of Colonial America* (New York: Alfred A. Knopf, 1978), 228–29.

3. Carolyn L. White, *American Artifacts of Personal Adornment, 1680–1820: A Guide to Identification and Interpretation* (Lanham, MD: Rowman & Littlefield, 2005), 3.

4. Stanley Olsen, "Dating Early Plain Buttons by Their Form," *American Antiquity* 28, no. 4 (1963): 551–54.

5. Cairns & Cos. was a British button maker based in Birmingham that produced buttons for the American export market between c. 1795 and 1810. "Button Makers and Their Backmarks." UK Detector Finds Database, accessed June 21, 2023, https://www.ukdfd.co.uk/pages/button-makers.html#anchorc; "Button Makers Backmarks," accessed June 21, 2023, https://oldcopper.org/makers/button_makers.php.

6. Elizabeth A. Perkins, *Border Life: Experience and Memory in the Revolutionary Ohio Valley* (Chapel Hill: University of North Carolina Press, 1998), 88.

7. Chester Raymond Young, *Westward into Kentucky: The Narrative of Daniel Trabue* (Lexington: University Press of Kentucky, 1981). While everyday apparel was probably fairly simple, the women of Mercer County were capable of dressing more formally. Daniel Trabue described an occasion when James and Ann Harrod, accompanied by McGary and possibly his wife, traveled to Louisville, where they had been invited to a "feast" hosted by George Rogers Clark after his return from the Illinois country in the late summer of 1779. Trabue commented that "when these Fort Ladys came to [be] Dressed up they did not look like the same."

8. Allan Peterkin, *One Thousand Beards: A Cultural History of Facial Hair* (Vancouver: Arsenal Pulp, 2001), 34.

9. George C. Neumann, *Swords & Blades of the American Revolution* (Texarkana, TX: Rebel Publishing, 1991), 231, 243.

10. Hume, *Guide to Artifacts of Colonial America*, 105–11.

11. Hume, *Guide to Artifacts of Colonial America*, 123.

12. George L. Miller, Ann Smart Martin, and Nancy S. Dickinson, "Changing Consumption Patterns: English Ceramics and the American Market from 1770 to 1840," in *Everyday Life in the Early Republic*, ed. Catherine E. Hutchins (Winterthur, DE: Henry Francis du Pont Winterthur Museum, 1994), 222.

13. Hume, *Guide to Artifacts of Colonial America*, 114.

14. Elizabeth Perkins, "The Consumer Frontier: Household Consumption in Early Kentucky," *Journal of American History* 78, no. 2 (1991): 486–510.

15. T. M. Hamilton, *Colonial Frontier Guns* (Union City, TN: Pioneer Press, 1987), 46.

16. Butler, *A History*, 44–45.

17. Adrian Mandzy, personal communication, 2008. Experiments in "biting the bullet" revealed that lead is much too dense to be modified by human teeth. Pigs have been documented as having the ability to deform bullets by chewing on them.

18. R. S. Yeoman, *A Guidebook of United States Coins* (Racine, WI: Western Publishing, 1992), 7–14.

19. R. Barry Lewis, ed., *Kentucky Archaeology* (Lexington: University Press of Kentucky, 1996).

20. Butler, *A History*, 43. Butler also noted that all but one of these horses were lost to Native American raiding; however, McGary may have benefited from trading them before they were stolen, in which case, their loss was someone else's misfortune. Perkins, "Consumer Frontier," 486–510.

12. Locating Archaeological Evidence of Daniel Boone's Station

1. Robert Channing Strader Estate to Kentucky Department of Parks, *Fayette County Deed Book 1618*, 175–80; O'Malley, *"Stockading Up,"* 171–78; O'Malley and Hudson, *Boone Station State Park.*

2. O'Malley and Hudson, *Boone Station State Park.*

3. O'Malley and Hudson, *Boone Station State Park*, 10.

4. Alex W. Bealer and John O. Ellis, *The Log Cabin: Homes of the North American Wilderness* (Barre, PA: Barre Publishing, 1979), 24.

5. Carolyn Murray-Wooley, *Early Stone Houses of Kentucky* (Lexington: University Press of Kentucky, 2008), 25. Architectural historian Karen Hudson contributed her expertise to decipher the drawing.

6. O'Malley, *Stockading Up*, 179, 181, 183, 185; O'Malley, *Boonesborough Unearthed*, 70–80.

7. O'Malley, *Boonesborough Unearthed*, 86–87.

8. When James Ray was living in Fort Harrod, he was pinned down by enemy gunfire behind a stump that stood outside but next to the fort stockade. Calling for help, he was rescued by the settlers inside the enclosure, who dug under the stockade to give him access. Accounts of stockades at other sites, such as Bryan's Station in Fayette County, mention that some of the puncheons or upright members forming the stockade could be removed to allow access. Chinking or mortar was used to fill in gaps in between the stockade log members. In one case, failure to maintain the chinking at Bryan's Station cost a man his life when a Native sharpshooter placed a well-aimed shot through a hole in the stockade. Letter from John Ray to Lyman C. Draper, Draper MSS 12C16; "Excerpt from the Boone Papers," Draper MSS 22C10k; Interview of Mrs. John Arnold, Draper MSS 22CC276–279.

13. The Boone Station Artifact Assemblage

1. Interview with Isaac Clinkenbeard, Draper MSS 11CC1-4.

2. Larkin, *Reshaping of Everyday Life*, 127; William Cobbett, *A Year's Residence in the United States of America* (Carbondale, IL: Southern Methodist University Press, 1964), 178, https://archive.org/details/yearsresidencein0000will/page/n7/mode/1up; Marley Brown, "The Use of Oral and Documentary Sources in Historical Archaeology: Ethnohistory at the Mott Farm," in *Historical Archaeology: A Guide to Substantive*

and Theoretical Contributions, ed. Robert L. Schuyler (Farmingdale, NY: Baywood Publishing, 1978), 178–83; Nancy O'Malley, *Middle Class Farmers on the Urban Periphery*, Archaeological Report 162 (Lexington: University of Kentucky Program for Cultural Resource Assessment, 1987).

3. Karl G. Roenke, *Flat Glass: Its Use as a Dating Tool for Nineteenth Century Archaeological Sites in the Pacific Northwest and Elsewhere*, Northwest Anthropological Research Notes, Memoir 4 (Moscow: Department of Sociology/Anthropology, University of Idaho, 1978).

4. Christopher M. Schoen, "Window Glass on the Plains: An Analysis of Flat Glass Samples from Ten Nineteenth Century Plains Historic Sites," *Central Plains Archaeology* 2, no. 1 (1990): 57–90; Jonathan Wieland, "A Comparison and Review of Window Glass Analysis Approaches in Historical Archaeology," *Technical Briefs in Historical Archaeology* 4 (2009): 29–40; Randall W. Moir, "Socioeconomic and Chronometric Patterning of Window Glass," in *Historic Buildings, Material Culture, and People of the Prairie Margin: Architecture, Artifacts, and Synthesis of Historic Archaeology*, ed. David H. Jurney and Randall W. Moir, Richland Creek Technical Series 5 (Dallas, TX: Archaeology Research Program, Institute for the Study of Earth and Man, Southern Methodist University, 1987), 73–81; Betty Sue Ison, "Window Glass in Kentucky, 1790 to 1940" (master's thesis, University of Kentucky, 1990).

5. Jay D. Edwards and Tom Wells, *Historic Louisiana Nails: Aids to the Dating of Old Buildings*, The Fred B. Kniffen Cultural Resource Laboratory Monograph Series 2 (Baton Rouge: Geoscience Publications, Dept. of Geography & Anthropology, Louisiana State University, 1993), 9–11.

6. Anonymous, "Builders' Hardware—III—Nails," *American Architect and Building News* 24 (1888): 73.

7. Amy Lambeck Young, "Nailing Down the Pattern," *Tennessee Anthropologist* 19, no. 1 (Spring 1994): 1–21.

8. George C. Neumann, *Battle Weapons of the American Revolution: The Historian's Complete Reference* (Texarkana, TX: Scurlock Publishing, 1998), 19.

9. Nancy Kenmotsu, "Gunflints: A Study," in *Approaches to Material Culture: Research for Historical Archaeologists*, 2nd ed., ed. David Brauner (California, PA: Society for Historical Archaeology, 2000), 197–221.

10. Daniel M. Sivilich, *Musket Ball and Small Shot Identification: A Guide* (Norman: University of Oklahoma Press, 2016), 30–35; Interview with Enoch Boone, Draper MSS 19C123; Interview with Isaiah Boone, Draper MSS 19C57; Bakeless, *Daniel Boone*, 180.

11. Merry W. Abbitt, "The Eighteenth-Century Shoe Buckle," in *Five Artifact Studies*, ed. Audrey Noel Hume et al., Occasional Papers in Archaeology 1 (Williamsburg, VA: Colonial Williamsburg Foundation, 1973), 25–53.

12. George C. Neumann and Frank J. Kravic, *Collector's Illustrated Encyclopedia of the American Revolution* (Texarkana, TX: Rebel Publishing, 1975), 158, 170, 249.

13. Ted Franklin Belue, *A Sketch of the Life and Character of Daniel Boone: A Memoir by Peter Houston* (Mechanicsburg, PA: Stackpole Books, 1997), frontispiece,

142, 181; Ted Franklin Belue, *The Hunters of Kentucky: A Narrative History of America's First Far West, 1750–1792* (Mechanicsburg, PA: Stackpole Books, 2003), 88–89; Neal O. Hammon, *My Father, Daniel Boone*, 37; Florence M. Montgomery, *Textiles in America: 1650–1870* (New York: W. W. Norton, 1984), 244, 271, 368.

14. Belue, *Daniel Boone*, 181; Nancy O. Bryant, "Buckles and Buttons: An Inquiry into Fastening Systems Used on Eighteenth-Century English Breeches," *Dress* 14 (1988): 27–38; White, *American Artifacts of Personal Adornment*, 57–58.

15. White, *American Artifacts of Personal Adornment*, 57–61; Olsen, "Dating Early Plain Buttons," 551–54.

16. White, *American Artifacts of Personal Adornment*, 57.

17. "The Militia Act of 1792," https://kynghistory.ky.gov/Our-History/History-of-the-Guard/Pages/The-Militia-Act-of-1792.aspx.

18. White, *American Artifacts of Personal Adornment*, 69.

19. White, *American Artifacts of Personal Adornment*, 61.

20. White, *American Artifacts of Personal Adornment*, 73–75.

21. White, *American Artifacts of Personal Adornment*, 31.

22. Harry Schenawolf, "Knives of the American Revolution," section on folding knives, *Revolutionary War Journal*, October 29, 2020, https://www.revolutionarywarjournal.com/knives-of-the-american-revolution; Bourbon County Will Book E: 471.

23. "Parasols: Dating, Buying and Restoring," accessed February 22, 2023, http://www.marquise.de/en/themes/howto/sonnenschirm.shtml#:~:text=As%20a%20rule%20of%20thumb,19th%20century%20or%20slightly%20earlier.

24. "Antique Mirrors: A Brief Social History of Mirrors," *Invaluable*, accessed February 2, 2023, https://www.invaluable.com/blog/antique-mirrors-a-brief-social-history-of-mirrors; Clerk of Court, Bourbon County Will Book F: 21, 25; G: 490–93; M: 4, 38–39, 305, 307.

25. Charles S. Bradley, "Smoking Pipes for the Archaeologist," in *Studies in Material Culture Research*, ed. Karlis Karklins (California, PA: Society for Historical Archaeology, 2000), 104–33; Iain C. Walker, "The American Stub-Stemmed Clay Tobacco-Pipe: A Survey of its Origins, Manufacture, and Distribution," *Conference on Historic Site Archaeology Papers* 9 (1975): 97–128.

26. Anonymous, https://www.loc.gov/resource/rbc0001.2003juv05880/?sp=35; *A Little Pretty Pocket-Book Intended for the Instruction and Amusement of Little Master Tommy and Pretty Miss Polly* (London: Printed for Newbery and Carnan, 1770), 24.

27. "Marbles," Forgotten Toy Shop, accessed February 25, 2023, https://www.theforgottentoyshop.co.uk/pages/marbles.

28. "Jew's Harp," accessed February 25, 2023, https://en.wikipedia.org/wiki/Jew%27s_harp.

29. Lewis, *Kentucky Archaeology*, 181–82.

30. "The History of U.S. Circulating Coins," United States Mint, accessed February 27, 2023, https://www.usmint.gov/learn/history/us-circulating-coins#:~:text=Finally%2C%20with%20the%20passage%20of,foreign%20coins%20as%20legal%20tender; Yeoman, *A Guide Book of United States Coins*, 83–84.

31. Mary C. Beaudry, *Findings: The Material Culture of Needlework and Sewing* (New Haven, CT: Yale University Press, 2006), 125–27.

32. Beaudry, *Findings*, 86, 89, 99–101.

33. Beaudry, *Findings*, 24–25.

34. "History of the Fine-Tooth Comb," Lice World, accessed March 2, 2023, https://liceworld.com/the-history-of-the-fine-tooth-comb.

35. "A Brush with History," National Museum of American History, accessed March 3, 2023, https://americanhistory.si.edu/blog/brush-history; "Dentistry, Charles B. Pelton" advertisement, *Kentucky Reporter*, December 16, 1829, accessed March 3, 2023, https://www.newspapers.com/search/?query=toothbrushes&p_province=us-ky&dr_year=1787-1854.

36. Elizabeth Ward's will, Clerk of Court, Bourbon County Will Book G: 142; Margaret Kenney's Inventory, Clerk of Court, Bourbon County Will Book H: 269.

37. Georgeanna H. Greer, *American Stonewares: The Art and Craft of Utilitarian Potters* (Exton, PA: Schiffer Publishing, 1981), 60, 65, 67, 112; Ivor Noël Hume, "Through the Lookinge Glasse: Or, the Chamber Pot as a Mirror of Its Time," in *Ceramics in America*, ed. Robert Hunter (Hanover, NH: University Press of New England, 2001), 162.

38. George L. Miller and Robert Hunter, "How Creamware Got the Blues: The Origins of China Glaze and Pearlware," in Hunter, ed., *Ceramics in America*, 154.

39. Ted Lofstrom, Jeffrey P. Tordoff, and Douglas C. George, "A Seriation of Historic Earthenwares in the Midwest, 1780–1870," *Minnesota Archaeologist* 41, no. 1 (1982): 3–29.

40. Miller, Martin, and Dickinson, "Changing Consumption Patterns," 219–48; George L. Miller, "A User's Guide to Ceramic Assemblages: Part Four," *Council for Northeast Historical Archaeology Newsletter* 26 (November 1993): 4–7; Geoffrey A. Godden, *An Illustrated Encyclopedia of British Pottery and Porcelain*, 2nd ed. (Leicester: Magna Books, 1992), xi–xxiv.

41. George L. Miller, "A Revised Set of CC Index Values for Classification and Economic Scaling of English Ceramics from 1787 to 1880," *Historical Archaeology* 25, no. 1 (1991): 11; Miller, Martin, and Dickinson, "Changing Consumption Patterns," 223.

42. Godden, *Illustrated Encyclopedia*, xvii.

43. Jonathan Rickard, *Mocha and Related Dipped Wares, 1770–1939* (Hanover, NH: University Press of New England, in association with Historic Eastfield Foundation, 2006), ix.

44. Lynne Sussman, "Mocha, Banded, Cat's Eye and Other Factory-Made Slipware," *Studies in Northeast Historical Archaeology* 1 (1997): 6–7.

45. Sussman, "Mocha," 26.

46. Miller, Martin, and Dickinson, "Changing Consumption Patterns," 219–248.

47. Geoffrey A. Godden, *Encyclopaedia of British Pottery and Porcelain Marks* (New York: Bonanza Books, 1964), 17; Miller, Martin, and Dickinson, "Changing Consumption Patterns," 237.

48. Miller, Martin, and Dickinson, "Changing Consumption Patterns," 232–34.

49. Robert Hunter and George L. Miller, "Suitable for Framing: Decorated Shell-Edge Earthenware," *Early American Life* 40, no. 4 (August 2009): 8–19.

50. "Underglaze Painted Earthenwares," Diagnostic Artifacts in Maryland, accessed April 21, 2023, https://apps.jefpat.maryland.gov/diagnostic/Post-Colonial%20Ceramics/PaintedWares/index-paintedwares.htm#mimimalcobalt.

51. "Underglaze Painted Earthenwares."

52. Ivor Noël Hume, *If These Pots Could Talk: Collecting 2,000 Years of British Household Pottery* (Hanover, NH: University Press of New England, 2001), 222.

53. "The Transfer Printing Process for Ceramics," National Park Service, accessed April 28, 2023, https://www.nps.gov/articles/transferprintprocess.htm.

54. Miller, "Revised Set," 9.

55. Miller, Martin, and Dickinson, "Changing Consumption Patterns," 225; Lofstrom, Tordoff, and George, "Seriation of Historic Earthenwares," 3–29.

56. George L. Miller and Robert R. Hunter Jr., "English Shell Edged Earthenware: Alias Leeds Ware, Alias Feather Edge," in *Proceedings of the 35th Annual Wedgwood International Seminar* (1990), 106–35; Hunter and Miller, "Suitable for Framing," 8–19.

57. Cynthia R. Price, *19th Century Ceramics in the Eastern Ozark Border Region*, Southwest Missouri State University Center for Archaeological Research 1 (Springfield: Southwest Missouri State University Center for Archaeological Research, 1979), 19–20; Miller, "Revised Set," 6.

58. Godden, *Illustrated Encyclopedia*, xxiv; Wolf Mankowitz and Reginald G. Haggar, *The Concise Encyclopedia of English Pottery and Porcelain* (New York: Hawthorn Books, 1968), 137.

59. Sussman, "Mocha," 6, 26, 29, 33.

60. Miller, Martin, and Dickinson, "Changing Consumption Patterns," 238.

61. Godden, *Encyclopaedia of British Pottery and Porcelain Marks*, 349; Robert Hunter and George L. Miller, "All in the Family: A Staffordshire Soup Plate and the American Market," in *Ceramics in America 2001*, ed. Robert Hunter (Hanover, NH: University Press of New England, 2001), 222–23.

62. "Job & John Jackson (Maker)," Printed British Pottery & Porcelain, accessed May 13, 2023, http://printedbritishpotteryandporcelain.com/who-made-it/jackson-maker; Godden, *Encyclopaedia of British Pottery and Porcelain Marks*, 151.

63. George L. Miller, "Common Staffordshire Cup and Bowl Shapes," accessed May 13, 2023, https://apps.jefpat.maryland.gov/diagnostic/Post-Colonial%20Ceramics/Cup%20Shapes/Essay%20on%20Cup%20&%20Bowl%20Shapes.pdf.

64. Fayette County Clerk of Court, Will Book L: 243–44.

65. Greer, *American Stonewares*, 14.

66. Greer, *American Stonewares*, 15, 27.

67. Nancy O'Malley, "Early Redware Production in the Bluegrass Region of Kentucky," paper presented at the 43rd Southeastern Archaeological Conference, Nashville, TN, November 5–8, 1986.

68. US Bureau of the Census, Industrial Census for Kentucky, 1820.

69. K&V Cultural Resources Management, LLC, *Constant's Station: Mitigation of Site 15CK461, Winchester, Clark County, Kentucky*, technical report submitted to Winchester and Clark County Industrial Authority, Union, KY, 2012.

70. William C. Gates Jr. and Dana E. Ormerod, "The East Liverpool, Ohio Pottery District: Identification of Manufacturers and Marks," *Historical Archaeology* 16, nos. 1–2 (1982): 3–4.

71. Edward Meigh, *The Story of the Glass Bottle* (Stoke-on-Trent: C. E. Ramsden, 1922), 31.

72. Appraisal of John Floyd, accessed June 29, 2017, https://memory.loc.gov/award/icufaw/bmc0185/0001r.jpg; Sales of Jonathan Clark's Estate, accessed June 29, 2017, https://memory.loc.gov/award/icufaw/bmc0186/0001v.jpg; Clerk of Court, Bourbon County Will Book G: 138–41.

73. Ronald William Deiss, *The Development and Application of a Chronology for American Glass* (Normal: Midwestern Archaeological Research Center, Illinois State University, 1981), 24–25; Olive Jones and Catherine Sullivan, *The Parks Canada Glass Glossary for the Description of Containers, Tableware, Flat Glass, and Closures* (Quebec: Canadian Government Publishing Centre, 1989), 40, 80–81, 91.

74. Helen McKearin and Kenneth M. Wilson, *American Bottles & Flasks and Their Ancestry* (New York: Crown, 1978), 617–18.

75. Clerk of Court, Fayette County Will Book A: 446–47; Fayette County Will Book B:58.

76. Phil Dunning, "Composite Table Cutlery from 1700 to 1930," in *Studies in Material Culture Research*, ed. Karlis Karklins (California, PA: Society for Historical Archaeology, 2000), 33.

77. Dunning, "Composite Table Cutlery," 35.

78. Dunning, "Composite Table Cutlery," 33.

79. Dunning, "Composite Table Cutlery," 37.

80. Ted Franklin Belue, *The Long Hunt: Death of the Buffalo East of the Mississippi* (Mechanicsburg, PA: Stackpole Books, 1996), 128, 132, 153, 163; Followell Hunts, "History of White-Tail Deer Management in Kentucky," accessed June 7, 2023, https://followellhunts.wordpress.com/2020/04/09/1201/.

81. O'Malley, *Boonesborough Unearthed*, 95.

82. Paul A. Henlein, *Cattle Kingdom in the Ohio Valley, 1783–1860* (Lexington: University of Kentucky Press, 1959), 23–24.

83. Fred Taylor, "Use the Screws to Help Identify the Age of Your Furniture," WorthPoint, accessed June 11, 2023, https://www.worthpoint.com/articles/collectibles/screws-identify-age-furniture.

84. Frank T. Barnes, *Hooks, Rings & Other Things: An Illustrated Index of New England Iron from 1660–1860* (Hanover, MA: Christopher Publishing House, 1988), 20, 75–76, 86.

85. Barnes, *Hooks, Rings & Other Things*, 219.

86. O'Malley, *Boonesborough Unearthed*, 130.

Conclusions

1. Craig Thompson Friend, *Kentucke's Frontiers* (Bloomington: Indiana University Press, 2010), 13.

2. Jack Larkin, *The Reshaping of Everyday Life, 1790–1840* (New York: Harper & Row, 1988), xiv.

3. Catherine Hutchins, *Everyday Life in the Early Republic* (Winterthur, DE: Henry Francis du Pont Winterthur Museum, 1994), 1–2.

4. W. Stephen McBride and Kim Arbogast McBride, *Frontier Community Defense of Monroe and Summers Counties, West Virginia* (Summers County, WV: Summers County Historic Landmark Commission, 2022), 7–10.

5. Larkin, *Reshaping Everyday Life*, 184.

6. K&V Cultural Resources Management, LLC, *Constant's Station: Mitigation of Site 15CK461, Winchester, Clark County*, technical report submitted to Winchester and Clark County Industrial Authority, Union, KY, 2012.

7. Larkin, *Reshaping Everyday Life*, 118.

8. Draper MSS. 12CC247.

9. Kim Arbogast McBride, email communication, July 5, 2023.

10. Olive R. Jones, "A Guide to Dating Glass Tableware: 1800 to 1940," in *Studies in Material Culture Research*, ed. Karlis Karklins (California, PA: Society for Historical Archaeology, 2000), 155–56.

11. Robert Frank will, 184–86.

12. John Cockrell will, 58; Jillson, "Boone's Station," 215.

13. US Bureau of the Census, Population Census for John Hendley, 1810, https://www.ancestry.com/imageviewer/collections/7613/images/4433225_00050?treeid=&personid=&rc=&usePUB=true&_phsrc=ksw2&_phstart=successSource&pId=556258.

14. Theresa A. Singleton, "The Archaeology of Slave Life," in *Images of the Recent Past: Readings in Historical Archaeology*, ed. Charles S. Orser Jr. (Walnut Creek, CA: Altamira Press, 1996), 143, 148–49; Aaron E. Russell, "Material Culture and African-American Spirituality at the Hermitage," in *Approaches to Material Culture Research for Historical Archaeologists*, comp. David R. Brauner (California, PA: Society for Historical Archaeology, 2000), 428–31.

15. Russell, "Material Culture and African-American Spirituality," 428, 434; Singleton, "Archaeology of Slave Life," 149.

16. Singleton, "Archaeology of Slave Life," 151.

17. Larkin, *Reshaping Everyday Life*, title page; Harriett Beecher Stowe, *Poganuc People*, 73, accessed January 7, 2025, https://archive.org/details/bwb_P9-EIZ-136; Francis Underwood, *Quabbin: The Story of a Small Town with Outlooks on Puritan Life*, 29, accessed July 10, 2023, https://archive.org/details/quabbinstoryofsm00underich/page/28/mode/2up?q=infinite+details.

Bibliography

Abbitt, Merry W. "The Eighteenth-Century Shoe Buckle." In *Five Artifact Studies,* edited by Audrey Noel Hume, Merry W. Abbitt, Robert H. McNulty, Isabel Davies, and Edward Chappell, 25–53. Occasional Papers in Archaeology 1. Williamsburg, VA: Colonial Williamsburg Foundation, 1973.

Abbott, John S. *Daniel Boone, Pioneer of Kentucky*. New York: Dodd & Mead, 1872.

Alexander Robertson v. Ambrose Gordon. Lincoln County Circuit Court Records, Stanton, Kentucky.

Anonymous. "Builders' Hardware—III—Nails." *American Architect and Building News* 24 (1888): 73.

Anonymous. *A Little Pretty Pocket-Book Intended for the Instruction and Amusement of Little Master Tommy and Pretty Miss Polly*. London: Printed for Newbery and Carnan, 1770.

Aron, Stephen. "Putting Kentucky in Its Place." In *Bluegrass Renaissance: The History and Culture of Central Kentucky, 1792–1852*, edited by James C. Klotter and Daniel Rowland, 36–52. Lexington: University Press of Kentucky, 2012.

Attendance Book for the House of Delegates of the Commonwealth of Virginia. Accession #35171, BC #1078198. The Library of Virginia, Richmond.

Bakeless, John. *Daniel Boone: Master of the Wilderness*. New York: William Morrow, 1939.

Barnes, Frank T. *Hooks, Rings & Other Things: An Illustrated Index of New England Iron from 1660–1860*. Hanover, MA: Christopher Publishing House, 1988.

"Battle of Blue Licks." *Register of the Kentucky Historical Society* 47, no. 169 (1949): 247–49.

Bealer, Alex W., and John O. Ellis. *The Log Cabin: Homes of the North American Wilderness*. Barre, PA: Barre Publishing, 1979.

Beaudry, Mary C. *Findings: The Material Culture of Needlework and Sewing*. New Haven, CT: Yale University Press, 2006.

Beckner, Lucien. "Reverend John D. Shane's Interview with Pioneer William Clinkenbeard." *Filson Club History Quarterly* 2, no. 3 (April 1928): 95–128.

Beckner, Lucien. "Rev. John Dabney Shane's Interview with Mrs. Sarah Graham of Bath County." *Filson Club History Quarterly* 9 (1935): 222–41.

Belue, Ted Franklin. *The Hunters of Kentucky: A Narrative History of America's First Far West, 1750–1792*. Mechanicsburg, PA: Stackpole Books, 2003.

Belue, Ted Franklin. *The Life of Daniel Boone by Lyman C. Draper*. Mechanicsburg, PA: Stackpole Books, 1998.

Belue, Ted Franklin. *The Long Hunt: Death of the Buffalo East of the Mississippi*. Mechanicsburg, PA: Stackpole Books, 1996.

Belue, Ted Franklin. *A Sketch of the Life and Character of Daniel Boone: A Memoir of Peter Houston*. Mechanicsburg, PA: Stackpole Books, 1997.

Boyd, Julian P. "The Sheriff in Colonial North Carolina." In *Essays on American Colonial History*, edited by Paul Goodman, 312–29. New York: Holt, Rinehart and Winston, 1972.

Bradley, Charles S. "Smoking Pipes for the Archaeologist." In *Studies in Material Culture Research*, edited by Karlis Karklins, 104–33. California, PA: Society for Historical Archaeology, 2000.

Brookes-Smith, Joan E. *Master Index Virginia Surveys and Grants*. Frankfort: Kentucky Historical Society, 1976.

Brown, Marley. "The Use of Oral and Documentary Sources in Historical Archaeology: Ethnohistory at the Mott Farm." In *Historical Archaeology: A Guide to Substantive and Theoretical Contributions*, edited by Robert L. Schuyler, 178–83. Farmingdale, NY: Baywood Publishing, 1978.

Bryant, Nancy O. "Buckles and Buttons: An Inquiry into Fastening Systems Used on Eighteenth-Century English Breeches." *Dress* 14 (1988): 27–38.

Butler, Mann. *A History of the Commonwealth of Kentucky*. Louisville: Wilcox, Dickerson, 1834.

Calloway, Colin G. "'We Have Always Been the Frontier': The American Revolution in Shawnee Country." *American Indian Quarterly* 16, no. 1 (1992): 39–52.

Carter, William G. *The McGary Frontier Family*. Undated manuscript on file, Harrodsburg Historical Society, Harrodsburg, KY.

Chinn, George Morgan. *Kentucky Settlement and Statehood 1750–1800*. Frankfort: Kentucky Historical Society, 1975.

Cist, Charles. *The Cincinnati Miscellany or Antiquities of the West and Pioneer History and General and Local Statistics Compiled from the* Western General Advertiser *from October 1st, 1844 to April 1st, 1845*. Vol. 1. Cincinnati, OH: Caleb Clark, Printer, 1845.

Clark, Thomas D. *The Voice of the Frontier: John Bradford's Notes on Kentucky*. Lexington: University Press of Kentucky, 1993.

Cobbett, William. *A Year's Residence in the United States of America*. Carbondale, IL: Southern Methodist University Press, 1964.

Coleman, T. Henry. "Early Marriage Records of Mercer County." *Register of the Kentucky Historical Society* 20 (1922): 9–20.

Collins, Richard H. *History of Kentucky*. Covington, KY: Collins, 1874.

Conkwright, Bessie Taul. "A Historical Error." *Lexington Herald*, August 1916.

Conover, Rebecca Wilson. *James Harrod: The Man and His Family*. Harrodsburg, KY: Harrodsburg Herald, 1972.

Cook, Michael L. *Lincoln County Kentucky Records, Volume C*. Evansville, IN: Cook, 1988.

Cotterill, R. S. *History of Pioneer Kentucky*. Cincinnati, OH: Johnson & Hardin, 1917.

Crabb, Anne. *And the Battle Began Like Claps of Thunder: The Siege of Boonesboro—1778—As Told to the Pioneers*. Richmond, KY: Privately Printed, 1998.

David Williams v. Samuel Taylor et al. Mercer County Circuit Court, Box S-20. Harrodsburg, KY.

Deiss, Ronald William. *The Development and Application of a Chronology for American Glass*. Normal: Midwestern Archaeological Research Center, Illinois State University, 1981.

Draper, Lyman Copeland. Manuscripts. Wisconsin Historical Society, Madison.

Dunn, C. Frank. "Boone Station Site." *Register of the Kentucky Historical Society* 41 (1943): 304–309.

Dunning, Phil. "Composite Table Cutlery from 1700 to 1930." In *Studies in Material Culture Research*, edited by Karlis Karklins, 32–45. California, PA: Society for Historical Archaeology, 2000.

Edwards, Jay D., and Tom Wells. *Historic Louisiana Nails: Aids to the Dating of Old Buildings*. Fred B. Kniffen Cultural Resource Laboratory Monograph Series 2. Baton Rouge: Geoscience Publications, Dept. of Geography & Anthropology, Louisiana State University, 1993.

Enoch, Harry G., and Anne Crabb. *Crisis in the Wilderness: The Capture and Rescue of the Boone and Callaway Girls, 1776*. Monee, IL: Fort Boonesborough Foundation, 2021.

Eslinger, Ellen. "Migration and Kinship on the Trans-Appalachian Frontier: Strode's Station, Kentucky." *Filson Club Quarterly* 62, no. 1 (1988): 52–66.

Faragher, John Mack. *Daniel Boone: The Life and Legend of an American Pioneer*. New York: Henry Holt, 1992.

Filson, John. *The Adventures of Daniel Boon, Formerly a Hunter: Containing a Narrative of the Wars of Kentucky, with the Discovery, Purchase, and Settlement of Kentucky, and the Piankashaw Council, 1784, and Territory of North American Indians, and the Rights of Land in Kentucky*. Old Chillicothe, OH: Privately Printed by A. Salisbury, 1967.

Friend, Craig Thompson. *Kentucke's Frontiers*. Bloomington: Indiana University Press, 2010.

Gates, William C., and Dana E. Ormerod. "The East Liverpool Pottery District: Identification of Manufacturers and Marks." *Historical Archaeology* 16, nos. 1–2 (1982).

Godden, Geoffrey A. *Encyclopaedia of British Pottery and Porcelain Marks*. New York: Bonanza Books, 1964.

Godden, Geoffrey A. *An Illustrated Encyclopedia of British Pottery and Porcelain.* 2nd ed. Leicester: Magna Books, 1992.

Greer, Bill. "McGary Likeness." *Sunday Courier and Press,* February 12, 1974.

Greer, Georgeanna H. *American Stonewares: The Art and Craft of Utilitarian Potters.* Exton, PA: Schiffer, 1981.

Hammersmith, Mary Powell. *Hugh McGary, Senior: Pioneer of Virginia, North Carolina, Kentucky and Indiana.* Wheaton, IL: Nodus Press, 2000.

Hamilton, T. M. *Colonial Frontier Guns.* Union City, TN: Pioneer Press, 1987.

Hammon, Neal O. *Daniel Boone and Defeat at Blue Licks.* Minneapolis, MN: Boone Society, 2005.

Hammon, Neal O. *My Father, Daniel Boone: The Draper Interviews with Nathan Boone.* Lexington: University Press of Kentucky, 1999.

Hammon, Neal O., and James Russell Harris. "Daniel Boone the Businessman: Revising the Myth of Failure." *Register of the Kentucky Historical Society* 112, no. 1 (2014): 5–50.

Hammon, Neal O., and Richard Taylor. *Virginia's Western War: 1775–1786.* Mechanicsburg, PA: Stackpole Books, 2002.

Hardin, Bayless. "Whitley Papers, Volume 9—Draper Manuscripts—Kentucky Papers." *Register of the Kentucky Historical Society* 36 (1938): 189–209.

Heinlein, Paul A. *Cattle Kingdom in the Ohio Valley, 1783–1860.* Lexington, KY: University of Kentucky Press, 1959.

Hening, William Waller, ed. *The Statutes at Large; Being a Collection of All the Laws of Virginia, from the First Session of the Legislature, in the Year 1619, Volume X.* Richmond, VA: George Cochran, Printer, 1822.

Hunter, Robert, ed. *Ceramics in America 2001.* Hanover, NH: University Press of New England, 2001.

Hunter, Robert, and George L. Miller. "All in the Family: A Staffordshire Soup Plate and the American Market." In *Ceramics in America 2001,* edited by Robert Hunter, 222–25. Hanover, NH: University Press of New England, 2001.

Hunter, Robert, and George L. Miller. "Suitable for Framing: Decorated Shell-Edge Earthenware." *Early American Life* 40, no. 4 (August 2009): 8–19.

Ison, Betty Sue. "Window Glass in Kentucky, 1790 to 1940." Master's thesis, University of Kentucky, 1990.

James, James Alton. *George Rogers Clark Papers 1771–1781.* Collection of Illinois State Historical Library, 8, Virginia Series 3. Springfield: Illinois State Historical Library, 1912.

James, James Alton. *George Rogers Clark Papers 1781–1784.* Collection of Illinois State Historical Library, Virginia Series 4. Springfield: Illinois State Historical Library, 1916.

Jillson, Willard Rouse. "Boone's Station." *Filson Club History Quarterly* 8 (1934): 213–16.

Jones, Olive, and Catherine Sullivan. *The Parks Canada Glass Glossary for the Description of Containers, Tableware, Flat Glass, and Closures.* Quebec: Canadian Government Publishing Centre, 1989.

Jones, Olive R. "A Guide to Dating Glass Tableware: 1800 to 1940." In *Studies in Material Culture Research*, edited by Karlis Karklins, 141–232. California, PA: Society for Historical Archaeology, 2000.

Journal of the House of Delegates of the Commonwealth of Virginia. Session of 1781–1782. Internet Archive. Accessed February 4, 2002. https://archive.org/details/journalofhouseof178186virg/page/4/mode/1up.

K&V Cultural Resources Management, LLC. *Constant's Station: Mitigation of Site 15CK461, Winchester, Clark County, Kentucky*. Technical report submitted to Winchester and Clark County Industrial Authority, 2012.

Kamper, Ken. "An Accurate Summary of the Life of Daniel Boone." *Daniel Boone History Research Newsletter* 6 (2021): 1–14.

Kenmotsu, Nancy. "Gunflints: A Study." In *Approaches to Material Culture: Research for Historical Archaeologists*, 2nd ed., edited by David Brauner, 197–221. California, PA: Society for Historical Archaeology, 2000.

Lafferty, Maude Ward. "Destruction of Ruddle's and Martin's Forts in the Revolutionary War." *Register of the Kentucky Historical Society* 54, no. 189 (October 1956): 297–338.

Larkin, Jack. *The Reshaping of Everyday Life, 1790–1840*. New York: Harper & Row, 1988.

Lewis, R. Barry, ed. *Kentucky Archaeology*. Lexington: University Press of Kentucky, 1996.

Lofaro, Michael A. *Daniel Boone: An American Life*. Lexington: University Press of Kentucky, 2003.

Lofstrom, Ted, Jeffrey P. Tordoff, and Douglas C. George. "A Seriation of Historic Earthenwares in the Midwest, 1780–1870." *Minnesota Archaeologist* 41, no. 1 (1982): 3–29.

Mankowitz, Wolf, and Reginald G. Haggar. *The Concise Encyclopedia of English Pottery and Porcelain*. New York: Hawthorn Books, 1968.

Marshall, Humphrey. *The History of Kentucky*. Frankfort: George S. Robinson, 1824.

Mason, Kathryn Harrod. "The Career of General James Ray, Kentucky Pioneer." *Filson Club History Quarterly* 19 (1945): 86–114.

McBride, M. Stephen, and Kim A. McBride. *An Archaeological Survey of Frontier Forts in the Greenbrier and Middle New River Valleys of West Virginia*. Archaeological Report 252. Lexington: Program for Cultural Resource Assessment, University of Kentucky, 1991.

McBride, W. Stephen, and Kim A. McBride. "Border Warfare in Revolutionary Era West Virginia." In *Partisans, Guerrillas, and Irregulars: Historical Archaeology of Asymmetric Warfare*, edited by Steven Smith and Clarence Geier, 11–32. Tuscaloosa: University of Alabama Press, 2019.

McBride, W. Stephen, and Kim Arbogast McBride. *Frontier Community Defense of Monroe and Summers Counties, West Virginia*. Summers County, WV: Summers County Historic Landmark Commission, 2022.

McClung, John A. *Sketches of Western Adventure*. Philadelphia: Grigg & Elliot, 1832.

McKearin, Helen, and Kenneth M. Wilson. *American Bottles & Flasks and Their Ancestry*. New York: Crown, 1978.
Meigh, Edward. *The Story of the Glass Bottle*. Stoke-on-Trent: C. E. Ramsden, 1922.
Michigan Pioneer and Historical Society. *Historical Collections of the Michigan Pioneer and Historical Society 19*. Lansing, MI: Robert Smith, 1892.
Miller, George L. "A Revised Set of CC Index Values for Classification and Economic Scaling of English Ceramics from 1787 to 1880." *Historical Archaeology* 25, no. 1 (1991): 1–25.
Miller, George L. "A User's Guide to Ceramic Assemblages: Part Four." *Council for Northeast Historical Archaeology Newsletter* 26 (November 1993): 4–7.
Miller, George L., and Robert Hunter. "How Creamware Got the Blues: The Origins of China Glaze and Pearlware." In *Ceramics in America*, edited by Robert Hunter, 135–62. Hanover, NH: University Press of New England, 2001.
Miller, George L., and Robert R. Hunter Jr. "English Shell Edged Earthenware: Alias Leeds Ware, Alias Feather Edge." In *Proceedings of the 35th Annual Wedgwood International Seminar*, 106–35. 1990.
Miller, George L., Ann Smart Martin, and Nancy S. Dickinson. "Changing Consumption Patterns: English Ceramics and the American Market from 1770 to 1840." In *Everyday Life in the Early Republic*, edited by Catherine E. Hutchins, 219–48. Winterthur, DE: Henry Francis du Pont Winterthur Museum, 1994.
Moir, Randall W. "Socioeconomic and Chronometric Patterning of Window Glass." In *Historic Buildings, Material Culture, and People of the Prairie Margin: Architecture, Artifacts, and Synthesis of Historic Archaeology*, edited by David H. Jurney and Randall W. Moir, 73–81. Richland Creek Technical Series 5. Dallas, TX: Archaeology Research Program, Institute for the Study of Earth and Man, Southern Methodist University, 1987.
Montgomery, Florence M. *Textiles in America: 1650–1870*. New York: W. W. Norton, 1984.
Morgan, Robert. *Boone: A Biography*. Chapel Hill, NC: Algonquin Books, 2007.
Murray-Wooley, Caroline. *Early Stone Houses of Kentucky*. Lexington: University Press of Kentucky, 2008.
Neumann, George C. *Battle Weapons of the American Revolution: The Historian's Complete Reference*. Texarkana, TX: Scurlock Publishing, 1998.
Neumann, George C. *Swords & Blades of the American Revolution*. Texarkana, TX: Rebel Publishing, 1991.
Neumann, George C., and Frank J. Kravic. *Collector's Illustrated Encyclopedia of the American Revolution*. Texarkana, TX: Rebel Publishing, 1975.
Noël Hume, Ivor. *A Guide to Artifacts of Colonial America*. New York: Alfred A. Knopf, 1978.
Noël Hume, Ivor. *If These Pots Could Talk: Collecting 2,000 Years of British Household Pottery*. Hanover, NH: University Press of New England, 2001.
Noël Hume, Ivor. "Through the Lookinge Glasse: Or, the Chamber Pot as a Mirror of Its Time." In *Ceramics in America*, edited by Robert Hunter, 139–72. Hanover, NH: University Press of New England, 2001.

Nye, Eric W. "Pounds Sterling to Dollars: Historical Conversion of Currency." Accessed February 10, 2025. https://www.uwyo.edu/numimage/currency.htm.

Olsen, Stanley. "Dating Early Plain Buttons by Their Form." *American Antiquity* 28, no. 4 (1963): 551–54.

O'Malley, Nancy. *Boonesborough Unearthed: Frontier Archaeology at a Revolutionary Fort.* Lexington: University Press of Kentucky, 2019.

O'Malley, Nancy. *Drawing Battle Lines at Fort Boonesborough: The Siege of 1778.* Lexington: Report Prepared for the American Battlefield Protection Program, 2012.

O'Malley, Nancy. "Early Redware Production in the Bluegrass Region of Kentucky." Paper presented at the 43rd Southeastern Archaeological Conference, Nashville, TN, November 1986.

O'Malley, Nancy. "Frontier Defenses and Pioneer Strategies in the Historic Settlement Era." In *The Buzzel about Kentuck: Settling the Promised Land,* edited by Craig Thompson Friend, 57–76. Lexington: University of Kentucky Press, 1999.

O'Malley, Nancy. *Middle Class Farmers on the Urban Periphery.* Archaeological Report 162. Lexington: University of Kentucky Program for Cultural Resource Assessment, 1987.

O'Malley, Nancy. *Searching for Boonesborough.* Archaeological Report 193. Lexington: Program for Cultural Resource Assessment, Department of Anthropology, University of Kentucky, 1987.

O'Malley, Nancy. *"Stockading Up": A Study of Pioneer Stations in the Inner Bluegrass Region of Kentucky.* Archaeological Report 127. Lexington: Program for Cultural Resource Assessment, Department of Anthropology, University of Kentucky, 1994 revised.

O'Malley, Nancy, and Karen Hudson. *Cultural Resource Assessment of Boone Station State Park, Fayette County, Kentucky.* Archaeological Report 316. Lexington: Program for Cultural Resource Assessment, Department of Anthropology, University of Kentucky, 1993.

Palmer, William P. *Calendar of Virginia State Papers and Other Manuscripts from January 1, 1785, to July 2, 1789.* New York: Kraus Reprint Corporation, 1968; originally published Richmond: Sherwin McRae, 1884.

Peck, John Mason. *Life of Daniel Boone: The Pioneer of Kentucky.* New York: The University Society, 1904 reprint.

Perkins, Elizabeth. *Border Life: Experience and Memory in the Revolutionary Ohio Valley.* Chapel Hill: University of North Carolina Press, 1998.

Perkins, Elizabeth. "The Consumer Frontier: Household Consumption in Early Kentucky." *Journal of American History* 78, no. 2 (September 1991): 486–510.

Peterkin, Allan. *One Thousand Beards: A Cultural History of Facial Hair.* Vancouver: Arsenal Pulp, 2001.

Price, Cynthia R. *19th Century Ceramics in the Eastern Ozark Border Region.* Southwest Missouri State University Center for Archaeological Research 1. Springfield: Southwest Missouri State University Center for Archaeological Research, 1979.

Ranck, George Washington. *Boonesborough: Its Founding, Pioneer Struggles, Indian Experiences, Transylvania Days, and Revolutionary Annals*. Louisville, KY: John P. Morton, 1901; reprint, Salem, NH: Ayer, 1986.

Ranck, George Washington. *The Story of Bryan's Station*. Lexington, KY: Transylvania Printing, 1896.

Rickard, Jonathan. *Mocha and Related Dipped Wares, 1770–1939*. Hanover, NH: University Press of New England, in association with Historic Eastfield Foundation, 2006.

Roenke, Karl G. *Flat Glass: Its Use as a Dating Tool for Nineteenth Century Archaeological Sites in the Pacific Northwest and Elsewhere*. Northwest Anthropological Research Notes, Memoir 4. Moscow: Department of Sociology/Anthropology, University of Idaho, 1978.

Russell, Aaron E. "Material Culture and African-American Spirituality at the Hermitage." In *Approaches to Material Culture Research for Historical Archaeologists*, compiled by David R. Brauner, 423–40. California, PA: Society for Historical Archaeology, 2000.

Schoen, Christopher M. "Window Glass on the Plains: An Analysis of Flat Glass Samples from Ten Nineteenth Century Plains Historic Sites." *Central Plains Archaeology* 2, no. 1 (1990): 57–90.

Scott, Hattie Marshall. *Scott's Papers: Kentucky Court and Other Records*. Frankfort: Kentucky Historical Society, 1953.

Singleton, Theresa A. "The Archaeology of Slave Life." In *Images of the Recent Past: Readings in Historical Archaeology*, edited by Charles S. Orser Jr., 141–65 . Walnut Creek, CA: Altamira Press, 1996.

Sivilich, Daniel M. *Musket Ball and Small Shot Identification: A Guide*. Norman: University of Oklahoma Press, 2016.

Smalley, Andrea L. "'They Steal Our Deer and Land': Contested Hunting Grounds in the Trans-Appalachian West." *Register of the Kentucky Historical Society* 114, nos. 3 and 4 (2016): 303–39.

Spalding, Martin John. *Sketches of the Early Catholic Missions in Kentucky*. Louisville, KY: B. J. Webb and Brothers, 1844.

Speed, Thomas. *The Wilderness Road: A Description of the Routes of Travel by Which the Pioneers and Early Settlers First Came to Kentucky*. New York: Lenox Hill Publishing and Distribution, 1886.

Staples, Charles R. "History of Circuit Court Records, Fayette County." *Register of the Kentucky Historical Society* 30, no. 93 (1932): 344–61.

Stewart, Richard W. *The United States Army and the Forging of a Nation, 1775–1917*. American Military History 1. Washington, DC: Center of Military United States Army, 2005.

Straker, Hazel Atterbury. *The Boone Family: A Genealogical History of the Descendants of George and Mary Boone Who Came to America in 1717*. Rutland, VT: Tuttle, 1922.

Sussman, Lynne. *Mocha, Banded, Cat's Eye and Other Factory-Made Slipware. Studies in Northeast Historical Archaeology* 1. Boston: Council for Northeast Historical Archaeology, 1997.

Talbert, Charles G. "Kentucky Invades Ohio—1780." *Register of the Kentucky Historical Society* 52, no. 181 (October 1954): 291–300.

Tarleton, Lieutenant-General Banastre. *A History of the Campaigns of 1780 and 1781, in the Southern Provinces of North America.* London: Printed for T. Cadell, 1787. https://archive.org/details/historyofcampaig00tarl.

Walker, Iain C. "The American Stub-Stemmed Clay Tobacco-Pipe: A Survey of Its Origins, Manufacture, and Distribution." *Conference on Historic Site Archaeology Papers* 9 (1975): 97–128.

Watlington, Patricia. *The Partisan Spirit: Kentucky Politics, 1779–1792.* New York: Atheneum, 1972.

Weiss, Kathryn H. *Daniel Bryan, Nephew of Daniel Boone: His Narrative and Other Stories.* Forbestown, CA: Privately Printed, 2008.

White, Carolyn L. *American Artifacts of Personal Adornment, 1680–1820: A Guide to Identification and Interpretation.* Lanham, MD: Rowman & Littlefield, 2005.

Wieland, Jonathan. "A Comparison and Review of Window Glass Analysis Approaches in Historical Archaeology." *Technical Briefs in Historical Archaeology* 4 (2009): 29–40.

Wilson, Samuel M. *Battle of Blue Licks, August 19, 1782.* Lexington, KY: Privately Printed, 1927.

Wooley, Carolyn Murray. *Early Stone Houses of Kentucky.* Lexington: University Press of Kentucky, 2008.

Yeoman, R. S. *A Guidebook of United States Coins.* Racine, WI: Western Publishing, 1992.

Young, Amy Lambert. "Nailing Down the Pattern." *Tennessee Anthropologist* 19, no. 1 (Spring 1994): 1–21.

Young, Bennett H. *History of the Battle of the Blue Licks.* Louisville, KY: John P. Morton, 1897.

Young, Chester Raymond. *Westward into Kentucky: The Narrative of Daniel Trabue.* Lexington: University Press of Kentucky, 1981.

Index

Page numbers in italics refer to illustrations.